D1559262

General Jacob Devers

This book is a publication of

INDIANA UNIVERSITY PRESS
Office of Scholarly Publishing
Herman B Wells Library 350
1320 East 10th Street
Bloomington, Indiana 47405 USA

iupress.indiana.edu

Telephone   800-842-6796
Fax   812-855-7931

⊗ The paper used in this publication
meets the minimum requirements of
the American National Standard for
Information Sciences – Permanence of
Paper for Printed Library Materials,
ANSI Z39.48–1992.

Manufactured in the
United States of America

Library of Congress
Cataloging-in-Publication Data

Adams, John A., [date]
    General Jacob Devers : World War II's
forgotten four star / John A. Adams.
    pages cm
    Includes bibliographical
references and index.
    ISBN 978-0-253-01517-4 (cloth :
alk. paper) – ISBN 978-0-253-01526-6
(ebook) 1. Devers, Jacob L. (Jacob
Loucks), 1887–1979. 2. Generals – United
States – Biography. 3. World War,
1939–1945 – Biography. 4. United
States. Army – Biography. I. Title.
    E745.D48A64 2015
    355.0092 – dc23
    [B]
                              2014030025

1 2 3 4 5   19 18 17   16 15

General Jacob Devers

World War II's Forgotten Four Star

JOHN A. ADAMS

INDIANA UNIVERSITY PRESS

Bloomington & Indianapolis

This volume is dedicated to the memory of Thomas E. Griess.

While chairman of the history department of the Military Academy at West Point, Colonel Griess conducted a large number of interviews that are well cared for at the York Historical Society, York, Pennsylvania. The collection of papers and artifacts of a proud son of York, General Jacob Devers, has grown to over 1,200 items, primarily interviews and documents. They provide a solid basis for my humble attempt to tell the story of a great American.

Contents

Maps

Acknowledgments

THANKS TO ALL OF THE HELPFUL STAFF AT THE YORK Historical Society; Eisenhower Library, Abilene, Kansas; Marshall Library, Lexington, Virginia; Military History Institute, Carlisle Barracks, Pennsylvania; and the Preston Library, Virginia Military Institute. Thanks to the editorial staff at Indiana University Press; to the faculty at the Virginia Military Institute, who gave me so much help and encouragement; and to my sister-in-law Geane Stevenson.

John A. Adams
Vero Beach, Florida, 2015

General Jacob Devers

At the turn of the twenty-first century, American armored forces ride in a honey of a fighting vehicle. The infantry version is called the M2 Bradley. Omar Bradley's service record as a senior commander during the famous battles in Western Europe is widely known, and naming the vehicle after him seems a fitting tribute. A somewhat more sophisticated version, the M3 Cavalry Fighting Vehicle, which carries the scouts into battle, was named after the other American army group commander in the European theater in World War II. Both vehicles, however, began to bear the name Bradley. Few can recall the other general's name. This is the story of Jacob Loucks Devers.

Prologue

WHEN APPOINTED CHIEF OF STAFF IN 1939, GEORGE C. Marshall faced a seemingly impossible task. Out of a small, second-rate peacetime army, he had to create what became an 8-million-man machine tasked with beating both the horror of Nazi Germany and the Japanese scourge of the Pacific. One of the first people to whom he turned is little remembered today. Out of a bag of good ideas, Jacob Devers created the Armored Force of sixteen armored divisions and a host of separate battalions that led to the retaking of Europe. As one of two American army group commanders under Dwight Eisenhower (the other was Omar Bradley), Devers led the invasion of southern France, commanding most of the French Army as well as the U.S. Seventh Army as they rampaged across southern Germany and into Austria.

While he worked for Eisenhower, the two did not get along well. Marshall had his hands full keeping both his star protégé and one of his first picks for general highly motivated and productive. Here is the story of Devers and his rise to four stars.

ONE

Early Years

BORN ON SEPTEMBER 8, 1887, IN THE PENNSYLVANIA DUTCH
town of York, Jacob Loucks Devers was the oldest of four children born
to the very upright couple of Philip and Ella Kate Loucks. Philip Devers
was a sturdy, good-natured Irishman, 5' 10" and 220 pounds or so, with a
thick crop of curly hair, olive complexion, and a moustache. Oddly, the
American who was to free Alsace descended on Ella Kate's side from
stock that hailed from Strasbourg. A heavyset semi-invalid, she needed
domestic help to raise her three sons and a daughter. Altogether they
were a gregarious and friendly family – a touch of the Irish in Pennsylvania Dutch country.

Father worked his way up to become a highly skilled watchmaker
and partner in the well-regarded jewelry store, Stevens and Devers. "My
father had to put those damned watches together – he had to do everything right or it didn't work. That impressed me," his son later commented.[1] Afterward, Philip became the only one in York who could repair the new "high tech" adding machines. As the junior partner in the
jewelry business, he often had to work late hours. He was a Democrat
active in civic affairs and a Thirty-Second Degree Mason. A boyhood
friend remembered him as "one of the great fathers I knew. He was a
real companion to the boys."[2] Jacob's sister remembered him as "a man's
man": "He had a horse and fancy pigeons which he trained. Father would
come home from work for meals on the trolley car. For the boys he made
the first skis in the area. He had a great deal of fun in him. Our childhood was happy and carefree."[3] The children remembered spending a
lot of time with their father. He helped them to build a coaster that the

boys endlessly took down hills. In warm weather, they might all go to the Susquehanna River and picnic. Honesty, integrity, dependability, and hard work were family trademarks.

In the autumn of his life, Jacob remembered his family as close-knit, even as they grew older. Family life was a source of strength. "My mother always kept us well stuffed with food and made us toe the mark and be on time. Mom was active at St. Paul's Lutheran Church and remembered for her skill at baking." Another time, the general recalled, "While she was warm and loving, there was always a cat-o-nine tails over the ice box. My mother never had to use it after the first time." Ella Kate disliked braggarts and admonished her children to be "very reticent" about their accomplishments. The Devers kids learned punctuality the hard way; be late for supper and you got none. From his mother, Jamie, as Jacob was called as a boy, inherited "a dogged determination and self-reliance" that were hard to shake, and a marked reticence that he overcame only with difficulty. Birthdays were a big deal, and Christmas was something to look forward to. "We did have chores, but I knew we could not have had a happier life."

In those days before universal automotive transportation, many people walked. In the part of town where the Devers resided, the streets were lined with boardwalks. Late in the evening, some people returning from the downtown taverns would stagger by, smoking. Jacob's mother would say, "See that man smoking? Putting another nail in his coffin." "And if she said that once," Devers recalled, "she repeated it a thousand times. I have never forgotten it and never had any desire to smoke. Besides, to play sports I had to run fast and if I smoked, I couldn't breathe. She counsels you when you really don't appreciate it. But you need it. But she always had several cans filled with cookies which you could share with your friends."

Devers also remembered the family's "six mule teams that pulled great rock trucks used to fix the roads. The gravel came from quarries not too far from the house. We always seemed to meet our bills but sometimes they would pile up. In the jewelry business, most of your money came around Christmas, so we would catch up then. The farm provided much of our food including butter."

Jamie's two brothers, Frank and Philip, were close in age. The housekeeper remembered the three boys were so close together and active that it was like looking after triplets. Catherine ("Kit") was six years younger. Frank and Phil were such good students that they each skipped a grade. Frank's placement put him in Jamie's class. Phil was always the man of science and later became an inventor at GE Labs. He held a number of patents, including one for the ultraviolet lamp. Jamie was always the energetic, active one. Frank, a little less active, was the thoughtful one. He became a banker. The three boys were always competitive with each other. Kit would later run a small bookstore in York. Said Devers, "We had a wonderful family life." That happy, carefree childhood induced him to set deep roots into the rich Pennsylvania soil, and he maintained close relationships in York until the end of his life. His parents lived out their lives there. Frank died at an early age in 1947; Philip passed away in 1969.

At the turn of the century, York was a budding, bustling manufacturing center situated along the Susquehanna River among the neat, well-cared-for farms in the rolling green hills that lie a hundred miles due west of Philadelphia. Small city life at the end of the nineteenth century is barely recognizable to those of us who dwell in the twenty-first. For the Devers children, grade school was only a few blocks away. Few residents journeyed outside of the county. Horse-drawn buggies and trolley cars were the principal transportation. It was a time when upright residents instilled the values of hard work, honesty, and good manners in their young and, expected them to be well-behaved.

The Devers family had a nice "fairly new" three-story brick home on West York Street (now known as Roosevelt Avenue). As was common at the time, the structure housed two modest, hardworking families. They had a horse and barn but not a lot of money. But no Devers ever wanted for the basics. Like his neighbors, Jamie grew up learning good manners and the value of hard work. Grandfather Jacob Loucks, the young Devers's namesake, owned the York Machine Shop, which matured into the York Manufacturing Company, later a part of Borg Warner Company. After selling the machinery business, he bought a 191-acre farm on Bull Road. During harvest, Jamie would be pressed into service as a farm hand. "He used my Park Street Gang to help pick potatoes," Devers recalled.[4] "He paid me one half what he paid his laborers, and I did twice as much work as any one of them and I always resented it. When I was much younger, he bribed us by taking us to Bierman's Ice Cream Parlor and giving us all the ice cream and cake we could eat, but we never were able to eat enough to pay for all the work we did picking those potatoes. . . . He taught us economics in a realistic way." Grandfather Loucks was an active Republican. Jamie used to listen over the fence to the political discussions of the adults. Still, he noted, "I have ended up after all these years as a Republican but not because of my grandfather." Grandfather Devers was a kindly but upright man. He had a lively blacksmithing business and shoed a lot of the neighborhood horses. The general fondly remembered his paternal grandfather's sense of humor. "Grandfather Devers was a great man in his own right and influenced me greatly. He was six feet tall with a fine soldierly posture and the best blacksmith and horseshoer in town. He saw that I got to Sunday school every week by walking me a mile and a half. I always remember he had a keen sense of humor and that he was kindly and helpful to everybody in every sense of the word."

Nearby stone quarries would flood during spring runoff. "Mom thought those old quarries were too dangerous," so the boys had to sneak off when they wanted to swim there in the summer or ice skate in the winter. "We didn't have much money. I remember going down and getting some of the woodworkers to make our bats and getting a shoemaker to cover our baseballs. He was a lame man and had been a ball player and taught me how to pitch." Somewhere along the line, Jamie learned to cook. When not tending to chores or schoolwork, the boys often were down along the Susquehanna River swimming, sailing, or catching shad. Surprisingly, Jamie was not a hunter. Sometimes they would canoe a mile down river to pick up supplies. "All of this had a lot to do with building my physique. The discussions we heard by the river men were generally clean stories about the progress the country was making and of the tremendous advantages that the counties of York and Lancaster had because of the kind of soil and the kind of people who inhabited the area." When it was in season, the kids picked watercress and sold it for 10 cents a bunch. As they grew of age, his buddy recalled, "We all pretty much liked the girls and we managed to spend as much time as we could with them." Jamie was popular with the fairer sex. Throughout his life, people commented on his pleasant, optimistic disposition.

Unlike his father, Jamie was slight of build, but he was well coordinated and showed athletic ability. His real passion was sports; they dominated his teen years and his outlook on life. From as far back as anyone could remember, he always seemed to wind up as the leader. Despite his demure size, only 120 pounds, he quarterbacked his high school football team. What he lacked in size, he more than made up in quick thinking and hard running. On the baseball diamond, he showed great enthusiasm and a willingness to play at whatever position the team required. He showed promise on the baseball diamond. Others who batted against him gave respect to his curve ball. Jamie's house was the headquarters for the school team. They kept their equipment in the Devers's barn. Even field hockey was given a try. But Jamie's favorite was the basketball court, where he captained the team for both his junior and senior years. Today some might dub him an "alpha male" or "Type A" personality. He was always highly competitive, an attitude that colored his entire life. "I was a poor loser; I didn't like to lose." He looked to excel at almost anything he took on, including beating his brothers. But the competition remained good natured – at least most of the time:

> I was the youngest of the group that played baseball. But I was first to be there and about the last to leave. I'd play whatever position the team needed, from catcher to pitcher. Broke my finger as catcher. I was captain of the basketball team and quarterbacked the football team. My father belonged to a club that gave him access to a cottage. Eleven miles down the river. We would go there for a couple of weeks and fish, the shad would come in a big run. Mr. Detweiler lived in a big house next door. He'd set out a net. I have seen hundreds of fish in the net on the beach. They would barrel them and haul them out with farm wagons to Columbia or Wrightsville.

Jamie was an earnest and serious student. Most everyone found him to be extremely intelligent though not bookish. His lessons were well prepared, and it was evident that he wanted to learn. Generally students of the period were respectful of their teachers. Jake described his student-teacher relationships as "good" and "friendly." The public high school Jake attended taught about four hundred students in four grades. While grade school was only a few blocks from home, the high school was several miles away. From the beginning, Jamie excelled, as did his brothers. Jamie finished third in his class; Frank, who skipped a grade, wound up in Jamie's class and finished second. In his own class, Philip also finished second. Jamie showed aptitude in mathematics, but languages, including English, were another matter. Later in life, Devers would come to feel that the Pennsylvania Dutch spoken around York limited his proficiency in English. Throughout his life, he was concerned that his writing might reveal this weakness so he avoided projects that required long, complex write-ups instead of short or verbal summaries. Overall, Jamie stood out as both popular and a leader among his peers. For three years he was voted class president, and from an early age, Jamie's social antenna seemed particularly attuned to interaction with others.

Jamie's father pushed him to be an engineer. In the Devers household, little thought was given to anything but doing one's best. At the turn of the twentieth century, engineers were big men in Pennsylvania. Mines, oil wells, and railroads were all created by these "can do" learned men, and joining their ranks promised a big future for an ambitious young man. He was going to study engineering at Penn State or Lehigh University.

Many famous men had to compete fiercely for West Point appointments. By contrast, Devers was sought out by his local congressman. The politician wanted a student who had good grades in math and science and could survive the tough engineering regimen for which "The Point" had a reputation. As with many new cadets, a free college education was just too valuable for Jamie to pass up. According to the general himself, he became interested in attending West Point as a high school junior, but he did not pursue the entrance process at the time. It was sports that eventually sparked the inclination. Jamie was enthralled at the exploits of the All-American Charlie Daly, who led Army's football team. "I had been reading about West Point graduates and the Indian Wars out there. Kit Carson was a hero to me."

Nevertheless, Jamie and one of his best friends applied and were accepted to Lehigh, a fine Pennsylvania engineering college, and the local Republican congressman appointed the son of a prominent family to West Point. Jamie's father, considered one of the town's more important

Democrats, inquired about an Annapolis appointment, but Jamie did not think he would take to the sea. Then the other West Point candidate turned down the appointment. It was the third time that this congress-man had had trouble with cadet appointments. Previously, one of his appointments had failed the entrance exam, and another had washed out academically. The congressmen was about to retire, and he was frus-trated with the record of Republican protégés. Despite being pushed by two families to appoint their sons, the congressman decided to appoint the son of a prominent Democrat – Jamie. He accepted. Prior to this, Jamie had never shown any interest in a military career or even playing "army" with his childhood buddies, but in this serendipitous moment, the army gained a youth that would become one of its four-star combat commanders. Said the congressman, "One day when some historian writes a history book on what small hinges the doors of destiny open and shut on, the story of the accidental general may lead all the rest."[5]

Jamie continued to worry that his Pennsylvania Dutch so interfered with his ability to communicate in clear English that he might have trou-ble with the entrance exam. Before entering the military academy, he engaged one of his former teachers as a tutor. After worrying about, and studying for, the entrance exam, Jamie was ultimately accepted on the basis of his good academic record compiled in York's public high school. After attending an Army football game, Jake informed Lehigh that he had settled on "The Point." His high school yearbook predicted "General Devers" would emerge from this decision.

Jamie was nervous about attending West Point. "I was the shy boy from York." His penmanship was atrocious, and he continued to worry that his reliance on the Pennsylvania Dutch of his youth would handicap him with better-spoken cadets who had been educated to express them-selves in clear, proper English. Neither was he a gifted orator. When he arrived at the academy, he was so intimidated, he almost turned around and left. "I was scared to death. But I'd been coached a little by older people. They'd say 'Jake somebody else had done it, and if they did it, you can do it.' So I always plunged in, and it worked. I got a lot of confidence built up in me that way. I think the real thing my parents gave me was a sense of justice. I've never had any trouble about what was right and what was wrong. I just knew that at West Point, you don't fail. And if somebody else could get through that place, I had a good chance of doing it, provided I worked at it."

"I was just a scared small town kid. I was awkward and had no poise. But the Army soon knocked all that out of me." As a first-year student, a plebe, Jamie's slight stature and boyish looks did not engender respect from always demanding upperclassmen. His meager 140 pounds and pigeon-toed gate instantly made him stand out as a bit of an oddity both on the parade ground and in barracks. Plebe life and its hazing were hard on him. His smile got him in a lot of trouble. Upperclassmen thought that expression was a smirk, meant to be trifling, when that was not what Devers intended. The slight plebe from York did not realize the image he was projecting. In his retirement, the general recalled, "I took an awful beating. I just went along as a plebe." Jamie picked up few demerits, but unlike some of his more adventuresome classmates, he was no prankster. He was known as a bit of a "goodie two shoes" who did not gamble or use coarse language, and seldom drank. He was just a young man from the wholesome Pennsylvania countryside who did not want to call attention to himself in barracks. From an early age, Devers wanted to achieve but not stand out for the wrong reason. There is little evidence from his cadet years that the proper, shy "nice boy" from small town Pennsylvania would mature into the self-confident, risk-taking man of action that would become his hallmark.

Despite his diminutive sized, he was a gifted athlete. As a school boy, he was a triple threat playing baseball, basketball, and football. Too small for the intercollegiate gridiron, he captained Army's basketball team. Later he would return to West Point twice as an instructor and coach or athletic director. Jamie also tried his hand at lacrosse and polo, but Devers lettered on the baseball team. He is remembered as one of the best shortstops the U.S. Military Academy (USMA) ever had. Likewise, almost from the beginning, Devers exhibited an equestrian aptitude. Many said he was a better rider than classmates like George Patton, who rode extensively while growing up on his family's California estate. At the beginning of the twentieth century, horsemanship was an important career skill for a young officer; Jamie's way with horses proved a valuable adjunct to his early career.

A young tactical officer, Joseph Stilwell, who became famous as chief of staff to Chinese General Chiang Kaishek, was the basketball coach while Jamie captained that team. Devers reminisced, "All the officers I admired had great integrity and were tough. In addition Stilwell had some sarcasm," which would later earn Stilwell the sobriquet "Vinegar Joe."

Jamie had never been a good foreign language student. "I pretty near got 'found' [flunked] in French," he later noted. Stilwell taught Spanish, so Devers transferred. "I went from being the goat [last place cadet] in French to the top in Spanish. . . . On the basketball court he was just as sarcastic as he could be. . . . He could burn me out to no end and I always produced for some reason. I loved the man. He knew how to get the most out of me."[6] Stilwell's techniques led Devers to investigate psychology to try to understand the mechanics of human motivation. For the cadet who was not known for using the library, this was major motivation itself. Captain Stilwell had cadets to his quarters for dinner, especially athletes, and he and Devers became fast friends. Stilwell taught Devers how to handle cadets. "I admired him greatly," Devers later recalled.[7]

On the banks of the Hudson, Jamie learned the elements of leadership with many of the luminaries of World War II. In later life, Devers recalled, "USMA firmed the values that count – hard work, meeting deadlines, being accurate, telling the truth." He found the history and English courses, many taught by recent USMA graduates, to be lacking, but overall he enjoyed the military academy. Outside of sports, Jamie did not stand out in his class. Unless it was assigned, he didn't read much, which proved a lifelong trait. While he had a quick mind, he never showed great interest in intellectual pursuits. Rather than inquiring deeply and looking for subtle differences, he was far more likely to survey the field to the horizon, quickly size up what he deemed important, and then take action. Religion was strong in Cadet Devers's life, and he attended chapel every Sunday. Strong language for him was "gol dang it." The 1909 USMA yearbook recorded that he had been a low-level ranker in his final year, a quartermaster sergeant. Said the book, he was "an exceedingly earnest youth, and enthusiastic worker with puritanical views." Jamie was "the model of a well-bred kaydet."

Upon commissioning in 1909, Devers (now "Jake") chose the artillery. He was drawn to that arm's mobility and fire power. Although not among the academic elite who chose the Corps of Engineers, artillery was a thinking man's branch. In an era that was just accustoming itself to the typewriter and couldn't imagine the computer, the ability to solve the geometry and physics required to turn a call for artillery support into precise firing instructions required a facility with mathematics.

Jake's first assignment was with the 4th Mountain Artillery, a pack artillery outfit in the far West. Duty began with stables before breakfast. "What you preach you have got to do."[8] First tend to the horses, then the men, and finally the officers. At Vancouver barracks in Washington state, Jake's sparse room in the bachelor officer's building contained a chair, table, bed, and little else. But he had a single room to himself. Not permitted civilian clothes, the young second lieutenant went to Portland in uniform. Some young officers got into trouble over gambling debts, so Jake stayed away from poker, especially since he didn't know the game. Mostly he was interested in his job, and had plenty of work on that post. After a short stay at the Vancouver barracks, the young artillery subaltern found himself in Fort D. A. Russell, a forlorn old cavalry post on the windswept Wyoming plains. Jake learned to handle mules and men as well as gunnery tables. Both man and beast required a steady hand, guided by a person with sensitivity to their needs.

In 1911, Cheyenne was still full of cowboys and Indians. There were enough "rough and rowdy places to go but we didn't go."[9] Still, with little recreation, the men drank heavily. Jake, however, by contrast, almost became a teetotaler. Back then, there were lots of details, including KP (kitchen patrol), necessary to keep the post running. Most of the time, less than a full battery turned out for training. Bugles still punctuated the day. Added duties were common assignments for junior officers, and Jake's was to serve as post communications officer with a focus on the rudimentary telephone system. That was high technology and something of a rarity in the far West before the Great War. Devers later remembered that the relatively simple switchboard was a constant problem. Showing some aptitude for things electrical and mechanical, he tinkered with it to keep people communicating. If he had stayed with his first collegiate choice, he might have earned a living as a passable engineer.

The 4th Mountain Artillery was made up of big tough men accus-tomed to lifting heavy weights and skinning mules. On pay day, they just disappeared. This was the West, and in Wyoming, it was still pretty wild. One of the older soldiers showed Jamie how to draw a holstered pistol with speed, which fascinated the young lieutenant. While it was quite a change from West Point, Devers had little difficulty making the transition from cadet to lieutenant. Without fanfare, he was the boss. He recalled, "You had to train your solders how not to get kicked [by mules]. If they get kicked you have to train them to keep going if they can. This is the way you build a team. I learned a lot about life because we had to go in and get them straightened out."[10]

There were other social issues as well. "We had 9th Cavalry [one of the famous Buffalo Solder units full of black troopers] at Fort Russell," Devers recalled, "so we had to be very tactful. We had trouble with some soldiers from the South because in Wyoming, blacks could sit anywhere on the trolley. Had a little trouble with the black chaplain from the 9th who would get very worked up about this. We were going to live with them, and by golly we did. In Rome, do what the Romans do."[11]

While out in Wyoming, Devers and the 4th Artillery made a 1,000-mile march from Cheyenne to southern Colorado and back. Most of the roads were little more than dirt tracks. The artillery formed up as a battalion of three 4-gun firing batteries and a headquarters (HQ) battery. Each battery had thirty-five mules and the battalion had three Quarter-master trains of fifty mules each. Mules should only carry 250 pounds apiece, but often the 4th Artillery overloaded them with 300–400-pound packs. Jake commanded all of these pack trains. With two hundred men to a battery, Devers had quite a task keeping the mules and mule skinners in line, especially for a young officer recently from West Point. Devers later recalled that they were a tough lot. Most of the men had had little education and came from the lower edges of society. The arduous trip took two months.

A typical march for this trip was twenty miles a day, five days a week, with Denver as an intermediate destination. Of course, the enlisted men walked while officers and senior noncommissioned officers (NCOs) rode horses. Care of feet and hooves was paramount. Devers learned the im-portance of proper shoes for both pack animals and men. After a few days on the trail, junior officers and NCOs often relinquished their mounts for several hours each day to give the most blistered men a little bit of relief. On the high plains and in the mountains, a part of the country called "the empty quarter," cold permeated the camp each night. Fog shrouded the mornings; the men broke ice most sun rises. Several times, the 4th Artillery stopped and conducted live fire exercises that reverberated in the mountains. Jake's battery commander was First Lieutenant Lesley McNair, with whom he would work for many years. They got to know each other and got along very well.

With little else to do in Wyoming, a post dance was an important social event. On the raw, isolated Wyoming plain, a young, well-turned-out Army officer was quite a catch, a ticket to escape the howling wind and see something of the world. Devers recalled that many of the young ladies in the area made it to post for social occasions. In 1911, the post commandant's daughter came out from Washington to stay for a month. Devers first met her on the street in town. Soon, he noticed that she seemed to come by the post guardhouse when he was on duty. After dating Jake a few times, Georgie Hayes Lyon decided to stay for another month. Jake taught her how to ride. She was already a good skater, and they frequently skated together outside on the pond. By the time she was to return to Washington, the couple was formally engaged.

They married on 11 October 1911. Until her death, the pair remained close, supporting each other. Georgie was known to be a charming wife who easily made friends with other officers' wives. Always ready to help out when an army family was having difficulty, she gained the reputation of an eloquent southern lady and had a huge impact on Jake's life. She stayed abreast of current events, and the Devers's dinner table was known for its lively conversation. Long after retirement, the general still began his letters "My Love" and closed with "lots of love." Human emotion contains the foundation of much human behavior. Adoration by the Japanese of their emperor. Love of Mother Russia. Deep love as between two people like the Deverses. Even though it's not quantifiable, never underestimate its fundamental influence as multiplied by millions of servicemen and their families.

In 1912, lieutenants lived modestly. Like most newlyweds, in the early days they had money problems; every nickel was important. Georgie recognized that a lot of sorrel grass graced their lawn, so she boiled and served it. The Deverses rode out to the dump to gather edible mushrooms. Little did Georgie know then that, in retirement, they would live in a fine house with a domestic staff. She was a great factor in Jake's career. As an "Army brat," Georgie knew what was expected of a young officer's wife: a life of genteel poverty, a closed society of officers' families on post. She was a gracious hostess. Unlike many officers' wives, Georgie did not attempt to play politics in order to advance her husband's career.

The Devers spent only a short time listening in Wyoming's high plains. In 1912, Devers was assigned back to the military academy as an instructor. There, he taught mathematics and artillery to classes that contained many cadets that would rise to become senior generals in World War II's European Theater of Operations (ETO). As baseball players, cadets Omar Bradley and Dwight Eisenhower served under Coach Devers. Bradley recalled that he saw a great deal of Devers, especially when he played plebe baseball, and was not favorably impressed with Devers.

Promotions were painfully slow for Devers. After seven years of commissioned service Devers made first lieutenant on April Fool's Day 1916. He thought that if he was lucky, he might retire as a lieutenant colonel. While ambitious, he felt that the opportunity for fast promotion was less than slim.

In the classroom, every cadet had to recite every day, particularly in mathematics. Typically the instructor would write a problem on the board. Each cadet would take his place along a line of blackboards and work the problem he was assigned. Since grammar school, math had been Jake's best and favorite subject. But he was concerned that he wasn't sufficiently prepared to teach the subject at West Point. After all, he had no more formal instruction than passing the required courses to obtain his diploma and commission. A Colonel Echols was head of the mathematics department at the time. Typically, recent graduates who had done well returned as instructors. The colonel, recognizing the lack of depth in these teachers' subject knowledge, gathered them together and had the budding instructors recite the work that they were to teach the cadets a few days later. By the end of Devers's tour, Echols had rated the young instructor as excellent. General William Palmer remembered

Devers while Palmer was a cadet: "He was very highly regarded at West Point. In addition to teaching math, he was attached to the Artillery. He became the protégé of the commanding officer of the West Point artillery detachment, Colonel William P. Ennis."[12]

Devers's four-year posting as an academy instructor ended in 1916. In Europe, World War I raged, and most professional officers readied themselves for the great battles that lay ahead. Adventuresome young men, like classmate George Patton, sought to join "Black Jack" Pershing down on the border of the American Southwest to chase Pancho Villa and his armed banditos back into Mexico. Instead, the young Devers requested a posting to the 9th Artillery at Schofield Barracks on Oahu.

Hawaii was comfortable duty, and assisting in the formation of the first motorized artillery broadened Devers's knowledge. Medium artillery was just entering the American army. Formed from the 1st Artillery, the 9th had a battalion of 155mm guns and a battalion of 4.7-inch guns. As Devers recalled, "Mediums were too big; we didn't have any way to horse them." The 9th became the first tractor-drawn artillery in American service. "Mobility is very important to the artillery, and it was the coming thing. So I was very enthusiastic about the assignment."[13] The first tractors were slow and clumsy, often jackknifing while descending grades, creating accidents. Soon the army substituted four-wheel-drive trucks, brutes in their day. Such line batteries needed a lot of mechanics to handle the cantankerous, rough-hewn motorized equipment. "I was very much for truck-drawn over draft animals," recalled Devers.[14]

At first he was just another officer with the regiment. Then, unusual circumstances led to his being designated as F Battery commander while still a first lieutenant, after only four months in the 9th Artillery. F Battery had essentially mutinied and lost its captain. Due to expansion pressures throughout the army, no other officers were assigned, so the Hawaiian battalion commander called in Devers: "These are hard men. If I give you F Battery you will be new to the battery and the only officer there. I am not telling you what to do but look to your NCOs and see what the problem is. I'll back you up 100%. If you need advice or help come to me." Devers willingly took on the assignment.

He discovered that the first sergeant was gambling with the men and had gotten many into debt. The mess sergeant also was doing a horrible job, and food being served was cold and unappetizing. The first thing Jake did was replace the first sergeant with a junior section sergeant. Then he called the battery together and promised that the food would improve. He replaced the mess sergeant with the chief cook. But that wasn't enough. Devers had to be present during the preparation of every meal or something would go wrong. "I got a lot of ideas from the men. When the battery showed skill at their drill and on my timeline, we would break and play baseball." Essentially, the less than fully seasoned first lieutenant was thrown into a cauldron of fire. That would have been a test for an experienced captain. But his leadership worked, and Devers learned much.[15]

At Schofield, Jake and Georgie had a nice house and help from a Chinese domestic. They were very happy in the islands. And soon they were three – Georgie delivered a baby girl named Frances.

While assigned to F Battery, Devers was also made judge advocate general – the legal officer. In those days, finding a trained lawyer out in the field was rare. The army held that any officer could perform as either prosecutor or defense counsel in even a general court martial. Devers was involved in about a dozen major cases. He also caught the duty of managing the officers' club. This included the need to collect past-due bar bills from senior officers, many of whom were not fond of being reminded of their obligations. Jake learned how to manage these delicate interpersonal jams.

Officers as a group did not study war the way they do today, and Jake did not read deeply like his classmate Patton.[16] Hostilities in Europe expanded the army, bringing much welcomed promotions. The proud father pinned on captain's bars on 15 May 1917 and a major's oak leaf on 5 August of the same year.

When America declared its participation in World War I, Jake was ordered to Fort Sill, Oklahoma, and the School of Fire there, which was turning into a major school for artillery. A new post recently built, Fort Sill was just coming into its own. Most of the instructors were raw, nowhere near the level they would attain in World War II. The youthful Major Devers was sent to be an instructor and the executive officer in the gunnery department. During the war and its immediate aftermath, Devers was promoted first to lieutenant colonel (30 July 1917) then colonel (24 October 1918). He was considered one of the school's experts in virtually all phases of artillery and was called upon to troubleshoot many projects at the post. A senior officer on post at the time commented, "Devers was very effective as a battalion commander. His professional knowledge was of the highest. He was recognized by his compatriots as an expert in artillery. He was a man of highest integrity and one of the most energetic officers."[17] A subordinate recalled, "He knew how to handle things in a simple, forthright manner. Everyone liked Jake."[18] Recalled Devers himself, "I didn't have time to read [the manuals]. My instruction was more practical than theoretical. I liked Fort Sill and its way of life."[19] For a while, Devers commanded two artillery regiments, the 14th Artillery and the 60th Artillery, a 155mm outfit that was being readied to be shipped to France when the war ended. Anyone who read the papers knew how important the big guns were in the battle of the trenches. But Jake developed a distaste for heavy artillery, decrying its lack of mobility and requirements for heavy maintenance and logistic support.

All three Devers brothers served as officers during World War I. Frank successfully completed officer's training and achieved the rank of captain. Phil became a lieutenant in the Balloon Corps. During the Great War, both sides relied on balloons tethered just behind friendly lines to maintain visual observation of enemy movements along the front. Airplanes were armed with machine guns to counter the menace of observation balloons. During interviews conducted in the 1960s, Devers said he never volunteered to go to France. He claimed he wasn't bothered about not seeing action in World War I. "I knew more than the guys that had been in combat."[20] His sister, Kit, however, dismissed Jake's recollections about not serving at the front: "He hated the fact that he missed going overseas during the war and thought his military career was over."[21] Right after the Great War, Jake was heard lamenting, "I was left standing at the starting post."

TWO

The Interwar Years

IN MAY 1919, WHILE MOST SOLDIERS WERE RETURNING HOME, Devers was one of the few American officers sent to France to attend the French artillery school at Treves. Jake never tried to use his influence to get assignments but was happy with this one. When he went to France, he retained the rank of colonel, thereby outranking many officers who had outranked him before the war, causing a great deal of embarrassment.

The French conducted staff rides of former battlefields to point out practical lessons of field artillery employment, an approach Devers liked. The British officers didn't impress him, but he got to know several French officers who were experts at their profession. Little did he know how much this background would help him during the world war that was to come. Unfortunately, the tour was unaccompanied, so Georgie and Frances stayed home with Georgie's parents while her husband was abroad. Jake left France with a very favorable impression of the French Army.[1] After completing the French school, Jake served shortly with the Army of Occupation in Germany, returning to the United States in August.

After his return, Devers again was assigned to West Point as instructor of field artillery tactics, a post he filled until 1924. Upon arriving at the West Shore train station for West Point along the Hudson, Jake had reverted to his permanent rank of captain (following his various wartime promotions). His elevation to major would not become effective until 1 July 1920. He commanded a demonstration horse battery of two hundred men and five officers, armed with 155mm howitzers and 75mm guns. Jake knew both pieces well and personally gave cadets instruction.

Again, because pulling the 155mm weapons was difficult for horses, Jake organized a complement of tractors, which also allowed his students to receive instruction in more contemporary artillery methods. Despite (or perhaps because of) what he had seen in France, Devers did not believe in trench warfare and favored mobile firepower in a war of maneuver.

Unlike both Dwight Eisenhower and George Patton, Devers did not immerse himself in the study of strategy or the reasons why men fight. While intelligent, he was not a deep thinker who pondered the intricacies of humans at war. His conversations and reminiscences were not laced with references to Carl von Clausewitz or examples of the great battles through history. Instead, they feature sports similes and analogies to the field of play: "A football team has to use all eleven men in order to win."

A longtime subordinate recalled, "I never did consider General Devers to be an intellectual giant, but he has sound judgment, a great sense of timing, tremendous energy and the enthusiasm and drive to get any job done. He is completely honest. No one could ever convince me that Jake Devers, however great the pressure, would submit to any wrong or dishonest act. He is a man of great compassion and sympathy for the under-dog."[2] While Devers headed the artillery section, Omar Bradley served West Point as a company tactical officer, providing guidance and an example for cadets. All of the instruction was in horse-drawn artillery. Major Devers was remembered as a meticulous instructor, with a keen interest in cadets, and an athletic enthusiast. Devers spent a lot of time on cadet athletics. Again, he didn't use the library much.

The Devers family received good quarters at West Point. Georgie displayed her knack for gardening and helped with post committees, as many of the officers' wives did. The Devers family usually had a couple of cats and at least one dog. As Frances showered her cats with attention, she picked up the nickname "Cat Girl." Always they had horses. The family thought the army a fine life.

Unlike most officers promoted during the war, Douglas MacArthur retained his new pair of stars. He was assigned as superintendent at West Point. MacArthur, however, was upset that the academic course of instruction at the USMA was out of date. Despite intense resistance from old-line officers, MacArthur worked hard to bring instruction at the academy into the twentieth century. He did not involve himself with trivial concerns, instead concentrating on what was important. For instance, MacArthur initiated intramural athletics so that most of the corps benefited from participating in competitive sports. Jake admired this approach. He did not have a personal relationship with the superintendent but was in MacArthur's office frequently. Early in this tour, he was called to the superintendent's office. Instead of coming directly to the point, the general, pacing back and forth as was his custom, expounded on impending international problems. "It was the most brilliant conversation I had listened to in a long time," Devers noted. Then the general handed Jake an inspector general report critical of the area maintained by the artillery detachment. MacArthur told Devers to clean it up. "I will be down to inspect," said the superintendent. "If you can't come see me, just walk in here. Don't tell the adjutant, he will only delay you."[3] His direct, simple orders left an impression on Devers.

At another of his visits to the superintendent, Devers and MacArthur talked about the academy's baseball season. MacArthur told Jake that he was in charge of winning it, plain and simple. Then they discussed a matter concerning the league West Point played in. Devers told the superintendent about a strong letter he was about to mail to the president of the Eastern Collegiate League in which West Point played. Devers commented that he might make enemies.

MacArthur responded, "Well, it is the truth isn't it?"

"Yes, sir"

"Devers, always tell the truth, then you can attack from there on. If you don't tell all of it there, then you have to go back and rearrange everything. This way you get things moving."[4]

At a time when the military academy did not have an honor code, this statement made a big impression on Devers.[5]

In retirement, Devers recalled that both

MacArthur and [George] Marshall operated in more or less the same way. They gave you a job to do. They didn't tell you how to do it. They expected it to be done in a hurry. . . . Everybody tried to build up that General Marshall and General MacArthur disliked each other. Well, I know they were in competition with each other to some extent, but I think those two men admired each other and they knew the abilities of the other. I don't think that General Marshall ever crossed up General MacArthur and I don't believe General MacArthur ever crossed up General Marshall.[6]

While not perfectly accurate, this assessment sums up Devers's beliefs about the two men. "They called me a Pollyanna but I always defended General MacArthur and his methods."

Despite Devers's stint in Hawaii using clumsy tractors as prime artillery movers, Jake understood that the army had to learn how to move faster and shift fire with more agility. Oversized weapons like the 155mm howitzer were difficult to transport and even harder to emplace. Their gun tubes wore rapidly, introducing accuracy errors, and they were difficult to replace. "You have to be flexible," said Devers. The first tractors used to replace horses to draw caissons also had their problems. They tended to get bogged down in the mud, jackknife, or get pushed over when going downhill by the weapons they were drawing. Devers knew that horses could not generate the required mobility, and that better all-wheel trucks had to be developed. As his career progressed, Jake was repeatedly involved in the development of artillery transport.

Throughout his early career, the officers that served with Devers noticed his energy level and his focused attention to detail. His enthusiasm was infectious. Known as a bright officer who could make all the pieces fit together, he was both a talented planner and a man who could get things done. Devers became expert at field artillery and was a recognized authority at the tactics and techniques of "cannon cockers." While not keen on studying warfare on the theoretical level, Jake was always studying the tactics and techniques of his profession.

About 1925, Jake started to pull together his own approach to command. He attended the nine-month "short version" of the Command School at Leavenworth, Kansas, that year. An officer that did not make it through Fort Leavenworth did not get very far, and Jake found the syllabus not hard but exciting. The instruction helped him to understand better the principles of war and overall army policies. As a cadet at West Point, Devers felt he had not received much grounding in history; Leavenworth helped a little. He remembered reading a little Clausewitz at the academy but felt he never really corrected his weakness in the history of warfare.

Jake emphasized practical experience over classroom instruction. The map problems presented by the instructors tended to favor approved "school" solutions, which were often somewhat rigid. Nevertheless, Jake received good grades. He found lessons about army administrative policy and tactical principles especially useful. While some of the student officers talked about military strategy after class, Jake's conversations were more likely to be laced with polo. "Eisenhower always said I was a good administrator but he intimated that I didn't know anything about strategy."[7] Devers graduated 42nd in a class of 258. Eisenhower graduated at the top of his class.

Emerging from Command and General Staff College as a distinguished graduate, Devers recalled, "I never tried to outguess the instructors; I just took the problem based on the principles that they lectured about and [that] I thought I remembered. I worked hard because this takes a lot of concentration."[8] When Devers returned to Europe in World War II, "I followed everything they taught me at Fort Leavenworth about forming a staff: how to form it, what each element of that staff meant, and how to handle it with some leadership and with the experience of the people that you are putting in the spots that are going to count."[9]

During the years right after the war, the army formed an artillery school at Fort Sill. Devers had developed a reputation as the one officer that knew about all types of artillery, and, following command school, Jake returned to his beloved mobile artillery in a key position, director of gunnery, serving from 1925 to 1929.[10] He taught classes at the artillery school for many years but was never a student. At the time, he was one of the few officers who knew details of both horse and motorized artillery. "I know more [about artillery] than the guys that had been in combat," Devers commented. He did not believe in the tenants of a broad education grounded in theory. His instruction concentrated on practical training, on "how to do it." At the school, he acted as pinch hitter in every subject. "If he came up on something he wasn't familiar with, he'd ask the students, who knows this piece of equipment? Instructor Devers always emphasized the practical over the theoretical."[11]

Jake had twelve instructors, one executive officer, and a scheduler assigned to his department at the school. Each instructor taught a section of ten to twelve officer students. Typically, they were in the classroom in the morning and firing artillery problems in afternoon. Devers discovered during these exercises that many of the students needed glasses. After ordering all students to take eye examinations, students' accuracy with controlled fire improved tremendously. Similarly, afternoon firing problems had been controlled by whistle command, which seemed to put everyone on edge. To relax the student officers, Devers dropped the use of the whistles. He organized advanced sections for field grade and some general officers and took on their instruction personally. For the advanced course, he eliminated the mathematics of probability and chance, which he felt was too much for senior officers, and instead described how the mathematics was employed. He stopped grading. Everyone relaxed and pulled together, and gunnery hits improved.

It was important for advanced students to understand the capability of artillery and how it fit into the battlefield team, rather than specific techniques that were usually handled by company grade officers. Many instructors improved elements of fire control. Devers concentrated on getting fire on target early. This drove advances in observation procedures, communications, and fire control. Lesley McNair later recalled that Devers was the "go to" guy when someone had a technical question for which no one else seemed to have the answer. His expertise was recognized throughout the artillery branch.

Devers's personal papers contain his notes on the development of fire direction centers. They show how he traced the centralization of fire control and the use of a battery or even a single weapon to register fire on an entire battalion. He outlined internal artillery organizations, the addition of fire control personnel to the artillery battalion, and the migration of computation of fire direction orders from officer's work to that of enlisted personnel.[12]

In between the wars, hardworking men at the artillery school developed revolutionary procedures to allow fires from battalion A to be called in by observers for battalion B so that the fires of both could be massed. Controlling massed artillery fires started at Fort Sill in 1925 in Devers's Department of Gunnery. Devers recognized that junior artillery officers' accompanying each maneuver company would provide far better target development than the battalion observation post that most armies had used in the past. To free up junior officers, he advocated using well-trained enlisted men as communicators and fire control computers instead of relying on officers. This became the basis for the incredible flexibility American artillery demonstrated in World War II. Jake carefully analyzed firing procedures and made additional changes to fire direction procedures. Procedures that previously had required thirty rounds to put steel on target were reduced to six rounds. When some older officers questioned the faster registration procedures, Devers dug out their gunnery records from an old safe and bettered them with his weakest crew. At the end of World War II, Devers's procedures were still in use.[13] Artillerymen from many nations, including Germany and Russia, were amazed at the lethality Americans wrought from a given set of artillery pieces with centralized and accurate fire control. American artillery was the greatest killer on the World War II battlefield, and Jake was there at its creation. Devers estimated it was the two hundred or so dedicated officers at Fort Sill during the interwar period that had given the field artillery the necessary tools they employed so effectively in the war.[14]

During this tour at Fort Sill, Jake met Edward "Ted" Brooks, who served as an artillery instructor. Jake found the young Brooks a good and earnest teacher, and thus began a lifelong friendship that included multiple tours together both at Fort Knox and later in Europe.

Jake was a great leader. He was on top of things all of the time, and everyone liked him.[15] From April 1928 to July 1929, he commanded the 1st Artillery at Fort Sill. From that position, Jake was transferred to the Office of the Chief of Artillery. The next year proved eventful. Jake's father passed away, and his death was hard on Jake. That same year, Jake was put on the short list to become commandant of cadets at West Point. Army senior leadership had marked him as an up-and-coming field grade officer with a bright career ahead of him. He served on the chief of artillery staff, mostly in the G3 (operations) section, until he left to attend the Army War College in August 1932.

Grading at the Command and General Staff School at Fort Leavenworth was highly competitive. Class standing often determined who would get prime, career-enhancing assignments and who would return to forlorn posts. Pressure was intense; student suicides were not unknown. On the other hand, the War College was essentially ungraded with the intent of providing attendees time to think more deeply about their profession. Jake, who attended in 1932, did not find the syllabus all that difficult, and perhaps not that enlightening. Upon graduation in

June 1933, he was ordered to the 6th Artillery at Fort Hoyle, Maryland, with additional duty as executive officer of that regiment's parent, 1st Field Artillery Brigade. In 1934, newly promoted to lieutenant colonel as of 26 January, Devers was assigned to Fort Myer near Washington, D.C., and the 16th Field Artillery Regiment, the other major organization of the 1st Field Artillery Brigade, "a plum assignment for up-and-coming field grade officers."[16] It provided salute cannons for state functions as well as horses and caissons for funerals at Arlington Cemetery. The arduous horse-drawn annual march to Fort Hoyle for maneuvers and firing exercises convinced Devers (if he needed further convincing) that the animals had to be replaced with motorized transport. He consequently led a series of tests of alternative rigs for tractor-towed artillery.

Devers retained his avid interest in sports and horses. Patton was also on post as the executive officer of the 3rd Cavalry. Both the 3rd Cavalry and 16th Artillery supported burials at Arlington Cemetery, sometimes as many as eight a day. After work, the two classmates played a lot of polo together. Many thought Jake the better player. Devers recalled, "We lived next door to the Pattons. His wife Beatrice was one of the finest personalities. Patton and I were congenial."[17] Being given command of the crack artillery unit at Fort Myer seems further evidence that senior leaders, in contemporary jargon, thought Devers was a "fast burner," destined for quick advancement. Jake too felt as if he was on his way to greater things. Jake recalled that during the interwar period, when many promising officers left the service due to limited opportunities, he never considered it.

While at Fort Sill, Jake had observed huge advances in fire direction. At Fort Hoyle for tactical maneuvers, he participated in improved artillery mobility. From a technical point of view, he became well informed about cutting-edge developments in field artillery, even though he continued to spend time playing polo. Although he was an accomplished horseman, he knew that horses would never be able to move artillery pieces fast enough to keep up. Initially, tractors were employed. While they could move weapons mounted on hard-rimmed tires through the mud, they could not develop enough road speed to keep up. Development of armored forces might have been more timely had larger numbers of cavalry officers had similar experiences trying to accomplish this feat. Jake was to have intense firsthand experience with this phenomenon.

As a practical artilleryman, Jake knew the importance of being able to keep artillery up with the movements of maneuver units. Even though he started out in coast artillery, which specialized in large, fixed guns designed to duel with battleships and moved little or not at all, Devers never became a fan of large-caliber artillery. During 1933–1934, he worked on other ideas to improve mobility of firing batteries. In the civilian sector, large trucks had begun to make their appearance. But their hard rubber tires, paired with little or no vibration-absorbing suspension, meant that howitzers would be shaken to pieces from high-speed towing. Initially innovators looked to hoist the venerable French 75mm guns and their hard-tire carriages up on the beds of powerful trucks. Dubbed "portee artillery," this arrangement showed great promise. But it seemed certain that even light artillery was going to increase in caliber and weight.

Emplacement and displacement times for "portee artillery" left much to be desired. Derricks and additional heavy trucks had to be added to each battery, increasing its logistical footprint and shipping weight, when the battery would likely be deployed overseas. Pneumatic tires and carriages mounted on trucklike suspensions offered dramatically increased road towing speeds. While stationed at Fort Hoyle, Jake was involved in experimentation in truck-drawn operations, and road march speeds increased. At first, experimental 75mm carriages were developed, which led to the familiar sight of mobile American artillery in World War II: the 105mm cannon towed behind a 2.5-ton truck.

By the time he had completed his tour with the 16th Artillery, Devers's command style had gelled. The notes he wrote to himself are revealing:

Personnel problems: one of the biggest that habitually confronts unit commanders. They must know intimately officers and men, [their] capabilities and limitations. Eliminate the dead wood. [You are] judged by what you produce, be sure the tools are sharp lest you be considered dull. Overwork comes from inefficiency. Orient officers and men – let them in on things. Ability should be rewarded with increased responsibility and promotion. Morale reflects the leadership of the commander, [be] tolerant sympathetic of personnel and [their] problems. Treat them as men – do not coddle them. Think before you act, but having thought – ACT! Proper utilization of personnel is a command function. Keep officers and men hard – constant daily exercise. . . .

Administration
Every breach of dress, neatness and saluting must be spot corrected . . . problem does not belong to senior officers alone.
Paperwork and reports should be pared to the bone.
Maintenance crews must function 24 hours of the day.
Keep fatigue details to a minimum.
Reduce administrative overhead to a minimum.
Make transition of new men smooth and without confusion, talk by commanders and by chaplain.
Keep regimental and unit areas neat, clean, and well policed.[18]

Elsewhere he noted,

Strategy is selecting the right objective.
Tactics is simple: you have force, fire power, and mobility.
Be careful not to hurt anybody's feelings. – Can't be arrogant.[19]

Always looking for immediate and practical solutions to problems, Devers did not stand on protocol and ceremony. While he was viewed as the expert, no one could master every detail and piece of artillery kit. Said Devers, "I didn't have time to read every manual," and instead focused on how to operate the equipment at hand.[20]

In the summer of 1936, General W. D. Connor, the West Point superintendent, asked Devers to return to West Point as graduate manager of athletics. Devers recalled, "A lot of people were afraid of General Connor. He called me a moron once a week."[21] This treatment, however, did not restrain Jake's enthusiasm or energy one iota.

As manager of athletics, Devers didn't interfere with the methods of individual coaches and was highly regarded.[22] He would select highly regarded subordinates, give them a job and the resources to accomplish it, and then allow them wide latitude to get the job done even if a mistake or two was made in the process. These characteristics were the essence of orders given to individuals to carry out a mission. It was an approach that became the hallmark of Devers's command style throughout his career. It also made for happy organizations able to achieve a great deal with limited resources. It required a patient leader who trusted his subordinates and had a good feeling for what they could accomplish. Jake was meticulous about getting the details right and set high standards. A subordinate who was having difficulty received more attention. But he never reprimanded a subordinate for an honest mistake.

Eugene Harrison and Jake encountered each other again at Fort Myer. Jake was well liked by junior officers there. Harrison played a lot of polo against him. On Jake's third USMA tour in 1936, Harrison was on Jake's staff. Devers made him assistant athletic director. Harrison thought Devers one of the best, as he concentrated on bringing talented youth into the corps of cadets. For a short time, Devers, who was the second most senior regular officer on post, became acting superintendent when Connor retired.

Despite the Great Depression, West Point's Athletic Association had accumulated $5 million to create first-rate athletic facilities. At the time, this was roughly the amount required to build a heavy cruiser. But instead of focusing on the performance of current-year athletic teams, the association built up the academy's sports facilities and sought to obtain the best cadet athletes possible. It was the sort of "out of the box" objective at which Jake excelled. He was never one to take his crayons and carefully color within the lines.

Jake needed blueprints for these facilities, however. Instead of going to an architectural firm, he sent Hank Holorook, West Point's master of the sword, to Yale to obtain plans of their recently completed gymnasium. With these, Jake and his staff rounded out the military academy's plans, resulting in a world-class gym that served for decades.[23] The academy also needed a fieldhouse. A study was made of a fieldhouse large enough to play football in. Again Devers sought out experts and found an old man who was extremely knowledgeable. Jake asked him, "If you had all the money in the world, what would you do to improve the [West Point] athletic field?" The gentleman responded that he would change little except the venue for shot put. But there was a major topographical problem. Tracks of the West Shore railroad had altered the riverfront. The old polo field, now the primary athletic field, lay below river level and had to be raised an average of 5 feet, no small adjustment. Some experts said soil conditions would prevent this. Devers knew little about soil bearing strength. Nevertheless, he came up with a plan and found an army dredge that was about to be laid up in Albany to complete the job, but only after Jake reached into the fund's coffers to finance the work.

Those familiar with the grounds at West Point are impressed with the stone palisades that rise up from the Hudson. Unfortunately, the palisades also restrict the land available for the academy. Added room was needed for both the new gym and a mess hall. Soon, Devers had detonations taking down rock, which was used to stabilize the dredging project. The civilians that operated the dredge said it would take three years for the dredged land to become stable enough to build on. Devers pointed to the gravel that lay deeper in the riverbed and told the operator if all he pumped in was sand and water, he would shoot him. Reluctantly, the contractors made the necessary adjustments. Gravel from upriver had to be used to complete the project. Jake did not worry about permits; he directed the dredge to move the material. To insure the relaid train tracks would not wash away, Devers had some special clay brought in and mixed with cinders from the locomotives. The railroad men supported Jake's idea since the revised track bed ran straighter, thereby making rail operations faster and more efficient. While Devers was not an engineer, Superintendent Connor was a good one. Under Connor's sometimes sharp comments, Jake learned about landfill construction. In the end, Connor laughed and told Devers that his improvisations reminded the senior officer of what he had had to do when he had been responsible for controlling a large stretch of the Mississippi. In 1938, midway through his third tour at West Point, Devers was promoted to full colonel.

Jake had a lot of stories about wheeling and dealing in relation to various games venues and construction. He recalled how a Boston contractor won the job of tiling the USMA swimming pool. The Newburgh, New York, union had demanded that he hire two local workmen for each one he brought in from Boston. Jake bristled, but the Boston contractor acceded to the demand. Still, Devers said he would throw off post any local workman he caught malingering, and he moved out quite a few. Other union problems cropped up. He came upon the fieldhouse worksite, and, instead of offloading construction steel, everyone was standing around. The union boss complained that the crane operator hadn't paid his dues. Jake promptly paid them, and everyone resumed work. Secretly, most of the workmen were pleased as they were about to lose a day's pay.

Jake picked up a lot of goodwill that made the job go easier. Rules may have been bent for many of these projects, but never the law. Devers got things done.

In 1939, the U.S. Army carried only fifty general officers on its active rolls. Made chief of staff on the day Hitler invaded Poland, 1 September 1939, General George C. Marshall was up to his eyeballs in problems created by the rapid expansion of a tiny army that was unprepared to enter World War II. The American army was about to expand from a few hundred thousand men to an 8-million-man behemoth. The new chief of staff was desperate to find trained officers to staff the leadership.

Hawaii and the Panama Canal Zone were two distant outposts that guarded key assets to the approaches to the United States. General Malin Craig, the chief of staff prior to Marshall, selected a bright, creative officer, Daniel Van Voorhis, to command the Canal Zone. Van Voorhis was a cavalry officer who had been instrumental in creating the first mechanized force in the American army. For those countries that championed democracy, 1940 brought many dark days. Britain stood alone facing the Nazi monster that had devoured Western Europe. Germany and Britain fought a desperate air battle to see who would control the English Channel and the invasion route into Britain. As Marshall communicated to Van Voorhis, "We cannot take any chances with the Panama Canal. If it is blocked our whole situation in the Atlantic becomes immensely critical should there be a tragic result in England."[24] To organize air defense of the canal, Marshall detailed a bright up-and-coming airman, Colonel Frank Andrews. The canal was defended by some of the largest coast artillery pieces in the American arsenal, including 16-inch guns, as large as America had ever mounted on a battleship. To round out the team, the ideal executive officer would be an artillery expert.

As the war clouds gathered over Europe, Devers was detailed to Panama in the spring of 1940. He was initially tasked with mechanizing the elements of Panama's defenses, including the maneuverable heavy coast artillery pieces that moved among the fixed emplacements that housed the 16-inch rifles, and with coordinating canal defense plans with the Navy. The canal zone had received poor marks for administration, which Jake cleaned up immediately. Army-navy cooperation was always difficult. In the years immediately before Pearl Harbor, the command climate in Panama between the services was especially challenging. Jake did a lot to improve day-to-day cooperation at the working level between the services. Grabbing a hold of the situation with Jake's trademark energy and vast detailed knowledge of artillery, including the artillery mechanization efforts, Jake and Van Voorhis made a great team and became lifelong friends. When asked by Marshall about Colonel Devers, General Van Voorhis opined that his executive officer was one of the best he had ever seen. Devers's reputation as a "can do" officer had become well-established.

While Jake was in Panama, there was a wild rumor that pilots of German origin had established a "Fifth Column" with the objective of stealing Pan Am Clippers at a critical time and somehow utilizing them to bomb the canal. While technically impractical, Devers personally hunted this lead down. At the time, the Nazis seemed omnipotent, and even improbable stories about them could be believed. American planners worried that the Germans might introduce forces into Dutch or French Caribbean possessions, threatening commerce. Others envisioned Nazis descending from North Africa down into West Africa and jumping the narrow point in the South Atlantic between Africa's western bulge and Recife, Brazil.

THREE

Marshall Recognizes Devers

ONE OF FRANKLIN ROOSEVELT'S MOST PERSPICACIOUS personnel decisions was making General George C. Marshall the army chief of staff. In recognition of his integrity and overpowering command presence, Winston Churchill dubbed him "The Noblest Roman." His official biographer, Forrest Pogue called him, "distant, austere, formal and humorless. He never did talk a great deal." Over his career, Marshall earned a reputation of being competent, severely fair, and impeccably honest. An early riser, he often said that no one ever had a good idea after 1 PM. He was taciturn to a fault and never had time for small talk. No one, save his old friend "Vinegar" Joe Stillwell, called him George. He did not like excessive drink, infidelity, or off-color humor. Among the army's senior ranks of officers, he was one of the most airpower minded. Early on, he selected Harold "Hap" Arnold to lead the army air forces and resolutely backed him throughout the war. Marshall had no time for stupid or unprepared people. Before one went into his office, that person needed to know exactly what he wanted from the chief of staff and have a concise and well-laid-out supporting argument. Still, "if you had a good reason, Marshall would shift," recalled Devers.[1]

For those who aspired to senior command during World War II, a prewar interaction with the coldly efficient Marshall was a seminal event. During the interwar years, the future chief of staff constantly searched among his brother officers for those who showed the skills required for leadership at the highest levels. Marshall was an infantryman. During his extended service as deputy, then commandant, of the Infantry School (1927–1932), his perceptive gaze fell on many future generals. It was a little unusual for Marshall to have encountered Devers, the artilleryman. Devers was on the Chief of Artillery Staff; he was detailed to Fort Benning and then introduced to Marshall. Instructor to instructor, Jake had the opportunity to ask about writing orders from a map and introducing new ideas to students. Marshall carefully described the methods he used. Jake recalled, "that was the first time I really got to know General Marshall."[2]

The interwar period was a time when branch rivalry tended to divide the army's officers into competing tribes according to the branch insignia worn on their uniforms. Marshall had plucked the brainy Lesley J. McNair from his post as commandant of the Command and General Staff College and made him commander of Army Ground Forces. In that role, McNair designed most of the army combat organizations from engineer battalions to infantry divisions, oversaw the creation of thousands of units, and was responsible for overseeing their training. An article in *Harper's* magazine said, "In a real sense, he was the prime builder of the American Army of World War II."[3] Marshall put him in charge, offloaded an enormous amount of detail onto this trusted subordinate, and then left him alone to do his job. That is the way Marshall worked. He demonstrated an unusual ability to show great confidence in his subordinates and to leave them decisions in their areas of responsibility. Lieutenant Colonel Mark Clark was to join General McNair and gain Marshall's recognition as McNair's right-hand man. By 1944, Clark would rise to command all U.S. troops in Italy.

McNair was Marshall's closest deputy at the time. Based upon McNair's experience with Devers both in Wyoming with the 4th Artillery and at Fort Sill, he had recommended that Jake receive his first star. Devers's current supervisor, Lieutenant General Daniel Van Voorhis, a senior officer whom Marshall greatly respected, also recommended Jake highly, as did General Frank Ross McCoy, Devers's previous supervisor during a short assignment in Nicaragua. Jake remembered McCoy as "a wonderful person who was always willing to talk to a younger man. That is where I learned to be tactful and at the same time get things done."[4]

In 1942, Secretary of War Harry H. Woodring wanted a brigadier general to be the liaison between the secretary and Marshall as chief of staff, and the chief liked the idea.[5] Much has been said of Marshall's "little black book" (which, incidentally, no one has ever seen), allegedly compiled when he was at the Infantry School. Devers was given the post. Promoting Devers was an early incidence of Marshall's making a personnel choice primarily on recommendations from men whose judgment he trusted. This substantially expanded his reach for the leaders that would take the American army to war. Devers was neither an alumnus of the Infantry School nor First Army staff from the Great War, but he was Marshall's first general officer selection. In doing so, Marshall jumped over 474 more senior colonels, something that was just not done prior to the international emergency. On 6 May 1940, Devers pinned on his first star. Classmates George Patton and Robert Eichelbergher were still colonels. Dwight Eisenhower was an obscure lieutenant colonel out in the hinterlands with the 15th Infantry.

Brehon B. (Bill) Somervell, an engineer colonel and chief of the Quartermaster Corps construction division, was made a brigadier general and assistant chief of staff for supply about the same time. He would ultimately become the lieutenant general chief, Services of Supply, in March 1942. Known to cut a corner or two, Marshall looked to Somervell to clean the cobwebs out of the Ordnance Department and put this group, known for its bureaucratic ways, on a wartime footing. Devers liked Somervell's approach – Devers felt you could call Somervell on the phone, not go through a lot of staff work, and get things done. As Marshall's team took shape in late 1941, McNair, Eisenhower, Somervell, and Devers emerged as his four horsemen, the officers he depended on when the situation at hand was especially tight.

When he was selected for promotion, Devers was chief of staff in the Panama Canal Zone. He barely knew Marshall, having met him only a few times during courtesy calls in the course of official business. As Devers recalled, "All of a sudden, out of a clear sky, secret orders came in 1940. 'Take the first transport and report to the Department of the Army.' I could get no one to tell me what this was about. When I arrived in New York, a courier came aboard with a letter from General Marshall. It said, 'The duty for which you were ordered back here no longer exists. You will report to me in Washington, and I will explain.'"[6] For a short period, Devers commanded the various units and activities in what became known as the Military District of Washington. When Devers made brigadier general, he called Eugene Harrison, who was at West Point, to come down and be his aide. During the Great War, many officers serving at the USMA were frozen there for the duration and did not see combat. Harrison looked at Devers's offer as a good way to avoid a similar fate. Devers cited Harrison as "one of the greatest can-doers."[7]

"The Military District of Washington was not that well organized," Harrison later recalled. "Devers shaped it up." Essentially, Devers handled routine matters for Secretary of War Henry L. Stimson. Harrison began a long-term association with Devers as an aide and staff member, one which lasted for the duration of World War II. Right from the beginning, Harrison told the newly minted flag officer, "General, you are now a general and nobody is going to say 'no' to you. From now on, I'm going to say 'no' to you every time I think that something is going wrong." Jake responded, "That's precisely what I want you to do. I think in that way you can help me."[8]

Not long after Devers had taken up his position, he heard from Marshall: "You have been appointed to a board of experts – the president's board of experts on selecting air and naval bases. You are to report at once to Admiral [John] Greenslade who is head of this board, and you will probably take off within two hours for Bermuda." Marshall commented to another general officer, "I had only a few hours in which to get together the Army representation so Devers was selected."[9] Apparently, Jake never became aware that Marshall had first tentatively selected the commander of army units in Puerto Rico to handle this task. Nevertheless, Devers proved a good choice, given his familiarity with Atlantic defense from his assignment in Panama and his reputation as a quick study.

The task was to figure out which of the British North American installations would be "leased" from the British and used to accommodate American hemispheric defense forces as part of the famous "Destroyers for Bases" lend-lease deal. The British were desperate for additional escorts to fight off the German U-boats that were ravaging North Atlantic shipping. Roosevelt agreed to lend Churchill forty overage American destroyers. The quid pro quo was to allow U.S. use of bases established on British territory in the Western hemisphere. Devers was on the committee that oversaw the selection of the bases. Lend-lease was quite a political football then, and no one, including Marshall, wanted to stub his toe in the spotlight. Initially, the committee selected Bermuda, which was to be fortified with coast artillery and several divisions. Devers had never been to Bermuda, but the board staff began to brief him. Serendipitously, Jake had just read about Bermuda in a *Reader's Digest* article, which noted the paucity of fresh water on an otherwise ideally situated island. The committee was projecting vast air and naval facilities guarded by an army division. Jake's first comment was, "Where are you going to get the fresh water to support a long troop list?" The committee agreed that Bermuda was not such a good idea.

Devers recalled that the committee was allowed to make their own pick of base sites to achieve American interests. Devers realized that fledgling air routes would be critical. The neophyte brigadier general knew he would have to have additional staff technical aviation expertise. This led to Devers's first meeting in General Marshall's office:

"Three hours ago you put me on the board to select new bases. Was that appointment temporary or permanent?"

"The latter," responded Marshall.

"I will need an air officer," Devers continued.

"Take the man outside my door," which was Colonel Townsend E. Griffiss.[10]

With his mission and new staff in tow, Devers proceeded to undertake studies of Newfoundland, Bermuda, Guantanamo (not part of lend-lease), and Trinidad as bases for the outer air defense of the United States. The navy officers were thorough but had focused on ship and seaplane bases. Jake had an idea. To get the best information on the most recent air surveys, he contacted the office of Juan Trippe, the founder of Pan Am Airways. Soon, Pan Am engineers were sharing their information with Devers and his small staff.

General Marshall was impressed with how Devers handled the unusual assignment of selecting island bases.[11] In turn, Jake was impressed with how quickly the no-nonsense Marshall got things done. Marshall told Devers that he did not need permission to come into the chief's office. "Sit down, say what you have got to say, and we'll clean it up in a hurry," Devers recalled Marshall saying. "He gave you a job to do but didn't tell you how to do it. He was concise, direct, to the point and expected all assignments to be done in a hurry. Marshall couldn't stand a man who asked too many questions. Everything I requested from Marshall I got." With a touch of pride, he added, "Both of us operated in more or less the same way. Once Marshall picked a man he left him alone until something went wrong. I did the same thing."[12] General Devers continued, "General Marshall is one of the finest men I have come in contact with. He knew how to handle me. He was a man of great integrity, straight to the point, he knew what he wanted, he told you what he wanted, and then he set you loose. He was fair. He was ruthless at times but necessarily so. He backed up those he gave authority to. . . . [If they didn't perform] he simply relieved them, which is the only way to do it."[13]

In October 1940, Marshall had yet another problem that he handed off to Devers. Major General Francis Honeycutt, commander at Fort Bragg, North Carolina, had recently been killed in a plane crash. Marshall told Devers, "I'm sending you down to Fort Bragg to command 9th Infantry Division [effective 9 October]. Construction [of the post] is three months behind schedule." The 9th Division had been thrown together from otherwise dissociated units, and hadn't much time to train together. "Go down there and let me know [what the holdup is]. I will back you up to the hilt. When can you go?"[14] Jake remembered some good advice General McCoy had given him some time ago: when they give you a job, say yes – and get some help.

Major General Honeycutt had been a fine officer, but he hadn't had much time to work on the problems of the post before the plane crash took his life. Now a division commander, Devers earned a second star with the assignment on 1 October 1940. Devers became the youngest major general in the army. He took Gene Harrison along with him to Fort Bragg. So began an almost father-son relationship that continued for the rest of the war. (Harrison left Fort Bragg to serve a stint as aide to Stimson before rejoining Devers at his next duty assignment. Harrison recalled that the secretary thought highly of Devers.[15]) During Devers's tenure as Commanding General, 9th Infantry Division, Colonel "Sandy" Patch was commander of the 47th Infantry Regiment, one of three in the 9th, and was about to have quite an odyssey himself. We will hear much more about him a little later.

Many tiny posts were engulfed with efforts to expand into world-class military bases. In North Carolina, 31,000 workers were enmeshed in a tangle of problems, trying to transform Fort Bragg from a small post designed to house 300 people into a training site for as many as 60,000. An aide recalled that Devers's principal task was to rejuvenate the failing effort to construct the base. Marshall needed a leader to bring order to this gargantuan problem. At fifty-three, Devers was trim with jet black hair, a boyish face with a grin to match, and slightly protruding ears; he looked and had the restless energy of someone ten years younger. At the time the youngest division commander in the army, he scorned red tape, cut corners, built Fort Bragg, and whipped a division into shape despite all obstacles. The *Washington Post* wrote, "By drive, cajolery and picking the right subordinates at Fort Bragg, [Devers] performed brilliantly.... [This] newly chosen commander is an outstanding younger member of the high command."[16] An Associated Press reporter noted, "He enjoys people and likes to talk with the troops. A human dynamo full of restless energy.... Ignoring red tape, he cuts corners and gets a job done in spite of all the obstacles.... In command at Fort Bragg, North Carolina, he is given credit for the speedy efficient development of that post."[17]

When directly asked about his reputation for slicing through the bureaucracy, Jake responded, "I always work within the Establishment in an unorthodox way.... My staff officers have authority to make decisions on the ground."[18]

Cutting through the many knots that impeded the Fort Bragg project displayed Devers at his best. Once he identified what he wanted to do, Jake was not about to be denied by some arcane regulation. Nor was he going to wait around while some far-off bureaucracy studied a question to death before granting him permission to proceed. When "who is in charge" was vaguely defined, he never hesitated to assume responsibility for getting things done. Devers was fond of saying, "Rather than sit still and get shot at, it's better to do *something*, even at the risk of making some mistakes."[19] An unidentified army historian observed, "He smashed into red tape with deliberatively destructive fury." Euphemistically, the scholar continued, "His penchant for getting things done was incomprehensible to those who could not see long range objectives as clearly as he [Devers] did. Once he told a buck private, 'The answer to red tape is to keep going and the tape soon breaks.'"[20] Devers himself stated, "I still have lots of trouble with the conservatives. They just cannot see the light and are afraid to move. . . . If you ask permission, you never get it in time."[21]

One longtime staffer observed that "Devers was so fundamentally optimistic that it was impossible for him to take counsel of his fears. Always an enthusiast, Jakie was an innovator, with imagination and leadership ability. My God, nobody was more enthusiastic than he was. . . . When a fellow like that gets the opportunity, he just bursts out, and that's what he did."[22] The sign behind Devers's desk summed up his attitude: "DO SOMETHING."

The state road network into the location where Fort Bragg was to be constructed was essentially nonexistent. When he first drove to the base, it took Devers two and a half hours to go 5½ miles. Efforts to build roads to the remote post typify the Devers style. Construction workers swarmed over the site, so that it became impossible to move. At the time, the very inexperienced constructing quartermaster, the officer charged with developing the camp, was completely overwhelmed. He couldn't get approval to get anything even started. "The real power was Colonel Norman S. Peace, and the prime contractor was Loving and Co.," recalled Devers. "I called them my peach-loving machine."[23]

Devers called in all the contractors and construction engineers. Drawing a little on his brief construction experience along the Hudson, he announced that all work except road construction would stop. Construct the road system. If you have to, use troops. Work weekends. Someone complained that Devers had no authority to commit the required funds. The constructing quartermaster shuddered at Jake's methods, stating that Devers did not have funding authority to finance his commitments. A less aggressive commander might have stopped. Devers responded, "Before we get through this project there is going to be so much money spent that it won't make any difference. We will get the money. I'm the commanding general. I'm responsible for the constructing. You have to carry out the contracts and see that the work is properly accounted for. All you have to do is sprinkle [oil] over the road, let it soak in, roll it properly, grade it, and you've got a good road. Now we can build roads pretty fast can't we?"

"Yes," responded the general contractor.

"Go to work tomorrow and build that road."[24]

It is amazing what an aggressive, self-starting commander can get done when he is confident he has the full backing of his commander and understands his superior's intent.

Devers directed them to first concentrate on the main entrance road to clear the bottleneck that had so slowed his arrival. Then they were to improve all roads into work sites so that traffic could really move. Fortunately, Devers had a skilled reserve engineer who handled all the drawings. Still, further state approval had not been completed but was needed. Nonetheless, Devers approved the road network on the spot. Bulldozers began roughing the roads in. With the equipment on hand, basic roads that met state requirements were graded, graveled, and oiled. The traffic snarls eased.

Even though it was Saturday, Jake called Bill Somervell: "His secretary said he was in conference. I said I'd wait all day for a return call. Bill was a real operator." Devers would not be deterred. The way Devers intervened in road construction was, to say the least, outside of procedure. Devers confided to Somervell that he had hijacked the Fort Bragg construction project from the quartermasters and directly awarded contracts to local firms to build much-needed roads to access the fort. Somervell said he would get Devers's actions covered and to keep on going. That is exactly what Marshall wanted. Construction at Fort Bragg was progressing again. Somervell called building designer Leslie Groves in Atlanta, who handled such matters in the Southeast.[25] Jake recalled, "He was a big help in a lot of things. Groves didn't know how we could do some of the things we had done, but he didn't say no. So I didn't have any trouble there."[26] The harvest was in, so Jake engaged a lot of farmers who arrived with their own tools to help. Employing local farmers squelched any union problems. Devers had no labor unrest at the time, as everyone had more work than they could do. Everyone worked together to meet the national emergency, and they were proud of it. Locals also liked the additional income, which lubricated local businesses.

Somervell then set about handling public relations. He sent his road man for North Carolina to meet with the state. Within forty-eight hours, he had an approved plan for the needed road system into Fort Bragg.[27]

Troops at the camp were living in tents heated by wood stoves. "Tents and no overcoats; this would not do," Harrison recalled. "At Fort Bragg, Devers's principal job was to get the base constructed. He stepped in his very aggressive way. Almost overnight you'd see a new group of barracks go up."[28] Devers made sure that his staff knew the priorities and gave them the authority to do them. Decisions were made quickly. Buildings were completed and occupied before they were authorized. Twenty-five hundred buildings, large and small, were erected. At the peak of construction, one went up every thirty-two minutes. When central heating in some barracks failed, Devers cajoled the railroad to "lend" him several steam locomotives. These were positioned on a nearby siding, and their steam was piped into the chilly barracks. Fort Bragg was woefully short of churches to handle the multitudes arriving on base. Constructing new churches to essentially be used one day a week seemed incredibly inefficient when there were so many other construction needs to be met. So Jake divided the troops into sevenths and let each group have its day at the one existing chapel.

There was a constant litany of impediments from an army that had not yet cast off its frugal interwar ways to ready itself to tackle world-sized enemies. Often the issues were small. Although Fort Bragg was authorized only 449 typewriters, Devers requisitioned 1,299. Despite the gathering war clouds, the commander of the Washington Quartermaster Depot thought it was appropriate to complain to Marshall about the discrepancy, and generated a memo from the quartermaster general to the chief of staff. Marshall replied that an additional 840 typewriters for a 62,000-man post seemed reasonable, as there was no letup in the amount of paperwork required by the War Department.[29] "Leaders like General Marshall will always back you up," observed Devers.[30] That the chief of staff had to intervene in a dispute over an order for a few hundred typewriters demonstrates the hidebound bureaucracy that Marshall had to rip through if he was going to get the American army ready to fight the Nazi war machine. Marshall followed up with a second memo castigating the quartermaster general for late delivery of equipment, inadequate laundry facilities, inadequate baking ovens, and lack of sufficient furniture for the number of men moving into Fort Bragg.

During the summer, Devers noticed that his military police (MPs) were frying in the heat and sun. According to army protocol, prescribed uniforms were sacrosanct. Not to Jakie. He acquired a supply of tropical pith helmets to shield his men from the Carolina sun. The men recognized that the "old man" was watching out for them.

Jake created an open and friendly but results-oriented command style. Simple, forthright, honest, and direct, he got things done. He said, "I never saw a commander worth anything that stayed around his headquarters. . . . When you have troubles, you have got to go yourself. You don't need to go where things are going right."[31] He left his chief of staff at HQ to keep the communications open and went up to the front. Devers told his subordinates, "Do the best you can with what you have in an honest and forthright manner," and he gave them a lot of authority to make decisions on the spot.[32] When it came to resources but where authority was not clear, Jake told them, "If you need it, use it."[33]

Marshall was impressed with Devers's attitude. General Omar Bradley recalled that Devers's performance at Fort Bragg caught Marshall's eye.[34] In early 1941, the chief of staff wrote to Devers, "I want to tell you formally how highly I appreciate the splendid job you are doing there."[35] Marshall increasingly relied on his four horsemen to assist in organizing the army for war.[36] McNair, commander of Army Ground Forces, created the organizational design and formation of the hundreds of units that had to be assembled.[37] As commander of Army Service Forces, Somervell oversaw all aspects of army logistics. All four men shared some common characteristics. Each had tremendous organizational skills, and could complete large, difficult tasks with little supervision. All of them were bright and known for their staff abilities. Interestingly, none of them had much experience in commanding large organizations or much combat experience. While Marshall advanced all four rapidly through the general ranks, he did so only after they repeatedly performed well under pressure. Capable men, like General Leonard "Gee" Gerow, who was bright but lacked the ability to make decisions without a lot of input from Marshall, were shunted into important but far less demanding tasks. Marshall himself was very direct. "I think the great thing was that General Marshall called you on the phone," noted Devers. "You don't go through a lot of staff work. He had a staff, yes. He listened to them, yes, but he cut across their lines when it was necessary to get something done."[38]

Marshall remarked that it took an extraordinary leader to pull together, essentially from scratch, a base to house sixty thousand men. Clearly he was impressed with what Devers had accomplished. Marshall wrote to Devers about the "reversal of form that is almost revolutionary. The greater part of the reason is your capable management and leadership." Writing to Daniel Van Voorhis, Marshall said, "Devers has gone a long way since he left your place. He is now a Division Commander, and making a fine job of it. We want to find more men of the same type and I am willing to go down the list quite a way to get them."[39] Martin Blumenson, the noted historian who was present during the European campaign, wrote, "Devers had the quality of persistence and enjoyed the reputation of having accomplished successfully every task he was assigned. Marshall saw him as a dedicated, dependable officer who eschewed publicity and flamboyance and who projected a quiet air of authority and no nonsense." Patton, fellow tanker and West Point classmate, referred to Devers as "a clever man."[40]

While commanding the 9th Infantry Division, Devers matured a command philosophy that he had been developing throughout his career: "First assemble a good staff. . . . I always called in the guys that talked the loudest."[41] Plan the division's training schedule. Make sure the training is relevant, and that it motivates the men. Insure teamwork both with the staff and up and down the chain of command. Then stand back and let your subordinates do their jobs. That develops them as well as the men. "You can't do everything. You have to have people you can depend on." Give staff authority but insure that they report to you. You will get more things done even if you have to allow for mistakes. "If you have a small staff, you don't have too many people passing on your decisions." Furthermore, "a small staff comprised of keen-minded alert officers of unquestioned integrity is the key to unity and success in action. You can never have a staff too small."[42] A staff should be made up of "men who will express their convictions in the planning stage and men who, when a decision is made, know how to carry it out loyally and properly. . . . Avoid layers that keep anything from getting done."[43]

As the 9th Infantry was fleshed out, a lot of new men arrived in newly activated units. Jake instituted a "buddy system" where a longer-serving battalion took a new one under its wing. In 1940, much mission essential equipment was in short supply. Through the buddy system, new units borrowed equipment for training and instruction from their partners. The senior unit had methods and procedures on which the new unit could pattern itself. Jake insisted on unit discipline and on adhering to the schedules in the training plan. Traffic accidents were reduced, and field exercises got off on time, reducing maneuver area congestion. Combat training took place at all hours. He instituted night exercises, which were executed without a single casualty. Devers was always out in the field inspecting and encouraging. This boundless ball of energy was legendary for never letting a day go by without personally attending to every operation.

John Turnispeed, a strapping black cook, started working with the Deverses at Fort Bragg. Even though he was in the Deep South, Devers told Turnispeed, "You come by the front door, not the back door."[44] When he was transferred to Fort Knox, Jake was going to leave him, but John wanted to stay with the general. So Devers took him. Turnispeed did not make the transfer to England but joined up with Devers again in North Africa and stayed with him thereafter. Wherever he went, Jake was known to be open to the needs and problems of nonwhite troops. They knew that they could talk with John, and John would talk to Devers. At Fort Knox, Devers was informed that some landlords in nearby Louisville were discriminating against black officers. Devers set up special bachelor officers' quarters for them. A Mrs. Collier ran the Fort Knox Service Club. Devers always stopped by to see her. On post, Jake had a brigade of black soldiers organized in the coast artillery and a black engineer regiment, both commanded by white officers. Devers commented, "Good as they were, they always seemed to be singing when they weren't double timing around post. Troops that enthusiastic deserved the very best in support."

While Devers stove to be fair and give each man a second chance, he would relieve an incompetent quickly. He believed that the way to make a person responsible was to give him responsibility. "Give a kid responsibility when he is young," he said.[45] Likewise, "Do the best you

can with what you have in an honest and forthright manner."[46] Devers
preferred to use company punishment instead of courts martial. A man
could make a mistake, pay for it, but not be branded for the rest of his
hitch. Devers's approach dropped the post's stockade population from
two hundred to sixty.[47] When faced with a controversy, Devers said,

> You must look carefully to get the facts. Don't make up your mind or take sides
> before everyone has had his say.... When you want to get rid of a man you
> better not write him. Go in and see whether he is doing the job and talk to him.
> You might find that your judgment might not be as good as it ought to be. First,
> establish if a man is no good. Did the man believe he was right; is he weak or is
> he deliberately no good? Get rid of the ones who are not willing to do a good job.
> Often a man is put in a job he cannot perform. Look around to see if there is a
> place where he can do well. If there is, give him a second chance at something he
> can succeed at. If someone is not working out, put in another alongside to do the
> job. Then move the failure to something he can do.[48]

Devers recalled that many prewar officers were "top notch." At that
time, many married officers were accompanied to North Carolina by
their families. Jake knew the importance of maintaining some semblance
of a good family life. He worked hard trying to improve the lives of de-
pendents. Most of the officers he met in his first fourteen years of service did not see action in World War II. Many of the enlisted men were
rough and ready; most did not have high school diplomas and a number
had never attended high school. The draft brought in a more intelligent,
better-educated group of enlisted men. But they needed to be kept use-
fully occupied. Leaders needed to remove the drudgery from daily life
that their long-serving predecessors would tolerate. In World War II,
Devers felt the weakness was in noncommissioned officers. The best
were always being selected for officer or other specialized training. The
new sergeants simply didn't have the long-term experience that their
predecessors possessed.[49]

Devers's friends took to using the more familiar "Jakie," a nickname
that does not elicit images of a towering, fierce warrior. Jakie had the face
of a choir boy even into his fifties; he looked more like a kindly school
teacher than combat commander. But he grasped problems quickly, reduced them to fundamental elements that could be managed or changed,
and came up with a solution or course of action in short order. The *Washington Post* said, "He had a pleasing personality. One immediately sensed

he was extremely intelligent."[50] Everyone who commented about Devers described him as "a human dynamo full of restless energy," noting that, "By drive cajolery and picking the right subordinates, he performed brilliantly."[51] But some observers also said, "He wasn't flamboyant like Patton, nor did he have Bradley's publicity machine. Like Eisenhower, [he] had never heard a shot fired in anger at him." One continued, "He had none of the fire and flair of leaders like [Lucian] Truscott, Patton, and Terry Allen."[52]

His friends and associates remembered him as a perpetual motion machine. "He talks off the top of his head all the time, which is just a matter of thinking out loud." Some saw this as "wild talk. Often [he] seemed to expect more than was humanly possible. Devers did not operate on 'what's in it for me.'"[53] "Devers never hit the panic button about anything. You could never get Devers excited about anything! The only time was when he was enthusiastic and almost jumping up and down he was so enthusiastic. But to get him gloomy or panicky, that's just not in the cards for General Devers."[54] During some risky situations during his command of the 6th Army Group in combat, a subordinate noted, "I saw absolutely no hesitation or sign of stress."[55] Devers was a meticulous record-keeper and left a large trove of papers. Devers did not let details overwhelm him. He selected good subordinates and let them do their jobs with little interference. Devers said, "I always called in the guys that talked the loudest," "issue orders broad and general," and "be seen; lead by example."[56]

The U.S. Army preaches the value of "mission type orders," where the commander tells a subordinate what to do and when to do it but leaves the "how" up to the creativity and ingenuity of the subordinate. While it is an official policy, many commanders cannot resist detailed instruction. Bradley, an army group commander, sometimes issued orders on movement of individual divisions, three levels below his station (army, corps, and division). Devers issued his intent and broad instructions to his immediate subordinates and let them handle their own operations. In order to speed responsiveness, he eschewed the micromanagement so prevalent in command-oriented spheres. It meant he had to tolerate solutions that were not exactly what he would have done and also some mistakes on the part of his juniors. In return, he got a more agile and

responsive organization, which he prized. And good subordinates flourished under the freedom of action they enjoyed. Devers's style would
later give the French under his command the independence of action
they needed to handle the problems that arose due to conflicting orders
from their army group commander, Devers, and their national leader,
Charles de Gaulle. Said Devers, "If things are running right, no reason to
go up there and stir them up. When there was trouble, Marshall helped.
I emulated that."[57]

Devers was incisive and straightforward. He thought a great deal
about a problem ahead of time. When called on, he was ready to make
a decision with dispatch. He washed a problem of its clutter, identified
the main issues, and then took action quickly. The combination of a
quick mind and the ability to delegate smaller issues to his subordinates
allowed Jake to concentrate on the essential. Patton, Devers's classmate
and one-time subordinate, was always saying, "Fill the 'unforgiving minute' with sixty seconds of distance run. That is the whole art of war."
Devers agreed entirely. "Time is just an important element in planning
and fighting as in anything else. Give them the policy guidelines but
they don't have to follow it rigidly or you'd never get anything done. This
builds up the judgment of the staff officer. Even when they are wrong,
you accomplish more than if you took a whole week to get it turned out
right because you have the rest of that week in which you've done a lot
of other things that will help cover up that deal."[58]

This bright coin in Devers's pocket also had a problematic side.
While he assembled a lot of objective data before he acted, occasionally
Devers would bridge across some fact he did not command. Sometimes
he won this bet. On several occasions, his lack of thoroughness forced
him to guess wide of the mark. He made some important mistakes in
front of Eisenhower that caused him enormous trouble.

A colleague later said, "He was a man of tremendous leadership ability; a very strong personality who is decisive but always willing to listen.
[He] won't listen to a dumb person very long. When a decision is made,
he expects that to be carried out without question. Jake is understanding,
with a warm personality. He is a great enthusiast. He can associate and
be a friend of a wide range of people." Furthermore, he was "universally
respected, well liked, he had a knack of getting along with the French."[59]

Another general officer colleague reinforced those observations: "General Devers is probably as fine a natural leader as I have ever known. . . . He always expects that everything is going to work all right, and the weakness of that [is], of course, that he often envisions more than can possibly be accomplished in the time and with the resources that he is thinking of. . . . He inspires people who work for him."[60] Devers stated, "Men are trained to follow leaders because they respect them, and the idea of compulsion is always in the background. Respect authority without being overawed by it."[61] He was deeply interested in other men and, after Fort Bragg, had practical experience with handling large organizations in the field. Devers watched out for his men: "Divisions should be in the line no longer than 21 days. Men get tired and sick. This induces lack of enthusiasm and makes them careless."[62]

FOUR

Chief of Armored Force

IT WAS ABOUT NOON, AND DEVERS WAS IN HIS OFFICE WHEN
the phone rang. It was General Marshall:

> Is anybody listening on this phone?
> Well, if they were they are off, General Marshall.
> I want you to get into your plane this afternoon and fly to Fort Knox,
> Kentucky. [General Adna R.] Chaffee is dying, and I don't want to announce it
> right now, but I am going to put you in command of the Armored Force. There is
> something wrong down there [at Armored Force]. I want to know about. I want
> you to go down to Fort Knox and find out what the trouble is and spend as much
> time as you want and then fly to Washington and tell me what the trouble is. In
> the meantime, we will get your status cleaned up and decide what we have got
> to do.[1]

"As I sat back in my chair to catch my breath, after hanging up the
telephone," recalled Devers in retirement, "the first thought that occurred to me was General Van Voorhis is going to get a big laugh out of
this."[2] Van Voorhis had been Jake's commanding officer in Panama, and
had earlier been instrumental in shepherding mechanized cavalry into
reality in the early 1930s. On sultry afternoons back in the canal zone,
he and Devers had sometimes talked about mechanized forces. Jake was
somewhat ambivalent. Initially, Devers viewed the tank as a method of
getting a large-caliber gun into position to fire directly on the enemy.
That did not embody the concept of slashing, high-speed warfare. What
little he saw of interwar tanks appeared "clumsy" to him.

The American army had tanks in World War I. George Patton, then a
temporary colonel, commanded the American tank brigade for a couple
of days in combat before he got shot in the seat of his pants. Back in

America, Colonel Dwight Eisenhower ran the tank training center near Gettysburg, Pennsylvania. The military reforms of 1920 abolished the World War Tank Corps and transferred its fleet of claptrap machines to the infantry. Most viewed the tank as an infantry support weapon that aided dough boys in breaking through lines of enemy trenches and machine gun nests. Some cavalry officers who could pull themselves away from their beloved horses saw cavalrymen mounted in vehicles but still conducting the traditional cavalry roles of operational reconnaissance, deep penetration of combat power into the enemy's flank and rear, and pursuit of defeated enemies as they ran from the battlefield. A mechanized brigade was briefly reconstituted in 1928, but quickly disbanded as no one could keep its antiquated vehicles running. In 1931, a collection of motorized units reconstituted the mechanized force that then-Colonel Van Voorhis commanded, the 7th Cavalry Brigade (Mechanized). The indefatigable tank proponent Adna Chaffee served as his executive officer. A handful of tanks were procured, and cavalry-like tactics pursued.

Daniel Van Voorhis has been called the grandfather of the Armored Force. Under his portrait, which hangs at the Armored School at Fort Knox, an inscription reads, "The Armored Force sprang from the seeds he planted." Throughout the interwar period, the chiefs of Infantry and Cavalry fought bitter turf wars over control of tank and mechanized forces. This and a reactionary Ordnance Department stunted the growth of tank and armored forces. Van Voorhis recommended Fort Knox as a home for mechanized forces, as "it would not be dominated there by the chief of any branch."[3] He envisioned the brigade as an exploitation force to capitalize on infantry success at creating a breach or turning the flank of prepared enemy defenses. Chaffee championed fast, light tanks to continue the mobility differential that the horse enjoyed over foot troops. He stated, "The primary role [of the tank] is in offensive operations against hostile rear areas."[4] But in the branch dominated interwar years, the more tank-minded in the infantry were effectively excluded from further mechanized development. Those "light cavalry" roots retarded development of heavier, more capable vehicles. The infantry branch continued to develop heavier "infantry accompanying tanks," and did develop the "tanks lead" concept as an auxiliary tactic to concentrate tanks to crack an exceptionally hard enemy position. A few farsighted infantry men also foresaw the possibility of using these lead tanks to exploit enemy reserve positions to defeat a counterattack before it could get started.

The Armored Force had been revived because the last chief of cavalry, Major General John Herr, could not grasp the concept of mechanization in a future war.[5] General Herr preferred horse-mechanized cavalry, which transported horses around in tractor-trailers, to acquiring anything resembling a main battle tank. The energy and effectiveness of the Armored Force's first commander, Adna Chaffee, was legendary, and he is most associated with the creation of the Armored Force. For many years between the wars, he, at times almost singlehandedly, had advocated a mobile tank force capable of wide maneuverability through the thicket of competing fiefdoms and critics who said that a mobile force could not survive on the battlefield. It was he who came up with the title for the new branch. Chaffee told Frank M. Andrews, then Marshall's G3 (operations), "Call the division Armored, then no branch can kick."[6] History has granted him the title "Father of Armor" for his persistent efforts to drag a reluctant, tradition-bound army into the age of mobile warfare. Van Voorhis also remained steadfast in his support of a mechanized combined arms force. After the Plattsburg maneuvers of 1939, the largest peacetime maneuvers ever held in the United States to that time, Chaffee recognized the value of mobile divisions with a heavier punch than the lightly armed cavalry units and began advocating "armored" divisions incorporating fast but cannon-armed tanks and some infantry. He still, however, had not solved the problem of mobile artillery support, and advocated a much more tank-heavy organization conducting traditional heavy cavalry missions than Van Voorhis and other mobile warfare advocates.

The actual creation of the Armored Force was almost matter of fact. Chaffee met with General Herr to plead again for an American armored division. Herr responded, "Not one more horse will I give up for a tank."[7] In long hand, Chaffee wrote out a proposal for an independent armored force and took it into the army's operations officer, the very capable and open minded Frank Andrews of Andrews Air Force Base fame. Andrews looked it over and said he would have it typed and read by Marshall. In his no nonsense manner, within an hour, Marshall had read and approved Chaffee's plan. Horse cavalry was doomed, and an armored force created.

Devers had known Chaffee well. After Chaffee's presentation at the War College on mechanized forces, the college's commander, Robert M. Danford, had called Chaffee "visionary."[8] His untimely death left the Armored Force to meander just when it needed to go full-speed ahead. A few eyebrows were raised when Marshall appointed artillery-man Devers to become the second Armored Force commander. After all, the Armored Force had been propelled by hard-charging cavalrymen like George Patton, who had commanded the American Expeditionary Force's tank operations and was an officer well known to Marshall. Actually, Marshall did discuss a number of armored force issues with Patton "in some detail."[9] But Patton wasn't familiar with British procedures at the time. Patton favored the "cavalry school" approach of a horde of lightly armed and armored fast tanks making sweeping envelopments into the enemy's rear. The tanks he had commanded in the Great War were light French Renaults, not armed to fight opposing tanks. So Marshall turned to Devers instead of the recognized "experts."

Marshall and Chaffee had been fighting a major institutional problem. Before the war, the chiefs of the combat arms (Infantry, Cavalry, and Artillery) had had a great deal of independence from the chief of staff. Each chief had direct access to members of Congress, who controlled their budgets, and therefore could steer independent courses. And all three were opposed to high-speed combined arms mechanized forces.[10] Even after panzers had overrun Poland, General Herr lectured a group of War College attendees that "that the machine could not replace the horse."[11] Major General Robert M. Danford, chief of artillery, held that the horse was the proper prime mover for light artillery and blocked self-propelled artillery. Major General George A. Lynch, chief of infantry, wanted nothing but heavily armored carriers armed with low-velocity assault guns, good for machine-gun-nest-busting but poor at penetrating tank armored plate to crawl along at the pace of his beloved foot infantry. As late as 1939, Lynch said, "the Infantry did not want any Panzer divisions." In the 1930s, MacArthur held that the army should buy only a small number of tanks as they were expensive and quickly outmoded.[12]

Lieutenant General Lesley McNair, head of Army Ground Forces, principal architect of the army organization that would fight World War II, and Marshall's right hand, strongly held that towed antitank guns, aggressively deployed, could eliminate the armor threat. Evidence from the Spanish Civil War indicated that the flimsy vehicles committed there had great difficulty in dealing with antitank guns and were vulnerable if they advanced faster than the infantry.[13] The notion of lightly armed and armored mechanized units penetrating into the depth of the enemy seemed an outdated relic of horse cavalry days and had no place in a 1940 army. Earlier, McNair had objected to an armored force due to its cost. A pamphlet used at the Command and General Staff College as late as 1938 decreed, "There will be no Panzer Division in our Army."[14] McNair, an artilleryman and advocate of fire power and attrition warfare, as opposed to the cavalry tradition of maneuver warfare, "had exhibited evidence of a distinct bias against an armored force."[15] One author went so far as to call McNair "armor's nemesis."[16] In December 1941, he would tell Secretary of War Stimson that the concept of the Armored Force was flawed, and that antitank guns should be stressed.[17] Before Congress, General Chaffee had stated that the army had "failed to evaluate properly the importance of combined arms in armored units."[18]

Although believing that big guns could stop tanks, Marshall was unhappy with previous Armored Force answers. Given McNair's prejudgment and the conflicting evidence from European battlefields overrun by German panzers, it is easy to see why Marshall needed a separate organization reporting directly to him if the American army had any chance of creating a competitive armored force. Still, Marshall was very much a proponent of heavy guns. His instruction while at the Infantry School featured the artillery-infantry team with little said of cavalry. At the time, Major General Charles L. Scott, the much-respected armor leader and commander, I Armored Corps, was an obvious choice to continue in Chaffee's tradition. He was reaching retirement, however, and Marshall appeared to be looking for a different slant than the light cavalry charges favored by Patton.

In a 1972 interview, General Anthony McAuliffe revealed additional information regarding Devers appointment, which in some ways was as matter of fact as the creation of the Armored Force. Back in 1941,

McAuliffe was carpooling with Walter "Beadle" Smith, who was then serving as the powerful secretary of the army staff, an important aide to General Marshall. During one such commute, Smith said that Devers was a man of action. Groping around for Chaffee's replacement, Smith recommended Devers to Marshall.[19]

Marshall leaned toward antitank guns as the way to fight tanks and wanted to see heavier armament on tanks. Devers, the artilleryman, saw the tank as a way to move a big gun around the battlefield. In his early Armored Force notes, Devers commented, "This is a gun war. Airplanes, tanks, battleships, and so forth, are merely means of transporting guns to a place where they can be used to destroy the enemy."[20] Marshall described McNair as having expert knowledge of artillery and infantry combined action, a combination Marshall strongly supported when he was at the Infantry School.[21] Devers's early position was not inconsistent with the views of the other two generals. But Devers's view would evolve. McNair, who had a well-earned reputation as an honest broker, promised Devers that he would do his utmost to see that other branches would be schooled in the armored doctrine that came out of Fort Knox. McNair told other senior officers that Armored Force doctrine and policy "are out of our line," meaning this was not the expertise of the Army Ground Forces staff.[22] Devers and McNair would be the only subordinates of Marshall routinely picking division commanders, so harmony and trust at this level immeasurably smoothed out the process.

Devers had some grounding in armor development: "I had been in the training section of the chief of artillery for nearly four years. Every time they had a tank demonstration on tanks, I went over to Aberdeen as representative of the chief's office," recalled Devers. He picked up ideas from Edmund L. Gruber, a good tactician of German descent who read that language and knew what the Germans were doing. Gruber said, "You haven't got any vehicles to do this [German Doctrine] with." He had talked to "slow anti-machine-gun-nest" infantry branch representatives and to Christie-suspension "fast light tank" promoters.

After his inspection trip to Fort Knox, Devers personally reported to Marshall, "The Armored Force is in trouble. I found a pretty bad mess down there."[23] Chaffee had been sick for a year. Cancer had robbed him of any productive ability. His executive officer's fondness for strong drink effectively immobilized his second. For lack of a senior decision-maker, staff work had come to a halt. The existing staff of the Armored Force had a lot of holes in it. A good tank school, mostly composed of civilian instructors, however, was turning out competent mechanics and crewmen. Soldiers at Fort Knox dubbed it "Newtona College," referring to Sir Isaac Newton, because it provided such good training. Many good officers clamored to transfer into what was perceived to be the up-and-coming Armored Force, but branch chiefs, all under pressure to expand their own organizations, held on to their best. Out of the 3,665 officers assigned to Armored Force, only 116 had previous tank or mechanized cavalry experience.[24]

Meanwhile, the Ordnance Department had not come up with an acceptable power plant for even a medium tank. Armored Force was a bunch of cavalrymen with a single good light tank design, the M3 Stuart. It had only sixty-six vehicles that passed as medium tanks, but none of them could survive in Europe.[25] The branch needed an organization to transform some vague ideas into well-engineered metal on the ground, organized into units trained, supported, and ready to fight. Devers talked a lot with Marshall and Stimson about how to organize the Armored Force.[26] "The cavalry didn't have any real tanks," Devers told Marshall. "They had pieces of tanks. We didn't have any power plants to drive the tanks, and industry told me that it would be a year to get the power that I needed to drive those tanks and carry the guns and get the fire power. We didn't have any projectiles to fight tanks. They had no [functioning tank] transmissions."[27]

There was no shortage of ideas among the protagonists of Armored Force. Marshall had been closely following the development and knew the American army was in trouble. Not much was getting accomplished. Devers, who did not have a well-established position but had a proven record of "get it done," seemed to be a good choice. Marshall also knew that the unsettled nature of mechanized field artillery support called for some artillery expertise. Devers was a doer. Conceptualizing a new idea was not his strong suit. But give him an outline and he quickly sharpened a vague idea and commenced action that turned it into reality. He readily took input from the field. "Tell us what you want and we will get it," he said. According to a member of the original armor advocates, "One of his strengths was the ability to sort out competing ideas, recognize the strengths and weaknesses of each alternative and make decisions." General Charles D. Palmer said, "Devers became the driving force behind the Armored Force."[28]

Things immediately began to change upon Devers's arrival. The new chief of Armored Force was as bold and aggressive as the tactics of armor. He cut into red tape with deliberatively destructive fury. "Devers is a good judge of human beings," recalled Bruce Clarke, who went on to become a noted combat armor commander and ultimately four-star commander of the army in Europe during the height of the Cold War. "He could get a difficult decision from his staff on almost anything in five minutes. He delegated the authority to staff. They relaxed and worked as a team."[29] Palmer said, "Initially, Devers had a good, thinking tanker, Ernie Harmon, as a chief of staff. However, he soon was selected for a command slot. Then Jake selected a man who would also become his chief of staff later in Europe, Jack Barr. Barr knew more about the basic problems of the Armored Force than anybody I could find."[30] The official history of the Armored Force would later observe, "General Devers, with his boundless enthusiasm and optimism, overcame a host of difficulties and got the Armored Force reoriented toward a better outlook on life, and in no time things were moving."[31]

In his lengthy interview with Forrest Pogue, Devers made some very revealing comments about his leadership style and offered perhaps a little insight into why Marshall was so attracted to him: "One of the things or troubles they have in the Pentagon today, and the reason General Marshall has been a great and successful administrator as well as a general, he had a staff. Yes, he listened to them, but he cut across their lines when it was necessary to get things done. His directions to me were 'you are under me.' He didn't put me under McNair or anybody else – thank goodness. I would have never gotten anything done."[32] George Patton put it another way: "The best is the enemy of the good. A good plan executed in time is far better than the perfect plan not ready to be executed until you are overrun."[33] Devers could make a timely decision, get it into execution, then modify it as events unfolded. That speed of action is what makes organizations adaptive and agile. Devers had that skill. When difficult decisions had to be made under extreme time pressure, Marshall was renowned for stepping into the breach. Devers also had a reputation for accomplishing an assigned task under severe deadlines. The results might not be nicely packaged and impeccably presented, but they were there in time to get the next critical step completed by its own deadline.

One of Devers's first tasks was to decide what key characteristics the army needed in its tanks. Then he had to outline the specifications of each needed type and freeze the designs so that American industry could produce them post haste. He was confronted with two divergent concepts. It was a case of the cavalry's "raised pistol and charge" versus the infantry's "look before you leap."[34] Chaffee had promulgated the notion of a slashing formation of light tanks in the traditional light cavalry role of reconnaissance. The cavalry's motto was "Through Mobility We Conquer." Initially, Chaffee believed that Armored Force should be strictly mechanized cavalry that executed traditional operational missions: pursuit, envelopment, and exploitation of the breakthrough. To generations of cavalry officers educated at Fort Riley, Kansas, this made sense. In battle it was assumed that infantry tanks would play the role of supporting the foot troops and battering down the strongest points of the enemy line. In the 1920 reorganization, the Tank Corps was abolished, and the infantry branch assumed the mission to develop tanks and cavalry to develop "combat cars" for reconnaissance and exploitation. While the cavalry-oriented officers looked for a fast, maneuverable light tank to slice into the enemy's vitals, the infantry looked for big, slow-moving tanks with low velocity guns adept at blowing apart enemy defensive positions and machine gun nests.

Devers recalled, "The InfantryT2 tank mounted only a 37mm gun, and they had barely 100 of them. The T2 could not possibly compete in Europe." Devers, a lifelong artillery man, was surprised that the largest gun mounted in a tank turret at the time was only 37mm. The Germans derisively called that caliber "the army's door knocker" and were getting rid of them. In 1940, German Mark IV tanks were already packing 75mm guns. Until 1939, the U.S. infantry branch eschewed even medium tanks, holding that a light tank capable of crossing the Engineer Corps' bridges of the time was best suited to accompany the "queen of battles." Now, the chief of infantry wanted to develop a heavily armored, 50- to 80-ton monster that could smash through enemy positions, breaking them open for foot soldier to follow.[35] Such a behemoth need not be either fast or maneuverable but had to be very survivable. Prior to this, Ordnance had shied away from vehicles this size, canceling the request for a heavy tank in 1936.[36]

As a "red leg cannon cocker," that is, an artilleryman, Jake wanted the largest high-velocity gun he could haul around the battlefield. But against a well-armed enemy, a tank needed armor to protect against return fire while retaining the most lethal gun it could maneuver with to defeat its adversaries. Conceptually identified characteristics led to a medium tank with a gun big enough to fight other tanks, enough armor to stand its ground while doing so, and enough speed to maneuver rapidly to concentrate and exploit changes on the battlefield before the enemy could react. As an artilleryman, Jake's initial inclination was to mount perhaps a 105mm on his theoretical medium tank. But mounting one in a turret on a fast-moving chassis was beyond the capability of American industry in 1941. Unlike the Germans, neither the British nor the Americans had the metallurgy to build a large enough turret ring and have it support a heavily armored turret. American shops could not produce a turret large enough to mount anything bigger than a 75mm gun. German metallurgy permitted stronger engines to power larger tanks, German instruments facilitated better fire control optics, and German FM radio technology outpaced the Allies and badly handicapped tank development. German tank technology simply could not be matched.

Armored Force was the end user of tanks, but actual development was left to the Ordnance Department. Before 1940, Ordnance listened to the chief of infantry and his need for assault tanks moving with dismounted riflemen. By statute, Infantry "owned" anything called a tank. As late as 1930, Major General Samuel Hof, a reactionary Ordnance Corps chief, refused to spend funds already appropriated to buy the 16-ton Christie tank. As justification he said, "I do not want a medium tank. I want a light tank," which by rule meant it must weigh less than 8 tons.[37]

Prior to 1940, American tanks had been limited to 15 tons. Right after Armored Force's creation in July of that year, General Chaffee finagled a conference at Aberdeen Proving Ground, home of Ordnance, to discuss tank armament. Ordnance, Infantry, and Armored Force, cognizant of Germany's blitz of France, agreed that a 75mm weapon was needed. This meant a 30-ton vehicle, a true medium tank. But no one in the United States had ever worked on, let alone created, a vehicle of this size. The best medium tank anyone had come up with was the M3 Grant, which was fitted with a 75mm cannon on a limited traverse arc on a hull-mounted sponson that resembled the secondary gun fittings on the battleship *Maine*.[38] Atop this was a turreted 37mm. "Ordnance was an iron curtain," recalled Devers. "They were against proposals from industry. They had to develop everything and had to show us [Armored Force] up. They had to have the first idea."[39]

Devers's understanding of the armored concept evolved rapidly. This was the most important breakthrough of all. Notes on a report prepared by General Scott records Devers's epiphany:

> The power, the tremendous power of surprise. How highly intelligent minds are numbed, absolutely numbed by surprise. The effects last for days or even weeks. . . . The decision in any action will be determined on the basis of man, surprise and maneuver with the advantage in the latter with the tank . . . massed tanks.
> The most outstanding qualities of the tank are firepower, speed and armor. Troops are easily liable to "tank fright."[40]

It has been written about armor's trinity – mobility, armor protection, and firepower. But command and control and its underpinning discipline, communications, are equally important. In 1940, most Allied tanks were not equipped with two-way radios. The great German armor commander Heinz Guderian saw that two-way FM radios (an invention of the American army's Major Edwin Armstrong) were installed in every panzer. In this way, German armor commanders could rapidly learn of enemy movements detected by forward scouts, react to their attacks, and exploit opportunities before the enemy could close them. Mobility is not just cross-country speed. It is the ability to react – to understand what is happening and to move faster than the enemy. This ability is crucial in armored warfare. Once he met it in combat in Europe, Devers realized that a major strength of the Wehrmacht was its ability to react.

The need for radios had been recognized but not really met when Devers arrived at Fort Knox. The Signal Corps had proposed a radio that needed a set of 125 crystals to operate, which could not be mass-produced. As he had done with artillery, Jake turned to industry, this time to a bevy of radio experts led by David Sarnoff of RCA.[41] While better known for his service on Eisenhower's staff in the use of broadcasting, Sarnoff contributed a great deal to lightening and simplifying radio equipment provided by a Signal Corps that was much more comfortable with field telephones that produced communications mobility at boot leather speed. Devers oversaw the creation of a series of radio nets in armored units that simultaneously allowed intense communication within tank companies and clear reporting and orders channels from company all the way through division level.

With this understanding, Devers moved beyond the notion of the tank as a method of transporting a big gun around the battlefield – which, in essence, is a tank destroyer, armored or not. Tanks needed to maneuver against a thinking opponent. Just like the cavalry of old, when the tank slammed into the enemy, it had to induce fear, to get the enemy formation to break and run. Then the tank had to have the mobility to chase after the remnants and destroy them. But it had to have the heavy firepower to create that fear. What some earlier armor proponents failed to emphasize, and what Devers immediately saw, was that the tank had to have sufficient protection to slug it out with enemy tanks until it defeated them, and then be able to advance against surviving enemy infantry and scatter them. Old-line cavalry had the mobility and shock effect but not the firepower, and thought in terms of lightly armed tanks. The artillery had big guns but no way to maneuver into position against enemy direct fire. It took all three elements, including sufficient armor protection, to survive in order to generate shock and surprise. This was the missing element in McNair's tank destroyer doctrine. Lightly armored guns that could not stand up to their enemies could never induce the enemy, protected by its own armored tanks, to run. At this point, Devers changed from an artilleryman to an armor commander who understood that mobility, armor protection, and heavy armament were all needed in a single package in order to win. A handwritten note in his personal notebook reads, "A separate tank destroyer lightly armored and trained solely to 'seek, strike and destroy' has no place in this war. The defensive role will lose every time."[42] Many cavalrymen, including Chaffee and Patton at first, did not clearly see the winning trinity. Neither did McNair or even Marshall. Recognizing the need for all three elements, and *continuing to advocate* this position despite its being out of favor with respected senior officers, was a major contribution by Devers. Other armor leaders had moved beyond the view of a single branch and understood it was firepower, mobility, and armor protection in combination that won. But without Devers's speaking out from his prominent position, armor might have been eclipsed by the artillery-oriented powerful proponents of tank destroyers.

Several days after he assumed command of Armored Force, Devers observed testing of the M3 tank. He quickly recognized the problems. In order to penetrate tank armor, the projectile being fired must transmit an enormous amount of energy into the enemy's armor plate. Devers knew enough physics to know that energy equals ½ mass times the square of velocity. The formula demonstrates that the velocity of a tank round is more important than the weight (or mass) of the projectile. As an artilleryman, Devers knew that long barrels meant higher projectile velocity. But the developers of the M3 Lee tank had cut off the barrel of the already inferior sponson-mounted 75mm gun because it kept getting caught on trees as this poor tank attempted to maneuver, robbing the gun of much of its muzzle velocity. Devers concluded, "The Grant was overweight, underpowered, and insufficiently armed."[43] The British welcomed the Grant, which could overcome the 50mm armed German Mark III's during the first Battle of El Alamein. But this benefit would be fleeting; the M3 would not be able to hold its own against the latest German tanks, long-barreled 75mm armed Mark IVs. At the time, "there was no gun, no engine, and no suspension from which to build a better tank."[44] The staff thought it would take at least twelve months to develop a suitable power plant. Devers insisted it had to be completed in eight.

General Devers did not make decisions on a whim. He embarked on a short, rapid testing program to determine what could be achieved technically and which manufacturer could provide the best components. Devers initiated extensive evaluations to measure the tradeoffs between heavy and light tanks. Bigger guns and heavier armor added weight that was difficult to move around. Tradeoffs had to be made. "Weight is the critical thing in everything you develop," recalled Devers.[45] Two years prior, no one in American industry had seen, let alone manufactured, a combat vehicle that weighed more than 15 tons. The army turned to locomotive builders for additional help. They had the forges, overhead cranes, and experience in assembling heavy equipment. Early tests trended toward sacrificing armor and armament in favor of lightness and speed. Devers agreed with the "cavalry" need for a light tank for reconnaissance. A recon tank needed to be fast and light so it could quickly close in on the enemy to gain information, then get away so it could report back. A few calculations indicated a 15-ton weight limit could not be exceeded to move quickly. The M3 Stuart had been developed prior to Devers's arrival, and it fit the bill so well that the British dubbed it the "Honey." An improved version, the M5, did even a better job of meeting the 15-ton requirement.

But a medium capable of defeating a German Mark IV had to be the general-purpose fighting vehicle. Thirty-five tons was the maximum weight a tank that retained a mid-20-mile-per-hour speed and good battlefield agility could have, given the state of engines. Transmissions, clutches, and chassis of the day could not reliably handle anything more without breaking down. All of this was determined in Devers's first month at Fort Knox.

Plans for the technical advances needed to manufacture a turreted 75mm gun tank had been started but not finalized when Devers arrived at Fort Knox. Thirty tons was sufficient to handle the recoil of a medium-velocity 75 mm gun, which was the largest that could be mounted in a turret traversing on the largest turret ring that could be developed and manufactured in sufficient numbers by the deadline that Devers had set. So much for the larger caliber gun that was Devers's initial concept. Analysis of European bridge specifications indicated that vehicles over 35 tons would have a hard time getting around. Pontoon bridges being developed at the time indicated a similar limit. So did port cranes and shipboard considerations for the transatlantic crossing. Devers's quick mind grasped the chain of events, the tradeoffs among armor protection, armament, and vehicle speed that could be contained within a 35-ton vehicle and the sequence of development required. "Every anti-tank solution we tried led back to the medium tank. It could shoot and move before anybody could shoot back. It could shoot on the run."[46]

Preliminary sketches that included a good armor-protected gun on a reliable, fast-moving chassis pointed to a need to develop a 400 horsepower plant. But these requirements drew Devers into a nest of automotive problems. No one had any experience with suspensions heavy enough to support a good medium tank. The Armored Force did not have a power plant sufficiently robust to power a 35-ton tank, nor did they have a transmission that could handle the requisite power. Devers wanted 800 horsepower, enough to propel a 50-ton monster with heavy armor and a high velocity gun like the Panther and Tiger. But American industry couldn't produce it. Devers and his staff began a rapid review of alternative power plants to meet even half the 400 horsepower requirement. Cadillac's proposal to use two engines – which did supply the necessary power but only when the two were perfectly synchronized – was rejected. So was a fantastic Chrysler five-engine proposal to do the same thing. Under rugged, dirty field conditions, two engines were more than most crews could handle. Neither could industry come up with a clutch that could handle the high horsepower. Still, Cadillac had just developed an "automatic" transmission that fed power through a closed oil system that did not require a clutch. Devers told them to put it in.

Many historians and tankers have pointed to the fire hazard of the gasoline-powered Sherman tank. Troops called it the "Ronson" after a popular 1940s cigarette because it caught fire so easily. Why not use diesel? Devers provided an answer. The armor school tested diesel engines closely and were impressed with the added cruising range, almost double. But Jake noticed that, at idle, crews never shut the diesels down. Vapor lock proved to be the problem. The diesels were started with a shotgun shell. Turn them off on a battlefield and you might never get them started again. While trying to, crews literally blew cylinders apart. When running at idle was factored in, the potential range advantage mostly disappeared. Any workable solution in 1941 would have required so much additional weight that armor protection would have to be reduced. Jake went to William Knudsen, a leading automotive executive from General Motors, about keeping injectors for diesel engines under oil because of dust.

Diesel is less flammable because it is less likely to create a cloud of explosive vapor than gasoline. Recent advances in American metallurgy had developed tough steel that could safely and reliably operate at the pressures and temperatures associated with 70-octane gasoline. British tank engines of the period were not tough enough to handle it. The weight savings from the lighter, high-octane tank engines translated into more armor on a tank and was thus a good tradeoff. At the time, using a diesel power plant resulted in a package that was too large and too heavy to fit within the 35-ton limitation that the design outline could accommodate.[47] Devers ordered the performance of extensive flame tests. The speed at which heat reached the powder in ammunition carried in ready racks had a greater impact on tank fires than fuel type. Tests on Sherman tanks demonstrated that it was ammunition, not fuel that was most likely to be set ablaze by enemy fire, thus improving the case for a gasoline-fueled engine.

Grabbing a promising solution, sometimes before it was thoroughly proven, was Devers's way. When time is paramount, this approach has its merits. But it is not an unalloyed solution. Finding a workable air-cooled 400-horsepower engine would eliminate the weight of water for cooling. To keep the Sherman within a maneuverable weight, the armor board – the steering committee – had already selected thinner armor than what was really needed. Looking for a solution, Jake came across a Guiberson air-cooled engine from Dallas that developed good base horsepower. At first, internal engine pressures threatened to exceed what steel of the period could withstand. Again, Knudsen came to the rescue. When tested, the manufacturers found inconsistencies within each batch of steel, which could result in engine failure. The metallurgy industry demonstrated that, if thoroughly beaten to remove a little more impurity in the final manufacturing process, steel could be produced that consistently met the requirement. Devers ramrodded a $7 million contract to build an engine plant, and all seemed well. After the initial engines were manufactured, however, they demonstrated the same vapor-lock problem that had plagued diesels. No one could find a solution, so the brand new plant had to be shut down. Inadequate testing to save precious time resulted in frightful waste. A more cautious decision maker would not have made such a mistake. Eisenhower would not have done so. As the war progressed, there would be other circumstances from which Eisenhower would conclude that Devers was an unreliable "hip shooter."

Too high a compression ratio resulted in vapor lock and a tank that was stopped cold just when it was needed most. The automotive industry demonstrated that 400 horsepower was the best Devers was likely to get. There had been lots of controversy among manufacturers of tank engines.[48] Jake would go up to Detroit to inspect new developments or resolve issues. He decided to seek a tough gasoline engine and stick to it. Engines installed in early M4 tanks were rated at 400 horsepower with the promise of a little more, which hadn't been available a year before. A 400-horsepower engine that could run four hundred hours before breakdown became his new target. Battlefield mobility also required battlefield reliability. Broken, immobile tanks don't scare anybody. Those goals sound paltry in the twenty-first century, and demonstrate how little progress American engineering had made by 1941. Manufacturers promised to have the engines within eighteen months. True to form, Jake demanded that they do it in twelve.

Given the weak state of the manufacturing base, Devers insisted that the engine be easy to produce. Thinking of the mechanics in the Armored Force School, he also wanted it to be easy to maintain. Using a radial aircraft engine to propel a 35-ton tank was entertained, but there was no way that the Air Corps would release any of them for tank production. After extensive testing, Ford's product came out best. The light M5 was equipped with Cadillac engines. These were reliable power plants and proved to be the main U.S. tank advantage. The big German tanks gave superior performance in a set piece fight, but they were difficult to produce, and the Tiger German tank was prone to breakdown as it had insufficient power for its great weight. Despite being the terror of Allied tankers, the Tiger fulfilled the role of the infantry tank – great armor protection and firepower, but due to its mechanical unreliability, poor mobility. Devers observed, "It was heavier than its automotive system could handle. The clutch was too weak to do its job. . . . The trick to defeat them was to out maneuver them. . . . It had trouble going up hills."[49] A careful study of Tigers found on the battlefield in Germany determined that most of them had been abandoned not from battle damage but from mechanical breakdown. The study concluded, "Who killed Tiger? He killed himself."[50] Shermans outmaneuvered their heavier opponents, and America drowned German fine craftsmanship in a flood of production. Without someone like Devers solving problems and pushing suppliers forward on production, that might not have happened.

Devers worried less about the thickness of armor plate (which was dictated by weight) than about how it was assembled. Tests, soon validated in the North African desert, demonstrated that bolts quickly took flight when the plates were struck, potentially killing crewmen. Devers again went to industry for a solution. K. T. Keller of Chrysler organized a group of expert welders from all over the country. In forty-eight hours, they had come up with a method to weld armor plate. This led to electric arc welding.[51] Teamwork also led to a way to beat steel used to make engine cylinders in order to make it tough enough to withstand the compression ratio required to develop the needed horsepower. A number of historians have quipped that the American automotive industry was America's secret weapon. But it took Devers to burst the "not invented here" mentality that straight-jacketed the Ordnance Corps and to employ that weapon. Jake welcomed outside solutions, remained flexible, and was always ready, with unorthodox methods, to speed things up. As Eugene Harrison later noted, "If it had not been for General Devers pushing, we would never have had the tank to fight in World War II. I feel that he must be given credit for the development of the Armored Force."[52] Devers's better tank engines, suspensions designs, communications, and ammunition attracted young and vigorous officers, and facilitated dissemination and discussion of new ideas.

"Jakie Devers and Joe Holly on top of a tank were the most creative armor board available," recalled General Williston B. Palmer.[53] The 30–35-ton specification led to the finalization of the M4 Sherman tank, which initially weighed in at 31 tons. It mounted a medium velocity 75mm gun that was obsolete before it left the drawing board. It could penetrate only 60mm of armor inclined at 30 degrees at 500 yards, which was nowhere near world class. But the M4 was the best they could get from the Ordinance Department given the time and technology constraints.

Americans like to pride themselves on their automotive technology. Given the state of that industry in 1941, the American industrial base could not support development of a tank in the 50-ton Panther class such as was being assembled on a German chassis. A heavy tank mounting thicker armor and a higher velocity 3-inch gun capable of penetrating the German Mark IV was under consideration.[54] In fact, American tankers would clamor for it the first time they went up against Tigers and panzers. But such a vehicle would sacrifice the mobility needed for rapid maneuvering. The M6 heavy tank had a great deal of developmental trouble. For example, a transmission was developed by General Motors but never actually installed. A 50- to 60-ton tank presented major shipping problems and could not traverse the typical European roads and bridges of 1941. Because of mobility and transportation problems, Devers wrote to General McNair that, "due to its tremendous weight and limited tactical use, there is no requirement in the Armored Force for the heavy tank."[55] Later, he recommended killing the heavy tank altogether.[56] Unfortunately, this played into the bias against arming tanks to kill tanks, even after events in Africa demonstrated Devers's long-held view that the tank destroyer was a badly flawed concept. As late as November 1943, McNair stated, "The conception of a tank vs. tank duel is believed to be unsound and unnecessary."[57] It was not that Devers did not see the need for a fast, reliable Panther. In 1941–1942, American industry was simply incapable of delivering them in quantity.

Developers looked at different ways of killing tanks but always returned to medium tanks with more firepower.[58] With the demise of the heavy tank, Devers knew improvements to the M4 medium were necessary to better allow the machine to survive intense combat and defeat the more advanced German tank, including heavier armor, a 105mm gun, and a periscope sight. To that end, Devers convened a new board. He recognized that further development of much of the newly created technology required stretching the weight limit to 40 tons in 1943.[59] This resulted in the M4A4E1 "Jumbo" tank. Additional development led to the "Easy 8" with a much higher velocity 76mm gun. Jake pressed hard to make these advances a reality. The added armor and 76mm gun were welcomed by tankers hard pressed by Panthers and Tigers, but did not close the gap between German armor and American counterparts. The 17 pounder mounted on the Sherman Firefly brought with it more than a heavier shell. It embodied the secret of sabot. Today, any gunner can explain the sabot principle. A smaller subcaliber, hardened penetrator is mounted on a full-sized propellant charge. The charge accelerates the smaller penetrator to a much higher velocity. Energy = $\frac{1}{2}mv^2$. As energy goes up with the square of the velocity, the penetrator hits the targeted panzer with much more force than a larger penetrator. The sabot principle allowed high-speed penetrators to punch through engine blocks as "silver bullets" during the Gulf War. Bernard Montgomery was willing to release 17 pounders so Americans manned Shermans in 1944. Devers and Edward Brooks salivated over the weapon. But the combination of excessive secretary and a "not invented here" attitude on the part of American ordnance officers blocked American tankers from becoming armed with an effective tank for the last twelve months of the war.

FIVE

The Debate over Doctrine

IN THE BEGINNING, GEORGE S. PATTON PROVED TO BE A LARGE problem. He had a lot of ideas, some good, some very unbalanced. Patton stressed mobility and tended to use the light tank as a horse. Despite the need demonstrated on European battlefields for more armor protection and heavier guns, he remained wedded to the light 15-ton cavalry tank. Patton handled light tanks as cavalry.[1] A committed cavalryman as late as 1933, he wrote in the *Cavalry Journal,* "Machines will always be preceded by horsemen." Patton, then subordinate to Devers as commander of the 2nd Armored Division (AD), had enjoyed a long association with Secretary of War Henry Stimson, which he exploited to challenge Devers's mechanized warfare expertise and hence his authority to command. Devers could not tolerate the situation if Patton became de facto *the* man in charge. Patton, who felt he was the armor expert, was feeding Stimson notes via Undersecretary John McCloy, questioning what Devers knew about armor.

Prior to assuming command of Armored Force, Devers had gotten to know Patton, the mercurial Californian. Pejoratively in retirement, Devers recalled that his classmates didn't think "Georgie" was the "sharpest knife in the drawer." When both were assigned to Fort Myer in the 1930s, they played a lot of polo together. Jake was one of the few riders that could swing a polo mallet with more skill than his famous classmate. They wound up with adjacent quarters on post and became friendly neighbors.[2] But in 1941, Devers had to demonstrate that he could handle his truculent classmate.

Devers traveled to Fort Benning to confront Patton. The Pattons had him to dinner at their residence. After dinner, Jake asked Beatrice to stay as a referee, since it appeared certain that Patton and Devers were going to fight. The men's heated conversation lasted until two in the morning. "We're not going to put any more holes in that armor on that turret to mount extra machine guns because it just weakens it," argued Devers. "These are the decisions. They've been made. I'm going to tell you right now. I went up and talked to General Marshall – just as I'm talking to you – and he has given me the go ahead. Now are you going to fall in line and be on the team and work with me on this, or are you going to send these notes to Mr. Stimson?" Patton got up, came to attention, saluted, and said, "Jake, you are the boss and I'm one of your commanders, and I'll play ball."[3]

Patton had a lot of the horse cavalry in him. Initially he had opposed a better armored and armed but slower medium tank in favor of light, fast tanks that could, in cavalry fashion, slash into the enemy's rear. Devers demonstrated to Patton the need for much more firepower and armor plate to allow a tank to move in the face of enemy fire and beat back their tanks. Patton wrote to Devers, "When you remember my one time aversion to the medium tank, you may be surprised at my suggestions concerning them, but you and they have certainly made a convert of me."[4] Later, Patton told Devers that he would never recommend a change to armored organization to Lesley McNair without Devers's approval.[5] As Patton began to recognize Devers's skills and the tank knowledge he had acquired, the confrontational tone receded. Devers wrote to Beatrice Patton after his inspection trip to say how well George was performing "an exceptional job." As was his approach to those who outranked him, Patton wrote somewhat obsequiously to Devers, "I want to thank you from the bottom of my heart for the many good turns and magnificent backing you have given me particularly since I have been serving under you."[6] Of course, Patton still thought he was the better armor commander. But on more than one occasion, he acknowledged Jake's command skills and contributions to the creation of the Armored Force. Not everyone was impressed with Jake's demeanor, however. One contemporary officer complained that "Jake bragged that he knew more about armor than either Patton or Eisenhower." Successful people often have strong egos. Then again, neither Eisenhower nor Patton had a clear conception about tanks except that they were going to use the tanks as cavalry.

Upon his arrival at Fort Knox, Devers might have thought his first task was to deal with high-velocity, flat-trajectory tank cannon. Instead, he ran into a major controversy about the need to integrate a strong field artillery contingent into large tank formations. Before his death, General Adna Chaffee had felt strongly that the allocation of seven batteries of towed 75mm artillery was far too little for the proposed "heavy" armored division that contained two tank regiments (a total of six tank battalions) and a full infantry regiment. The counterpart "triangular" infantry division contained three battalions of light howitzers, a medium battalion, and a cannon company of light artillery organic to each regiment. Chaffee wanted the artillery pieces upgraded to 105mm, and all artillery placed under a single divisional artillery officer, instead of being parceled out separately to the armored brigade and the infantry regiment. On these points, he had the backing of the chief of artillery. But the War Department insisted that the lighter, more mobile, but less deadly 75mm be retained.

Devers wanted then-Colonel Edward H. Brooks to accompany him down to Fort Knox, and talked to the young officer about the assignment. Brooks had been an instructor under Devers at Fort Sill and would have done just about anything to get out of Washington staff work. Pending his getting approval from the chief, Devers had mentioned the change as a possibility. When Devers brought up the issue with Marshall, Marshall told his secretary that he wanted to see Brooks right away. He was nowhere to be found. Fearing that he would be stuck forever at a Washington desk, Brooks had already taken the night train for Fort Knox. Marshall smiled and, according to Devers, never quite got over chuckling about the incident.[7]

Brooks, a proud graduate of Norwich University, had been working hard to correct the serious problems stemming from improper integration of artillery into the Armored Force. Speed of an armored formation depends on more than the speed of its tanks. Many people envision an armored division as a thundering herd of tanks plowing across an open field, tearing up everything in its path. Actually, the concept of a mobile force is to give speed to a group of combined arms, infantry, tanks, and artillery, supported by fast-moving engineers, communications, and logistics. Even if infantry and tanks are moving forward on armored caterpillar tracks, the entire formation is paced by the ability of the artillery to pack up, redeploy, and get ready to execute a fire mission. For towed artillery, this is a time-consuming activity. Chaffee never came up with an artillery piece that could keep up with the Armored Force. Brooks had suggested either a "portee" pack howitzer loaded onto the rear end of a flatbed truck and offloaded to fire, or a gun mounted on a halftrack. Neither of these ideas panned out.

Brooks had just started looking at self-propelled artillery in 1942. Every idea came back to the medium-tank chassis. Brooks began working on a scheme to mount a 105mm howitzer on a medium-tank chassis. Devers suggested removing the heavy-tank turret to eliminate enough weight so that the chassis could carry the howitzer and its equipment.[8] Chassis armor was also reduced to increase speed. While some others talked about the idea, nothing happened until Brooks outlined a proposal to employ the weapon. Devers saw where Brooks was heading and provided steam to power the bureaucracy into motion. In a matter of months, the obstructionists at Ordnance were pushed aside. American locomotive workers took up their hammers and got down to work.

In November 1941, two prototypes of what would evolve into the work-horse self-propelled artillery piece of World War II, the M7 Priest, stood on the pavement. Devers saw to it that the new weapon was immediately put through its paces. Three days later, tests were completed. Chalk marks on the prototypes indicated recommended changes. Without even final engineering drawings, the pilot models were shipped off to American Locomotive Company, where production began. By the summer of 1942, the first production models were in the hands of troops. By October 1942, General Bernard Montgomery had deployed them as a new secret weapon in his advance from El Alamein. They participated in the invasion of North Africa right after Election Day.

Before the war, Jake preferred that the traditional four-gun battery be expanded to six guns with only the marginal addition of the extra gun crews. Artillery units have extensive manpower devoted to observation, fire control, and communications. Jake strongly felt that well-equipped artillery could support more pieces in existing batteries and generate more firepower. Armored Force was organized with three six-gun 105mm self-propelled M7 batteries per battalion and three battalions per division artillery, while other units retained their four-gun configuration. Late in the war, most of the rest of the army changed to six-gun batteries.

Today, most combat arms officers can rattle off the benefits of operations that blend the effects of infantry, artillery, tanks, and other supporting arms. The idea of combined arms is to present the attacker with multiple threats. When defending against one, the enemy becomes vulnerable to another. His machine guns, which keep infantry from moving across open fields, are easy targets for armored tanks that directly fire into their nests. Enemy soldiers hiding in woods or towns hoping to ambush tanks are at the mercy of infantry watching for their presence. Artillery pounds defenders while tank-infantry teams advance. Most of artillery's firepower is directed to keep the enemy pinned down so that he cannot shoot, move, or even think. Artillery blocks reinforcements and additional ammunition from reaching defenders, so that clumps of them become isolated and no match for the armored firepower rolling against them.

In 1940, opinions on the organization of tank forces were more bifurcated. German thought emphasized three principles – combined arms, armor en masse, and mobility. Task-oriented organizations, called *kampfgruppes,* emphasized the use of combined arms forces and often were specifically assembled for the immediate task at hand. They were supported by air power that could strike deep to inhibit the enemy's ability to react, permitting large combined arms and armored formations to attack at critical points.

Fire and movement by combined arms units was not initially emulated by either the French or British. Instead, they favored independent action by tanks. The French tended to distribute tank formations in a manner that supported larger infantry units. As a result of the lightning German success in Poland, the French had just begun to organize three combined arms armored divisions, but they were not fully operational when the Germans struck through the Ardennes. In 1940, France had more and heavier tanks than the Germans. But the Wehrmacht prevailed due to superior tactics and agility. Devers and a number of forward-thinking Armored Force officers perceived one of the reasons why. As Jake said, "Superior power at a decisive point, or *schwerpunct,* was key to their success. When a weak point in the enemy's line is penetrated, the resulting flanks are rolled up to allow the armored force to pour through."[9] Germans moved from light to medium tanks. Americans modified their own cavalry tradition and built on what was learned from the clashes in Europe.

Lesley McNair, who always favored general-purpose large organizations augmented by smaller specialized units when needed, decreed that corps should be general-purpose headquarters commanding a collection of units specially organized for the mission. Separate tank battalions would be parceled out to infantry divisions as required. When a larger task was at hand, a tank battalion might be attached to an infantry division. As previously discussed, Devers did not agree with this doctrine. He wrote to McNair that infantry divisions "have their place in the scheme of affairs to protect lines of communication, to hold ground to assist armored units in supply and the crossing of obstacles such as rivers, defile, etc. They do not carry the spearhead of the fight and never will when tanks and guns are present."[10] In other words, combined arms led by medium tanks capable of slugging it out and then rapidly exploiting any resulting opening could both break through enemy positions and maneuver deeply into the enemy's rear to exploit the breakthrough. This vision describes what was to become the basis of mobile combat as prosecuted by GIs in Europe in 1944–1945, and it remains the basis of large-scale armored doctrine into the twenty-first century. Devers also advocated mechanizing infantry in a great many divisions in order that the entire force be armor protected and mobile, a development that, starting in the 1960s, would become standard in most armies projected to fight over ground that was conducive to mobile combat. Often overlooked, this was one of Devers's most important contributions.

McNair hung onto the notion of small units of heavy tanks to break through, antitank guns to fight enemy tanks, and finally light tanks, in McNair's words, "not greatly different than horse cavalry," as an agent of exploitation.[11] He persisted in this belief even after the British experience in North Africa. Without a proponent like Devers, the American army that fought in Europe would have looked and operated quite differently. Still, army plans sharply reduced the projected number of armored divisions throughout much of 1942–1943 to the numbers that were subsequently organized, while the number of infantry divisions in the plan continued to rise.[12] By late 1943, McNair was recommending that only six armored divisions be retained.

Hardly had Devers assumed his new command than the 1941 Louisiana maneuvers began. Staged over August and September, these were the biggest maneuvers the army had ever held. Among the major questions to be answered by the maneuvers were the efficacy of the Armored Force and the effectiveness of defense by antitank guns. In the short amount of time the force had to work up under Devers, tank-artillery coordination was emphasized. Devers held that artillery could bombard a hole in enemy defenses, allowing the tanks access into enemy rear areas. Jake had not transitioned most of the force to combined arms when the maneuvers began. He sought to increase mobile force speed and ability by reducing the reaction time of divisional staffs through streamlined procedures. During these maneuvers, while Devers reshaped the Armored Force, Colonel Dwight Eisenhower was chief of staff for one of the participants, Third Army, at that time commanded by General Walter Krueger.

The results of the Louisiana maneuvers did not reflect well on the Armored Force. Armored divisions were not able to bring their massive power to bear. In the British style, then-current armored division organization separated the tanks into a pure tank brigade and the infantry into its own regiment. Instead of integrating the separate arms into combined arms teams, divisions tended to use only one arm at a time. In essence, the armored divisions tended to operate as regiments of a single arm, instead of being a team of combined arms. Reconnaissance elements were poorly coordinated with the main body units moving to the attack. As a result, tank columns blundered into antitank defenses with no advanced warning. Umpiring rules emphasized the use of infantry or artillery to counter antitank guns. Instead, pure tank units took them on with disastrous losses as assessed by the umpires.[13] Poor organization induced poor tactics. Afterward, most analysts found the data confirming Mc-Nair's bias and Marshall's inclination, but also found that the umpiring rules for antitank engagements were unduly biased toward the guns.

Devers attributed the poor performance to undertrained junior officers and poor staff work at the regiment and division levels. Alluding to the lack of use of combined arms, Patton told his 2AD officers, "Each time we fight with only one weapon when we could use several weapons, we are not winning, we are making fools of ourselves."[14] Major General Charles L. Scott, commander I Armored Corps, directed his troops to correct the most glaring error, a lack of infantry-tank coordination, which improved performance during the subsequent Carolina maneuvers. He sought to employ armored divisions as a combined team and achieved decisive results, something that did not occur in Louisiana.[15] But organizational and doctrinal weakness was responsible for a good many shortfalls. Devers and other armor officers now saw that it was the combined arms of the tank-infantry-artillery team that would win engagements, a needed adjustment in Devers's outlook. Infantry added eyes and the sensing ability to feel out antitank defenses before they announced their presence by setting tanks on fire. The infantry dug out defenders ensconced in city rubble, wooded thickets, and entrenchments. Tanks directly reduced hard points that survived the accompanying artillery bombardment. Still, mechanized formations were gaining notice. Reflecting the gain in respect for the new organizations, "Mechanized cavalry was first called the mosquito, then the hornet, then the Devers."[16]

A man who adapted to new information, Devers saw the need to reorganize armored divisions to get effective combined arms battle groups. Devers wrote in his notebook, "A breakthrough of a stabilized defensive position by infantry followed by exploitation by armor is *our doctrine*." In the subsequent Carolina maneuvers in October and November, division commanders attempted to give their tanks more infantry support. But they had only a pair of infantry battalions to support eight organic tank battalions. Scott emphasized the need to use advance guards composed of reconnaissance troops and not to commit main bodies until enemy defenses were uncovered. It was movement in the right direction but still insufficient.

Along with most Armored Force officers, Devers was not convinced that antitank guns were anywhere near as effective as the apparent results of the Louisiana maneuvers: "We were licked by a set of umpire's rules."[17] In an address to civilian industry executives, Devers categorically stated, "The only way to defend against enemy tanks is to bring up tanks of your own."[18] But McNair still didn't see it that way. Antitank gun battalions were far cheaper in both money and scarce space on transoceanic freighters. Devers's decision to make this speech favoring tanks to fight tanks within a month of the Louisiana maneuvers and at a time when leaders he admired were going in the opposite direction demonstrates the conviction he harbored, the willingness he had for change, and the moral courage he possessed to press home his convictions.

Devers wanted the combined arms aspect of the Armored Force expanded. In armored corps, he wanted to see motorized infantry divisions, and armored MPs, medics, engineers, and maintenance companies to deal with all of the automotive equipment.[19] He was not impressed with emerging antitank doctrine, calling it little more than use of direct-fire artillery in the defense. McNair sought to pool large groups of antitank assets at corps level, and to employ them in what became the tank destroyer motto, "Seek, Strike, and Destroy." No other army in the world followed such aggressive concentration or tactics.[20] At one time, planners projected 220 tank destroyer battalions in what was then a planned 55-division army. In this endeavor, McNair had the support of General Marshall. The chief of staff authorized the establishment of the Tank Destroyer Center at Fort Hood and supported even more antitank battalions.[21] While Marshall had retained an open mind about the value of large combined armored formations, he had been one of the initiators of the tank destroyer concept so championed by his protégé, McNair.[22] With the evidence of the Louisiana maneuvers, he leaned back toward antitank guns as the solution to the panzer division.

After several antitank conferences, the early war tank destroyer became a 75mm gun mounted on a half-track. Devers's efforts to enhance the organization of armored corps fell on deaf ears. McNair believed that massed armor was "not very different in principle from horse cavalry of old. . . . An armored division is of value in pursuit and exploitation."

Instead, he felt "the infantry division, backed by artillery, would remain the basic instrument of warfare."[23] Marshall was comfortable with this conclusion, as evidenced by the book of combat examples that was a standard treatise in army circles, *Infantry in Combat,* compiled before the war under Marshall's direction while he was at the Infantry School. It was not far from Chaffee's line of thinking and would have received some support from Patton. The War Department disapproved the motorized infantry division, stating that standard infantry divisions, augmented with truck companies as required, would fit the bill.

Poor showings in the two large maneuvers diminished the stature of the Armored Force, but Devers emerged as a true advocate for combined arms armored teams. Rejecting the antitank gun trend, he flatly stated that the best way to fight a tank is with another tank. Only in this way could the Americans maneuver their guns to bring them to bear on panzers while retaining the protection of armor plate. While tank destroyers were effective from ambush, it was too much to ask crews with little armor protection to advance on deadly panzers. Furthermore, Devers convinced many armor officers that massed tank formations unsupported by closely supporting infantry, artillery, and other supporting services was not the best way to employ tanks. German thinking had already developed in this direction. Panzer divisions were reorganized to contain more infantry than tank battalions, along with a strong artillery component. The British continued to advocate a separate tank brigade paired with a pure infantry brigade, which was supposed to provide a "pivot" around which the tanks were to maneuver (as in Montgomery's tactic at El Alamein). This organization proved far less successful.[24] In defense, antitank guns could add combat power, but the notion of unlimbering towed guns within sight of enemy armor was ludicrous. Another solution was the track-laying antitank gun. The first 75mm guns mounted on thinly armored half-tracks proved a failure in North African combat.

Initially, U.S. Armor was organized under centralized general headquarters control. Many armored leaders advocated armored armies and the retention of as much centralized mass as possible. Initially, the Armored Force was to contain four armored corps headquarters. Jake's picks for corps commanders were Willis Crittenberger, Oliver Gillem,

Walton Walker, and Patton. On 8 December 1941, Devers wrote to Marshall recommending that Patton be moved up from commander 2AD to commander I Armored Corps.

General McNair had included an armored corps in the Louisiana maneuvers with the hope it would strike deeply into the depths of enemy position. He was disappointed when it failed to achieve decisive results. Subsequently, McNair held that corps and armies should be general purpose, with no fixed organization. Their organization was to be custom-organized to meet the task at hand. Thus, the armored corps disappeared. After the war, a number of German armored experts criticized the Americans for not building higher headquarters with officers skilled in mobile warfare. As a result, they felt that the Americans had not sufficiently developed mobile warfare at the operational level.[25] McNair did not believe the purpose of the tank was to fight another tank. He said that tank-versus-tank combat was "unsound and unnecessary." The concept of employing tank destroyers instead of medium tanks "would prove to be one of great doctrinal wrong turns of the century."[26] Had someone else been in charge of the Armored Force, it might have had fleets of light tanks but few of the tank-mounted 75mm guns that most soldiers in the field felt should have been even heavier.

The large-scale maneuvers saw the end of horse cavalry and inspired emphasis on the light tanks that had been advocated by Chaffee, Patton, and a number of like-minded officers. Chaffee did not want to get any heavier until he saw a mobile medium tank ready to be issued to troops. Devers foresaw the weakness of lightly protected self-propelled antitank vehicles that had insufficient armor to stand up to enemy tanks. A lot more mediums were needed. He reversed the ratio of medium to light tanks from 1:3 to 3:1. With this change, Devers brought firepower and armor protection back into balance with mobility. To provide sufficient infantry, he lowered the ratio of tanks to infantry from 3:1 to 1:1. Divisions were reorganized around three combat commands, similar to German *kampfgruppes,* balanced around one tank, one armored infantry, and one artillery battalion. Doctrine encouraged combat command commanding officers (COs) to cross-attach tank companies to armored infantry battalions and vice versa, so that combined arms were fully integrated throughout the organization. Cross-attaching tank and infantry platoons became common practice. Engineers often accompanied lead battalions, and artillery observers were pushed down to the tank-infantry company level. Fully integrated combined arms were a much-needed alteration that produced the teams that won World War II.

A division commander could form three balanced combat commands each with a battalion of tanks, one of armored infantry, and another of self-propelled artillery. But he could mix them differently depending on the mission. One combat command might have two tank battalions to meet a large tank threat, while another, scheduled to take a town, might receive the fire of two artillery battalions. At times a combat command was detached and given to an infantry or even an airborne division. Additional infantry regiments were frequently attached to armored divisions assaulting the German main line. Devers and his officers created a very flexible, balanced concept that was the basis of American armored formations right up to the Gulf War.

Always attending to details, Devers ignored neither the division's whiskers nor its tail. The reconnaissance battalion, the unit that was supposed to feel ahead of the division to detect opportunities and risks, received increased combat power. This reflected evidence that units would rather fight for information about enemy dispositions than sneak up on them. Artillery could not hit anything without some forward observer (FO) identifying the target and adjusting the fall of artillery shells upon it. In fast moving armored battles, this was especially difficult. While artillery forward observers rode with the lead tanks, they often had difficulty pinpointing enemy antitank guns among the smoke and careening hot metal. Devers reasoned, why not put the observer in the air? In a light plane, just out of range of light antiaircraft fire, an observer could better understand the situation as it unfolded. Devers ordered that light planes be assigned directly to the artillery and dedicated to observation, so they weren't purloined for other pressing duties. Eight light planes were added to each armored division's artillery organization. Originally armored division logistical support was fractured and uncoordinated. Devers created a central divisional support organization called the trains (after the wagon trains that supported nineteenth-century forces). Armored divisions had an unprecedented number of contrary vehicles. A centralized ordnance maintenance battalion pooled resources and allowed the division to concentrate repairs on those items in greatest need. Similarly, a medical battalion allowed support to be directed at any given unit in great need and avoided overworked doctors supporting one command while those behind another command remanding idle.

Much armor force energy concentrated on creating new armored divisions. McNair directed that infantry divisions contain no organic armor. Separate tank battalions would be attached only when required. This proved to be a good approach in the atolls and jungles of the Pacific. But virtually every infantry division deployed to Western Europe had a tank battalion attached. Chaffee knew that independent tank battalions would be needed. The 70th Tank Battalion was the lead organization, with four more organized in 1941. From their inception, separate battalions became neglected, causing Devers to label them "the lost children of the Armored Force." Supposedly, provisional tank groups were to supervise them, but little life was breathed into these organizations, and the independent tankers became orphans. As the commander of the 70th Battalion recalled, five different headquarters, thinking they were in the chain of command, issued orders to the hapless commander. Armored Force at Fort Knox changed them from light tanks to medium tanks, and then back to light tanks, all before the battalion received the requisitioned medium tanks. Devers was particularly concerned about senior leadership in these independent units. Remedial action was necessary to bring them up to snuff.

By 1942, almost everyone was sold on the 6×6, 2½-ton trucks. The next question became, how about one that can float? Initially, most officers turned their noses up, but Jake instantly saw possibilities. The DUKW (amphibious truck) proved to be seaworthy and became ubiquitous in amphibious operations. Beach masters quickly learned that DUKWs could do more than deposit cargo on the beach. Avoiding manpower-intensive cargo transfers from landing craft across a sandy beach by hand and then onto a truck, DUKWs could drive up from the surf, across the beach, and onto inland supply dumps. They became the lighter of choice, and were often seen aside all types of ships that busily deposited their cargoes for delivery even in ports lacking sufficient undamaged wharves to accommodate oceangoing ships. Marshall commented, "In the very early stages in this matter, he [Devers] was the only man in the Army who fully saw the possibilities [of the DUKW] and his encouragement was much needed."[27] Throughout the amphibious campaigns, the vehicle proved invaluable. Admiral Bertram Ramsay, commander of the British Navy, called the DUKW "a magnificent bird." Even after he left Armored Force, Devers watched over his fledgling. Upon arriving in London, he found that managers without foresight had zeroed out DUKW production in 1943. Stating that thousands of them would be needed, he was instrumental in getting production restored.

Devers met the inventor of the LCT (landing craft, tank) on a train. When the inventor explained what he was doing, Devers recognized the same problem and easily agreed on the solution. "We didn't have to issue orders, write a letter or anything," recalled Devers. The concept was an LCVP (landing craft, vehicle, personnel; also called a Higgins boat), enlarged to accommodate a Sherman tank, and built of steel in order to carry a tank's weight and discharge it through a metal drop ramp. The first LCT prototype was built at Fort Knox, and production continued.[28]

Devers endorsed General Scott's observation that unarmored, unarmed vehicles could not recover damaged tanks from an active battlefield. This led to armored recovery vehicles based on M3 and M4 chasses equipped with winches and booms capable of removing immobile 35-ton tanks from soft fields and deep mud. Again following Scott, Devers oversaw the development of huge "dragon wagon" tractor-trailer rigs that could haul many tons of cargo when they were not transporting broken tanks.

Devers brought to the Armored Force an appreciation that was a much larger part of the army than the old cavalry. He wanted division commanders to bring in engineers, transportation, artillery, or whatever was needed to complete the mission. The Armored Force started with two armored divisions and a separate tank battalion. Before Devers arrived, plans for the third and fourth divisions were in their advanced stages. By the time he left for his next assignment, the pool had expanded to fourteen armored divisions. Subsequently, two more would be added, and all sixteen entered combat.

Marshall allowed Devers to select new armored division commanders, subject only to the chief's final review. "Few men can lead divisions," recalled Devers. "I know them. I picked leaders with demonstrated ability, motivation and brains." He made sure that infantry, cavalry, artillery, and engineer officers were included at all levels. Devers advised new division commanders to first get staff, then immediately plan out the division's training program. "All training must be realistic or you will lose commitment from the troops," he said. "Insure teamwork. I had a great influence on all this planning."[29]

The promotion of John Leonard to command is indicative of the matter-of-fact way Marshall had of solving problems, and the closeness that then existed between mentor and protégé.[30] Leonard commanded the infantry regiment in 4AD at Pine Camp (now Fort Drum) in northern New York. Devers asked Leonard, "Why aren't you a general?" Leonard replied, "I fought with the Chief of Infantry." The chief of infantry had placed a zero on Leonard's efficiency report because he put in a minority report disagreeing with the chief.

Later, when Devers went in to Marshall, the senior general asked, "What do you want?" Devers responded, "I want you to make John Leonard a general." Devers had known Leonard since they were cadets, and Leonard had always been a top performer. Marshall responded, "Who is he? He is just a name to me." Devers briefly described Leonard, his attributes, and his problem with the chief of infantry. "Who was the Chief of Infantry?" asked Marshall. "General Lynch," responded Devers. "I never saw a man punch a button faster [than Marshall]," Devers recalled. Beadle Smith, then an assistant to the General Staff, responded to the buzzer. Marshall barked, "Put Leonard's name on top of the list for promotion."[31]

Devers never paused to relieve or reclassify an aging or incompetent officer, and crushed branch jealousy whenever it showed its head. He possessed a flexible and open mind, and was more than ready to modify his approach to new problems in training, tactics, and equipment.

Organization charts and pages of combat doctrine are valuable tools. But they are nothing if not employed by trained, motivated, and confident warriors. Devers never took his gaze away from this essential truth, producing those warriors from often capable civilians with little relevant experience or training, even if they wore spanking-new uniforms straight from quartermaster issue. Jake wrote in his notes while he brought up the Armored Force: "Junior officers capable and equal to their responsibility are their men's best chance of survival. . . . Officers must know capabilities and limitations of men intimately. . . . Morale [is] reflected by leadership of their commander, tolerant and sympathetic understanding of personnel and problems. Treat men as men, don't coddle them. Think before you act, but having thought, ACT!"[32]

Lieutenant Charles R. Williams advocated a program to develop within the individual fighter a high degree of self-confidence, courage, and aggressiveness in battle: Train him to coordinate both mental and physical condition during close combat. Emphasize cover and concealment afforded by terrain. Accustom him to the noise of battle, advancing under fire, and shooting at surprise close-in targets with poor visibility. Emphasize urban fighting from rooftop to rooftop, entering and searching buildings, booby traps, and forest fighting methods. Devers directed that this approach be incorporated, noting, "war is a young man's game." In his own handwriting on a battle report from North Africa, he wrote, "Leadership training and spirit are of prime importance. . . . The decision in any action will be determined on the brains of man. . . . Surprise and maneuver will be the advantage."

Devers was deeply interested in other people's motivations. "Men are trained to follow leaders because they respect them, and the idea of compulsion is always in the background. . . . Keep respect for authority without being overawed by it."[33] He believed in management by walking around; talking with and listening to the troops that served in his command. Henry Cabot Lodge, who went on after serving as Devers's principal liaison with the French to become President John F. Kennedy's ambassador to Saigon, recalled, "Devers had the knack of taking men who had not always been successful and, by making them understand that he expected the best of them, thereupon getting their best."[34]

During his tenure at Fort Knox, Devers did not want to give the impression that Armored Force was in crisis. To set a more relaxed pace and to keep in shape, he golfed twice a week and wanted his entire staff to take up some athletic pursuit as a conduit to let off steam. Jake said he learned a lot about what was really going on by talking with young staffers as they golfed together. Devers had always been acutely aware of the importance of community relations. He said it was necessary to maintain good relations with the local civilian community and to dissipate the notion that the military on post was a closed society. After the war, Forrest Pogue, a native Kentuckian, said that those at Fort Knox remembered Devers pleasantly.[35] To an extent, a number of the men Jake served with felt he was quite naive for a person of his age and experience. He was too sincere and humble to seek publicity, as some of his better known contemporaries have done.[36] Marshall saw Devers as a dedicated, dependable officer who eschewed publicity and flamboyance, and who projected a quiet air of authority and no nonsense.[37]

Desert warfare was likely for the Armored Force in the not too distant future. Jake flew out and selected the area that became the Desert Training Center at today's Fort Irwin, a facility that again became crucial for training at the end of the twentieth century. Devers felt that the California desert would make an ideal training ground. While McNair was against the site, Devers sold Marshall on the location – and on sending Patton to command the training center.[38] When Patton heard, he called Devers, saying, "What are you trying to do, can me?" Devers replied, "I am giving you the greatest opportunity of your life. Actually, I didn't select you, Marshall did."[39] Devers was hard-driving but did not play favorites. "Under me, Patton wouldn't have been allowed to abscond with anything he could get."[40] Devers drove himself hardest of all: "You don't need to go where things are going right. When you have troubles and you know where it is, you have got to be there. You have got to go yourself."[41] Patton asked for permission to fly his private plane out there. In doing so, he tripped over another of Jake's methods for eliminating red tape: "You can do anything you want but don't ask permission."[42] It's far easier to ask for forgiveness than to face retribution for being denied and doing something anyway.

By the end of 1942, no one in the American army really had any practical experience of taking armor up against German panzers. All service schools treated armor from a theoretical point of view. They had no idea of the capabilities of a tank. Little thought had been given to how tanks were to fight and survive against the likes of German Mark IIIs and IVs, let alone the monster Panthers and Tigers that they would face in 1944.

Devers wanted to be more than a chair-bound warrior, so he pitched the possibility of a trip to Africa to inspect the British Eighth Army. As he told Forrest Pogue, "I made the trip out there to inspect the Eighth Army to learn about tanks so that I could talk with authority and not just as a desk soldier. I'm tired of being told that we don't know what we are talking about and they are fighting them."[43] On 1 December 1942, Devers flew to Washington and went directly to Marshall's office. Waved in with no fanfare, Devers addressed the chief of staff: "General, I have got this Armored Force pretty well running now, and at least for another two months, there isn't much I can do, and it is in good hands. I have got the staff formed and the training is going on, and I want to go out and inspect the [British] Eighth Army" fighting the Afrika Korps in the desert. Marshall cut him off. "When can you take off? Why don't you take Ted Brooks?"[44]

The trip to Africa, which took place from 28 December 1942 to 28 January 1943, included Devers, Brooks, Williston Palmer, and General Gladeon Marcus Barnes from Ordnance. According to Palmer, "We studied the Hell out of the operations in the Libyan desert. We learned a lot from the trip."[45] Right after they returned, the debacle of the U.S. First Armored Division at Kasserine Pass shocked many. Heavy German panzers in combined arms formations had demonstrated that American antitank doctrine was "a fundamentally flawed set of principles."[46] One learning experience they would gladly have skipped was a crash landing in Ireland that destroyed the B-17 carrying Devers's party home from Africa. "Anyhow, the Irish let us escape . . . and then I made all these inspections [in England]."[47]

The principal findings from armored operations in North Africa were contained in a written report:

M4 (Sherman tank) and the M7 (self-propelled artillery) are the best in the world (an overstatement for the former).
The present war is definitely one of guns.
The separate tank destroyer arm is not a practical concept on the battlefield.
Sooner or later, the issue between ground forces is settled in an armored battle, tank against tank.[48]

In the same document, Devers stated, "The doctrine of TD's [tank destroyers] chasing tanks is absurd." No one was surprised when McNair was not convinced. Surprisingly neither was Marshall.[49] In his report, Devers glossed over the firepower advantage that high-velocity 75mm and 88mm tank guns had over the relatively short-barreled Sherman. Would a more forthright report have accelerated the M4E8 tank with the higher-velocity 76mm gun?

In his own hand, Jake scrawled across a summary of Charles Scott's notes from an earlier Africa trip: "Quality wins rather than quantity." His notes continue, "Train commanders, staffs, individuals, units to be physically ready, mentally alert and emotionally set for the realities of war." Devers, Eisenhower, and many officers returning from the battlefield repeated a common theme. In North Africa, American soldiers were not ready for the shock and intensity of the enemy advancing with intent to kill. In a comment that Devers would repeat throughout his wartime service, "A higher standard of discipline of American troops must be obtained."

"The US armored division with its crushing firepower, its high battlefield mobility, its shock action, and its ability for sustained action over a considerable period of time," Devers maintained, "remains the most powerful ground force in existence."[50] He summarized his views as follows:

1. The decision in any action will be determined on the basis of men, surprise, and maneuver with the advantage in the latter in the *tank*.
2. A breakthrough of a stabilized defensive position by infantry and artillery followed by exploitation by armor is *our doctrine*.
3. Assaulting infantry cannot stand up against machine gun fire. It is easier for artillery to destroy gun defense [meaning direct and indirect artillery] than it is to destroy machine gun defense. The latter is the tank's meat.[51]

This simple list of principles unties the knot that bound both the infantry and cavalry view of tanks. The problem before interwar tacticians was how to break through a continuous line of entrenched machine guns with enough power to maneuver to operational depth. Focusing on the breakthrough, infantry wanted a heavy tank that could survive and smash through the machine guns. Cavalry wanted a light, fast, mostly all-tank force to exploit with. Under Devers, Armored Force developed an all-purpose medium tank *embedded in a combined arms team* to complete both phases of the attack without pause, so the enemy had insufficient time to react. In the initial assault, tank-infantry teams took out the machine guns while artillery suppressed or destroyed enemy artillery guns. As the breakthrough continued, medium tanks, such as the fast, mechanically reliable Sherman, could rapidly exploit into the enemy's rear, tearing up its entire organization. This is where the heavy Panthers and Tigers did not measure up. But the medium tanks had sufficient armor and firepower to take on enemy tanks that had moved to block the exploitation.

The armored division moved away from primarily a tank formation to balance tank, mechanized infantry, and mobile artillery teams. Devers was not the only one to see the solution. But he was the wrangler who rescued the Armored Force from some unbalanced solutions in less than two years while a war raged. Armored Force did not have to lose a war to make this critical change. It was Devers's ability to quickly recognize the right solution and turn ideas into action that was his genius.

Prior to his North African trip, Devers had identified serious shortcomings in the M4 tank to Marshall: "The weakness that I reported to you personally last November are that the tanks are underpowered and that the gun had too low a velocity." But he had also written, "The trouble in the Middle East is leadership and training and not equipment."[52] Devers has been criticized for being too effusive about the standard M4 tank as late as 1943, after it became apparent that it could not defeat the new German designs. While he had endorsed a major improvement with the 76mm gun, he has also been criticized for not paying more attention to an even better solution, the British 17-pounder weapon mounted on what became known in British service as the "Sherman firefly," which was even more effective against Panthers and Tigers.[53]

During 1941–1942, most American two-star generals were overseeing the initial training of divisions formed around small seasoned cadres and a lot of new soldiers and freshly minted junior officers. These senior officers had their hands full organizing this human raw material into a military organization that could perform the basics. Before the war, few officers handled anything larger than a regiment. Devers spent these years thinking and experimenting with how armored divisions were to fight, and how such a division fit into a large force made up of corps and field armies. During the early part of the war, army military historians wrote a short history of the Armored Force that remains unpublished. In it, they summarized Devers's enormous impact on American armor: "The man primarily responsible for developing and expanding the Armored Force far beyond the original dreams of its first chieftains was Lt. Gen. Jacob L. Devers. [His] phenomenal energy, superior administrative ability and refusal to be bound by traditions welded the Armored Force into sixteen armored divisions and many more separate tank battalions."[54]

Devers brought many improvements. Still, American armored doctrine, especially at the level of operational maneuver, was woefully underdeveloped, especially when compared to German and Soviet doctrine. The shortcomings of the Sherman are now well known. In one of the best histories of the development of American armor, one author wrote, "When U.S. ground forces finally entered World War II they engaged the Wehrmacht with inferior tanks, equipment and doctrine."[55] Without Devers's energy and efforts, the situation would have been far worse. His huge contribution in developing the Armored Force into a world-class competitor in time for battle has gone largely unheralded. The Armored Force Department he inherited in 1941 was a clear war loser. If another officer was viewed as the father of armor, then Jake was the physician that delivered and nurtured the baby so that it grew into a strong, healthy young adult.

Not everyone approved of Devers's fast-paced, damn-the-red-tape methods. One such person was General Lesley McNair, who was convinced that the Armored Force was the most wasteful of the ground arms in the use of men and equipment because of its custom of doing big things in a hurry.[56] Another was Eisenhower, whose by-the-book approach was almost diametrically opposed to Devers's. So, in late spring 1943, when Devers was relieved of command of Armored Force and sent to replace Eisenhower as commander of the European Theater of Operations (ETO), rumors abounded that Jake had gotten crosswise with McNair on the issue of tanks versus antitank guns and was being sent to a backwater command as a punishment.[57] That simply was not true. Forrest Pogue later examined the issue carefully and found no evidence supporting the rumor. Marshall did not abandon his "go-to" commander. Instead he had another hot potato to throw to Devers.

During the course of his career, Devers built new staffs at seven different postings, as he did not believe in taking a huge entourage from post to post. The German command model effectively "married" a commander and his chief of staff. By contrast, Jake would only take a few key individuals along. He felt the job at Armored Force was not done, so he left most of the staff in place. As he later commented, "I am against the clique system anywhere."[58]

In 1940, the British said they were surprised by the quality of German armor, and despite many tank duels in the desert, they never had the time to catch up. Had a leader with less decisive speed and energy than Devers taken over the mess of Armored Force in late 1941, despite some good extant concepts, America would not have had a competitive combined arms armored team with which to defeat the Nazis in Europe. While preparing for battle in France, Patton was heard to say, "Thanks to Jake Devers, we are ready."[59]

SIX

Commander, ETO

EARLY IN 1942, MAJOR GENERAL JAMES CHANEY WAS SENT TO the United Kingdom to take command of the American army in Europe. Yes, there was a war into which America had just been thrust. But old habits die hard. Chaney maintained a pace as if it was peacetime.

In June 1942, to shift into high gear, George Marshall dispatched his most rapidly rising star, Dwight Eisenhower, to London. For the past year, he had performed well as Marshall's war plans officer. The two men found they had parallel views on how to conduct the war, and their judgments on a range of issues were compatible. Eisenhower was destined for even more lofty heights. Soon he would be selected to lead the invasion of North Africa.

Marshall selected another rising star, Lieutenant General Frank M. Andrews, to fill the soon-to-be-vacated position of American army leader in Europe. He was the first army aviator to become assistant chief of staff for plans. The official history of the period records that his death in a plane crash "ended a career of large accomplishment and larger promise."[1]

In World War II, all army logistical support emanated from the Services of Supply in the United States, which was headed by Brehon Somervell, who reported directly to Marshall as assistant chief of staff for supply and head of Services of Supply. To eliminate duplicate communications that had created problems during World War I, Somervell was adamant that the Services of Supply organization in Europe closely mirror his own. To affect this, he arranged for J. C. H. Lee, a protégé, to head Services of Supply in Europe under Eisenhower. Before he left for

North Africa, he became entangled with many organizational concerns with the imperious if hard-working Lee. The choice of Lee for the job was one of the most controversial personnel selections that Marshall ever approved.

During his truncated tenure, Andrews had ever larger problems with Lee, and it turned out that Chaney had similar troubles. All supply questions and much administrative paperwork routed through Lee. Andrews was convinced that Lee had been granted too much power, and he decided to request that Lee be sent home.

Before arriving in London, Andrews had not been given extensive instructions about grand strategy. During his tour in London, Eisenhower had become heavily involved in these questions. Apparently, Marshall had wanted Andrews to concentrate on what Marshall considered the true prize, build-up for the Allied invasion of northwestern France.

It was about 1100 hours, and Jacob Devers was sitting in his office when the call came from General George Marshall: "I want you to pack up. You are not going back to Fort Knox. Come up to Washington immediately. You know Andrews was killed. I am going to send you to England. That is all I can tell you on the phone."[2]

Marshall valued the organizational skills Devers had exhibited in North Carolina and in raising a real Armored Force out of a cloud of ideas, wishes, and plans. While others wrestled with world strategy, Devers had a full-time job created concrete action as men and equipment landed in the United Kingdom.

Devers recalled, "I don't think he [Marshall] gave me very definite instructions except the general policy that we did want to cross the English Channel eventually. The British were not very much for the cross-Channel operation. I had to form a staff. We were going to build up supplies and men. He would be in further touch with me and that is all. I was sent over there with pretty much freedom as a matter of fact."[3]

Marshall admonished Devers to maintain a close relationship with British Major General Frederick E. Morgan, who was detailed to head up planning for the invasion of France. Some quipped that he was more American than anything. Lieutenant General (and simultaneously Vice Admiral) Louis Mountbatten also gave Devers a great deal of encouragement. Americans on Morgan's staff were seconded from G5 (plans) of Eu-

ropean Theater of Operations, United States of America (ETOUSA), an
administrative organ to manage the huge job of bedding down millions
of newly arrived Americans. Morgan was the British officer detailed to
head up planning the cross-Channel attack. Although he was not among
the innermost circle of senior British officers, it was clear, at least to Devers, that the British did not want the Allies to make a cross-Channel
attack. The two had many frank discussions about getting across the
channel. "I had wonderful relations with [Frederick] Morgan," Devers
recalled. "He was very honest with me. Morgan told me a lot of things
that I can't repeat because he'd get direction from Mr. Churchill or the
chief of the British Army, on these things, he did keep me informed but in
secret." Still, Morgan and Devers stayed in communication throughout
the war. Bernard Montgomery, too, had a decent opinion of Devers. If
ETO was split into two army groups, he opined, Devers was capable of
leading one. Chief of the Imperial Staff Alan Brooke agreed. This specu-
lation was exactly what Devers hoped for. Likewise, Marshall's principal
biographer, Forrest Pogue, stated that he found no evidence to a report
that Marshall had removed Devers as commander of ETO because he
wasn't getting along with the British.[4]

Devers had to fight constantly to overcome obstacles that appeared
from above Morgan's level to retard invasion planning. He compiled a
list of the initial things he needed to do:

1. Build a proper staff.
2. Cross the Channel.
3. Assist the Eighth Air Force.
4. Make second priority Service of Supply personnel.
5. Provide training grounds for arriving troops.
6. Assist efforts to defeat the submarine menace.
7. Step up the building of landing craft to allow an assault with
   six divisions.
8. Check on DUKWs.
9. Reduce the command in Iceland.
10. Increase troop carriers (air drop capacity) to one or two
    divisions.

Devers felt that assembling a good staff was the first and most important task of any commander. He later noted, "No criticism, but when Eisenhower left for Africa, he left all the bums behind, and I found out in a hurry. We had to clean those out. This was a very difficult job for me."[5] Devers remembered some advice given to him by an old friend: When given a job, say, "Yes, sir. Get to work right away and get some help."

Devers picked up David Barr as his operations officer and Dan Noce, who joined the Armored Force as an engineer and now became chief of staff. Devers described Noce as a plainspoken, honest farm boy, and a little stubborn at times. "I always felt that when I wanted some real sharp advice, I should call Dan Noce."[6] He remained with Devers throughout much of the war.

Everyone was still feeling their way into the intricacies of assembling in the United Kingdom the huge American army that Franklin Roosevelt, Winston Churchill, and their respective service chiefs had envisioned. It was the summer of 1942, and the Battle of the Atlantic was raging. German U-boat commanders dubbed it "the Happy Time" as they sank ship after ship. The U.S. Army Transportation Corps was established only in July of that year. There was a tremendous shortage of officers with training or experience to ship the vast quantities of materiel that were piling up on American wharves en route to England. Neither operating procedures nor manuals existed, and there was little to guide a neophyte supply handler. In an effort to economize on the use of limited eastbound space, dispatchers ordered their men to top off every ship with cargo from the mountains awaiting a ride. Soon record-keeping completely broke down. Shipping manifests bore little resemblance to the contents of ship holds. Ships sailed the high seas in large convoys but were directed one by one into available quays in sundry British ports. For the most part, civilian British stevedores unloaded cargoes and send them off to various available warehouses and storage sites with little regard to documentation. Soon, control and materiel were lost. All of us have experienced difficulty in locating a tool that has been neatly tucked away God knows where. Imagine this with millions of tons of unfamiliar supplies and equipment being shuffled about by an undertrained labor force of inadequate size. One can appreciate the size of Devers's headaches. A less competent, less optimistic commander would have been overwhelmed.

With the exception of the destroyers for bases deal, Devers's career had concentrated on the deployment of ground combat power. Upon being posted to England, he expected his horizon to expand. During the summer of 1942, however, little did he expect to be thrust into the most contentious geopolitical controversy between the two allies while having breakfast with the prime minister and secretary of war in July 1943.

Henry Stimson had come to the United Kingdom to meet the prime minister. Devers and the secretary had a friendship that extended back a long ways. As one of the most senior American officers in Britain, it was only natural that Devers escort Stimson. The trio motored down to view the cliffs of Dover. Hardly had they sat at the table when the secretary directly confronted Churchill. "Mr. Prime Minister, when are you going to cross the Channel?" For emphasis, he struck the table top. Devers's egg flew onto the floor. Churchill replied, "I give you my word that we'll cross the English Channel providing my military commanders agree."[7]

Devers thought Stimson was one of the most competent civilian leaders. Later, during the same trip, Devers confided that, in his opinion, Marshall was the best choice to command the invasion. "Churchill trusted him and he had the power to say Yes."[8] If not Marshall, then Eisenhower. Devers thought that only these two officers could command sufficient respect to keep the British in line with an operation that they supported reluctantly at best.

A cross-Channel invasion by ground forces was for a distant future date. At present, B-17s and B-24s were making constant daylight bombing runs into the heart of the Third Reich and getting slaughtered. Loss rates on the infamous Schweinfurt and Regensburg raids would top 20 percent, with another 20 percent of the bombers landing safely but not able to fly again. A few similar losses would essentially destroy the American bomber force. The Army Air Corps put on its best face but was in trouble. At first, General Henry Arnold would not accept low operational rates among the surviving aircraft. He did not understand the amount of battle damage that was not repairable in the United Kingdom. ETO simply did not have the trained manpower, heavy equipment, and repair parts to handle these jobs. Heavily damaged aircraft often needed to be returned to America, only there was no way for non-flyable aircraft to make the trip.

Major General Ira Eaker commanded the bombers in England during those dark days. At first, Eaker was suspicious of Devers. He soon, however, saw that this ground officer was enthusiastic and wanted to help. When interviewed after the war, Eaker had nothing but accolades for Devers: "He supported us completely, enthusiastically and was, I think, the best commanding officer I served under during the war. I always found that the staff seemed to take the color of his personality. I always had excellent cooperation from them."[9] Eaker was a fighting man, not a wild-blue-yonder flyboy. He and Devers became close friends.[10] Eaker recalled, "Devers interceded on my behalf with Arnold. His effort was essential to the success of Eighth Air Force operations. Without support from Devers, we might not have been allowed to continue until we proved our case." Eaker extended the highest accolade an airman could bestow on a ground-pounder: "Devers understood airpower."[11] Often Devers sat in of the daily air operations conference and was more interested in air operations than logistics.

While he was impressed with Eaker, Devers said that Eaker had a lot of older men in command there, and they were beginning to think more about their men than they were about the fight. "Arnold had the pressure on, so I had to take action." Devers saw that the older commanders were rotated back to training slots in the United States, and men like Generals Carl Spaatz and Curtis LeMay elevated. "We revamped that whole set up. Somebody had to have drive and keep going. Otherwise we would have been in trouble." Jake also recalled, "I can say with a great deal of authority that we got more information from the German Air Force through their broadcasting in code than we got from anything else over there. We could break that code in twenty-four hours once we got on to it."[12]

Midway through his command of ETO, a tiff over assignment of four bomber groups brought Eisenhower and Devers to loggerheads. At the time (July 1943), Eisenhower and his staff were looking for a way to gain air superiority for the invasion from Sicily onto the Italian mainland. Naples was the primary candidate for the invasion, but it was at maximum fighter range, and planners wanted additional multiengine support for the operation. Spaatz and Eisenhower wanted bombers transferred from ETO to the Mediterranean. As theirs was the active theater, they reasoned, the Mediterranean should have priority. Eaker advised Devers that this would eviscerate the strategic air war just when it appeared that the "corner" was about to be turned – a major overstatement.

Eisenhower's request hit Devers's desk on 28 July. Intelligence at the time indicated that the Luftwaffe was about to back off their intense attacks on daylight bombers. Devers bitterly protested Eisenhower's request for the bombers. The Eighth Air Force was already too small to carry out its mission. The campaign had barely gotten underway, and it was not going well. An even-handed assessment would have concluded that the German airmen retained the upper hand. By cable, Devers told the combined chiefs, "The German high command would be delighted if the shift were made. . . . The Eighth Air Force should never be diverted from its primary task. Summing up I must be guided by the greatest damage to the German army and I must never lose sight of the imminence of Overlord."[13] In the summer of 1943, losses during daylight American bomber raids were heavy. While no one wanted to admit it at the time, the Allies were losing the air war over Germany. These raids were, in fact, suffering war-losing loss rates, and British night bombing was not delivering sufficient target destruction. Yet the infamous raids on Schweinfurt and Regensburg were being planned and would be dispatched in mid-August, only a few weeks after Eisenhower's request.

Eisenhower appealed to Marshall to overrule Devers. Marshall ran the bomber issue by the joint chiefs, who were in agreement. To Eisenhower's surprise, the joint chiefs supported Devers. On the last day of July 1943, Marshall cabled both theater commanders saying Devers was right and that the heavy bombers had to stay in England. Four groups represented a major slice of frontline bomber strength, as the Eighth Air Force mustered only six heavy groups with an average daily strength of 153 bombers.[14] Further, it would take a month to move the four thousand ground crew and equipment associated with the bombers, essentially taking those bomber groups out of the fight for three months. The Mediterranean officers lost sight of the strategic importance the chiefs had assigned to the bombing campaign over Germany.

Some historians have felt that Eisenhower's embarrassment at this decision might have been the root of the enmity he felt toward Devers. Air Chief Marshal Sir Arthur Tedder was Eisenhower's air commander at the time and became deputy supreme commander for Operation Overlord. He observed, "For understandable reasons, the idea [of an inter-theater bomber transfer] was turned down."[15] While people in the Mediterranean Theater of Operations (MTO) might have been frustrated at the time, Tedder's observation hardly sounds like a reason Eisenhower would use to down-check a senior commander. But historian Stephen Ambrose noted that "Eisenhower was not accustomed to having his requests to Marshall turned down and found it difficult to accept."[16] An aide noted, "Ike is furious with Devers."[17] The decision served as another crack to allow acid to attack the foundation on which Devers stood. When it came to Devers and the bombers, "Eisenhower could be sullen and petty."[18] The interrelationship among Marshall, Eisenhower, and Devers gained complexity. Marshall had been the mentor and cultivator of the careers of the two less-senior generals. The ties among them were being drawn into ever more troublesome knots.

On 22 August, Marshall finally admitted that a 1943 invasion of the continent was infeasible. Top priority would go to equipping the forces Eisenhower was about to lead in the first major American invasion across the Atlantic, the three simultaneous landings in North Africa (Operation Torch). Eisenhower sought out the man most knowledgeable about what was on hand in the United Kingdom to supply and equip his invasion forces. That was Lee, not Devers. Undoubtedly this led to the diminution of Eisenhower's estimate of Devers. At first, Eisenhower sang Lee's praises. The myriad logistical snarls, however, soon became apparent; Lee had massively overrepresented his control of the chain of supply.[19] For example, no one could find the artillery pieces that were to arm the 1st Infantry Division (1D) about to invade African beaches. Available artillery ammunition was corroded and of little use. Despite the stores stacked somewhere, American sources would be unable to supply much of what was required in North Africa. Eisenhower turned to his deputy, Mark Clark, and his chief of staff, "Beetle" Smith, for solutions. Much materiel would have to come directly from the United States, though

Smith turned to the British for food, fuel, and heavy construction supplies. British General Humfrey Gale was instrumental in making these
arrangements and became Eisenhower's senior logistical officer for the
remainder of the war.

Devers was a touch more tolerant of Lee's machinations. In any
event, Devers's leadership style had always been to tell a hard-charging
subordinate what to get done, assign him the means to do it, and then
step back and let the subordinate do his job without interference from
above.

Obvious to Devers, there was a lot of duplication in the staff effort
between Services of Supply, European Theater of Operations (SOSETO)
and ETOUSA. Supposedly the ETOUSA staff was responsible for planning
logistic operations and SOSETO was to execute them. To Devers, this
sounded like bureaucracy binding things in red tape, which was anath-
ema to him. He readily agreed to eliminate the planning function from
ETO and to consolidate it with Lee's operating authority at Services of
Supply. While outside of established doctrine, it appeared the best way
to solve local issues and keep the important useful Somervell happy.
This pleased Lee, who said, "For the first time an American Army has
. . . what we regard as a sound organization, bringing together these two
organizational functions."[20] Peace between the warring bureaucracies
brought a little respite for Eisenhower, although not for long.

Controlling both the flow of supplies and paperwork, Lee held tremendous administrative power skillfully. But an official study of the
history of World War II logistics makes an unfavorable judgment on
Lee's operation: "The Logistic structure was probably inferior to that
devised during World War I."[21] The essential traits of those logisticians
who succeed are great initiative, a can-do attitude, and a willingness to
improvise, traits J. C. H. Lee lacked in abundance.

Lee asked for twenty-nine brigadier general slots for his staff and
subordinate organization of logistics. Such an outsized request was a
major problem for Devers and Eisenhower, who was still in theater. Devers finally put his foot down and trimmed this back. Many field commanders held a low opinion of Lee and his entourage. Patton remarked,
"Lee is a glib liar."[22]

Devers, no stranger to controlling headstrong subordinates, firmly cut them off when necessary. Devers was the boss. Major General Everett Hughes, SOSETO's chief ordnance officer, who would become one of Eisenhower's most trusted logisticians, confided, "Devers set up the present organization in order that he might keep Johnny Lee under his thumb."[23] Still, jostling among American control organizations in the United Kingdom continued. It was apparent that the Supply of Services operations in the United States continued to have its influence. Devers wrote in his diary, "It seems to me that Washington tries to interfere too much with the command of a theater where conditions and relations between the arms and services are not happy."[24]

The bedrock on which supply plans are based is the troop list, the summary of personnel and equipment that individual units will require. Overall troop strength, composition, equipment required, and the supplies to support these are compiled. Organizations can be evaluated. Andrews had been working on the first comprehensive troop list for ETO. Without it, there could be no master plan for transatlantic shipment. Cargoes would arrive as catch can. Devers was experienced in working on them. Given his critical thinking skills in past work in building Fort Bragg and assembling the Armored Force, it was his forte. As many staff officers and senior commanders have observed, logistics dictate everything. While less glamorous than strategy, such calculations created an ocean of work into which Jake enthusiastically dove. Both large issues and enormous amounts of detail had to be ground out in rapid order. No one had ever heard of a desktop calculator, let alone a computer.

The first master troop list was completed in three weeks, under the supervision of Army Air Corps Major General Follett Bradley, who completed an air-oriented first draft. Approved by General Ira Eaker, the plan called for over 485,000 men and 113 air groups. Devers had a number of objections. He felt that the air component was too large, the ground component insufficient, and the service element too small. By the time the massaging was done, Devers had approved and sent to the War Department on 18 July a ground forces plan calling for 18 divisions and over 635,000 men, supported by an Army Service Forces (ASF) troop basis of 375,000.

Table 6.1. Cumulative arrivals of U.S. Army in Great Britain, 1942–1944

	Troops	Army Cargo (tons)
December 1942	248,139	2,179,996
December 1943	918,347	7,943,790
May 1944	1,792,512	15,573,989

Source: Bykofsky and Larson, *Transportation Corps,* 104–105.

Devers got on well with Admiral Harold R. Stark, the senior American naval officer in the United Kingdom who was senior to Devers by two stars. Often they coordinated ship arrivals and unloadings on a daily basis. Some numbers help to summarize the magnitude of incoming men and materiel that had to be accommodated, as shown in table 6.1.

Before he left at the end of 1943 for the Mediterranean, Devers had bedded down in a foreign land more men than the armed forces had in total strength before the war. He had to deal with an immense pile of organizational problems, more than all the prewar army bureaucracy.

A major shortage of Service Force troops developed. Eisenhower needed even more in North Africa, which became the priority. A lot of cargo arrived from the United States, more than British port labor could handle. Devers was acutely aware of the limitations on British railroads and ports, which prevented even greater shipments. By the end of 1943, he had hoped to have landed even greater volumes.

Devers had displayed base development skills at Fort Bragg. Now he graduated to Theater of Operations scale. For example, 120 airfields needed to be built or renovated to accommodate incoming American war birds. Even ones that had served as British airfields needed lengthened runways, added hangar space, and expanded accommodations. Devers was at his best cutting through administrative delays, managing a myriad of details, and getting things done.

Unbeknownst to Devers, General Marshall had just lost a major debate over strategy. From the beginning, Marshall had strongly agreed with "Plan Dog," which placed the defeat of Germany ahead of all other strategic tasks. Marshall felt that the only way to accomplish this was for the Western Allies to invade northwest France, directly take on the Wehrmacht, and defeat it in the field. By contrast, the British, led by a vehement Winston Churchill, surmised that American strength was nowhere near the level nor their skills sufficient to directly take on the Germans. The British surmised that the only way to get involved in ground combat against the Germans was to invade North Africa. Stephen Ambrose, a principal biographer of Eisenhower, agreed with the British assessment: "Perhaps the strongest argument against a cross channel attack in 1943 was that the Allied high command was too inexperienced to successfully direct such a complex operation."[25] By cutting off debate, Roosevelt forced Marshall's agreement.

Americans under the command of Eisenhower landed in North Africa the day after Election Day in November 1942. From touchdown of the first landing craft, little went according to plan. It was a testament more to the inexperience of the American war machine than anything else, and underscored the lack of readiness to directly take on the Germans, who had been beating up on the armies of Europe going on four years. Logistical foul-ups allowed only 10 percent of American forces landed to get to the front that, by February 1943, was in Tunisia, several hundred miles from the initial landing zones. It took direct intervention from Somervell back in the United State to dispatch an additional 5,400 line haul trucks, 2,000 trailers, 100 locomotives, and railway engineering supplies to keep transport from Oran to the front from collapsing. Somehow, twenty additional ships were conjured up to carry them to North Africa. This was on top of an already full sailing schedule. These quantities on such short notice were unprecedented and strained ASF beyond what many thought was possible. Somehow, Somervell always came through.

Fortunately, the Allied forces moving through northwest Africa met little initial resistance. Except for the valor of the soldiers, little in the opening months went right. Poor tactics precipitated the horrible defeat at Kasserine. Eisenhower himself confided to Lieutenant General Thomas Handy, Marshall's de facto vice chief of staff, that the North African campaign "had violated every recognized principle of war, was in conflict with all operational and logistical methods laid down in textbooks, and will be condemned, in their entirety, by all Leavenworth and War College classes for the next twenty-five years."[26]

"Victorious Eisenhower" felt the weight of his myriad problems and recognized that his missteps on the road to Tunisia hardly merited any medal. As early as November, Chief of the Imperial Staff Alan Brooke wrote in his diary, "It must be remembered that Eisenhower had never commanded even a battalion in action when he found himself commanding a group of armies in North Africa. No wonder he was at a loss as to what to do. . . . He had little confidence in his having the ability to handle the military situation confronting him and he caused me great anxiety."[27] Marshall recognized a number of serious mistakes, sometimes doubting Eisenhower's ability to master the problems before him, but ultimately Marshall remained highly supportive of his protégé. Still, at Casablanca, he dressed down Eisenhower for not being more decisive, especially with the internal organization of his theater headquarters. Nevertheless, Marshall lobbied for Eisenhower's fourth star, a rarified rank in the American services at the beginning of 1943. At first the president balked, due to the slow advance in Tunisia, but, recognizing the inter-Allied politics and wanting to retain an American supreme commander, acquiesced. Also recognizing the political realities, the British chiefs retained Eisenhower but insisted on inserting a British overall ground commander, General Harold Alexander. Essentially, this kicked Eisenhower upstairs.

Due to logistical errors, five American divisions were immobilized in North Africa, while the forward-most Americans were distributed in small packets and were about to be trounced by superior German forces at Kasserine. With his own eyes, Marshall had seen the poor conditions and lax discipline of American soldiers in the base section and replacement depot in Casablanca. These men did little in the rear area, while their brethren farther east facing the Afrika Corps were badly outnumbered. Marshall privately took Eisenhower aside and ordered him to get tough, instill some discipline, and "clean up the mess in his rear."[28] The chief of staff had been less than impressed with Eisenhower's summary presentation to the combined British-American chiefs, and was beginning to doubt his ability to regain control of the situation. Eisenhower was frustrated with events to the point of tears.

During the initial combat in North Africa, Eisenhower found himself becoming closer to Omar Bradley. This created a bond that lasted for the remainder of the war. Agreeing that a commander should be able to choose his lieutenants, Marshall, at Eisenhower's behest, picked Bradley to command the U.S. First Army because of this calm stability and proficiency at battalion tactics, demonstrated as an instructor of tactics at the Infantry School. Marshall chose Bradley when it became imperative to choose someone with extensive combat experience as a corps commander. It also gave Eisenhower the field army commander he wanted and would soon rise to army group commander. Everyone was happy – except Devers.

This requirement crossed Devers off the list of possible Overlord commanders. Despite Eisenhower's selection, Marshall retained his good opinion of Devers. Actually Marshall had other plans for him: little did Devers know that he almost became commander of Army Service Forces in October 1943. The constant friction between General Joseph Stilwell, one of Marshall's true friends from long before the war, and Chiang Kaishek in China was taking its toll. Marshall sent Brehon Somervell to investigate, and, if required, to replace Stilwell. Marshall in turn planned to replace Somervell with Devers.[29] At the time, Marshall could have given Devers no higher an accolade. It is clear that, at the end of 1943, the chief saw Devers as one of his most valuable (but not *the* most valuable) officers in the army.

Devers's biggest problem was that he was not Dwight Eisenhower. During his tenure in London from late June until mid-September 1942, Eisenhower had "wowed" both the British public and its leadership with his winning ways. Eisenhower's principal biographer, Stephen Ambrose, observed that "Eisenhower was more successful than any other VIP of the twentieth century. . . . He used the press to sell the idea of Allied unity. . . . London took him to her heart."[30] He got on well with all of the senior British leadership except Brooke and Bernard Montgomery. A regular visitor to the prime minister's country home, Chequers, Eisenhower engendered a close friendship with Churchill, despite their differences on strategy. Eisenhower's informality appealed to Churchill. Even when differences were heated, the two could talk with each other.

Devers also faced clandestine opposition from within his own organization. Eugene Harrison had served with Devers as far back as West Point athletics. Over time, they had developed something of a "father-son" relationship. Devers brought him over to London as a member of Devers's staff. At one point, Harrison informed his boss that a senior staff member, a holdover from the Chaney days, was "cutting his throat."[31]

Using his access to COSSAC staff, the staff member was bad-mouthing Devers to the British and creating a great deal of dissention. Devers was flabbergasted. Such behavior, while not unknown, was rare in the prewar American army. But he believed Harrison and dealt with the problem.

In interviews after the war, Devers also recounted many instances of good cooperation. But they came from the ranks of those assigned either to work with the Yankees in getting them settled in the United Kingdom or in preparations for the cross-Channel operation.

Both Eisenhower and Devers were brilliant, capable men. But they had very different styles. Eisenhower carefully assembled information from many sources, looked at the alternatives, and came to deliberate conclusions. Often he avoided making decisions he could postpone and made them only at the last minute possible. The more mercurial Devers looked over the situation and, sometimes shooting from the hip, came to rapid conclusions, cutting through whatever stood in the way of quick action. Both approaches had their advantages. Patton was fond of saying "the best is the enemy of the good," that a good plan executed in time always beat the perfect plan readied after the enemy has overrun your position. Some instances favored Devers's approach. But his quick summing up sometimes overlooked important nuances and resulted in less than accurate solutions. Not surprisingly, men with such varied approaches sometimes had difficulty getting along.

Devers recalled later that senior British leadership became irritated with him because "they had to do something with me and I would not give in on it [the earliest possible cross Channel attack], and they all knew it. There is no doubt that the British wanted to do one thing and we wanted to do another. . . . People are always going to tell you are ambitious and wanting this and you did this because of that. That isn't always so."[32] After Devers had been reassigned, however, reports in British newspapers that Marshall had removed Devers because he was an obstructionist were false.

In 1942, Devers was one of the biggest proponents of the medium Sherman tank. But reports of the Tiger from North Africa and later the Panther opposing the Soviet Union convinced him that a heavier vehicle was needed to survive fights with heavy German armor. When Devers had been chief of armor, he had rejected the M6 heavy tank for being under-powered and under-gunned for its weight. Ordnance had gone back and come up with the T20, the precursor to the 90mm armed and heavily armored M26 tank. Devers recommended that 250 of these be immediately shipped to ETO. General Lesley McNair, however, still advocating heavily armed but lightly armored tank destroyers, blocked the shipment.

Devers also had to deal with seemingly extraneous personnel problems. One source was soldiers who had access to classified information and couldn't resist showing it off. Weeding out soldiers, especially over-age officers that needed to go back to the states, generated myriad headaches. Someone was always alleging waste, fraud, or abuse. Often reports resulted from people new and unfamiliar with the job at hand. Getting Coca-Cola and other soft drinks into local pubs proved a problem. Existing brewers didn't want to lose the beer business, but lower alcohol consumption by troops led to fewer incidents. The trick was to get the brewers involved in the soda distribution chain so that they could make a profit. Jake recalled an episode with his intelligence officer (G2): "G2 was new to me. I found almost nothing in the existing ETO organization. So I brought in the Armored Force G2 who both read and spoke German. He met Mr. Big of British Intelligence," the unidentified head of British Intelligence whom the British took very seriously. An Englishman informed Devers that the American G2 had an English mistress living in his room. Besides the moral lapse, the American officer opened himself up to blackmail from foreign agents. Devers immediately sent him packing, cabled General Handy with particulars, and recommended a start-over. "I never heard what happened to him."[33]

A lot of the Army Service of Supply soldiers were African American, and the British were concerned about racial incidents. There were problems with the locals and festering racism among many Americans. African Americans from the North and MPs from the Deep South often had trouble with each other. Devers, who maintained that black troops could perform well if only given a chance, had to handle interracial problems with tact and determination.[34] Jake was convinced that "colored troops," as they were known in 1945, had not been given a level chance to display their combat ability. To that time, the combat record of many small colored combat units had been poor. Many white officers honestly believed that colored men simply did not have what it took to become first line soldiers. Devers was sure that actual performance would correct this mistaken attitude.[35]

General Albert Wedemeyer, an influential strategic planner on the army staff, was sent over to England to have a look at things. He reported back that Devers was "a happy selection as CG [commanding general] ETO. He is rapidly winning the respect and confidence of the British, and the Americans are uniformly pleased with the manner in which they receive decisions and sound directions."[36] A subordinate recalled, there were "very few officers in service that were as good as Devers was." He inspired his subordinates and was very patient with them. . . . Devers was a man who gives second chances. He had qualities of a theater commander but didn't have Ike's diplomatic facility."[37] Devers's chief of staff, Dan Noce, remembered, "Devers was direct. That is an admirable attribute in a commander but one that may lead a diplomat into trouble."[38]

Army Ground Forces performed a Herculean job raising and training new divisions. But Devers noticed that the quality and training of many nondivisional units, corps, and army-level artillery, engineers, quartermasters, and such were far below standard. Many GIs did not seem to take impending combat or the Germans as mortal enemies very seriously. Similar traits had surfaced among GIs as they entered North Africa, and Devers strongly believed it was due to a lack of leadership. Less care had been taken in the selection of nondivisional unit commanding officers, often separate battalions, than the efforts of divisional commanders to build their own teams. Devers recommended a better CO selection process.[39] Throughout his wartime service, Devers would make this a recurring theme. On 1 March 1943, during a North African inspection tour, Devers cabled General Marshall, "1 armored division and 1 infantry division have a softness or complacent attitude. Need to understand that the enemy are killers." When he took over ETO, he removed the commanding general of 51D, which was occupying Iceland at the time, due to the unit's low morale and level of training. "From the highest to very lowest they must learn that this is not a child's game and [be] ready and eager to get down to business."[40] In this concern, Eisenhower and Devers were of a similar mind. Eisenhower made the same

observations to Marshall: "A certain softness or complacent attitude.
. . . I don't know how we are going to get over to unit commanders the
sternness of the proposition with which they are faced. You have a real
problem on your hands." From his own experience interacting with the
British government, Devers recognized the need to have officers trained
in civil-military relations. When the American army landed on the continent, this requirement would likely expand dramatically. Therefore, he
decreed that a civil affairs course be instituted and that the school report
directly to ETO staff, where the latest lessons learned could constantly
be used to update the curriculum.

Whether Devers realized it or not, his tenure as commander, ETO, was
coming to an end. Bit by bit the foundation of his command was erod-
ing. Devers could be a very charming individual. He strongly believed
that "public relations were an important part of your command. A commander must be proactive."[41] But while he commanded good interpersonal skills, he did not have the endearing touch that made Eisenhower
so favored by Churchill and his staff. Devers felt it was his place to keep
the invasion on track. He openly and strenuously resisted British attempts to delay or divert preparations. The British found him prickly
and difficult. While relations were overtly cordial, Churchill had little
use for Devers. By Marshall's design, Devers was not really involved in
large questions of grand strategy as Eisenhower had been. Eisenhower's
superlative skills and authority clearly identified him as the man to talk
to. As a replacement, Devers had nowhere the same gravitas. A more objective observer than Jake would have been able to recognize Marshall's
rank ordering of his subordinates.

Devers's methods created interpersonal damage that slightly accelerated his decline, while Eisenhower's skill at handling people left a
better impression. Admiral Sir Andrew B. Cunningham, commander of
the Royal Navy, was the epitome of what the British liked in a First Sea
Lord – a cool, competent, refined gentleman of dignity and grace. He
would seem to have had little in common with the homespun Kansas
farm boy with an infectious grin, but the admiral "liked him [Eisen-
hower] at once. He struck me as being completely sincere, straight for-

ward and very modest.... Eisenhower grew quickly in stature and it was not long before one recognized him as the really great man he is – forceful, able, direct, and far seeing with a great charm of manner."[42]

Marshall's first choice was to have Lesley McNair command the American Army Group with Devers and Omar Bradley as army commanders. But McNair was almost deaf. If he was disqualified, Marshall's backup plan was to put Devers at Army Group with Bradley and Courtney Hodges commanding the armies. Devers himself would have liked to see McNair in Overlord's senior command structure.

Devers was Bradley's senior by six years. They had served together at West Point; Devers had been the baseball coach when Cadet Bradley played on the team. For three years in the early 1920s, Devers was in the tactical department when Bradley was a math instructor. Bradley recalled, "I was not overjoyed at the prospect of Jake Devers being elevated to high command in Overlord. I may have been initially prejudiced against Devers by Ike, who recently had several long distance set-tos with him over airpower [the transferring of the bombers]. The matter was referred to the Combined Chiefs who sided with Devers. That made Ike furious."[43] Bradley thought little of Devers: "I found him to be overly garrulous, egotistical, shallow, intolerant, not very smart, much too inclined to act on impulse and rush off half cocked."[44] Bradley added, "He talked too much, said nothing, and made a poor impression. He struck us as a great egotist and told us how he alone was responsible for the progress and development of the Army."[45]

In the many interviews Forrest Pogue and especially Thomas Griess conducted with Devers after the war, one gets the impression that he had very sensitive antenna for the opinions and desires of others. The transcripts are laced with comments and observations about other officers and stories about his interactions with them. Of course, Devers knew that Bradley was a rival who was not likely to think highly of Jake. Bradley was now one of the few seasoned commanders of a corps in combat, and had been with Eisenhower through both North Africa and Sicily. Devers's deputy operations officer recalled Jake's guidance in regard to Bradley: "When a question come up that concerns Bradley and his area of responsibility, first give it careful thought. Think of terms that will bring Jake and Omar in agreement, then take the matter up with

Devers."[46] While Jake, like anyone else who had attained high office, watched out for his own interests, he would not allow that to color the discharge of his professional duties.

Eisenhower commented on the people he wanted on his staff: "Fake reputations, habits of glib and clever speech and glittering surface performance are going to be discovered and kicked overboard."[47] Eisenhower's low opinion of Devers's military abilities was well known among the staffs in Europe.[48] In his book *Crusade in Europe,* Eisenhower described Devers "as a very fine administrator," which is faint praise for a combatant army group commander.[49] Carlo D'Este, a major Eisenhower biographer, opined, "Eisenhower was ruthless in accepting only men he knew and trusted. Those who crossed him paid, among them LTG Jacob L. Devers." Blocking transfer of bombers "angered Eisenhower who thereafter bore ill feelings toward Devers."[50]

One of Eisenhower's first actions was to convince Marshall to order Devers out of ETO.[51] On 17 December 1943, in a letter to Marshall, Eisenhower indicated that he had no need for the services of Devers and suggested he be reassigned to the Mediterranean theater.[52] After the war, Bradley related, "Ike sought to remove Jake Devers from the scene by sending him to the [Mediterranean] . . . since Devers was a Marshall man, Marshall was naturally miffed."[53] Apparently, Marshall viewed this as an attempt by Eisenhower to move out a potential rival for the command of Overlord and was disturbed by it.[54] Marshall by contrast sought to include Devers in ETO command structure. In a 27 December 1943 communication, Marshall suggested two alternative sets of combat commanders to Eisenhower: either appoint McNair as army group commander with Bradley and Devers as army commanders, or make Devers army group commander with Bradley and Hodges commanding armies.[55] Eisenhower preferred the former. Later, he would comment on McNair's deafness, which opened the way for Eisenhower to elevate Bradley to army group command. The dates of the communications indicate that Marshall still had confidence in Devers's skills, and that Marshall and Eisenhower did not see eye to eye. In time, Marshall would insist on Devers's commanding the army group that landed in southern France. Now it was time for Eisenhower to not disagree with his boss. His letter to Marshall of 12 July 1944 stated that he did not know Devers well. Reports that Eisenhower had received from the Mediterranean indicated that Devers had done a fine administrative job and had an ability to inspire the troops. But if Eisenhower believed that was true, why did the bad talk of Devers around SHAEF headquarters continue? Eisenhower maintained decent relationships with British decision makers in London. They viewed Devers as something of a hair shirt. Undoubtedly that got back to Eisenhower, with detrimental impact on Devers. Later, Forrest Pogue would comment that Eisenhower seemed ill at ease when discussing Devers.[56]

Still, for now, Marshall felt that Eisenhower should be able to pick his own team and acceded to his request. Making Devers deputy to Jumbo Wilson was Eisenhower's attempt to put Devers somewhere out of the way. Nonetheless, Marshall retained a large hat for Jake as 6th Army Group commander. Although Devers didn't know it at the time, Marshall would later be brusque with Eisenhower's early attempts at removing Devers from the Mediterranean Theater of Operations and into his own ETO. Always moving carefully, Eisenhower followed up with a cable to Marshall on Christmas day stating that "I have nothing whatsoever against Devers.... If you want to leave Devers in England I have no doubt I will find a useful job for him. I have no repeat no reason in the world to doubt his ability and I know that he has enjoyed your confidence for a long time."[57] But he agreed only reluctantly, said Bradley.[58]

Under Harold Alexander, George Patton and Bernard Montgomery led armies into Sicily. Later Mark Clark, one of the few American amphibious experts in MTO, led the American invasion of the Italian boot at Salerno. Relying on unimaginative frontal attacks, he led a maddeningly slow advance up the boot toward Casino, while Montgomery took the Eighth Army up the east coast. Clark increasingly was a problem down in Italy, which was part of the Mediterranean Theater. Eisenhower suggested to British Field Marshal Henry Maitland "Jumbo" Wilson, who had been selected to replace Eisenhower as supreme Allied commander in the Mediterranean, that Devers might be slotted into Fifth Army command, which would have been a disaster if Clark were then moved up to 15th Army Group command. Per Allied policy, the commander and deputy would come from different countries (so an American com-

mander would have a British deputy or vice versa). Deputy commander
ETO and commander of U.S. forces in the Mediterranean was an ideal
position for which Eisenhower could recommend for Devers. It placed
him in a position that would be out of Eisenhower's way, and Devers was
senior enough to Clark to be his commander. As a deputy, Devers was
acceptable to the British.[59] Marshall approved, if reluctantly. As he told
Eisenhower, "you list your final desires and so far as I can see now they
will be approved."[60]

Devers was coming down the elevator in his London hotel when
he saw someone reading the London *Times*. The headline announced
that Devers and Eisenhower were changing jobs. That is how Jake was
informed of his new assignment.[61] Over Marshall's signature, a supple-
mentary letter to Devers followed the announcement informing Devers that he would probably be assigned as American commander in
the Mediterranean under Wilson.[62] Jake was reassigned as deputy Allied commander, Mediterranean, and commander of U.S. forces there.
The latter was an administrative job, not a combat command. Bradley
recounted, "Marshall was naturally miffed, but he finally agreed, al-
beit reluctantly, to the transfer. Although Devers had graduated from
West Point several years ahead of Ike, they had been professional rivals
for some time."[63] Eisenhower was now one star superior in grade. The
transfer was a comedown for Devers, and thereafter his relations with
Eisenhower were frosty.[64] Later, Eisenhower would be unhappy when
Marshall recommended to the president that Devers, along with Bradley,
be promoted to four-star rank in March 1945.[65]

On 13 December, Devers wrote Marshall what he considered an important assessment of progress within the theater to date. He observed
that "air forces are steadily improved. Services of Supply has accomplished much. [As for ground troops] all seem to need jacking up as to
standards, this being particularly true for those units below division."
Apparently Marshall sensed that Devers felt left out. In his role as chief
of the Armored Force, Devers had become accustomed to weekly meetings with the chief of staff. Now, some of what Devers considered important cables to the chief went unanswered. Marshall knew that Jake
was disappointed when he did not make the list of designated Overlord
commanders. In the margin of his copy of the cable, Marshall wrote,

"General Handy, Please draft reply. Devers has been hurt by the fact that I have not answered his letters. GCM." Then again, once General Marshall picked a man for a job, he didn't pay much attention to him until there was something going wrong, Devers recalled, and he always provided some good help.[66]

Wrote the noted historian Martin Blumenson, who was present during the European campaign, "He [Devers] had the quality of persistence and enjoyed the reputation of having accomplished successfully every task he was assigned. Marshall saw him as a dedicated, dependable officer who eschewed publicity and flamboyance and who projected a quiet air of authority and no nonsense."[67] Marshall thought Devers could command in combat; he had recommended Devers to Eisenhower as a possible commander for the Central Taskforce in the North Africa invasion.[68]

The personnel issue was not about Devers's performance. It was about Marshall and Eisenhower straightening out their relationship vis-à-vis personnel. Despite Marshall's endorsement, Devers didn't fit with Eisenhower's preferences for team members. Perhaps some men could reconcile themselves to the vagaries of team selection and accept a less prestigious but still valuable job. Marshall did. Jake tried to pretend that he did – but his bitterness about what he considered a raw deal in his personal case became obvious to everyone. Undoubtedly, that made matters worse. He could not see it from another point of view. He had come so close to fulfilling his desire for a senior European command; he had a hard time believing that the stars above him caused a miss at so close a range.

While he was highly competitive in the heat of the moment, Jake did understand the immense importance of the bond between commanders and their subordinates. In one of his postwar interviews, Thomas Griess asked Devers what it was like after orders were issued and before the battle had begun. Devers responded, "A commander is lonely. He's made his decisions. He's wondering what's going to happen. He is depending on his commanders."[69]

In his retirement, when questioned by Forrest Pogue, Devers was extremely defensive: "Ike, I think, has held something against me which somebody has printed on his mind. In the fighting days I was always extremely loyal to him, but I always got a little brush-off or thought I did." Devers always held that Eisenhower was a man of integrity. "I think he has got the integrity and the things that count to make this go, but I don't think he thinks that way about me."[70] For his part, Pogue speculated that Eisenhower listened carefully to his English friends and that rough edges left from Devers's tenure as commander, ETO might have been the source of some adverse stories.[71] Then again, it was natural that Devers and Eisenhower were rivals. Marshall had raised both of them from obscurity, Devers first. While McNair and Somervell were slotted into specific support positions and had little competition at their level, both Devers and Eisenhower were commanders, still competing for the highest command jobs.

While Eisenhower, Beetle Smith, Humphrey Gale (a highly regarded British logistician), and a host of senior officers packed for England. Mark Clark, increasingly distanced from Eisenhower, remained in North Africa as commander of the newly fleshed out Fifth Army. Initially, the Fifth Army was held in reserve, against a possible Spanish attempt to intervene in Africa and to prepare for future events in the Mediterranean. Eisenhower still found use in Clark. Increasingly, Eisenhower warmed to the idea of an invasion of southern France as an important adjunct to Overlord. He proposed that Clark, with his extensive knowledge of amphibious operations, lead an American field army in an invasion onto the beaches of the Riviera.

On 15 January 1944, Eisenhower opened the Supreme Headquarters Allied Expeditionary Force (SHAEF). Despite his reservations about John Lee, he amalgamated the ETOUSA and SOSETO into a single operation under Lee, who became second in command for purely U.S. matters. The post that Devers had filled ceased to exist.

SEVEN

Deputy Supreme Commander, MTO

AS JACOB DEVERS REPLACED DWIGHT EISENHOWER FOR command of the United Kingdom in November 1942, Eisenhower replaced Devers in 1943. While Eisenhower returned to Washington to meet with George Marshall and Franklin Roosevelt, and to spend a little time with his wife, Devers left Europe for North Africa. There was no in-person hand-off. In preparation for his trip to Washington, Eisenhower had asked Devers's opinions about ETO organization. Just before Christmas, Jake wrote in his diary that he and Ira Eaker had felt deflated by the reassignment from the big leagues of ETO to what was now the MTO sideshow. The decisions at Casablanca had much reduced the importance of the Mediterranean. Devers's longtime aide Colonel Eugene Harrison thought Devers was shunted aside.[1] Jake was likely miffed. But he stepped off the airplane running onto the shores of the Mediterranean. According to the man who would be his chief plans officer for the next year and a half, "Devers was supposed to be a fireball."[2]

Had Devers known how important the deputy supreme commander, MTO, would be, he might have not felt so slighted. Bedell "Beetle" Smith, Eisenhower's chief of staff, had wielded power far beyond his apparent rank. He was the one officer that Marshall had considered retaining in his Washington headquarters, despite Eisenhower's adamant request for his services, and relented only with the greatest reluctance. With Eisenhower headed back to the United Kingdom to command Overlord, Winston Churchill argued strongly that Smith be retained in the Mediterranean as deputy supreme commander. The prime minister had great plans for the Mediterranean Theater. Senior British officials did not object to Devers's being the top American voice there. Despite his difficult reputation on strategic issues, the British thought well enough of Devers to have him in close proximity to southern France.

Despite British criticism of the starch Devers had shown as the senior American in ETO, Marshall expressed his pleasure for the way Jake had discharged his duties. The chief believed that, beyond knocking Italy out of the war, further advance up the Italian peninsula had virtually no strategic value and would only weaken the effort that needed to be placed into Overlord. He wanted the officer that would represent future American interests to be more than able to hold his own against the best arguments the British, especially Churchill, could muster for wasting more effort in what was now a superseded theater. Marshall down-checked Eaker for failing to maintain this. The backbone that Devers had exhibited suited his mentor just fine.

To staff Overlord, Eisenhower looked for every senior American commander with combat experience he could obtain. As most of them were in the Mediterranean, he leaned heavily on MTO, which Devers had just inherited. Churchill and Alan Brooke agreed with Devers that Eisenhower was stripping the Mediterranean of talent. As part of the transition, Beetle Smith, who had been intimately involved with aspects of MTO, accompanied Jake to Algiers on 4 January. Smith's real motive was to wheedle additional talent from Devers's new theater. Devers and Smith, of course, had been friends, and back in 1941, Smith had dubbed Devers "a man of action" and recommended him to Marshall to take over Armored Force. But positions around the table had changed. Eisenhower had been very cool about Devers, and Smith was renowned for his loyalty to Eisenhower in his new role as SHAEF chief of staff. Eisenhower, and many other officers, viewed Lucian Truscott, 3rd Infantry Division (ID) commander, as the best division commander in the army. Eisenhower wanted this combat-experienced leader to command one of the two American corps that were to land in Normandy. Devers tried to be accommodating to SHAEF's call for personnel. He consented to Patton's transfer but drew the line at Truscott. Jake also saw Truscott as leading a corps in an amphibious landing, but in southern France. Back in 1942, Truscott had wanted to get into Armored Force. Knowing his ability and record, Devers said then he would be delighted to have him.[3]

No neophyte to intra-army wrangling over talent, Devers assigned one of his staff to see who else Smith might be looking to poach. Enraged, Smith strode into Jake's office with his list and demanded to go down it name by name. It wasn't just Truscott. Devers held his ground on names like General Clarence Adcock and General Thomas B. Larkin and a legion of individuals less well known. Frustrated, Smith called Jake a lightweight, as if to validate Eisenhower's opinion of Devers. The reality, however, was that the interests of each theater were being properly advocated by its respective leaders. They were in legitimate conflict. If things were to be reprioritized, it was up to Marshall to do so. The chief of staff was aware of the conflict, and he chose to maintain the status quo. Marshall was, after all, the principal initiator of the concept of a second landing in the south of France to insure against a stalled Overlord invasion, which Eisenhower ultimately experienced.[4]

Marshall disapproved of the way Eisenhower took almost all of the good Mediterranean staff with him to England and his maneuverings to send Devers and Eaker to the Mediterranean. Resistance by Devers to Eisenhower's personnel actions was exactly why Eisenhower labeled Devers "uncooperative." Marshall thought Devers should be retained in London and Beetle Smith in the Mediterranean, to help the new incoming theater commander, General Henry "Jumbo" Wilson (Jumbo stood 6-feet 7-inches tall but had received his sobriquet for his ears, not his height). Marshall thought Devers was a good selection for the principal army group command.[5]

Devers said, "When I took over Africa, it was pretty much of a mess. Ike had done a job. He had won a battle, a big battle, but there was chaos all over the place. The clean-up is always bad."[6] According to Jake, Eisenhower left the GHQ there in disarray.[7] Accurate or not, Devers immediately began to improve its efficiency. In his 4 January diary entry, Devers recorded, "[I] will soon have the African HQ stepped up in tempo and reorganized. This is one of the most difficult jobs I have inherited." Jake was prone to commenting on what he thought at the moment, and apparently the press picked up Devers's off-the-cuff remarks. When this got back to Eisenhower, he was again angry with Devers. He took great offense, and this incident has been repeatedly cited as a source of deep enmity by Eisenhower for Devers. Perhaps the remark kindled an already smoldering personal dislike. Of course, Marshall had said much the same thing about the situation in MTO, but he had the tact to say it in private.

There were piles of supplies sitting in North African depots. World War II logisticians in North Africa ran into the same problem that has defeated generations of their brethren, inventory control. Devers sought to segregate supplies into branch-oriented depots (quartermaster, ordinance repair parts, ordinance ammunition, engineer, etc.) in order to get a handle on inventory, but, like many, he had difficulty in climbing the "iron mountain" the American logisticians had built.[8]

Devers wore two hats: administrative commander of all American army and air force activities in Italy, and North Africa deputy commander of the Mediterranean under Wilson. While he had both a good deal of combat and high-level command experience, he was not considered by the British as one of their best. Harold Alexander, the commander of all Allied ground forces in Italy and Eisenhower's favorite, hated Wilson and ignored his erstwhile superior when he did not agree with him.[9] Alexander, the real power remaining in the Mediterranean after Eisenhower's departure, called Devers a "pleasant fellow" but regarded him as a boy who never grew up, and who had little influence on tactical operations in Italy.[10] Wilson himself rarely interfered with the conduct of the war in Italy. Like Devers, he was new to the position but not to the Mediterranean. He commanded all combat operations in Italy, kept track of numerous British intrigues and schemes in Eastern Europe, and would command the initial landings in the invasion of southern France. He held the reins loosely and preferred that his subordinate commanders use their initiative.

Right from the beginning, Wilson and Devers hit it off, working closely on everything.[11] While Devers was right in line with Washington's position on Mediterranean strategy, which was frequently at odds with London's, the pair developed a warm, deep relationship. Devers said that Wilson was "by far the best British general in the whole damned war," because he had so much experience. "He handled me 100 percent right," recalled Devers. "Wilson always sent me up when there was any trouble. I went up and handled the Poles and the French and in one case I handled the group [French]. I spent quite a bit of time with [Alphonse] Juin (the senior Free French Commander). I liked him." Devers found

Juin easy to work with and a leader who had the love of his men.[12] Furthermore, Devers noted, "As deputy, I was in the frontlines in the critical places."[13] Given the logistical flavor of the U.S. Mediterranean HQ and being deputy to Wilson, Devers might have expected to become deskbound. Instead, he spent most of his time in the field.

In addition to being Wilson's deputy, Devers was also commander of the American organization North Africa Theater of Operations (NATOUSA). Initially, all logistical support for both Operation Anvil and American units in Italy emanated from Services of Supply NATOUSA, which was commanded by the very able General Larkin. He was completely independent from General John Lee's Services of Supply for the European Theater. Devers's energetic tackling of problems in the Mediterranean overcame any reservations Marshall had had about his performance.[14] Devers was Marshall's personal choice to protect American interests in the Mediterranean, which must say something about what the chief thought of Devers's performance in ETO.

Churchill had many designs on Eastern Europe that were motivated more by potential postwar politics than toward defeating the Germans. Devers reasoned that Wilson could not outwardly disagree with his prime minister, but he really did not believe in these Eastern Europe escapades.[15] Devers noted, "When he [Churchill] found that soft underbelly there wasn't a British officer there that [thought] they could ever go through those passes [in the mountainous Balkans]."[16] Devers never realized how well Wilson manipulated him at times. As late as May, Devers signaled Marshall, "General Wilson never has had any thought of sending any troops into the Balkans."[17] In fact, Wilson truly agreed with Churchill that an invasion at the head of the Adriatic and into the Balkans would be profitable.

Lieutenant General Mark Clark was also a Marshall man. On a trip to Panama before Pearl Harbor to witness the army's first amphibious operation, Marshall had commented to Devers that if all the senior people with amphibious experience were to be retired, he would depend on Clark to fill in the gap.[18] He was young and perhaps overly ambitious. He had been Lesley McNair's deputy commander, Army Ground Forces. Administratively subordinated to Devers under the NATOUSA structure, Clark commanded Fifth Army and was the principal U.S. combat commander in Italy. For tactical purposes, Clark reported to Alexander but still had to listen to Devers, even if he did not take battle orders from Devers.

Devers and Clark did not like each other. Devers said, "Clark had brains enough but he was very difficult. . . . Here is Clark and he is fighting the Fifth Army and doing it very badly I thought. . . . They [Fifth Army] were in the doldrums, standing before the [Rapido] river."[19] At the end of his tenure as MTO commander, Devers wrote in his diary, "Noted two cables from Clark to me which show quite well his lack of judgment and tact and indicate definitely that he is not a team player nor has he the instincts of a fighting soldier and a gentleman. . . . I should reprimand him."[20] Generals Guenther and Lyman Lemnitzer on Clark's Fifth Army staff, unlike Clark himself, were most helpful to Devers.[21]

Clark was also candid about his feelings for Devers and once referred to him as "that dope."[22] The two dueled with each other openly. Later, Devers recorded in his diary, "He [Clark] did not know how to command or handle troops. That is why his operations in Italy produced such heavy casualties." Lieutenant General Joseph T. McNarney, Devers's successor as American commander in the Mediterranean, would later tell Devers that Clark felt abused when VI Corps and the French Expeditionary Corps were taken from him to conduct the landings in southern France. Lemnitzer recalled that Clark's staff worried that their leader would be removed every time he and Devers met. Devers recalled, "He is a headache to me and I would relieve him if I could, but I can't. Marshall wouldn't let me relieve him."[23] Devers kept very close tabs on Clark's Fifth Army. Clark was worried lest Devers dictate to him. But that wasn't Devers's style.[24]

They had known each other for some time. Clark had been a student in Devers's mathematics class many years ago at the military academy. He did not do well. When Clark heard Devers was going to become his superior in MTO, he wrote to Eisenhower looking for a job in ETO. Later, Clark felt that Devers's fiddling with the replacement system was his way of diverting all the replacements into divisions headed for southern France at the expense of the Fifth Army. Clark was uncomfortable about what Devers, as Clark's immediate American superior, was passing back to Washington. Clark thought Devers might not be communicating the

Fifth Army's predicament in the most sympathetic manner. In fact he wrote, "I am convinced of that." He also believed that Devers diverted supplies for the Anvil buildup at the expense of the Fifth Army. Devers disagreed, stating, "I am absolutely confident that they got all the troops they needed in Italy to go all the way if they had just pushed a little harder when they got the jump."[25] After the war, Devers, as chief of army field forces and again Clark's superior, wrote in Clark's performance rating, "A cold, distinguished, conceited, selfish, clever, intellectual, resourceful officer who secures excellent results quickly. Very ambitious. Superior performance."[26]

The War Department was very concerned about manpower availability and the number of men that old theaters wanted to hang onto. On 26 January 1944, Marshall wrote to Devers, "Our shortage of service troops has become critical. . . . Use native resources and Italian war prisoners. Get ready to close down North Africa Depots when south of France is opened." Devers worked hard to close old bases and clean out organizations that were no longer heavily tasked. As he told Marshall, "We are trying in every way to roll up our tail as fast as possible."[27] Italian service volunteers released 25,000 U.S. service troops.[28] Ever since the first landing on the Italian boot at Salerno, Eisenhower, Alexander, and Clark had begun to think in terms of another invasion farther up the west coast to outflank stubborn German defenders dug into the mountainous terrain along the Winter (Gothic) Line. Clark selected Anzio, a sleepy coastal resort 35 miles south of Rome because of its proximity to choke points along the principal supply roads (Routes 6 and 7) in the Alban Hills from Rome to the Winter Line near Monte Cassino. A landing had two objectives: cutting off the supplies to Germans farther down the boot, causing them to withdraw, and opening an expedited route to Rome (see map 7.1). Anzio had been a controversial and much debated issue. Eisenhower and Alexander had initiated the concept in the fall of 1943. Lack of landing ship, tanks (LSTs), and arguments over prioritizing these ships among Overlord, the Italian campaign, and the Pacific limited the size of Shingle, the proposed Anzio landing, to one or two divisions with limited logistical support.

Eisenhower was concerned that an effort this size had little chance of success but also felt that, since he had been transferred to command

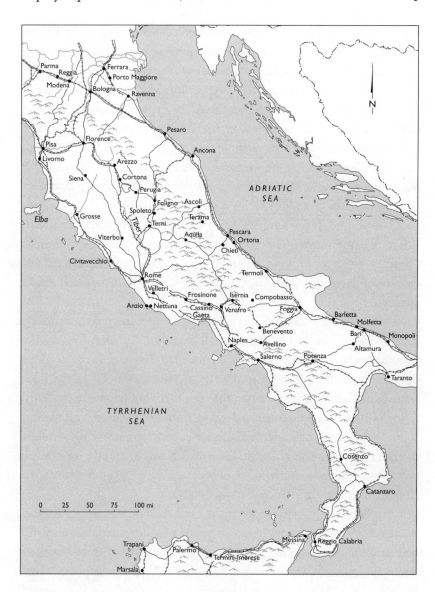

7.1. Central Italy

Overlord, he should not actively insert himself into the ongoing debate. Instead, as the new ETO supreme commander, he needed to concentrate on bringing forth the invasion of southern France. Eisenhower was worried about the inadequate port infrastructure along the French Channel coast. This almost mandated that the Allies capture Antwerp (or, less likely, Rotterdam) at an early juncture. Seizing Marseilles, the largest French seaport, would be a valuable insurance policy against deadlock along the Channel coast. At one time, Eisenhower had considered Clark for the top American Mediterranean job. But he thought it better to keep Clark with his beloved Fifth Army until Rome was captured. Then Clark could be shifted to the Seventh Army to lead the invasion of southern France where his amphibious skills would be well employed.[29] Before Eisenhower left for London, he had designated Major General John Lucas, commander, VI Corps, as the commander of the projected Anzio landing.

Under the direction of Colonel Reuben E. Jenkins, who became G3 (operations officer) to Devers, Colonel Theodore Conway drew up the plan for Anzio.[30] From the beach, an armored division was to head for Valmontone, while an infantry division headed east north of the Pontrane Mountains and then down into the Liri Valley to meet the Fifth Army. None of the American leadership, from Lucas on down, however, thought that the Anzio plan was strong enough to cause the Germans to withdraw from their Gothic Line, which was currently frustrating any Allied attempt to move north of Monte Carlo or to open the road to Rome. For a time, the Anzio plan was shelved.

The British were still leery of the cross-Channel invasion at Normandy. They were in a position to dominate Mediterranean strategy and had imperial objectives in the eastern end of that sea not shared by their American allies. With Eisenhower gone and Wilson as supreme commander of the Mediterranean, there was little to stop Churchill. Harold Alexander advocated a strong "left hook" against the Italian peninsula, that is, an invasion at Anzio. In this he was heavily supported by Alan Brooke.[31] Winston Churchill, always a champion of British objectives in the Eastern Mediterranean, claimed the landing at Anzio "would decide the Battle of Rome." Britain's prestige in the postwar period hinged far more on their primacy in Italy and Eastern Europe than in playing second fiddle to the liberation of France.[32] Wilson was hardly in a position to counter both his prime minister and a general of Alexander's stature.

No one thought a small-sized Anzio landing was a good idea except the British prime minister. He tugged at General Alexander to reinstate the landing. Now designated "Shingle," landing at Anzio was reproposed as a two-division landing. In the initial revised plan, troops would not land in Anzio until the Fifth Army had broken through the main German defense line that currently prevented its advance.

This would free the U.S. 1st Armored Division to roar up the Liri Valley to Anzio – and ultimately to Rome. The initial projection anticipated a link up with the landing force in about a week. Clark continued to believe the Germans would withdraw up the Liri Valley when the Anzio landing threatened their supply line to Rome. If the invasion force landed and held on, the Fifth Army breakthrough via Anzio would lead to a major success. Major General Lucian Truscott, who would command 3ID in the landing, was far more pessimistic. He wrote, "A worse plan would be difficult to conceive."[33] Clark's Fifth Army was deadlocked along the Rapido River, which anchored the German Winter Line near Monte Cassino. Without a breakthrough across the Rapido, the Anzio landing made little sense. And there was nothing creative in the works to break the deadlock. Without a link up with the main Allied force, the beachhead would languish. Truscott recalled, "No one below Army level believed that the landing of two divisions at Anzio would cause a German withdrawal on the southern front, or that there was more than a remote chance that the remainder of Fifth Army would be able to cross the Rapido River and fight its way [north to the Anzio beachhead] within a month."[34] This remarkable disconnect demonstrated that senior leadership, save one, was out of touch. Marshall recalled that Eisenhower was aware of Anzio planning before he left the Mediterranean and still was not in favor of the operation (see map 7.2).[35]

Devers arrived in-theater just in time for a 7 January conference at Marrakech to decide final details of the much-faulted plan for the upcoming landing at Anzio. Eisenhower (who did not attend) had warned the prime minister about the pitfalls of landing a small force behind German lines without the means to constantly resupply the beachhead from the sea.[36] That was not what Churchill wanted to hear. British Chief of

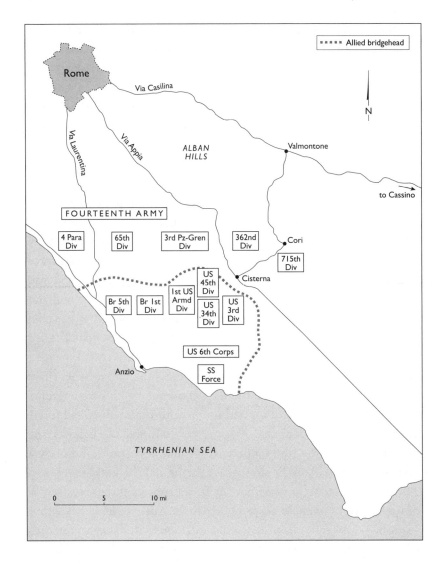

7.2. Anzio

the Imperial Staff Sir Alan Brooke observed that Clark's "penny packet attacks up from Naples on to the Winter Line were achieving little," and that nothing would happen "unless we make greater use of our amphibious power."[37] Both Clark and Lucas believed that the operation was trying to do too much with too little.[38] But Clark wasn't present at Marrakech as he was immersed in problems along the Rapido. Neither Jumbo Wilson nor Harold Alexander wanted to tangle with an increasingly sarcastic Churchill, especially after he had grumbled that he couldn't get any commanders who would fight. Wilson was regarded as "putty in Churchill's hands."[39] In the British camp, only Brooke had the stature to stand up to Churchill. Knowing that Churchill was doing nothing but goading people into his way of thinking, Wilson, who was feeling his age, retired for the evening. As David Fraser, Brooke's biographer observed, Churchill had a "general dislike for those aspects of reality which impeded his grand design for victory."[40]

This left Devers and Alexander to fend for themselves. Despite many subsequent questions about the Anzio expedition, Devers noted that all participants favored the landing. The official historian, Martin Blumenson, recorded that approval came "despite the apparent impracticality of the Anzio operation."[41] Devers could not see why such a large meeting was convened to make a simple tactical decision. He had not grasped the difficult problems that predictably led to deadlock and almost resulted in failure at Anzio for the Allies. Not fully understanding the linkup problem but understanding the landing plan, Devers agreed to it as well.[42] He should have done more homework before opining on such a momentous decision. He had the resources of Jenkins and a lot of staff with which to educate himself. There again Devers showed his tendency to shoot from the hip. Later, Churchill would relate to Roosevelt that the 7 January review of the Anzio landing received unanimous support.

Brigadier Kenneth Strong, Eisenhower's intelligence chief and a British officer, was the lone dissenter. As he recounted in his memoirs, "The Landing Force could not achieve success in face of the opposition that could be expected. I was strongly supported by members of General Clark's staff, but we could make little impression on the others there."[43] Before the meeting in Marrakech, Devers noted in his diary on 4 January that Clark looked good but that Lucas, commander of VI Corps, which would make the landings, looked old. In his own diary, Lucas wrote, "The whole affair has a strong odor of Gallipoli and apparently the same amateur was still sitting on the coaches bench."[44] To improve coordination with the active theater, Devers convinced Wilson to move his headquarters from Algiers to Naples.

The largest problem was the plan to break through the Winter Line and ram northward. No one ever accused Clark of being a brilliant tactician. But Major General Geoffrey Keyes, II Corps commander, was. Patton said that Keyes "had the best tactical mind of any officer I know."[45] The II Corps would be the outfit that would have to cross the Rapido. Keyes observed that crossing that river would have to be done in full view of the commanding heights on the far side, including the Abbey on Monte Cassino. German guns could fire directly on any potential bridging sight, making construction efforts almost impossible. Similarly high ground that the Germans controlled would make an attack up the Liri Valley nothing more than an advance into a killing zone. The strongest division in Italy, the 15th Panzer Grenadiers, had sited hordes of machine guns behind carefully constructed defensive positions reinforced with mines and barbed wire. Nevertheless, Clark ordered a frontal attack into German strength. The 361D commander, Major General Fred Walker, penned into his diary, "We have done everything that we can, but I do not now see how we can succeed."[46] It was Alexander's job to correct Clark, but Devers did not comment.

Churchill, always the champion of attacking the Axis in its "vulnerable underbelly," stated that Rome must be taken "at almost any cost."[47] Planners knew that at least 14 LSTs would be required to bring the daily 1,500 tons of required supplies ashore given Anzio's modest port facilities. But the landing ships were scheduled to be released right after the landing so that they could be refurbished for the Normandy invasion. Sensing the planners' unease, Devers assured them that the LSTs would remain available and that they would not be cut off. That part Devers grasped and took on directly despite his short tenure. Still, while he took care of the detail, he did not see the huge flaw in the big picture.

Eisenhower felt it inappropriate to further influence the most important decision now facing MTO. He had warned Churchill, who wanted no warning. With Churchill under a full head of steam to attack at Anzio and with most British generals approving of the concept, if not the size of the force about to be deployed, only Devers could throw down a red flag. Perhaps this was too much to ask of a deputy commander who had barely enough time in theater to unpack his footlocker. Also, countering

Churchill when all British officers save one agreed with him was a daunt-
ing endeavor. A master of the operational art might have taken it on. But
demanding that an officer with only two weeks on the job call a halt to
such an important operation? Clark, Lucas, and Devers's own assistant
G3, Colonel Dan Noce, all concluded the invasion was too high risk. But,
according to Devers's own statement, it was "a simple tactical decision."

But on the 15th, three days after the landing, Eisenhower insultingly
called Devers ".22 caliber." Six days after the landing, when the operation
was in deep trouble, Beetle Smith echoed Eisenhower's observation, saying Devers was narrow indeed and a "lightweight."[48] Given Eisenhower's
derisive comment on Devers's handling of the Anzio invasion and his
strong misgivings about that operation, is it reasonable to conclude they
are linked? If he linked them, was he being reasonable? After all Eisenhower had been deeply involved in the basic Anzio decision from inception and had not dissuaded Churchill and the British. Devers came in
at the last minute. On the other hand, Devers's initial involvement with
Anzio was not his most shining hour. Jake failed to grasp the severity of
the tactical problems that commanders he respected, such as Truscott,
well understood and were deeply disturbed about. Regardless of the link-
age, Eisenhower's opinion of Jake in the winter of 1944 is unmistakable.
It also emphasized the differences in depth of understanding and the
method of approaching a problem between the two generals.

Ultra intelligence – the Allied decryption of German signals – reported the landing at Anzio would meet with little initial resistance.
Because Allied airpower had shredded German aerial reconnaissance
capability, German intelligence noticed nothing unusual in the very busy
port at Naples. A German intelligence summary stated, "There is not the
slightest sign that a new landing will be undertaken in the immediate
future."[49] Based on this, German Air Marshal Albert Kesselring sent his
two best mobile divisions south to oppose Clark's attack on the Gustav
Line. That attack, which had gotten off to a good start on 12 January, was
now bogged down. Attempting to cross the Rapido River, 361 D met with
disaster.

The Anzio invasion achieved complete tactical surprise. As Allied
intelligence predicted, VI Corps came ashore on 22 January against al-

most no opposition. Some of the defenders, exhausted from fighting down south and moved to a quiet rest area, were captured while sleeping in their beds. Others were rounded up as they attempted to lasso Italian cows for dinner. The towns of Anzio and Nettuno were secured by mid-morning. That was the time an aggressive commander would have moved into the Alban Hills. Against a prepared position, an attacker needs between three and six times the enemy's combat power at the point of attack in order to prevail. A four-division Allied force had a shot at holding a 12-by-18-mile piece of prepared ground, especially with the huge amount of artillery and airpower that Lucas had available. But he had virtually no chance of taking it once German reinforcements had organized a defense. The conservative option, which eschews opportunity, is frequently *not* the least risky alternative.

While it achieved tactical surprise, the landing did not achieve strategic surprise. Kesselring believed that the Allies could not achieve much without additional landings up the boot, as Alexander was not about to give up on Italy.[50] To thwart that threat, the Germans insured that mobile reserves were held near the coast to quickly seal off the expected Allied invasion, even though its location had not been identified. While Lucas hesitated, Kesselring reacted. Woken at 0300 with news of the surprise landing at Anzio as well as Allied naval bombardment of Rome's port of Civitavecchia to the north, Kesselring immediately recognized the real threat was to the choke points in the Alban Hills. Immediately, alarm orders went out for units from every direction to close on the Alban Hills and contain the beachhead. By evening, lead German elements were digging into the hills. Kesselring was an outstanding German field commander. Anzio may have been his finest hour.

At the beginning of the invasion, Devers flew into the beachhead. He later recalled,

> Lucas was in his dugout, and he never believed in the [landing]. I go up to Lucian Truscott and I say, "Lucian, why have you stopped here?"
>
> Truscott responded, "I wanted to go on but they wouldn't let me go. I could go all the way up to the foot of the mountains [the Alban Hills] and I would be through this thing, but this is where we drew the line and here is where they want me to stop."
>
> Devers asked, "Who issued those orders?"
>
> "They came from Clark – Fifth Army."[51]

Regarding the visit from Devers, Lucas wrote in his diary, "Devers came by to see me. He seemed to understand things and to appreciate my situation."[52]

Clark had very mixed motivations. While he badly wanted to break free of Kesselring's difficult defensive line south along the Rapido River, he felt the small size of VI Corps made for a risky operation at Anzio. Just before the landing, he advised the already timid Lucas, "Don't stick your neck out the way I did at Salerno."[53] Lucas had no thought of moving either into the Alban Hills or north to Rome during the first two days. In his diary, he wrote, "I must keep my feet on the ground and do nothing foolish.... I will not be stampeded.... Had I been able to rush the high ground around Albano ... nothing would have been accomplished ... because the troops sent, being completely beyond supporting distance, would have been completely destroyed."[54] He had no thought of serious offensive action over the next ten days when the buildup would be completed. By that time, Allied chances of taking the Alban Hills had fallen to zero. A horrible deadlock ensued, with German observers able to direct heavy artillery fire over every square inch of the shallow beachhead. A British guardsman noted in his diary, "25 Jan. Carroceto is in our hand. With how much less cost could it have been captured two days before!"[55]

On 28 January, when Clark inspected the Anzio beachhead, the situation appeared even better. From Ultra, Clark knew that German intelligence forecast no Allied invasion threat and that Kesselring had ordered his last two mobile divisions in reserve to head south to oppose the pending Allied attack. This was a priceless opportunity for an aggressive commander. Lucas and his VI Corps landed Friday morning against almost no opposition. While Kesselring scrambled to bring everything he could find from southern France and Yugoslavia as well as northern Italy, little showed up near Anzio on Saturday. VI Corps had established a perimeter 15 miles wide but only 3 deep, all of it subject to German observation and artillery fire. VI Corps would receive a British division and most of the U.S. 1st Armored in short order. Pushing the invasion divisions into the Alban Hills and readily defensible terrain would cut the main supply roads to German forces along the Rapido and remove the artillery threat from the Allied innermost beachhead logistic sites. A 15-by-15-mile beachhead was too much for a two-division force to defend against strong counterattacks. But a four-division force, on defendable ground, covered by naval gunfire and Allied air power, had a chance. Of course, there was risk, but not as much as clinging to a narrow, marshy, difficult-to-defend coastal strip while under constant German observation.

But Lucas continued to hesitate to advance into good defensive positions in the Alban Hills. He followed his orders literally. Prior to the operation, Clark had cautioned Lucas to be careful. Now, Clark's urgings to be bold had little effect. In a postwar interview, Reuben Jenkins stated that, when Lucas realized he had completely surprised the Germans and encountered the flimsiest of defenses, he should have disregarded his orders and "tear out of there." He thought Lucas should have been relieved from duty when he didn't tear up his orders as soon as the force landed.[56] In his diary, Lucas recorded that his orders and the explanation given him by the Fifth Army operations officer gave him the latitude to do so if he had the opportunity.[57] Alexander met Lucas in the beachhead on D-Day and D-Day plus 3, but did not use either opportunity to order Lucas to take the Alban Hills.

Critiquing the operation for the U.S. Army right after the war, German General Eduard Hauser observed, "Why didn't [General Lucas], in a daring quick dash to the Alban Hills, push through to Valmontone and cut the supply road to the south flank of the Tenth Army?" He answered his own question: "He felt himself not strong enough and thereby missed his great chance."[58] The great naval historian, Samuel Elliot Morison, concluded flatly, "There is no doubt that the 3rd Infantry Division could have rolled into Valmontone on the second or third day.[59] Churchill was more caustic: "I had hoped we were hurling a wildcat onto the shore, but all we got was a stranded whale."[60] While Lucas hesitated, Kesselring accelerated his initial response. He rushed panzer reinforcements to the invasion area and secured the high ground for the Germans. Intense artillery fire rained down on the hapless Allied invaders, stalling the landing effort after eking out only a shallow beachhead. This led to four months of deadlock. Neither side could dislodge the other.

On 9 February, Marshall cabled Devers, "We feel some concern about the situation in Italy," and instructed Devers to see if Wilson was happy with the senior American commanders. Devers responded immediately, "General Wilson is always frank and open to me." He was favorably impressed with Eisenhower, but "Lucas was slow at first although no one needed to be relieved."[61] On the 16th, Devers went ashore at Anzio. Despite the shelling, he found the supply situation sound. The Allies had a tremendous amount of firepower available – 350 tanks and 498 guns. There was no spark, however, among either the leadership or the men. Devers spent some time talking with all of the division commanders. He recalled, "Lucas hadn't been out of his dugout for 48 hours. He didn't know what the British divisions were doing. Later I found out he didn't believe in it [the Anzio landing]. If a man doesn't believe, he shouldn't be placed in command."[62] Meanwhile, Alexander went to Eisenhower about Lucas. Eisenhower took Alexander's action to be more evidence of Devers's incompetence. The real fault was Clark's and his inability to tell Alexander and Churchill that Shingle lacked the resources to succeed.[63]

While Lucas strongly objected to aggressive advance, Devers felt he should have made for the Alban Hills earlier when few Germans were present. Devers later recalled that the British commanders in the beachhead "were scared to death," and that Lucas wasn't doing a very good job.[64] Alexander finally concluded that Lucas had to be relieved.

Later, Devers had a long conversation with Clark, who blew off some steam about dealing with the British, saying he was the lone American holding up the flag in a sea of British procedures and foibles. At this point, Devers outlined his plans for Anvil, the invasion of southern France. To the surprise of Clark, Devers advised him not to get involved in the invasion of southern France and remain in command of his beloved Fifth Army. It did not dawn on Clark that Devers didn't want him. Instead, Clark thought everyone was ganging up to take the Fifth Army away from him. When there is flux, humans often react by assuming that which they perceive to be the worst that can happen to them. But the business at hand was the timid command of General Lucas and the resulting deadlock. Both generals agreed that Lucas should be returned to the states in a fashion that would not hurt him professionally. Marshall followed up with Devers on the 19 February, stating that Brooke was voicing dissatisfaction with the Anzio landing. Devers responded, "Lucas is tired and appears very old but he has been fighting hard." It was becoming apparent to Devers that Lucas had to be replaced, and he so advised Clark.[65] On the 22nd, Clark returned to Anzio and relieved Lucas of VI Corps command but without prejudice. He explained to Lucas that "he could no longer resist the pressure from Alexander and Devers" to do so. Before Anzio, Eisenhower had considered Lucas to succeed Clark as Fifth Army commander, if Clark slid over to command the Seventh Army in the upcoming invasion of southern France. Estimations of Lucas had fallen a long way in a short time.[66]

If the Anzio landing was in great trouble, the attack across the 50-foot-wide but deep and fast flowing Rapido River was a disaster. The British 46th Division on the south flank accomplished little. The two assaulting regiments of 361D that attacked the most heavily defended segment of the Rapido defense were wiped out. The Germans pounded them to pieces, and then captured what was left. Two thousand dogfaces either lay dead or were huddled in German cages. Their brief bridgehead was completely erased. Not a free American soldier remained on the Rapido's far bank. Bungling of this operation would be the subject of a later inquiry. An attempt to gain some room around Anzio resulted in an attempt to infiltrate several Ranger battalions into the crossroads town of Cisterna. Clark's British deputy commander, General Sir Charles Richardson, stated, "Anzio was a complete nonsense from its inception."[67] With all the reinforcements, Kesselring rushed to Anzio. German attacks almost split the beachhead in two. But the Germans were bled white in the process. The operation did not achieve its objective.

Another new arrival, the French Expeditionary Corps under the command of General Alphonse Juin, attacked the Winter Line north of Monte Cassino. Their skillful and well-fought attack dented the line badly but did not break it. Many North Africans fighting under the tricolor became casualties. Several additional Allied attempts to force the Rapido River ended in failure. The abbey atop Monte Cassino continued to look down on the Allies, but its bombing was very controversial. If Germans had not used the abbey for military purposes, bombing it would have been proscribed. But many, including Indians and New Zealanders who had fought bitterly to gain the mount, were sure German observers in the abbey directed the German artillery that had frustrated their attacks. They wanted the ancient religious monument obliterated. On 13 February, Ira Eaker, commander of Allied Mediterranean Air

Forces, and Devers took off in a Piper Cub and overflew Cassino. To avoid revealing their antiaircraft positions in exchange for a cheap target, the Germans had a pattern of not firing on light aircraft. The two American generals believed they saw a military radio antenna and Germans in the abbey. Allied Air Forces were cleared to bomb it. It appears, however, that the Germans had placed their observers farther down the mountain away from the abbey and had not violated its sanctity. Again Devers's involvement in an episode that did not require the services of a lieutenant general – although he did not give the order – did not bring him accolades. Later, intelligence interrogators concluded that the Germans had studiously avoided entering the abbey until after the Allies bombed it.

In his diary, Devers wrote,

> Battle of Cassino: Medium bombers good. Heavies needed tighter formations. It was a shock to me that our Allied Infantry was unable to advance when continuously supported by dive bombers and artillery fire. Emphasize the principle that there must be a determined attack. Need for experienced leadership. Culmination of a lot of little things that make a tough battle successful. Great care needed in selection of commanders. Troops must be inspired. Infantry might advance about 3 miles a day on road to Rome.[68]

On 16 March, Devers joined Alexander, Clark, Bernard Freyberg, and his old friend Eaker to watch the incredible air bombardment at Cassino. For a radius of 5 miles around the town at the base of the hill, the ground shook. Between bomber waves, artillery pounded away. Over 200,000 Allied shells were added to the 1,000 tons of bombs that struck targets in and around Cassino. Subsequent assaults resulted in little gain. After the war, Devers stated flatly, "Monte Cassino was a disaster."[69] After the failure around Cassino and the disappointment at Anzio, the Italian campaign devolved into a series of local tactical battles. Devers felt that "Clark is commanding the Fifth Army and doing it very badly." Devers tried to get the Fifth Army moving, but "they were in the doldrums."[70] Right after the Cassino engagement, General Marshall lost any expectation that much more would be accomplished in Italy. On the 16th, he cabled Eisenhower, there is "no probability of a decisive change in Italy." On the 18th, he cabled Devers "that 6–8 German divisions may contain our forces in Italy," and the rest of the German forces would be sent to France when Overlord began.[71]

Devers was learning from his exposure to the campaign in Italy. As later analysts also noted, bombing must immediately be followed up with ground troops. Airpower and land power are like the two blades of a pair of scissors. Separately, they don't cut. Together they do quite a job. Divisional artillery was not sufficient for combat in the hills. Their fires had to be heavily reinforced by large amounts of corps and army artillery. Active patrolling must be maintained. "Indian style" probes emphasizing stealth and careful observation worked best. Devers noted in his diary that combat troops should never be left in the line more than twenty-one days. After that, they lose their edge, become sullen and careless, and ultimately unable to press home an attack or mount a stout defense. Throughout his career, Devers remained very interested in the effects of combat on humans and an organization's ability to withstand the unbelievable pressures placed upon its members.

He thought American soldiers fought well but that there were some deficiencies in the regimental and battalion commanders. Devers remained especially critical of the American replacement system. Replacements were shunted around with no continuity of organization or leadership. They did not arrive in coherent units and were immediately shunted into "repple dapples" (replacement depots) where no one looked out for their needs or preparation to enter combat. Often they arrived at their new units not knowing what they were doing or how they fit in. As a result, Devers found replacements were below standard. "Only 1/3 make the grade. They are too soft and many immediately become sick."[72]

Marshall did his best to respond to the needs Devers identified. The chief sent his Mediterranean commander a list of twenty-three officers that might be replacement battalion and regimental commanders. Devers responded, "I am absolutely confident that they got all the troops they needed in Italy to go all the way if they had just pushed a little harder when they got the jump." A month later, Devers cabled Marshall, "Progress in Italy is slow and disappointing." After the war, Devers stated, "We wasted a whole lot of time in Italy. I think we should have thrown more behind the southern France invasion." Eisenhower agreed. He confided to Beetle Smith, "Where in Hell do they think they are going in Italy?"[73] One thing Devers had learned about his adversary: "That is the great thing about the German Army. It could react fast."[74]

Since the time both had come to Marshall's attention, Devers and Eisenhower had become rivals. At the time he was appointed chief of Armored Force, perhaps Devers had moved ahead. By the time Roosevelt designated Eisenhower as supreme commander in Europe and then commander of the North African operations, Marshall appears to have rank-ordered his two primary lieutenants. Both could make enormous contributions when placed into their respective slots. It was very clear that Marshall still found great value in Devers's service. On 6 June, Marshall wrote to Secretary Henry Stimson, "The personal leadership of Devers is a large factor in the fine showing American units have made." "Eaker thinks Devers is instrumental in getting air going . . . [Devers] enthused everyone with the will to fight and the spirit that is required to win." On 20 June, Marshall wrote to Devers, "Your numerous problems and effective manner in which you are solving them are an inspiration."

EIGHT

The French and a Southern Front

AMERICAN MILITARY HISTORIANS OFTEN DISMISS FRENCH actions and participation during the campaign in Western Europe. They praise the élan shown by the men of the French 2nd Armored Division (Deuxième Division Blindée) and its very capable leader, General Jacques-Philippe Leclerc, but echo the frustration of American commanders that Leclerc ignored American orders and struck out for Paris on his own. De Gaulle's intransigence on a range of issues frustrated many Americans from Roosevelt on down. For the Americans, the war's objective was straightforward: crush the Wehrmacht and eliminate Nazism as rapidly as possible, with minimum loss of friendly and civilian life. For the most part, the British agreed. Churchill, however, always had his eye on the shape of the postwar world and the map that reflected it. For the French, the issues were far more complicated. Their rapid collapse before the Nazi assault in 1940 and subsequent partial complicity in Nazi crimes from 1940–1944 left a deep stain on the fabric of an ancient culture. As First French Army Commander General Jean de Lattre de Tassigny often said, "French honor can be redeemed only by the spilling of French blood. . . . French command could not leave out the effect of our national pride."[1] The French had more complex war aims than simply destroying Nazism by the most efficacious means available.

The national collapse in 1940 left the French divided into many disjointed fragments with no credible, overarching national government. Who constituted the true government of France was up for grabs from a host of contenders, none of which had demonstrated the backing of French voters by the winter of 1943–1944. Several competing factions vied for the post. The Vichy French government, with the approval of their German masters, claimed to be the legitimate rulers of France. Free French that had fled the country and clandestine indigenous resisters, including many communists within the Maquis or FFI (Forces Françaises de l'Intérieur), claimed legitimacy. Charles de Gaulle's government in exile in London was a third. Jacob Devers quipped, "The French problem will always be with us for they do not seem to be on the level with themselves."[2] While becoming involved in Franco-American affairs, Devers stayed well clear of French infighting with the communists. Many French also questioned those who initially served the Philippe Pétain government in French Africa, which included officers who subsequently joined the First French Army. In addition, there were traditional class distinctions that characterized prewar Europe. Like many European countries, a large communist element, which predated the war, set itself against conservatives, royalists, and aristocrats. These complications made intrigue almost inevitable and colored many French actions. Now the French had to get by with little influence on how the Nazis were to be ejected from France. That was up to the British and the Americans. All of these issues generated legitimate French national goals. While nations join alliances, they rightly retain some national objectives that are not necessarily congruent with the alliance's goal. Lack of recognition of the legitimate conflict among friends created a great deal of frustration among Americans who saw the Allied task as solely Nazi defeat.

Charles de Gaulle, leader of the French Committee for National Liberation, sparred with General Henri Giraud, commander of the French Army that had been recreated in North Africa in 1943, to seize the laurels from among those defying Vichy. Subsequent to the assassination of Admiral François Darlan on Christmas Eve 1942, Giraud assumed supreme civil as well as military authority in French North Africa. After secret negotiations with the general, the Americans thought Giraud was the most likely leader to assemble useful forces to retake France. Both he and de Gaulle were initially copresidents of the French Committee, but de Gaulle had ascended to the sole presidency by October 1943. Roosevelt resisted de Gaulle's attempt to push Giraud aside. The president did not want the Anglo Allies to be kingmaker. Officially, he maintained that was for the French people to decide. Those "in the know," however, realized that Roosevelt perceived de Gaulle to be a very dangerous man, a "general on a white horse," who wanted to seize power. Secretly, Roosevelt did what he could to retain power in the hands of Giraud. Churchill was less anti–de Gaulle but would defer to Roosevelt on the issue. While the British were inclined to work with the London-based French Committee for National Liberation, the president convinced Churchill to steer a course in step with American policy. Neither leader wanted a large communist influence, which was active among the Maquis, to seize power. By the time Devers landed in France in August 1944, the French themselves had demonstrated that de Gaulle was their de factor leader.

As de Gaulle gained ascendancy, he wasn't on the best terms with the Anglophone leaders that, from his viewpoint, had impeded his rise. In his memoirs, the French leader mused, "We were obliged to depend on the goodwill of the United States. Their goodwill was scanty."[3] De Gaulle did not want to see Teutonic domination of Europe replaced by an Anglo-Saxon one. With that much distrust about the Americans, de Lattre, who in reality reported more to de Gaulle via national channels than through Devers to the combined chiefs who held him at arm's length, was in an almost impossible situation. The Anglo Allies dealt with de Gaulle's coalescing government in exile only on a military-to-military basis. As the official American history stated, "The U.S. Army staff, oriented to fighting an efficient and military war, could not be expected to be highly enthusiastic over the ambitious plans for raising and equipping new French divisions."[4] Eisenhower had assigned to the Sixth Army the task of bringing the French Army to combat readiness. But there wasn't enough equipment available for the far-better-trained U.S. Army. One can see the extremely difficult situation placed at Devers's feet for him to manage.

While at the top level, the powers that be wrestled with the fate of France, Devers dealt principally at the level of generating effective combat power from organized French Army units. In addition to the French First Army, a conventional force organized under de Lattre, Devers would also command the French Army of the Alps, which guarded the Franco-Italian border, and the French Army of the Atlantic based in southwestern France along the Bay of Biscay. This last force was more concerned with keeping order among competing French factions than in corralling the few remaining Germans in their area. The French First Army was the primary French instrument that Devers maneuvered against the Germans.

George Marshall is widely known for never showing favoritism and sticking to the point at hand. But he was not insensitive to the national political implications of military decisions. In November 1943, he pointed out that the matter of French rearmament "was a matter of national policy that should be decided by the President on the basis of its postwar implications."[5] Loyalties among various French groups were exceedingly complex. Both British and American counterintelligence had limited confidence in French security, so little highly sensitive information was shared. This further complicated the relationship and engendered its own mistrust among the Allies. Distain among many senior American officers for the French and their manifest and multilayered problems was thinly camouflaged. In a classified cable to Marshall, Eisenhower commented, "The French continue to be difficult. I must say that next to the weather I think they have caused me more trouble in this war than any other factor."[6] He had earlier noted, "French divisions are always a questionable asset."[7] Devers felt that Eisenhower did not really believe in them. Devers later noted, "He didn't think the French were doing the best they could. Eisenhower doesn't trust the French for anything."[8] Placing day-to-day supervision of the organized French Army at the army group level, with Devers as the interface instead of the Allied supreme commander, added further distance between the French Army and Eisenhower, thereby reducing his daily list of headaches.

On the other hand, Devers, who came into the war with memories of competent French officers from 1919, was empathetic with the French and their complex tangle of problems. He recalled, "I want to help the French because I believe in them. I want my whole staff to believe in them, and I don't want any ifs, and, or buts on it. We have got to depend on them. They have a big part of this to do and they can do it."[9] General Reuben Jenkins, who served as chief American planner in the Mediterranean under Devers, then as G3 (operations officer) for the 6th Army Group, remarked, "The French did a magnificent job in Italy so Devers had few preconceived notions."[10] Their German opponent, Field Marshal Albrecht Kesselring, who would also be Devers's last opponent in southern Germany, described the French Corps in Italy as "excellent."[11]

By April, Giraud had retired. The French under de Gaulle were disappointed to find that most organized French divisions were to be assigned to the invasion of southern France. The French government wanted to retain the ability to deploy them as the French saw fit, including using them to maintain domestic order. American planners envisioned an American army group consisting of the U.S. Seventh Army and a French Army containing eight of the ten French divisions, which were to be equipped by the United States. They would land in southern France, capture the huge port of Marseilles, advance up the Rhône Valley, and finally subdue southern Germany. Marseilles was the big magnet. The Normandy landings and subsequent advance up the Channel coast would not liberate enough port capacity to handle the huge supply tonnages consumed by the Allied armies. By capturing Marseilles and then linking into the logistics system by French rail, the tonnage problem would finally be solved. This is the primary reason why Eisenhower was so adamant about landing in southern France. On the other hand, French leadership felt that the assault on the Côte d'Azur was a sideshow. French arms would be denied their rightful place leading the force that would deal the death blow to the Wehrmacht, which would likely occur in the Ruhr Valley and the north German plain. Ultimately, that was also Eisenhower's plan. Southern France was an important support, but the main Allied effort would be north of the Ardennes.

When he learned that French divisions would outnumber American ones in the proposed army group, de Gaulle pressed for a French general to be appointed overall ground commander for the upcoming invasion of southern France. But with no independent source of supply, the French had little bargaining power. The initial landings as well as the French Expeditionary Corps in Italy were subordinate to General Henry Wilson's overall Mediterranean command. Wilson pointed out that the French had neither experience in nor equipment for amphibious warfare. The upcoming landings in southern France had to be under American command. The thought of untrained French troops attempting to deal with all the details, problems, and confusion of an assault landing while struggling to deal with support staff who spoke only a foreign language was a reality no one wanted. Reluctantly, de Gaulle agreed. So began the slow path to compromise, that is, accepting the American position. The French settled for an independent army, the minimum John Pershing accepted in World War I. Wilson agreed. During the Anvil invasion (the codename for the invasion of southern France, subsequently labeled "Dragoon" when the Anvil tag was compromised by a security breach), however, the French demanded that all French units be consolidated under a single headquarters. Wilson formulated the U.S. Seventh Army with one American and two French corps; the French agreed, but called their force under the Seventh Army French Army B. Such were the attitudes with which Devers continuously had to deal.

At the end of June 1944, Devers sent Marshall his confidential assessment of French capabilities and limitations.[12] The French were not able to operate independently and should agree to be bound by SHAEF orders, but they should also retain sovereignty forces not part of U.S. equipment plans. Except for strictly military reasons, commanders of French units should be French. Devers wanted General Alphonse Juin to command the French First Army, which would join the 6th Army Group as an outgrowth of Army B.[13] In Italy, Juin's corps compiled an outstanding record of solid military achievements. According to Devers, "They did a good job and they were well trained to do it."[14] Devers called Juin and his corps in Italy "magnificent." But he found other senior French commanders "erratic."[15] De Gaulle knew that the Americans favored Juin; Devers had even wheedled an American decoration for him from Marshall. Perhaps de Gaulle sensed that Juin might ultimately challenge him for leadership of the entire French Army, or that Juin's popularity with the Americans would bias him to readily agree with American decisions that would impinge on French national objectives. Either way, in April, de Gaulle appointed de Lattre instead to command the French First Army. Before its headquarters was activated, de Lattre would command first the lead French corps and then all French elements participating in the invasion. De Lattre also became de Gaulle's personal representative for the Dragoon operation. Juin, a brilliant officer, became de Gaulle's chief of staff. From that position, he might be of great assistance in keeping the Americans within proper bounds. Moving Juin to headquarters and assigning his old command to become part of de Lattre's organization, de Gaulle also cut Juin off from his old power base, reducing the risk of competition from a capable potential rival.

Rivals for the leadership of France, Juin and de Lattre hated each other intensely. Their rivalry began the day they graduated from Saint-Cyr, the French military academy, together. De Gaulle continued to divide and rule. Devers and his staff didn't really want de Lattre as French First Army commander. He was too difficult to deal with. Instead, they wanted Juin. Devers thought, "[His] corps was as good as there was in Italy. They did a good job and they were well trained to do it."[16] While they were very different personalities, Devers stated flatly, "in combat, I would put Juin and de Lattre as the top."[17]

In his introduction to de Lattre's *The History of the French First Army*, the noted British author B. H. Liddell Hart wrote of de Lattre:

> He was an aristocrat not merely by heredity but in reality. De Lattre succeeded in demonstrating the value of innate leadership and staking a claim for Genius. ... He was outstanding by force of mind and personality ... [with] a strong sense of mobility and could make the most of limited means. [He had a] dynamic and creative imagination, the two most essential qualities for supreme command ... love of the dramatic and a sense of history. One of the most sympathetic personalities I have known. He seemed to enjoy insubordinate subordinates.

One of de Lattre's biographers described the marshal as "unpredictable and more theatrical than even Patton."[18]

Born in 1889 to minor gentry in the small village of Mouilleron-en-Pareds, young de Lattre received a strict Catholic education followed by college under the Jesuits. Discipline, strong religious beliefs, honor, and duty to country came to permeate his entire personality. He was known for his mercurial temper and angry outbursts. After a year with the cavalry, he entered Saint-Cyr in 1909. The young cadet was disillusioned with the quality of instruction and graduated near the bottom of his class. He rode into World War I with the 12th Dragoons. During a horse to horse fight, the young de Lattre killed two German hussars with his sword before being almost unhorsed by a German lance. The wound nearly took his life. A cavalry sergeant placed his boot on de Lattre's neck and pulled the broken lance out of the wounded subaltern. Not to be kept down, after recovering at a hospital, he returned to combat, leading an infantry company. Wounded four times and decorated twice, he was mentioned in dispatches eight times.

Following World War I, de Lattre spent time fighting in French North Africa and was seriously wounded again. Posted to the École de Guerre and subsequently the Centre des Hautes Études de Guerre, he graduated both with distinction. In 1935, he came back to the École de Guerre as commandant. In 1940, as the youngest general in the French Army, he commanded a division that fought with distinction to stem the German onslaught. Upon hearing of the armistice, he appealed to the High Command to send his division, still full of fight, to North Africa or even England. Later, the Vichy government imprisoned him for fermenting resistance against the Germans by converting the 16th Division he commanded into an anti-German force. Subsequently he escaped from the prison at Riom.

De Lattre was a man of honor. He embodied a stain from the German occupation felt by many: "France can only win back her prestige by spilling the blood of her men in the conquering of Germany."[19] Over time, Devers believed that de Lattre and he built up good trust. "He was a fighter."[20] Because of the American's actions, de Lattre came to deeply trust Devers as a fellow officer and man of honor. It was Devers, as commander of U.S. forces in Britain, "who showed me the most friendly confidence from our first meeting."[21]

De Lattre could micromanage with the best of them. He kept in constant touch by radio or phone, often intervening in local tactical decisions. A martinet prone to frequent tirades about everything, he was an aristocratic authoritarian. Temperamental, mercurial, and, unfortunately, very energetic, he often amended orders as his mood changed. He frustrated his staff with constant changes to orders and his quest for perfection with details. Notoriously late for meetings and appointments, de Lattre refused to make decisions until the last minute. Nevertheless, he demanded instant performance from his staff, which always kept them on edge, attempting to anticipate which direction their commander would take next. Often he would change orders several times as he considered additional aspects. The French staff had trouble working with him.[22] But he knew his craft well.

Devers openly stated that de Lattre wanted to be loyal to the 6th Army Group commander but was pulled in opposite directions by two masters. De Gaulle ordered what he thought best for France, as opposed to what was best for the alliance. Britain had similar conflicts but was more likely to weigh in favor of the Allies if they could not sway the Americans. When they disagreed, Devers and de Lattre didn't write each other; they met face to face. As he did his entire career, Devers much preferred this approach to conflict resolution.[23] On occasion, Devers would ask de Lattre directly, "Will you obey me?" De Lattre would salute formally, open the door, salute again, and then slam the door. Devers recalled that the Frenchman would be mad for two or three days. But he would then obey.[24] When Devers said, "I have all the facts and this is my decision," de Lattre would sulk but always carried out his orders. Devers noted, "We didn't like de Lattre very much. I consider General de Lattre a very ambitious man who had a great deal of ability – tremendous ability – and a very difficult situation. He was a great orator but was hard to deal with. The French staff had trouble working with him."[25] Devers later noted, "I made a rule from the start that everything that I handled with de Lattre would be done with him and our two interpreters. We would never have staff in there."[26] De Latte would pace the floor in the manner of Douglas MacArthur.

Devers found that de Lattre's "temperamental personality causes more trouble within his own staff than he does with us. He hears only what he wants to hear."[27] With only a little exposure, Devers formed a far better opinion of this prickly French officer. In his personal diary, which was not intended for public consumption, he wrote, "General de Lattre is a great inspirational leader. He inspired all his commanders with the necessity of driving on, not letting the Germans get a foothold, if they stopped for one minute it would be harder." De Lattre had only a limited knowledge of English. Because of his selective memory, Devers made it an absolute rule to have another officer present when he met with the Frenchmen. Reuben Jenkins recalled, "Devers had real problems with de Gaulle's interference. Somehow Devers always landed on his feet. I don't think he was ever outmaneuvered by the French. They, including divisional commanders, liked him."[28]

In Henry Cabot Lodge, son of Boston Brahmins, future ambassador, and vice presidential candidate, Devers had a secret weapon. Lodge became Devers's alter ego with the French. Devers had gotten to know Lodge, who served with the 2nd Armored Division, when Devers was chief, Armored Force. In 1943, he had sent Lodge to North Africa as part of a liaison group to oversee British use of newly shipped M4 tanks. Colonel Lodge, who spoke impeccable French, understood French culture and the angst many Frenchmen felt about their 1940 defeat and the collaboration of many of their countrymen with the Germans. Devers rated Lodge as "top notch" and frequently used him as his special representative to de Lattre and the French.[29] De Lattre wrote to Lodge, Devers has "remarkable intelligence and obvious honesty captivated me at once.[30] Recalled Lodge, "Devers gave me wide latitude. He said he wanted to receive a lot of information but not to give a lot of detailed instructions. I felt like a man who is in business for himself and strained myself to the utmost to make the effort a success."[31] As a preliminary, de Lattre and his army took Elba, the sometimes prison of de Lattre's hero and model, Napoleon.

Marshall was a firm supporter of French rearmament. Early on, he instructed Eisenhower to issue the best of equipment for the French units and to use French forces rather than additional Americans whenever possible.[32] Initially, Henri Giraud led the raising of the eleven divisions (three armored and eight infantry) that the Americans had promised. Under his NATOUSA hat, Devers became responsible for the flow of U.S. equipment to the French. Devers ordered that French supplies delivery be regular. "The French always wanted more ammo than they needed," he observed.[33] The French had virtually nothing in the way of equipment. Initially, French soldiers even wore U.S. uniforms. In the days of curl-edged, rubber-stamped requisition slips, there was a lot of overage materiel in equipment stocks. America kept piling up stuff on their Iron Mountain of supplies. When the army needed an item, the supply people would rummage about until they found something in the pile that would work. Under Devers's sharp eye for detail, French requisitions for the required equipment began to be filled. Still, one snag after another backed up the flow of equipment from the United States. Using his authority as U.S. commander in the Mediterranean, Devers reached down into U.S. stocks to make up the shortages. Within a year and a half, significant reserve stocks and inventory overages gave him warehouses of materiel to work with. Of course, the French complained that they were being short-sheeted. Dealing with the myriad headaches of assembling eleven division equipment sets, Devers and his staff learned a lot about the French and the army they were putting together.

Modern armies are complex organizations. Less than 15 percent of the manpower soldiered in the infantry. A mechanized 1944 army had more cooks, supply handlers, and mechanics than it had riflemen. Perceiving combat units as measures of strength and prestige, the French did not want to divert any manpower to form service units. Hard-fighting infantrymen, not quartermasters and communicators, would restore honor to French arms. With shortages of service troops in all theaters jamming up every set of offensive plans, Marshall was not going to tolerate any such French tomfoolery. He demanded that the French create a balanced force or the United States would not provide the equipment, and he expected Devers to make sure that the French toed the mark. Neither would Marshall support endless arming of new units while existing ones weren't maintained with required replacements.

Marshall cabled Devers stating, "We are not justified in providing equipment for French units for which there is not an adequate replacement system."[34] French authorities viewed the American support structure as lavish and not required by French units operating within France.

By the end of February, the French General Staff was frantically searching for people with the requisite skills to fill support organizations. In the summer of 1944, many of the serving troops were men from North Africa, valorous but largely illiterate, and therefore not suitable for schooling in the skills needed to form support units. Few colonial troops had the requisite skills or education. The French repeated that "it was a pity to waste excellent combat troops by converting them into service units in which duty they were poor."[35] Devers replied that his command was short ten thousand service troops, and he could spare little to help the French support their unbalanced force. Devers offered some help with port and base service units but could not do more. Marshall informed Devers that the War Department "specifically decided and directed" that no American service troops be detailed to support the French.[36]

Quotas for basic skills such as truck drivers could not be met. The French shortage increased to sixty thousand slots.[37] French supply systems could not even move and distribute rations, let alone the thousands of spare parts a mechanized army requires. They didn't order enough stock, which led the Americans to infer that the French expected the Americans to fix or replace their broken equipment. Finally the War Department relented and allowed limited service support to French units about to enter combat. General Thomas Larkin felt the French were fiddling with the numbers and authorized equipment only from surplus stock already in ETO.[38] In a sense, the French Army was playing "chicken" with the Americans. As in Italy, the Americans would have to provide the missing support, or the French couldn't enter combat. Over 137,000 FFI joined the First French Army. Devers understood the support the French asked of him, but the Washington bureaucracy did not. These volunteers need uniforms, weapons, and basic equipment in order to perform as members of an organized army.

By early June 1944, a large percentage of the equipment to arm the First French Army had arrived, principally at depots in North Africa. On 23 June, Devers cabled the War Department to float the remainder on the highest priority to complete the equipment sets for French units scheduled for the invasion in August. Since mid-1943, Devers had managed supply to the French, overseeing the distribution of American equipment that constituted most of the materiel used to rebuild the French Army. American support for French forces flowed through another NATOUSA organization, the Franco-American Joint Rearmament Committee. Supposedly the French Army provided capability parallel to Larkin's, but it was never properly staffed. The French tended to see malevolent American motives behind virtually every supply shortfall. America furnished $2.3 billion in war materiel and another $548 million in supplies for civilians. France supplied American forces good and services totaling $868 million. During the war, France paid $232 million in reverse lend-lease.[39]

Devers called Lieutenant General Antoine Béthouart, a trim, white-haired figure of erect military bearing, a solid infantryman, "outstanding and thoroughly reliable," and a great Frenchman.[40] During the initial invasion of North Africa in November 1942, he commanded most of the French troops that defended the coast of Morocco. Americans brought him into the secret that they planned to invade near Casablanca. Béthouart led a group of his loyal officers against the local Vichy authorities. Unsuccessful, he was court-martialed and jailed until the Americans freed him. During combat north of Marseilles, de Lattre made him commander, French I Corps. De Lattre elevated General Joseph de Monsabert, commander of the 3rd Infantry Division, to become commander of French II Corps. He had done well during the fighting to break the Gustav Line in Italy and had a reputation of liking a good fight. In the field grades, the French had many good officers with prewar military experience. "French troops weren't as bad as we thought," said Devers. "The major French failure was at the junior leadership level. They didn't have replacement officers for their African army. For lack of junior leadership, they lost offensive capability."[41] Devers's cable to Marshall of 15 April 1944 summed it all up: "Our problems with the French are many and varied. They are very sensitive and at times very difficult."

General Marshall was the real father of the landing in southern France. Since early 1943, he had advocated a second landing to insure that Overlord, the primary Normandy invasion, did not get walled off by the Germans and go awry. Eisenhower concurred. Analysis of the logistics of a landing along the Channel coast immediately revealed that the Allies would not have enough port capacity to support the number of divisions needed to defeat the Germans until either Antwerp or Marseilles was placed into operation. In 1944, Marseilles had 13 miles of quays all linked to standard-gauge rails and hard-surfaced roads. After seeing the destruction at Cherbourg and the Brittany ports, planners assumed Marseilles and Toulon would be wrecked.[42] To overcome the port capacity problem, initial Overlord plans had simultaneous landings in both Normandy and southern France. Lack of sufficient landing craft, exacerbated by the Anzio landings and hoarding in the Pacific, caused the southern landing to lag behind the Normandy by about two months to recycle amphibious resources. From an early date, Henry Wilson turned to Devers as likely overall commander of operations in southern France to marshal the resources for the invasion. Devers retained his role as deputy commander for the Mediterranean while beginning to watch over Anvil preparations.

Eisenhower had more involvement with the gestation of Anvil than Devers did. Just before he left the Mediterranean for London, Eisenhower had supervised the drafting of a three-division invasion of southern France followed by exploitation north up the Rhône Valley. He believed anything less would be insufficient to provide much support to the invasion via Normandy.[43] Eisenhower had written a paper on how the Mediterranean landing would fit with Overlord. He knew that the Normandy invasion would be the decisive battle in 1944, but he was afraid of a deadlock there. A landing in southern France insured against that eventuality.[44] On 26 June, when it appeared the Allies would be bogged down in Normandy, Eisenhower wrote the combined chiefs about the necessity for an early landing in southern France. Wilson too wrote the combined chiefs that he was ready to commit to Anvil with 15 August as a target date. About the same time, General Alexander Patch sent General Lucian Truscott the army portion of the Anvil plan.

By the time Devers got settled in, the basic Anvil plan was in good shape. In London and wrestling with the port problem, Eisenhower reemphasized his desire for the quays of Marseilles. "Logistics is the biggest problem you had at senior command levels," recalled Devers.[45]

Churchill was adamantly opposed to what was now called Dragoon. At least since the nineteenth century, Great Britain had interests in Eastern Europe. Approaches to the Dardanelles and Suez were only part of British concerns. Churchill, fearing that Joseph Stalin would gain a hammerlock on postwar Eastern Europe, would have rather deployed the Dragoon forces to enter Eastern Europe, perhaps at the head of the Adriatic Sea.

Furthermore, the deadlock at Anzio began to consume the amphibious shipping and supplies that were earmarked for Dragoon. While Devers was inspecting the Anzio enclave, Churchill demanded that

Dragoon be canceled and the resources thus freed to be used to reinforce the Italian beachhead. By mid-February 1944, the prime minister's views prevailed, and Dragoon was canceled. Even Marshall was willing to throw in the towel. But thus began a convoluted set of maneuverings about Mediterranean strategy in which Anvil/Dragoon was canceled, reconfigured, and reinstated several times. The U.S. chiefs held that the additional support to the Normandy landings was absolutely necessary. The British chiefs held that either the Italian campaign should continue to be pushed above Rome or that a new front in Eastern Europe at the head of the Adriatic should ensue. Conversations between Roosevelt and Churchill, repeated the issues.[46] Marshall regained his moxie, stating he would rather accept halting the Italian offensive south of Rome than sacrifice Dragoon.[47] The final words between Eisenhower and Churchill were not spoken until mid-July, only a month before landing craft were to beach on the Côte d'Azur. It took a conversation between the president and the prime minister to resolve the issue. In the end, the British Joint Chiefs, while still maintaining that Dragoon was the wrong strategy, gave in on the landings in southern France in order to keep solidarity among the Allies.

The final objectives of the southern France invasion issued to Wilson were as follows:

1. Contain and destroy German forces that might otherwise oppose the Normandy landings;
2. Secure a major port in Southern France to land additional forces;
3. Advance northward to threaten an enemy flank;
4. Develop the lines of communication to support further operations.[48]

Devers was not heavily involved in this heated debate. But Wilson kept him very involved in Dragoon planning. Jake's principal duties in the Mediterranean and North Africa were to manage the organization that would enter France from the south and the build-up of American forces. Devers recalled, "I had logistics and worked hard to marshal the resources required for the invasion of southern France."[49]

As Eisenhower left the Mediterranean for London to command Overlord, Mark Clark was given a second hat as Seventh Army commander as well as Fifth Army commander. The Seventh Army would continue tactical planning for the campaign through southern France. Higher authorities planned for Clark to switch horses after Rome was secured and conduct the southern French campaign. But he preferred to stay with his beloved Fifth Army. Given the troubles at Anzio and total lack of progress near Monte Cassino, Wilson in mid-February removed Clark from any responsibility for Dragoon so that he could concentrate on Italy. Devers couldn't have been happier; Wilson set him in charge of bringing forth Dragoon.

If there was a dead end consuming supplies it was the Italian campaign.[50] Under instructions from Devers, SOS-NATOUSA switched first priority from supplying U.S. forces in Italy to equipping the three American division Dragoon force.[51] That action only reinforced Clark's enmity toward Devers. Before the temporary cancellation of Dragoon, a large amount of supplies and equipment for the amphibious operation in the south of France had reached the Mediterranean. The logisticians reported to Devers that virtually all supplies for the invasion for both the Americans and French were either on hand or on the ocean, heading in from the United States. Devers fought strenuously to keep this stockpile intact and not to reallocate it to combat forces fighting in Italy.

Most of the tactical landing planning was produced in Naples by Brigadier General Garrison H. Davidson and his staff under direct supervision of Patch and Admiral Henry Kent Hewitt, the Landing Force commander. Lucian Truscott recalled, "Few operations of such magnitude have been planned more cooperatively or mounted more efficiently than Anvil."[52] The team briefed the final plan to Wilson and Devers on 28 July. Rather than its creator, Devers was more Dragoon's midwife. As the birth was painful, that was no small feat. In his diary, Devers wrote, "It was a personal fight on my part from this end to get that operation [Dragoon] mounted."[53] Churchill continued to advocate landings at the head of the Adriatic. Clark wanted to prosecute the campaign up the Italian boot with the supplies collected for Anvil. Only constant work by Devers kept the resources for the landing in the south of France intact while the strategic debate raged.

When Rome fell on 5 June, Wilson communicated to the combined chiefs that he was ready to land east of Toulon by 15 August with the largest force that amphibious resources could handle.[54] On 17 June, Marshall met with Generals Clark, Devers, and Wilson in Rome. Wilson was especially impressed with Marshall's comment that another large port was needed to land additional American divisions that were ready in the United States to ship out but had nowhere to come ashore. Marshall had come to recommend that the Fifth Army be withdrawn altogether from Italy and committed to France. Devers's view reflected Marshall's on the subject.[55] Long after the war, Devers remarked, "They should have given me Fifth Army" as well as the Seventh.

The combined chiefs continued to debate the southern France invasion until only a few weeks before the actual operation. Senior planners concluded that French and American armies would be needed, and that a new army group headquarters would indeed be formed. In early July, Wilson created the nub of a new army group by establishing Advanced Detachment Army General Headquarters Mediterranean on Corsica. He placed Devers in charge and tasked him with overseeing the planned invasion. Always willing to grab the reins, Devers requested from Marshall that an army group be created with Devers as commander. He added that Wilson favored this course of direction. Marshall anticipated this request and thought highly of Devers and his demonstrated skill, but was concerned that Eisenhower would have a problem with Devers.

Devers personally organized the headquarters and headquarters company, according to the prewar Command and General Staff College outline.[56] Army group headquarters were supposed to be small. Logistical administration was supposed to pass from the field army directly to the army service force logistical section. Omar Bradley didn't do this, and as a result, the 12th Army Group headquarters grew to gargantuan size. The field army and below drew up detailed operational field orders. Army groups were supposed to concentrate on the big picture and write shorter letters of instruction. Devers selected his chief of staff, Brigadier General David G. Barr. Devers wanted Thomas Larkin to handle logistics and told Barr to select the rest of the staff. The nascent army group staff assembled on Corsica.

NINE

Dragooned

WINSTON CHURCHILL SAID THAT THE AMERICANS DRAGOONED him into the landings in southern France, hence the selection of that code name. Jacob Devers certainly had not been. British Field Marshal Henry "Jumbo" Wilson had set things up with the notion that Devers would command the invasion of southern France in August 1944. On 1 July, Wilson cabled George Marshall, "We will need AG [army group] and I want Devers to be commander." Marshall floated the idea of Devers's becoming the third ETO army group commander among the players – Bernard Montgomery commanded the 21st Army Group in the north; Omar Bradley led the 12th Army Group in the center. Dwight Eisenhower, however, was unpleasantly surprised when he learned that Marshall was considering Devers.[1] According to historian Forrest Pogue, Eisenhower recognized that Marshall wanted Devers. He had heard from General Carl Spaatz, commander of American strategic air forces in Europe, that Marshall was intent on placing Devers at the head of the 6th Army Group.[2]

More than likely, Eisenhower saw the appointment as necessary to get Dragoon aboard for a landing that was scheduled in less a month. In response to Marshall's suggestion of Devers, Eisenhower responded that previously he had had reservations about Devers "based completely on impressions . . . [which] never had any basis in positive information."[3] But, he continued, "I understand that Devers has been on the battle front a lot and that he has demonstrated a happy faculty of inspiring troops. That is enough for me. I would accept the decision cheerfully and willingly."[4] Given the tone of these statements, Marshall might reasonably have assumed that any past problem was obviated. But given what was being said about Devers around SHAEF headquarters, Eisenhower was not being completely candid with the chief. The official historian for the campaign in southern France mused, "[Devers's] appointment would further ensure that Anvil took place as scheduled, thus promising relief for the beleaguered forces under Eisenhower's command in Normandy."[5] Often important priorities run afoul of each other, and people do what they can. Eisenhower most likely sensed that, despite his misgivings about Devers, he should not get crosswise with both Marshall and Churchill at the same time. Devers was enthusiastic about the operation, and Eisenhower never doubted that he made the right decision about invading southern France.[6] Until Antwerp became available, Marseilles would become the largest port in Allied hands. During the Battle of the Bulge, more than half of American supplies would come through there.[7] Even in the final campaign in Germany, a quarter of the artillery ammunition for the American army came in through Marseilles.[8]

On 16 July 1944, Marshall radioed, "Devers, you will set up an army group . . . that is primarily an American headquarters with a carefully chosen French representation. The important thing is that we push Anvil to the utmost as the main effort on the Mediterranean." He added, "There should be no waiting for the perfection of arrangements. . . . Carefully planned and bold action will shorten the war."[9] In an effort to narrow Devers's responsibility for the French to the strictly military and local spheres, Marshall added, "Eisenhower favored the army group idea so as to keep control over all Civil Affairs as well as troop and supply priorities and major tactical decisions."[10] Marshall went on to say that Overlord was first priority, Anvil (Dragoon) was the Mediterranean priority, and if the Fifth Army stalled because Overlord and Anvil absorbed all of the resources in Italy, then its divisions should be transferred to the south of France.

Charles MacDonald, one of the most knowledgeable historians of the U.S. Army in Europe during World War II and author of two of the "Green Books," official U.S. Army histories, on the subject, summarized it thus: "One top American failed through no fault of his own to make [Eisenhower's] close knit team. Jakie Devers, who needed all of the charm of winning smile, protruding ears and boyish features to hold his own in company where he lacked the full confidence of the chief. Eisenhower knew Devers only slightly, he was Marshall's man. Devers and his 6th Army Group were Johnny come lately, the poor relations from out of town strangers to the established family."[11] Another historian argued, "Eisenhower disliked Devers's bombastic and cocky attitude. . . . Eisenhower and his staffers treated the 6th Army Group like the 12th Army Group's unwanted and ugly step sister to whom nothing was given and nothing was expected."[12]

Devers recalled Marshall stating that the principal Dragoon ground leader, commanding general, Seventh Army, had to be a combat-experienced commander. That seemed to narrow the choice to either George Patton or Mark Clark. Devers recalled that "I wasn't going to give either one of them the command of Seventh Army if I had anything to do with it."[13] Patton's slapping incident while he commanded the Seventh Army pretty well ruled him out. Devers was "very definite" about that. As we have seen, Devers thought little of Clark. Later, Wilson revealed that Eisenhower had intended for Clark to command the invasion of southern France.[14]

As the commanding officer of IV Corps newly arrived from the United States, Major General Alexander M. "Sandy" Patch, who had commanded both a division and a corps on Guadalcanal, entered Devers's theater. Son of a horse cavalry officer, he was born in Fort Huachuca, Arizona, in 1889 but grew up in Lebanon, Pennsylvania. He served with John Pershing in Mexico chasing bandits, and commanded an infantry battalion in the "Big Red One" during its service in the Great War. In 1942, Marshall selected Patch to lead a force in the southern Pacific that he turned into the Americal Division.[15] Later, he commanded XIV Corps, which cleaned out Guadalcanal. Patch gained the reputation of being a quiet professional, good with troops, and a commander who got the job done. Marshall had formed a good opinion of him during the Great War and thought he had done an outstanding job in the Pacific.[16] A West Point classmate and effective regimental commander during in Devers's tenure in the 9th Infantry Division (1D), Devers always had been impressed with him. "Sandy" as his friends called him was sensitive to the plight of his troops. During the European campaign, he wrote to his wife, "In my quiet moments, alone, I too get a great sense of depression – not too much of – but because I think I see too much serious incompetence – and I wonder how long it can continue – Am getting so very very many letters now from parents of boys who have been killed, wounded, or missing . . . there is so little I can say."[17]

Commending Patch as a cool-headed, frank, and fearless fighter who said what he thought, Devers recommended that he be promoted to command the Seventh Army.[18] Marshall concurred. After all, Patton was slated for the Third Army and Clark had his hands full with the Fifth Army in Italy. Later, after an inspection trip to the Seventh Army, Jumbo Wilson said Patch was the finest army commander in the Mediterranean Theater.[19] When de Lattre first called on Patch, the band played the "March of Lorraine," a thoughtful touch. De Lattre seemed to have a genuine affection for Patch, who was religious and a little bit the mystic.[20]

After the war, Patch wrote to Jake and stated candidly that, without Devers's strong and unceasing support, he never would have received the Seventh Army Command.[21] But Devers recalled, "For six months I tried to get Sandy Patch made a lieutenant general and I got turned down every doggone time."[22] Patch had run afoul of the navy by talking about the interception and shooting down of the plane carrying Admiral Isoroku Yamamoto. Patch had made an inopportune comment in the presence of a reporter and been formally reprimanded. The intercept was highly classified in order to protect the secret that the Americans were able to decipher Japanese codes.

Between March and July 1944, Devers and Patch had "become the primary movers within the theater for the continued planning for the Franco-American Anvil Assault."[23] Devers was not likely to produce a detailed and intricate multi-phased written plan. But he had an uncanny ability to rapidly recognize the critical objectives that must be achieved in order to solve the larger problem in front of them. As one army historian observed, "He saw long range objectives with a clarity which was seldom accompanied by any fuzzy whys and wherefores."[24] Major General Lucian Truscott commanded the invasion force, VI Corps. In Wilson's name, Devers retained overall control, while leaving tactics to Patch and Truscott. Eisenhower had requested that Devers release Truscott to command an invasion corps in Overlord, but Devers had refused. Patch and Truscott became close friends.

The plan for the invasion of southern France had two stated, over-arching strategic objectives. Logistic projections predicted the Allied landings in northwestern France would not capture enough port capacity to supply the number of divisions the Allies would need to destroy the German army. In 1944, the high-tonnage logistic system was a large working port linked to a railroad system that could move a lot of rail carloads of supplies. The Allies needed the capacity of Antwerp and Rotterdam or Marseilles to sustain their plans. This is why Eisenhower was so adamant about Dragoon. The naval fortress of Toulon might add capacity, but its much smaller system of wharves would be hard pressed to feed both France and the Allied armies. While accomplishing this objective, the southern France invasion force would link up with the troops streaming from Normandy and form a continuous front from the North Sea to the Swiss border, the second objective.

Events obscure a third, implied contingent objective. What if the Allies were bottled up in Normandy? Then the southern force would fall on the flank of the Germans and tear free the shackles restraining Overlord. Despite these goals, many British officers thought this mission was about to become one of the biggest strategic errors of the war. Churchill feared that the Americans were taking on much more than they could hope to handle.[25]

Detailed planning of the landing itself was under Truscott. Devers thought Truscott was "first class" and "the finest army combat commander," and had been instrumental in elevating him to corps command in the Anzio beachhead. Rarely did one see Patch's hand overtly moving pieces across the battlefield.[26] But it was he who made most of the critical planning decisions for Anvil.[27] Rather than intervening on the battlefield, he made sure his subordinate commanders, Truscott and de Lattre (before the activation of a separate Free French First Army), kept heading in the right direction, focused on the right tasks, and properly supplied. As noted, de Lattre liked Devers from their first meeting, finding him friendly and confident.[28] For his part, Patch found de Lattre a general of wide experience, "expressive in both speech and gesture," and "impeccably polite and agreeable in his acceptance of my command."[29]

Devers was not scheduled to take formal command of the Dragoon force until the 6th Army Group was activated a month after the landings. Wilson got around this by letting Devers work from the theater's "advanced detachment" in Corsica. While technically not in command, Wilson let him supervise in the name of the theater commander. Planning was collegial among Devers, Patch, and Truscott, incurring little rancor among the staffs.[30] Because the top Americans got along so well together, few written directives were needed. All three wanted to quickly establish a defendable beachhead and then be prepared to rapidly move inland if the opportunity developed.[31] The new VI Corps commander did not want to emulate John Lucas at Anzio and hold back if the opportunity to exploit presented itself. Devers the tanker backed up the cavalryman Truscott. There was to be no repeat of Anzio or the first month in Normandy, for that matter. Patch concentrated on campaign planning while Devers marshaled the supply buildup. Devers fought off both the Fifth Army's and the War Department's attempts to raid the supplies assembled to support Dragoon. He succeeded in retaining 75 percent of what was needed. Later, this would minimize the demand for hard-to-find shipping for the buildup.[32] Clark complained bitterly that Devers was short-sheeting the Fifth Army. But the official history states, "Without the strong support of Devers and Patch it is doubtful that Anvil would have ever taken place."[33]

Even though they did not know the specific beaches or even the size of the invasion force, planners began to pull together data. The baseline assumption was a two-division operation. Planning continued using the concept of a "division slice," a division plus normal nondivisional supporting artillery, tanks, engineers, and so on, so the work could be expanded or shrunk depending on the final decision of the combined chiefs. Work continued despite several cancellations of the landings. Patch refused to take charge of the tactical fight until the French had landed and called it an army. Until then, VI Corps soldiered under a very steady performer, Truscott. In a plan drawn up by Eisenhower with Clark's assistance before Devers arrived in the Mediterranean, Clark earmarked 3ID, 45ID, and 1st Armored Division (AD) as the invasion force. The two infantry divisions were experienced in amphibious operations and had fought up the Italian boot. Major General John W. "Iron Mike" O'Daniel, commanding general, 3ID, had been Truscott's deputy when Truscott had commanded that famous division at Anzio. William

W. Eagles, 451D's commander, had also served under Truscott as assistant division commander.

Events at Anzio and Salerno strongly colored the assumptions planners made. Both of those invasions had been tough fights. Critical Allied mistakes had been made. Given the near disaster at Anzio, planners expected strong German resistance along the Côte d'Azur.[34] Dragoon planners estimated that twenty days would be required to take Toulon, and Marseilles would not be cleared until D-Day plus 45.[35] This proved to be far too pessimistic. The French demanded the honor of liberating the two port cities. Recognizing the incredible inter-Allied risks of mixing tumultuous civilians with foreign combat troops in active combat, the Americans readily agreed. As de Lattre said, in Marseilles, "a few turns of the tracks, a tank covered with flowers was either taken by the assault of pretty, smiling girls or fired at by an 88mm."[36]

Devers asked Truscott if he was going to advance to a stop line to get adjusted after coming across the beach. "No if I have a breakthrough I have a special force set up that will go through the opening and keep going," Lucian responded. Initially planners thought that one advance division or elements thereof would be available. Devers said, "Good, let's not repeat Anzio, you will be in command," and not to let anyone stop "his exploitation."[37] Devers's staff officers could make significant changes on the spot given new information; their only requirement was to notify Devers immediately. As he had been with 91D back at Fort Bragg, Devers was a familiar sight at army, corps, and division levels, getting around in all but the worst weather in a light aircraft that he had pioneered for the artillery.[38] He left most planning to his army HQ staffs, thereby keeping his army group staff small, about six hundred men versus Omar Bradley's thirteen thousand. Bradley only talked with army commanders.

It did not take an Ouija board for German commanders to realize the most likely landing beaches lay between Toulon and Marseilles. But the beaches there were not the best. Instead, the Allied operational concept landed the invaders on Riviera beaches east of the French naval port of Toulon. The Allies knew to stay clear of the port defenses of those two large cities, with their monster coast artillery pieces and concrete fortifications. Landing beaches in and around picturesque St. Tropez Bay, between Toulon and Cannes, were selected instead. Truscott did

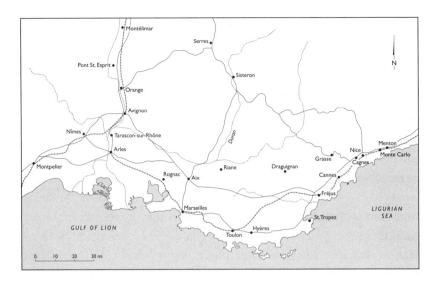

9.1. South Coast of France

not want to repeat Anzio, where German observers on high ground could direct observed artillery fire throughout the beachhead. On a map, he drew a line – the Blue Line – for a beachhead perimeter far enough inland to grab the Massif de Maures mountains, which dominated the landing beaches. The line ran roughly 15–20 miles from the coast, which excluded bombardment from medium and most heavy artillery.[39] From southwest to northeast, the massif ran along about 40 miles of coast. All three assaulting infantry divisions would land within this beachhead (map 9.1).

Initially, Patch envisioned the Americans' landing on the west beaches and the French disembarking on the east. After securing the beachhead, the first task would be to capture the port metropolis of Marseilles, however, so that arrangement was reversed. Then service troops would develop a large logistical base there while combat forces ran up the Rhône Valley as swiftly as they could to link up with a much more powerful American force advancing from Normandy and headed toward the German border. Neither the Allies nor the Germans seriously thought a major attack or counterattack would attempt to traverse the Alps along the Franco-Italian border.

As spring wore on, Jumbo Wilson concluded that he needed to retain 1AD in the Italian Theater. Again, it is reasonable to question why strategists did not overrule "localitis" and assign a scarce resource to the highest priority as Marshall designated it, the campaign in France. No subordinate "owns" resources required by his commander elsewhere. It was an opportunity for Devers, the prior chief of Armor, to shine. Only he didn't. Initially an inexperienced infantry division was substituted for "Old Ironsides." Finally, the experienced 36ID became the third team member. Major General John E. Dahlquist was new to the division, having recently taken command of the troubled "Texans." Because of the heavy casualties suffered in Italy, especially in the failed attempt to cross the Rapido River to link up with the Anzio invading force, as well as particularly poor performance of one of its regiments, an aura of hard luck hung over this outfit.

Until the beginning of August, plans onward from the beach were vague. Planners were thinking of the move northward in tactical terms. It was Wilson and his staff that identified weaknesses in German resolve and their plans to defend little east of Marseilles and to prepare for withdrawal.[40] He advocated even a deeper strike northward, all the way to Avignon, suggesting Grenoble as an alternative. Truscott, with Devers's hearty concurrence, grabbed onto Wilson's proposal and began planning for either of the objectives Wilson suggested. Truscott was absolutely convinced that an armored combat command would be required to propel the spearhead at the requisite speed northward.[41] Initial thinking proposed landing a combat command from the French 1st Armored that would charge up the small Argens Valley to link up with the airborne. But squabbles over American control of the French unit caused Truscott to reject that idea. A scratch force of a couple of tank companies, a mechanized cavalry squadron, along with supporting motorized infantry and artillery, dubbed Taskforce Butler after its commander, who was deputy VI Corps commander, assumed the mission.

The formal organization chart went from the Seventh Army (Patch) to Mediterranean Theater of Operations (Wilson). Devers acted as de facto commander as Wilson's deputy and in his name. Wilson approved the idea of advancing rapidly north from the beaches as did all three

American commanders. Devers recalled that each level of command was "flexible," and gave its subordinates a lot of latitude.[42] Patch left Truscott to make all of the tactical decisions on deployment of the three assaulting divisions. But he kept the larger decisions firmly in his own hand. Truscott wanted independent control of air and ground forces. Patch retained these at the Seventh Army. From the beginning, Truscott planned to advance rapidly inland with the intent to bottle up and destroy the German Nineteenth Army. There would be no repeat of the hesitation upon arrival as at Anzio. From the beginning, Truscott had his eye on a gorge through the Rhône passes called the Gate of Montélimar, just north of a town with the same name.[43] It was an ideal place to trap a retreating army.

VI Corps contained the only three American divisions in Dragoon. Elements of three French II Corps divisions, not trained for amphibious assault, would land the second day of the invasion on beaches cleared by Americans. Devers recalled, "The French were very nervous about this landing."[44] The French first echelon included 37,000 troops and 5,860 vehicles; the second included 28,000 men and an additional 3,500 vehicles.[45] Many of these divisions had fought in Italy, and they comprised two corps. Wilson felt that a second army headquarters should not be inserted into the beachhead until the campaign had moved up the Rhône Valley.[46] The French wanted their own army-level headquarters but knew they were nowhere near ready to command an invasion. A compromise was reached. Initially, de Lattre would command the first French corps that landed. He would move to "army" command (Army B), but that organization and its two corps would report to Patch at the Seventh Army. An additional French division would land on D-Day plus 9 (D+9). Four French divisions were slated to capture first Toulon and its Navy base, and then the metropolis of Marseilles.

Based on Maquis reports of enemy strength, planners anticipated a slow advance from the beachhead. Initially, they thought the Germans would fight tenaciously to deny the Allies use of the ports. A senior American planner recalled, "The French are going to have a bloodbath in Marseilles and Toulon. It is no place for American troops."[47] The French wanted three months to take Toulon. Devers, sensing a less tenacious fight, said thirty days.[48] The final plan estimated Toulon would fall to the French about D+20 and Marseilles on D+45. Supply would have to come in over the beach for the first thirty days. Commanders took a calculated risk that supplies for a deep exploitation would not be required and reduced POL (petrol, oil, and lubricants) and rations in the assault landings by 20 percent. De Lattre feared most that French troops would be tied down and ground to pieces in sieges of Toulon and Marseilles, and would not be able to participate in the liberation of the remainder of the south of France (map 9.2).[49]

Although the town of Le Muy was within the Blue Line, Truscott wanted paratroopers to seize it at the beginning of the operation. Le Muy controlled the Argens River Valley that exited the beaches toward the northwest. Major General Robert T. Frederick, the much-admired commander of the Canadian American commando outfit dubbed the 1st Special Service Force, was picked to command 1st Allied Airborne Taskforce. When Frederick reported to Devers for the assignment, he told Jake that he had never commanded an airdrop before. There was only five weeks to pull the operation together. When Frederick asked how many airborne troops the invasion force had assembled, Devers replied in his upbeat, optimistic way, "So far you are the only one we have."[50] Subsequently, the 1st Airborne Taskforce was cobbled together from a British airborne brigade group, a regiment plus two battalions of American airborne infantry, and several battalions of airborne and air landing pack artillery.

German intelligence had carefully watched the build-up of amphibious shipping in the Mediterranean and other Allied preparations. The Germans assumed that the Allies would undertake a major invasion of western France during the first four months of 1944 in conjunction with a major Soviet offensive on the Eastern Front. Some German analysts predicted landings in southern France before the attack in northern France. The January landings at Anzio were interpreted as a preliminary diversion to draw German strength away from southern France. While they did not know the exact invasion beaches, the Germans were forewarned.

In January 1944, the Germans had completely cordoned off the Anzio landing. For the six weeks after the huge Normandy invasion, the Allies captured little more than Cherbourg and the Cotentin Peninsula. Again, the Germans had almost achieved deadlock. Then at the end of

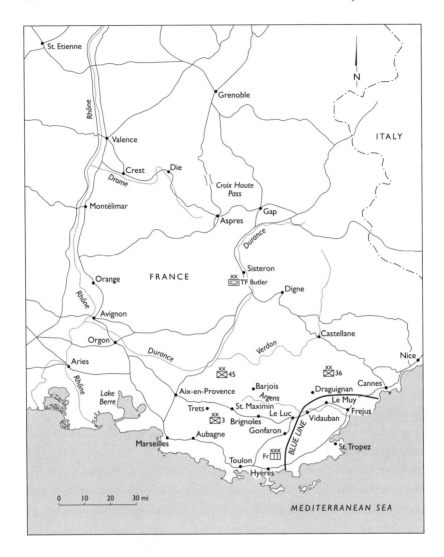

9.2. Breakout from the Blue Line

July, the magnificent American breakout, Cobra, tore open the front. Joe Lawton Collins's highly mechanized VII Corps burst out of Normandy, hell bent for leather. A German counterattack to seal the break did little except set up an opportunity for the Allies to surround virtually the entire German Army in Normandy.

It the middle of this, German Army officers almost succeeded in assassinating Hitler. On the Eastern Front, German Army Group Center was collapsing in the face of a determined Soviet Army, leaving hundreds of miles of front with little in the way of organized resistance. German soldiers left in France took off on the run for the Fatherland, feeling fortunate to escape with their own hides. Even Hitler could see that any attempt to hold southern or western France was not possible.

General Johannes Blaskowitz commanded German Army Group G, which defended France south of the Loire. Under him, General Friedrich Wiese, in command of the Nineteenth Army, was responsible for defending France's Mediterranean Coast. Wiese had a long history with radical opponents of the Weimer Republic and was considered an ardent Nazi by Allied intelligence. But, as de Lattre said, "the man knew his job."[51] Much of the Nineteenth Army's best units had already been stripped to shore up the Normandy Front. The Seventh Army contained the IV Luftwaffe Field Corps of three weak divisions, LXXXV Corps with two divisions, and LXVII Reserve Corps, also with a brace of divisions. LXVI Reserve Corps, with a single weak division, guarded the Italian border and the passes into the Pyrenees. Most of these units were under strength. To substitute for some of the huge shortages in German equipment, a motley collection of artillery and vehicles manufactured in almost any European nation engaged by Germany or under German occupation found its way into the Nineteenth Army. Many French tanks left over from 1940 were pressed into service. Fixed fortifications existed only at the seaward entrances to Marseilles and Toulon. Blaskowitz, however, recognized that Allied airpower that could reach the Côte d'Azur would only be a minor fraction of what appeared over Normandy. As a result, he would have greater latitude to shuffle kampfgruppes to counter Allied landings of up to a three-division size.[52] German airpower was limited to a handful of fighters and sixty-five Kriegsmarine torpedo bombers.

Dragoon came ashore on Napoleon's birthday, 15 August. Because of the high-level squabbling over whether or not to invade, the invasion force had little time to arrange and rehearse myriad details. The pressure on the responsible officers was so intense that one admiral took his own life. The day before the invasion, Devers made two trips out over the invasion fleet in a modified, two-seat P-38 and monitored the landings the next day from the same perch.[53] The invaders came ashore through the morning mist against little opposition. Only 361D met any serious resistance, which the Texans handled well. The famous commander of the 82nd Airborne Division, observing the air drop during the invasion of southern France, said it was "the most successful airborne operation of the whole war."[54] Seaborne invaders linked up with the airborne troops on D-Day and continued to move inland.

By day's end, 86,000 men and 12,000 vehicles had come ashore in small surf with only a 1-foot tidal range. Many reached solid ground with dry feet. The Dragoon landings have been described as textbook. That was due in part to the experienced invading teams but mostly to desultory and ineffective resistance. The defenders that did show up were of low quality and offered nowhere near the fight that the Allies had become accustomed to in Italy. Most of the two thousand plus prisoners taken were either overage or from Ost battalions. Only ninety-five Allied soldiers lost their lives on Dragoon's D-Day. Instead of losses increasing on subsequent days, as had happened at Anzio, daily casualties trended downward. VI Corps penetrated deeper against less resistance than anyone thought possible.[55] The Allied hold on the beachhead was solid, and airborne troops had linked up; Germans were unable to orchestrate their efforts to contain the beachhead. After securing the beachheads on the first day, VI Corps advanced across a deep arc toward the confluence of the Durance and Verdon Rivers. The 31D got into a violent firefight at Brignoles. Lieutenant General Brehon Somervell, commander of worldwide army services of supply and one of Marshall's closest lieutenants, wrote after observing Dragoon's coming ashore that it "was an inspiration to see the smoothness which characterizes operations in southern France."[56] Samuel Eliot Morison, the dean of American naval historians, called the landings on the Côte d'Azur "an almost perfect performance which contributed heavily to victory over Germany."[57]

Churchill observed the landings from the deck of a British warship and was impressed at the precision of the operation and the rapidity of the initial movement off the beach. He wired his cheerful approval to Eisenhower. After all the intense bickering over the landings in southern France, the supreme commander wired back to the prime minister, "I am delighted to note in your latest telegram to me that you have personally and legally adopted the Dragoon."[58] The Normandy breakout ordained that the Germans would not be able to hold southern France for long. Most of General Wiese's panzer and regular infantry divisions not already sent to Normandy now departed to staunch the flow of Allied armor in the north streaming toward the German border. The Nineteenth Army began making plans to pull most of its remaining defenders back up the Rhône Valley as soon as the Allies firmly established their landings in the south. Wiese had correctly surmised that the Allies would land east of Toulon. But defenders to the west stayed in place to deny entry to Marseilles and Toulon. Wiese cobbled together plans to leave defenders in the major ports, then pull the bulk of his forces back into the Vosges. Instead of the determined reinforcement bottling up the landing force indefinitely – the nightmare of a repeat of Anzio – the Dragoon force would only meet delaying parties as they advanced up the Rhône River Valley. VI Corps advanced much faster than planned.

Truscott and Patch envisioned a lighting move by VI Corps northward with two immediate objectives: first, surround the remnants of the German Nineteenth Army evacuating up the Rhône Valley, and, second, link up with the southernmost SHAEF organization, Patton's Third Army. After all, SHAEF's primary motivation for the southern landing was rapid infusion of supplies to Bradley's forces, primarily via the great port of Marseilles and French rail lines up the Rhône Valley. Pursuing the first objective, 45ID advanced west along the Durance River Valley, while on a parallel advance just to the south, the 31D moved up Route N7 toward Aix-en-Provence. While staying about 20 miles north of the coast, this offensive effectively interdicted the two Mediterranean ports from the north and was consistent with Devers's operational intentions.

As was his style, Devers did not get involved in the tactical details of the Dragoon landings or the drive up from the beaches. Instead he focused on logistical bottlenecks and sticking points in the Allied machinery. Back at the beach, DUKWs, the amphibious trucks that Devers had championed when he was chief of Armored Force, came up three on each side of a Liberty ship bobbling a mile or two out in the ocean. Boom operators reached into the ship's holds, lifted out netted loads, and set one in each DUKW, which then headed for the beach. The DUKWs crawled out of the water and then drove to inland depots, obviating any need for dumps on the beach. On shore, cranes lifted out the loaded nets, and stevedores threw empty ones in. Then the DUKW headed back for a new load. Patch accelerated the unloading of French II Corps since soon they would be needed to seize the entrances to Toulon. Devers, always in the middle of the action, moved his headquarters, nominally the Mediterranean Theater Forward Headquarters but actually most of what would become the 6th Army Group headquarters, from Corsica to St. Tropez on the 18th.

On the 17th, two days after the Dragoon landings, Ultra intercepted orders to the German Nineteenth Army to withdraw up the Rhône.[59] With that information in hand, senior commanders knew the rapidly expanding beachhead was secure. Truscott turned his troops northward.

The 11th Panzer Division, which became known by the Allies as the "Ghost Division" for its ability to slip away into the night, defended against an American thrust up the Rhône. Two good roads and a rail line led up the valley to Lyons. Ultra assured Patch and Devers that they would not be counterattacked by any substantial German reinforcements. Ultimately, French II Corps would take over defense of the area after French 21D, 31D, and 91D were landed to flesh out what would become the French First Army.

Marseilles is an immense city with large suburbs. Most of the Germans had already departed as the Seventh Army advanced behind the city.[60] Truscott was certain that U.S. 31D could take Toulon in two days, much ahead of the formal schedule. But both he and Patch felt it would be a mistake to divert 31D from northward advance. Further, the French were scheduled to take these important cities. Both Devers and Patch were sensitive to the political and cultural dimensions of the situation. Instead, Truscott continued VI Corps's westward movement, cutting off both Toulon and Marseilles, effectively defining the Seventh Army's area of operations, while giving the French free rein to maneuver against Toulon and Marseilles. Those two ports were each garrisoned by a German division and had been designated as fortresses by Hitler to be defended until the last man. Coastal artillery up to 340mm guarded the seaward approaches, but the Allies simply had to have these ports.

"The night de Lattre landed, we were going like a house afire," recalled Devers.[61] But de Lattre was upset with the speed-ups that were occurring, as opposed to the agreed-upon Allied plan. He was dragging his feet, and Truscott's staff couldn't get him to advance. After checking with both Patch and Truscott, Devers went directly to the Frenchmen's headquarters. He had told his American subordinates, "I am going down and I am really going to give [de Lattre] hell. I think he can take Toulon tomorrow." De Lattre was feeling the weight of the huge risk that attacking these port cities might hold. "Caution could mean a siege ... Boldness might mean that the French Army would be broken even before it had been brought together."[62]

Both de Lattre and Devers agree that the meeting about the timing of the advance occurred, but there the record splits. In his memoirs, published in 1954, de Lattre said he proposed to a surprised Devers a plan to rush to Toulon. It was he, not Devers, who wanted an immediate advance. The French general convinced Devers to go along.[63] In unpublished interviews given to credible official U.S. Army historians, Eugene Harrison's recollection was that Devers told de Lattre, "Now look, you are sitting and you can't sit still. Keep those Senegalese going. Get into Toulon tonight or tomorrow night. Then go on to Marseilles, and I think you will take Marseilles in the next two or three days. . . . Seventh Army was already behind Marseilles and many of the Germans that had been in the city had already evacuated."[64] After all, most of the German Army was retreating from their disaster at Falaise, where in mid-August, the town was nearly surrounded by the Allied armies advancing from Normandy.

De Lattre responded, "You demand the impossible."

Devers continued, "You asked the impossible [going up the left side of the Rhône in order to liberate the towns], and we are giving it to you."[65] So de Lattre accepted the new timeline – and met it.

The French advanced on Toulon six days earlier than planned. It was less than a week into the campaign. After capturing an arc of mountains just north of the city, which essentially isolated it, French II Corps plunged into Toulon. The Germans feared retribution from the FFI as much as the French Army. After pockets of intense fighting, the Germans surrendered a city littered with thousands of bodies. Marseilles was a similar story. By the night of the 18th, mobs only loosely controlled by the Maquis owned the streets. Germans who could find their way northward did so. The Maquis seized city hall and appealed to the French Army for help, even as de Lattre's units battled for Toulon. In responding to their pleas, de Lattre, through his subordinate, General Joseph de Goislard de Monsabert, took on some horrible risks. American planners were right. Liberation of such a large metropolis was best left to the French Army to sort out. Despite the best efforts of the resistance, the Germans thoroughly wrecked the port before they surrendered on the 28th, the same day that Toulon surrendered. Seventy-five ships were sunk in the waterways of Marseilles's port, which was sown with mines, and hundreds of cranes along the quays were left as little more than scrap iron.

Roads paralleling the Rhône were now choked with vehicles, horse-drawn and motorized, and burdened with fleeing Germans. Little planning for French pursuit northward had been laid out. It probably made little difference, as de Lattre and his men had already shredded the carefully laid out plans to capture the two large port cities.

Understanding their need for redemption, Devers gave the French additional plums. Devers would allow de Lattre to go farther up the Rhône's west bank and take both Lyons and Dijon, adding to the expanding list of French battle honors. Even before the ports were secure, Patch wanted to start moving north. Wilson had warned Devers about going straight north up the Rhône Valley. Streams feeding that river come straight down from the Alps and form gorges along some stretches of the river's course that are almost impossible to traverse. Wilson didn't think a large mechanized force could advance up the valley against defenders holding the tops of those gorges without suffering great delay and casualties.[66] Instead, Wilson recommended taking the old Napoleon road that paralleled the Rhône Valley to the east via Grenoble.

While all of this was occupying Allied leaders, the Germans were desperately trying to evacuate what remained of their forces along the Bay of Biscay and southwest France. Their commanders attempted to retreat behind the Moselle River and to create a defense of the Belfort Gap. Hitler approved the retrograde – provided a counterattack was mounted against Patton. Supply constraints began to retard the Allied forward surge, and the Germans were finally regaining their balance. French II Corps handled the politically sensitive issue of liberating southwestern France and re-establishing French governmental control. Many

Maquis groups and the FFI existed with differing loyalties to leaders who claimed to represent France. Communist influence hostile to de Gaulle pervaded many Maquis organizations, especially in the south. Only twelve days had passed since the French landing. Throughout southwestern France, seventy thousand armed members of the French resistance overwhelmed small groups of Germans that had not made good their escape. Celebrations went on for days, hence this offensive's nickname – the Champagne Campaign. In two weeks, the Dragoon force took 57,000 German prisoners while suffering 2,700 American and 4,000 French casualties. It was a victory of overwhelming proportions. Linkup with Patton's forces was imminent.

TEN

Up the Rhône Valley

REFUGEES WERE ON THE MOVE ALL ACROSS FRANCE, TRYING to return home. Jacob Devers was especially considerate of the Poles. In Italy, Poles had fought bravely and hard in an attempt to move the Allies up the Italian boot. "I was close to the Poles. So I made a deal to turn the Polish refugees over to the British, who were anxious to get them back to help the Polish corps in Italy." But the French didn't want to do it. Many prisoners in German uniforms readily volunteered to join the Polish corps. Devers agreed to ship them south in empty supply trucks and then send them back on empty ships already heading to Italy. "We sent back thousands that way."[1] In recognition, the Polish government decorated Devers.

Before the invasion, planners envisioned creating a small mechanized taskforce to exploit inland from the beachhead. Taskforce Butler (TF Butler) was big enough to knock over the usual rearguard forces but was nowhere near large enough to go hunting a panzer division. The vaunted "Ghost Division" lay out there somewhere, doing quite a job of covering the German withdrawal. Devers was anxious to let TF Butler loose. Lucian Truscott, ever the aggressive cavalryman looking for a weakness to exploit, was chomping at the bit. "Germans were retreating so fast, we had trouble keeping up with them," recalled General Eugene Harrison.[2] Ultra decrypts demonstrated that the Nineteenth Army was heading north under orders, and that the Nazis would not come across the Italian border in force and fall on the flank of the Seventh Army.[3] This allowed Sandy Patch to send Fred Butler's small force on a 100-mile mission. While he didn't make a show of appearing in the frontlines, Patch constantly moved around among his commanders and kept in close touch with critical points throughout his command. This is exactly the behavior Devers liked to see, so he left his gifted subordinate alone to run his own show. Truscott was made aware of "secret intelligence" regarding the whereabouts of the 11th Panzer Division (PzD). Nonplussed, that old cavalryman needed only permission to start the race. Truscott unleashed TF Butler on 20 August 1944, far earlier than anticipated in the initial plan due to the German "bug out." From Devers on down, everyone agreed that the route least likely to be blocked was not Route 7 through the Rhône Valley but via the old Napoleon Road (the one the emperor had taken when he returned from Elba) through the mountains to Grenoble then Lyons.

The operation resembled a textbook pursuit where the pursuing force takes a route parallel to the one the enemy is retiring on, rushes ahead, establishes a road block, and destroys the enemy force. Little hindered, Butler made a high-speed run up the Napoleon Road (N-85). Truscott told Butler to make his small taskforce sound and look like an armored division, which is exactly what he did. But the 3rd infantry division (1D) moved straight north up Route 7 in the Rhône Valley and onto Montélimar. Soon they began running into columns of horse-drawn vehicles and gaggles of trucks moving north, all covered by packets of 11PzD panzers fighting as rearguard.

During the exploitation northward, Truscott continued to call most of the tactical shots. Now the Americans would be the trappers. Truscott hoped to pin the Germans so they couldn't escape.[4] Devers understood what Truscott was attempting and fully approved of the maneuver. He focused on several logistical problems that rapid maneuver entailed, and marshaled the limited truck transport available to support this operation. It was the kind of problem that Devers excelled at solving, a bold and doctrinally correct plan.

TF Butler led up north N-85, the road from Le Muy toward Grenoble. This kept the Americans out of the traps in the Rhône Valley and allowed them to attempt to outdistance retreating Germans via a parallel road through the mountains. Had tenacious defenders constructed and defended strong roadblocks, this effort might have become bogged down. But that did not happen. TF Butler now had advanced 240 miles with only ten casualties. This route led them up down Routes 94 and 93 along the Drome River to the Montélimar gate.

Butler's lead elements approached the gorge from the west and began taking positions on the high ground to fire into the gorge. On the same day, French troops eliminated the last of the German rearguards in Toulon and Marseilles. Far to the north, Jacques-Philippe Leclerc's tanks, as part of Omar Bradley's army group, had entered Paris in triumph several days before. There simply wasn't enough space on the front pages of newspapers to extol all the good news.

One American armored car platoon drove right through German trucks on Route 7 from the east, blasting them to pieces. This set off a running battle, a "meeting engagement" in military terms. TF Butler had moved swiftly but not quite fast enough. Lead American scout cars were met by tank fire from Germans that had beat them to the high ground overlooking the Rhône. Infantry reinforcing TF Butler had their attack broken up by German artillery. The taskforce just wasn't strong enough to take the town. Additional German artillery and infantry from the retreating columns were thrown into the fray. Reinforcements swelled the German forces to the size of a corps. They charged the valley roadblock, bursting it apart and reopening the road. A 361D infantry battalion assaulted Montélimar head on. Some Maquis attempted to help but were scattered by concentrated German fire. General Butler described the attack as poorly organized and poorly led.[5] The attack was stopped and did not carry the town. The Seventh Army Report of Operations concluded that failure to carry the town prevented closure of the escape route.[6]

The Americans were not strong enough to retain even possession by fire of the gorge against the Germans trying to hold open Route 7, the way home. Butler had to pull his troops back under pressure from elements of 11PzD and a Luftwaffe infantry training regiment, which had already lost most of its transport to an American fighter-bombers attack along the road from Crest, about 17 miles east of the gorge. Route 7 lay open again. Butler radioed for more combat power. Meanwhile, he was in desperate need of both ammunition and gas. Some artillery unlimbered close enough to put fire on Germans retreating up the main road in the Rhône Valley but could not stop their retreat. Lack of ammunition limited their fires. Germans kept the road north open and also threatened to sever TF Butler's tenuous communications back to Grenoble. American artillery had to be shifted from pounding the traffic jams in the gate to securing TF Butler's own line of communications.

Truscott knew the objective was to kill Germans, not push them home. Frustrated, he sought battle to further devastate German formations. Unfortunately, Truscott had not declared TF Butler's move to interdict the Montélimar gate his main effort. Because of earlier 11PzD sightings, Truscott had canceled moving an infantry regiment into the area, an order for which he has been criticized. As a result, 361D continued to move toward Grenoble rather than Montélimar. Butler's force had to tag up a little and face west to fend off any aggressive move 11PzD might make. Because the invaders came ashore on assault shipping, many vehicles had been left in Italy to be shipped later. A lot of 361D infantry had to move at boot leather speed. When in command of 31D, Truscott became famous for the "Truscott trot," marching 30 miles with full pack in 8 hours. That training was put to the test (map 10.1).

Now Truscott sped to 361D HQ and cleared up orders that could be interpreted as making Grenoble and Montélimar joint objectives. He then sent two regiments to Montélimar on whatever transport could be found. Captured German fuel was used for the move. Patch and Devers labored hard to push gas-laden trucks and as much artillery as possible forward into the developing meeting engagement. Germans, led by the reconnaissance battalion of 11PzD, fought to unhinge the Americans. They blocked off roads to the south of Crest, which cut off resupply. The Germans were far from beaten. Late that night, after communication and orders were unsnarled, lead reinforcements from 361D finally began to arrive. The division delayed closing up because it received reports, later proved erroneous, that a large German column was advancing on the gate from Grenoble. Some criticize Patch and Truscott for not acting more quickly. To add to the pressure, Ultra identified more of 11PzD arriving in the battle area. Truscott expressed his displeasure with the 361D commander. He made it clear that two regiments of the division

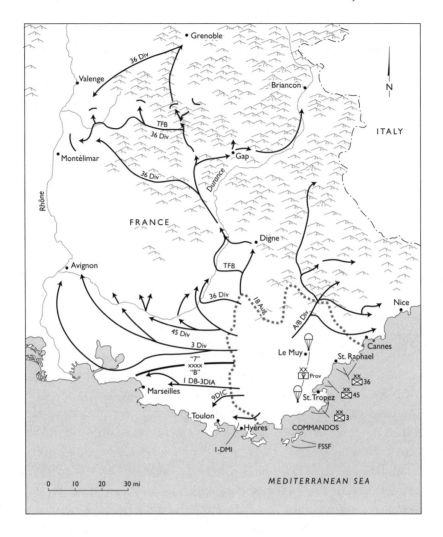

10.1. Allied Landings and Advance to Grenoble

were to move westward from the Napoleon Road and block the Rhône Valley. Lack of fuel hampered efforts to do so. The 45 ID began arriving and relieved 36 ID of responsibility for the advance to Grenoble.

Meanwhile, efforts by the panzers to push 36 ID away from the gate were shackled by their own fuel shortage. Fighting raged back and forth. Because of the paucity of trucks, companies were shuttled forward as best possible. Still, the misdirected move consumed limited transportation resources while the Americans were failing to project enough combat power along the Rhône Gorge. As a result, 361 D's move slowed. Neither of Truscott's immediate commanders, Patch or Devers, picked up the error of this slowdown. Truscott straightened John E. Dahlquist out on the spot, telling the division commander he was "considerably upset because my original instructions had not been carried out."[7] The first reinforcements from 361 D had to go into defensive positions to allow Butler to hold on. A few 361 D patrols made it back into the valley. But the division commander's report that his men were "physically on the road [Route 7]" was wide of the mark.[8] More Germans escaped. But many were being caught in the American artillery barrages fired into the gorge.

More and more artillery, a total of eight battalions, set up to pound the Rhône Valley. Meanwhile, additional Germans made good their escape north. Elements of 451 D arrived and closed parts of the German escape route. Carnage and wreckage began to choke the road leading north. Hundreds of slaughtered horses added to the horror. Bleeding flesh coated the ground in the killing zones. Fighter pilots also contributed to the carnage, and wreckage further constricted the herd attempting to thunder north. Other Germans, mostly without their vehicles, found paths by which to escape from the Montélimar gate. While many slipped through, the devastation brought about by American artillery and air power was shocking.

Try as they did, the Americans were not able to move sufficient armor and infantry to close the gate. Although the Nineteenth Army ran a gauntlet of American artillery, the bulk of German troops made it north, even if their equipment did not.

Essentially, Taskforce Butler had not been large enough to do the job. Later, Butler would say that if he had had a full armored division, he would have annihilated everything the German Nineteenth Army attempted to withdraw up the Rhône.[9] While the 1st Armored Division (A D) assisted in the drive north in Italy, leaving the division in Italy had proved in the end to be a clear misallocation of resources. Commanders of efforts that are not the main one are prone to want "nice to have" reinforcements that detract from the main effort. Carl von Clausewitz warned against such distractions. While compromise is essential to democratic government, it is the bane of the strategist. Senior commanders that do not jealously guard against such diversions often wind up with hard fighting but inadequately sized taskforces, such as Butler. Before quarrelling about retention of resources, commanders of secondary efforts need to reconsider and support unity of effort against the main effort.

The Montélimar fight was a close-run eight-day battle. To paraphrase the Confederate cavalryman Nathan Bedford Forrest, TF Butler arrived "firstest" but not with "the mostest." The taskforce was far smaller than a regiment, and it had to hold back German divisions clawing for their only way home. Small American roadblocks were repeatedly emplaced and then broken by the Germans. Devers recalled that the Germans had his forces outnumbered at times. If they had been "more coordinated and pulled together, they could have given us a bad time.... I think there was twenty miles of dead animals and broken down trucks."[10]

Truscott became so frustrated that he wanted to relieve 361D's commander for not reacting to a situation that Truscott thought was obvious on its face. Devers, who monitored the battle but, as was his style, did not "kibitz," stepped in and saved the division commander. The maneuver had been very difficult, and despite less than a complete success, there were good performances from many who scrambled to meet the challenge. German forces lost about 20 percent of their manpower, including 5,800 sitting in VI Corps cages. Truscott lost 187 killed and 1,023 wounded. While a sterling effort, it was not a decisive victory for the Americans. Parts of some 4,000 vehicles and wagons lay strewn across the gate of Montélimar. The 361D Artillery alone fired over 37,000 shells. But 11PzD remained a strong, effective armored force and did not begin its general withdrawal until the 27th. The 361D finally cleared the Rhône Valley on the last day of August, bringing the battle to its close. Devers would recall that "the Germans did all right until we cut them off in the pass. Then they lost a lot of people. They had us outnumbered, and if they could have stood and been coordinated, they could have given us a bad time."[11]

As soon as the two major port cities were taken, French 1AD and 11D of French II Corps followed up by traveling up the west bank of the Rhône. Blown bridges and lack of gasoline hampered their efforts probably more than the Germans. A second grouping of French divisions remained on the east side of the Rhône.

While VI Corps was busy smashing German transport trying to escape around Montélimar, Patch issued orders designating VI Corps's subsequent objectives. Devers noted approvingly in his diary, "Patch forgot flanks and kept moving."[12] While Truscott tried to keep the gate of Montélimar closed, Patch sought the point where the Seventh and Third Armies would meet. After the last German stragglers fled north from Montélimar, VI Corps would advance straight north up the Rhône to Lyons, 170 miles from Marseilles. Without any pause to regroup, Truscott would continue past the eastward bend in the Rhône, up the northward stream called the Saone, past Chalon, and then continue north to Dijon. There, he would meet Patton's recon cars and complete a continuous front. Patton's spearheads were 125 miles north in Lorraine along the Moselle River at Metz and Nancy. The Seventh Army's future laid to the northeast toward Besançon and from there on two alternative axes into Alsace and toward Strasbourg.

Patch was a master of carefully calculating what his forces could do, setting objectives at the outer limit of their capabilities, and then letting his subordinates fight the battle. Truscott and his staff fought the close-in battle, while Patch and his people looked deeper and thought farther down the timeline to set up and shape the next battle to create advantages for the Americans. This is the way staffs at different levels of command are supposed to work. Wilson told Devers that Patch was the best army commander in the theater among the four including Mark Clark, Jean de Lattre, and the 8th Army CG.[13]

During most of August, the bulk of available French forces were busy cleaning up Marseilles and Toulon. Because of extensive German demolition, Toulon would be of only limited use. Marseilles had to be made workable despite the destruction. For some time, liberty ships would pull up alongside ships sunk at the quays, and discharge troops onto planks laid over the sides of the sunken hulks.

Instead of wielding the two French spearheads as a single Army B, Patch continued to deploy one to either side of the main thrust conducted by VI Corps. French I Corps would relieve VI Corps from responsibility from the boundary east to the Italian border. Neither the Allies nor the

Germans expected any large military organization to traverse the Alps, so this was an economy of force operation. De Lattre objected to the split of French forces and the lack of a unified French Army. Both Devers and Patch tread carefully.

Ever conscious of French battle honors, de Lattre worried that his troops would continue to move behind the Americans fighting the Germans in the north. While he understood the necessity of quelling potential insurrection in southwestern France, Patch's Field Order 4 excluded French troops from the liberation of Lyons. Further, de Lattre didn't want to see French combat troops relieve British and American paratroopers guarding the Italian border. He appealed to Wilson as supreme commander in the Mediterranean to have the American plans modified to allow French elements to capture Lyons directly and be relieved of assuming defense of a large section of the Franco-Italian border. Sensitive to French needs, Wilson agreed. Devers recalled speaking to Patch: "Let them capture those big cities. The French like big cities. Let them have three days in the city. What do you care as long as Truscott can go up the other side? If we run into problems then we will handle this on our feet." At times, the French advance slowed as they seemed to have to celebrate Free France in every liberated city. Patch responded, "Sure that is all right."[14]

Ultra continued to report that the Allies had nothing coming at them through the mountain passes from Italy. The 1st Allied Airborne Taskforce had captured Cannes on 24 August 1944 and Nice on the 30th. As the last August pursuit beyond Montélimar began, Germans raided along the Italian border at Briançon. Devers employed the supernumerary headquarters of the 44th Anti-Aircraft Artillery Brigade to fill in along the Italian border and relieve the paratroopers.

SHAEF's Services of Supply commanded by the imperious General J. C. H. Lee was overwhelmed while attempting to reestablish supply for 12 and 21 Army Groups. So everyone readily agreed that the Mediterranean infrastructure would continue to service what became the 6th Army Group. Devers kept his second hat as commander NATOUSA, and Larkin continued to run NATOUSA Services of Supply independent of Lee and directly under Devers. This also allowed much excess stock that remained in North Africa to be channeled into resupplying the 6th

Army Group. Fresh supplies from the United States would bypass both the United Kingdom and the choked ports in northwestern France that were in Allied hands.

At this time, Devers and Larkin assured Eisenhower that they could "take two or three divisions from the United States and process them rapidly to the front lines."[15] On 9 September 1944, as hope for a quick capture of Antwerp faded, SHAEF began looking into landing an additional three division corps through Marseilles if the 6th Army Group could provide the service troops to support it. Without the logistical tail, nothing in available to support combat units, and nothing happens. Despite the added strain from an inadequate service structure to support the French, Devers was ecstatic at the prospect of having a second American corps to flesh out the Seventh Army and to add weight to its attack toward Saverne. Colonel Clarence Adcock, 6th Army supply officer, said he could find the necessary support for an additional U.S. corps.[16] Eisenhower and Wilson agreed that the 6th Army Group should switch to Eisenhower's command about the time the attack had advanced to Lyons.[17] He was to keep Wilson informed so Dragoon's advance would conform to SHAEF's overall plan (map 10.2).[18]

Truscott plowed ahead. Patch adroitly made a midcourse correction that allowed Truscott to better concentrate his forces by directing the French still east of the Rhône toward Grenoble. Still engaged in the big ports, they would be delayed. Patch concluded that VI Corps would have to proceed northward with little additional support. He viewed Lyons as an intermediate objective that oriented VI Corps in the right direction. He did not yet envision another attempt to encircle Germans running for the border. But Truscott was not to be denied. While 3ID continued to chew up German stragglers around Montélimar, 36ID made toward Lyons with 45ID in trail. Devers wrote in his diary, "It is the destruction of the enemy itself that counts. We must take our minds off terrain."[19]

With the frustrating conclusion of the battle to close the Montélimar gate over, Patch ordered the pursuit continued toward Lyons. Tactical reconnaissance indicated that the Germans were withdrawing from there, the third largest city in France. Complying with instructions that the French liberate major cities, Truscott held U.S. 36ID on the outskirts of the city so that French 11D of French II Corps could have the honor.

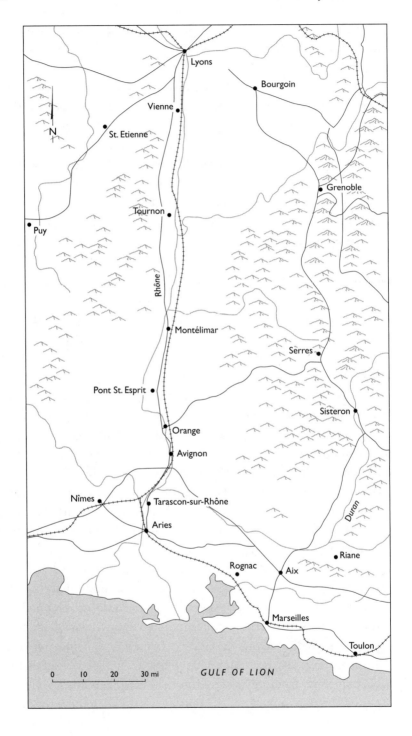

Truscott maneuvered 45ID to the northeast to cut off further German withdrawals to the east. Thunderbirds moved smartly to block all the roads. Its old nemesis, 11PzD, maneuvering aggressively, slipped past the block and fought the Thunderbirds for the town center. Again, cooks and supply handlers were thrown in as infantry. Finally, the German "Ghost Division" had enough and slipped off to the northeast that night; a chastised 45ID nipped at the German rearguard.

The Seventh Army had planned a pause after the capture of Lyons to allow logistics to catch up and to give the infantry a breather. Devers and Wilson anticipated further movement northward would be toward Dijon and the Plateau de Langres west of the Vosges. Now, Truscott wanted to continue his hot pursuit east of the Vosges and northward toward Belfort, that is, into the Belfort Gap. He radioed Patch, informing him that the Germans were capable of no more than delaying and asked for permission to continue pursuit. Truscott wanted to trap the remainder of the German force against the Vosges and destroy it. The Seventh Army commander agreed. Instead of crossing over and joining French I Corps to the east of VI Corps, II French Corps would follow the Saone directly north (the Rhône bends eastward just above Lyons) and stay to the west of VI Corps. De Lattre was very unhappy about the delay in pulling both French corps together into a single army with its own important zone of advance.[20] The VI Corps advanced northeast up N-83, which runs to Besançon and Belfort, attempting to shake off German delaying actions and French mud along the way. This logical tactical move led VI Corps on the operationally incorrect route north. Later, Devers would have to correct it.

German defenders attempted to make a stand at the old fortress guarding Besançon. Truscott ordered his lead 36ID to bypass, and invested the fort with 31D, which was in column. He was a hard-charging general willing to take risks, as he had done at Montélimar, to wreck the German Nineteenth Army. After a confusing fight, American infantry crossed the moat and were scaling the walls like medieval attackers when the Germans within finally surrendered on the 7th of August. But the

10.2. Topography from Marseilles to Lyons

battle slowed Truscott just enough to allow the remainder of the German Nineteenth Army to find refuge in the Vosges. A counterattack by 11PzD near the Swiss border stymied a French I corps advance on Belfort.

Moving supplies north of Marseilles remained a major problem. Railroad bridges spanning the Rhône had been blown. Despite this impediment to moving tonnage northward, Devers did not slow down. Supplying Dragoon was easily as difficult as directing combat. Unlike in Normandy and along the Channel coast, there was no shortage of quays onto which transoceanic ships could offload. Marseilles had 13 miles of quays. Toulon was expected to fall about 5 September, followed by Marseilles around the 1st of October.[21] Offloading of military cargo was concentrated along Marseilles's ample docks, France's primary transatlantic port. It fell to the Free French on 28 August, days earlier than planned. While Germans had created a lot of havoc, American engineers found useful dockage almost immediately. As frequently happened in all theaters, shipping load plans had shorted service units in favor of early landing of combat units. This almost universally diminished early available combat power due to lack of ammunition, food, and fuel. In a 29 August diary entry, Devers wrote that the port of Marseilles could be developed more rapidly than railroads up the Rhône. The Allies couldn't use the waterway itself. It would take a year's work to clear away the blockage.

"No question Devers had a good grasp of logistics," recalled Reuben Jenkins. "He demanded solutions. If we can't get 10,000 tons a day, Devers will find someone who will."[22] Devers rode everyone hard to see that the port met its throughput targets. "I was down there all the time and did everything I could do to raise a row with those people until it was done. My staff all worked hard on it."[23] During September, trucks moved 220,000 tons of cargo out of the southern ports and up the Rhône, while rail service moved only 63,000 tons.[24] The problem was moving supplies inland. Despite admonitions about the need for serviceable rail capacity, track along the Rhône Valley had been extensively damaged by Allied bombing. As in the north, the trucking shortage bottlenecked everything. VI Corps had Lyons in hand by D+15, far earlier than anyone anticipated. The supply system broke down almost completely. Captured German gasoline stocks met minimal requirements. But many American troops had but two meals a day because of a ration shortage. VI Corps's advance north of Lyons was severely hampered by lack of gasoline and supplies. Back on the beach, ample gasoline stocks were available – but not at the front. French units were in even worse shape. Care had to be taken lest "living off the land" create starvation among the local civilian population. In 1944, the south of France was not self-sufficient in food. Some enterprising GIs took a couple of truckloads of Nazi war souvenirs over to the Third Army and traded for fresh beef and pork. "I guess I was gambling a bit but we did it," remembered Devers. "We did it because we used everything to get these supplies up there."[25]

Dragoon force was going to have to rehabilitate a lot more railroad track much sooner than anticipated. "I didn't know anything about railroading," recalled Devers, "but if you can get the right man for the boss, he knows: and he knows where to get the skills he needs to do the job."[26] That man was Brigadier General Carl R. Gray, Jr. He seemed to know the officers and men with the requisite skills, and soon had crews hard at work on the rail system. An old-time railroad man back in the states, he had assembled a very able team with the requisite experiences and skills to handle the seemingly impossible construction job. They had been together since North Africa.

Gray had met with Devers in Rome before the invasion. The two men got down on their knees with a big map of southern France, took a red pencil to it, laid out the detailed railroad right of way they would use, and then identified the construction problems that had to be solved. The entire process took only two hours. Devers pointed out a particularly difficult bridging problem over the Durance. "Clay responded, 'Don't worry about that. I have a section chief who will have his gang and we will have it up in less than 30 days.' He did just that."[27] Devers added, "The things we were taught at Leavenworth were sound."[28]

To oversee work, Gray had the 703rd Grand Railway Division offloaded onto Marseilles quays almost a month earlier than initially planned. Railroads, not combat troops, were now the capability most in demand. French railroad workers willingly answered the call to repair and operate equipment and rolling stock. Downed bridges were the major impediment. Sometimes, railroads were run up to the downed bridge, DUKWs were used to ferry supplies, which were then reloaded onto another working train on the other side. It was a manpower-intensive job that no one had time for. Many bridges were major undertakings. Due to the gorges, some spans arched 92 feet above ground level. The skills of the 40th Engineer Combat Group frequently were put to the test. American engineers had to clean up after the effects of Allied airpower. In one case, 18 miles of track had to be laid to get around facilities that were devastated by American pilots. On 25 August, U.S. tactical air commanders recommended that all further bridge bombing be halted. The B-25s were doing more harm restricting American advance than in retarding German retreat. By 14 September, lack of rolling stock rather than destroyed bridges became the larger problem. Devers impressed upon Gray that 15,000 tons a day must move north from Marseilles.[29]

Still, the logistics flow was merely a trickle, not the gusher Eisenhower had planned to support the 12th Army Group. On the first of October, when Adcock, Devers's G4 (logistics), estimated ten divisions could be supported, only 500 tons a day were reaching the front by rail. That was enough for but a single division. As was the case with Normandy and the famous Red Ball Express – the stream of trucks supplying forward units – cargo trucks were at a premium. They pounded the light French roads to pieces, diverting engineers badly needed for rail rehabilitation to road maintenance and repair. Supplies piled up in Marseilles for lack of onward transportation. Meanwhile, Eisenhower and Bradley steamed over the lack of logistical support from the south. This did not help Devers's spotty reputation with these generals. SHAEF staffers questioned the veracity of information emanating from the 6th Army Group.

By mid-September, the main line was open as far as Bourg-en-Bresse, 220 miles from the invasion beaches. By 25 September, double tracked railroad could move 3,000 tons a day to as far north as Lyons; by the 30th, the railway had reached Besançon and the French First Army railhead near the Belfort Gap. This performance was much faster than the American effort in Normandy. Still trucks hauled 220,000 tons in September versus only 63,000 moved by rail. Lack of rolling stock and coal limited operations. American-supplied engines and cars weren't offloaded until mid-October. "We had two rail lines and a pipeline coming up the Rhône," remembered Brigadier General Eugene L. Harrison. "We could've supplied this attack probably better than the attack made later by 12th Army Group. . . . Certainly the Battle of the Bulge would never have been successful. By hindsight now we know that this attack probably would have succeeded. However at this time, it presented a dangerous risk and the more conservative policy was probably adopted."[30] Devers had bought the plan.

In early July 1944, General Clark had complained that he had insufficient troops left to force the Apennine Mountains of northern Italy. Unwilling to assault the Apennines, he requested two additional divisions, reinforcing artillery and more service troops in order to revitalize the Italian campaign.[31] He didn't seem to understand that the decisive campaign was the offensive from France into Germany, and that the priority of the Mediterranean Theater was to support that drive by adding to it with an attack from southern France. Allied efforts in Italy through the summer drove the Germans back up the Italian boot instead of destroying them. Devers felt nothing good would result from arriving on the Po River. Movement of VI Corps to southern France on 15 August had left Harold Alexander with twenty-seven divisions including Mark Clark's Fifth Army. That was a significant force as the 6th Army Group in southern France had only eleven. An agreement among senior Mediterranean officers, American and British, ruled out further talk of landing in the Balkans or at the head of the Adriatic.[32] Churchill was not likely to agree, however. Clark felt victimized as the Fifth Army was being shorted both attention and resources in favor of the Côte d'Azur landing. But such considerations are always out of bounds. Wars are not fought to satisfy armies or generals. They are fought to realize national objectives, regardless of which tools or means are employed.

"Clark was very depressing," Devers noted in his 21 August diary entry. After Rome fell on 5 June 1944, no one seemed to care about Italy. According to Devers's diary, "Clark complained the British would not fight and the Americans would have to drag them along." Furthermore, "I ran into considerable anti-British feeling," noted Devers. He felt nothing of consequence could result from pushing into the Po Valley from Rome. To advance from Italy and into Germany, Allied armies would have to scale the Alps. Germans were masters at delaying Allied advance, especially in the mountains. Why not reinforce the main strategic direction via France into Germany by taking strength from a secondary effort facing a blind wall?

Instead, Devers thought that the Fifth Army should cross the lightly guarded mountain passes between Italy and France. Suitably reinforced, the 6th Army Group could be across the Rhine and into Germany in forty-five days, he believed, and that when pressed, German defenders in Italy would fight a delaying action until they reached defensive positions in the mountain passes. On 9 August, Devers had cabled Marshall, "Since last writing to you the battle in Italy has bogged down. [There has been] lack of pressure by [the Allies] at the right time. The British are not trained for mountain fighting and don't like it. Withdrawal of French corps from Fifth Army has caused them to be more cautious about flanks. Alexander has decided he cannot force the Apennines; he will advance to Florence and Bologna. The American element should be withdrawn from Italy and moved into southern France," leaving the British to contain the Germans in Italy. Devers's 25 August diary entry contained his estimate of the situation in Italy: "When pressure is put on Germans, they will withdraw through the Apennines to the Po and then to the Alps. The Germans fully realize they have neither the equipment nor men to stop as big a force as Alexander's." On 9 September, Devers wrote that the Italian campaign was "not going well." He felt Clark had made a significant tactical error by stopping at the Arno River. General Willis Crittenburger's IV Corps could have taken it. Clark's mistake was driving the Germans back instead of destroying them. Devers could not understand why the British Eighth Army was bogged down on the Gothic Line.

ELEVEN

An End to Champagne

ON 3 SEPTEMBER 1944, JACOB DEVERS AND HENRY "JUMBO" Wilson, still the leadership of MTO, traveled to Dwight Eisenhower's headquarters to go over his overarching intentions for the order he would issue the next day. Much of the meeting revolved around logistics. The northern two groups were starved for supplies. George Patton's Third Army was grounded for lack of them. Eisenhower wanted tonnage trans-shipped up the Rhône Valley to supply them, which couldn't be done until the Third and Seventh Armies welded a firm connection.

About the same time, Eisenhower met with his current subordinates to give strategic guidance. The supreme commander was under intense pressure. Both of the army groups that stemmed from Normandy were running out of supplies, and their commanders, Bernard Montgomery and Omar Bradley, were screaming for more. Both were in the process of derailing Eisenhower's carefully set plans. Despite his explicit instructions to the contrary, Montgomery was circumventing the capture of the great port of Antwerp in an effort to tackle the Rhine. Bradley evaded Eisenhower's carefully laid out verbal instruction to concentrate the First Army in a strike through the Aachen Gap, which is north of that city, and instead splattered V Corps all over the Ardennes. Dealing with Devers and his supernumerary army group was almost an afterthought.

For the fall, Eisenhower outlined the same theme he had been pushing for some time. The First and Ninth Armies in Bradley's group would make the theater main effort north of the Ardennes toward the Ruhr. This would force the Germans to commit the bulk of their forces west of the Rhine in defense of their principal industrial base. There the Allies would smash the Wehrmacht in mobile combat on the Rhine plain. Patton would make a secondary effort south of the Ardennes toward the Saar, so, in Eisenhower's words, the Allies would have "two strings in their bow" and not get stuck on a single axis of advance. Despite Montgomery's characterization, Eisenhower did not want "everyone to attack everywhere."[1] He planned no effort in the Ardennes, which was to be lightly defended. Neither would there be a third effort in the 6th Army Group area of operations along the upper Rhine, or for that matter in the 21st Army Group area through the Netherlands west of Arnhem. Devers was to support Patton's drive through Lorraine by guarding his right flank and keeping the U.S. Seventh Army advancing in parallel west of the Vosges. The French would perform a useful task by defending the upper Rhine from a German incursion while cleaning up southern and southwestern France. Eisenhower didn't really see any significant offensive effort on the part of the 6th Army Group.[2]

But Devers wanted more than a minor supporting role in the great offensive. He recalled, "They should have given me the Third Army and then directed our efforts toward the Rhine.... We were moving as fast as we could."[3] By advocating the transfer of Patton's Third Army to the 6th Army Group, Devers was angling to take over the secondary thrust from Bradley. In isolation, this made sense. Bradley could manage the theater's primary thrust north of the Ardennes, while Devers concentrated on the secondary axis of advance south.

Eisenhower and his staff had their hands full dealing with competing demands from truculent subordinates like Montgomery, Bradley, and Patton, who had mutually exclusive ideas as to what the Allies should do immediately. Montgomery was about to begin operation Market Garden, a plan to allow the British to breakthrough over the Rhine on a carpet of airborne drops. Bradley was pushing his "American Plan," which featured a Patton-led advance into Germany via the Saar, and also bungling the First Army's attack that should have gone through Aachen. The main Allied offensive in northwestern Europe had ground to a halt because the Allies simply could not keep their spearheads supplied from the logistics infrastructure in Normandy and along the English Channel. An inability to truck supplies up from the Normandy beaches was bringing to a halt the pursuit by Eisenhower's other two army groups toward the German border. General John Lee, Eisenhower's logistical commander, said they had more troops than they could supply. Off the coast of western France lay 180 loaded ships that Lee's men couldn't unload. Cherbourg could handle only two Liberties at wharf side. There was a "general lack of confidence in the ETO Communications Zone which was widely prevalent in the field commands."[4] Field commanders held a universally low opinion of Lee and his ETO Services of Supply entourage. Patton remarked, "Lee is a glib liar."[5] Referring to the fall's supply problems, Patton further wrote in his diary, "He has failed in his supply setup. I cannot understand why Eisenhower does not get rid of him."[6] Actually, George Marshall had looked to his stateside commander of services and supply to find a solution. "[Brehon] Somervell did great things around the world. Only thing he failed to do was when I sent him to Europe to handle Lee. He didn't quite do it. Lee had been his roommate at [West Point]."[7]

The primary rationale for Dragoon had been its promise of additional logistical support for the Allied offensive into Germany. Devers knew Marseilles was handling ten. Perhaps that small piece of knowledge led Jake to state, brashly, that after 20 September, Marseilles could solve the logistical problem.[8] It was a promise he would not be able to keep, but it underscored the desperate need to connect the Marseilles quays into the supply system feeding Montgomery and Bradley. While that port had additional discharge capacity, rail lines up the Rhône were not sufficiently repaired to handle additional tonnages. And, as there was no operable train service to Toulon, that port could not be used for moving supplies forward either. As in Normandy, the available truck fleet was already overtaxed.

Given Devers's confidence in his supply capacity from the southern ports, Eisenhower suggested that an additional American corps of three divisions be brought in via Marseilles. Desiring a second U.S. corps for the Seventh Army, Devers readily agreed. He wanted to begin a powerful offensive in the Seventh Army zone as soon as possible. Later, Admiral Henry Kent Hewitt, Dragoon landing force commander, provided data that demonstrated the inaccuracy of Devers's report that Marseilles could handle any number of ships. In his own defense, Devers maintained that the operating quays of Marseilles could handle ten Liberties, but qualified his earlier statement by pointing out that insufficient transport capacity up the Rhône remained a bottleneck.[9] Devers's earlier overstatement reinforced the notion held at SHAEF that he would report widely inaccurate information in order to further his own point of view. Again, his optimism and lack of supporting detail got him into serious trouble. Officers at SHAEF were already sensitized from Lee's machinations. Needless to say, this did not sit well with senior officers at SHAEF, who were already ill-disposed toward the general about to become the 6th Army Group commander.

Following his meeting with Eisenhower, Devers met with Sandy Patch. Like the supply lines from Normandy, Dragoon's truck fleet was simply overtaxed. The railroad operating up the Rhône Valley would need to be extensively repaired, and the labor-intensive shipments eliminated. Tonnage sat on the docks at Marseilles because there was no train to Lyons. When Eisenhower finally sorted out the extent of Jake's overstatement, it proved nearly professionally fatal to Devers.

During Eisenhower's theater strategy conference from 4–6 September, arrangements for the transfer and onward operations of the Dragoon force were worked out. Marshall had already cabled Eisenhower that the U.S. chiefs would not accept a British proposal to give the Italian campaign priority over Dragoon. Devers was acutely aware of the rump nature of his organization. Initially, he wanted the U.S. Fifth Army transferred from Italy and made part of his army group in southern France. This transfer had logical underpinning. Rome had fallen, and the Italians had surrendered. Moreover, an advance into Germany from Italy would mean negotiating the Alps. But Jumbo Wilson and the British objected. Churchill, always the champion of attacking through the "soft underbelly" of Europe, pressed the Americans to keep the Fifth Army and Twelfth Air Force in Italy. That finished the matter. Devers lobbied hard to get just IV Corps, part of the Fifth Army, transferred so that Patch's Seventh Army would have two corps. Fearing a total stall on the Italian front, which would also jeopardize British designs in Eastern Europe, Wilson would not even entertain the notion. Neither did Devers get anywhere when he suggested that the Third Army be transferred to his army group. Eisenhower initially declined to take troops from Bradley's 12th Army Group, which was about to make both the theater's main and secondary efforts toward the Rhine. Eisenhower looked to fresh divisions from the United States disembarking on the quays of Marseilles to bring the Seventh Army up to strength.

Eisenhower would have preferred to simply add the Seventh Army to Bradley's army group and be done with it. But there was the French Army to consider. Creating another American army group and placing the French Army within it kept that nettlesome force away from both Eisenhower and Bradley. Good enough. Eisenhower wanted to insure that the American kernel in the 6th Army Group, Lucian Truscott's VI Corps, protected Bradley's and Patton's southern flank. The advance to Dijon met this requirement. Final agreement on the transfer from MTO to ETO was not made until additional consultations between Air Force Headquarters (AFHQ) and SHAEF took place on 9 September. Little air support was allocated to the 6th Army Group – just XII Tactical Air Command (XII TAC), controlling a single fighter group of thirty-six P-47s. That was it. In the other army groups, each army was supported by a TAC composed of three or four groups made up of seventy-two aircraft each.

Eisenhower was anxious to transfer the southern invasion force from MTO into his own area of command. Eisenhower and Marshall wrestled somewhat over the date Dragoon force would be severed from the Mediterranean Theater and organized as the 6th Army Group under SHAEF control. Several times Eisenhower cabled Marshall requesting it be cut over only to be uncharacteristically put off by Marshall. As the Southern Group passed Dijon and closed the gap between ETO and MTO forces, that time had come. As supreme commander, Mediterranean, Wilson focused on the fight up the Italian boot and other events planned for or transpiring in the eastern Mediterranean. During his tenure as deputy Allied theater commander and commander of U.S. forces, Mediterranean, Devers had championed the efforts of Marshall and the American chiefs and vigorously pursued their implementation.[10] He interfaced with various high commands and tended to the logistical and political dimensions of the operation, which due to a major Free French presence, loomed large. He left most tactical matters to the very able leadership of Patch and Truscott. From their perspective, advancing up the Rhône Valley, continuing through the Belfort Gap to Strasbourg, and then

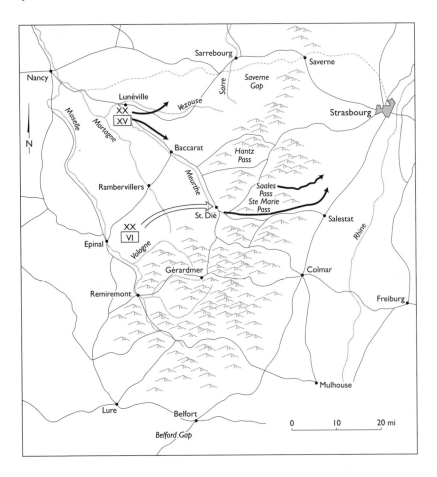

11.1. To Dijon and Linkup

over the Rhine somewhere downstream from the Black Forest, was the logical progression of the campaign. Wilson decided that an advance on the Belfort Gap and to Strasbourg would best satisfy this requirement (map 11.1).[11]

Just before the cut over to ETO, it appeared as if the Germans might be massing for a counterstrike against the Seventh Army. In his 12 September diary entry, Devers wrote, "Pleased that Patch is closing in tight, collecting disparate individual advances strung out over many miles of front." Jean de Lattre wanted to prepare for a major effort to liber-

ate Alsace by advancing through the Belfort Gap. Devers had already
decided that no American forces would be involved in such a maneuver.
He expected that a fight for Belfort Gap would last for only a few days.
Devers knew the constraint would be transporting supplies to his own
spearheads, and fretted that his truck fleet was extended to the utmost.
Sensing the constraints, de Lattre commented, "If I wished to continue
my offensive attitude, I would have to be content with a more modest
maneuver. . . . It was too late in the season to secure rapid access to Alsace through the Vosges."[12] Knowing the Vosges in winter, he worried
lest U.S. VI Corps become stranded in the mountains and vulnerable to
encirclement.

The granite massif known as the Vosges Mountains split the Lorraine gateway from the Belfort Gap and lowlands along the west bank
of the Rhine. The mountains run from southwest to northeast and are
bisected by the Saverne Gap, which connects the Lorraine to the Rhine
Valley just north of Strasbourg. To the southwest, they are called the
High Vosges. Peaks rise to 4,500 feet. The Low Vosges, which sound
easier to cross, are actually far more dissected, irregular, and difficult to
traverse. They present a far more challenging barrier to military movement than the High Vosges. Throughout history, these mountains have
been viewed as an impenetrable refuge. Ruins of pre-Christian redoubts
remain. No army in modern times had ever forced a crossing.

The Vosges road network in 1944 was sparse – barely adequate for
division-sized operations. Most roads followed valley floors, which were
flanked by forested, sharply rising mountains. The road surface quickly
broke up under the weight of even light vehicles. Communications were
so sparse that MPs released carrier pigeons from traffic control points
to division lofts to update weather, road, and traffic conditions.[13] Commanders on both sides described fighting in the close terrain of the
Vosges as being similar to jungle warfare.[14]

The Meurthe River was another major military obstacle. The
Meurthe originates in the mountains, flows past Saint-Dié and Luneville and finally empties into the Rhine-Marne Canal, which, in turn,
runs into the Moselle, forming a barrier across the axis that leads into
Lorraine. High ground to the north of the stream gave the Germans an
added advantage against an American attack that would have to be made

uphill. The Rhine-Marne Canal, which connects the Moselle and the Rhine, was a second water barrier to an advance via southern Lorraine. The canal runs from the vicinity of Nancy, past Sarrebourg, and then east through the Saverne Gap to the Rhine.

As Dragoon forces moved north through the Rhône Valley, it was Patch who created the initial operational design for movement toward Dijon. Above Dijon, the Allies faced a choice: advance west or east of the Vosges. On the eastern side lay the Belfort Gap, also called the Gate of Burgundy. It was level ground about 15 miles wide, running from the eastern foothills of the Vosges to the Rhine River. At first glance it appears to lead to a rapid crossing of the Rhine. The rough terrain of the Black Forest, however, extends for some distance on the far bank. The transportation network there was poor and led to nowhere of military importance to the Allies. Advancing up the western edge of the Vosges would place the Seventh Army in southern Lorraine on the right flank of the Third Army's major attack. To the north, a second opening in the mountains, the Saverne Gap, leads to Strasbourg, the capital of Alsace. Strasbourg is on the Rhine, but an army still would need to travel another 30 miles north, down the Rhine, before a good crossing site leads into a sensible avenue of approach into the German interior.

On 3 September, Patch had approved Truscott's plan to thrust VI Corps into the Belfort Gap. He stated, "The Belfort Gap was the Gateway to Germany," a view shared by neither Eisenhower, Devers, nor any of their principal staff.[15] Not having strong guidance for the advance above Dijon, Patch had been swayed by Truscott's arguments. Truck-mounted infantry from the 3rd Infantry Division (1D) motored up the road northeast to Besançon against little opposition. This rapid movement prevented the Germans from creating a defensive line along the Doubs River, but a major fight broke out over the old Vauban-era fortresses that guarded Besançon. All three regiments of 31D assembled in a formal attack to take the citadel from the Germans on the 7th. The 361D captured 175,000 gallons of lower-grade German gasoline that nevertheless was a godsend to VI Corps quartermasters who otherwise had little fuel to distribute. Patch thought there wasn't much left in front of him and was more restrained by supply shortages than German resistance.[16] To avoid being little more than an eastern flank guard for Patch, de Lattre pushed Antoine Béthouart's I Corps up from Grenoble and headed toward Belfort via a narrow strip between the Dobbs River and the Swiss border.

When he heard about Truscott's move toward the Belfort Gap, Eisenhower was irritated. Initially he had approved of the Seventh Army's striking for Belfort. Now, the theater plan envisioned that an attack from northern France toward the Ruhr, supported by supplies landing at Antwerp (and perhaps Rotterdam), would be the main effort. The Third Army would make the secondary effort from Lorraine toward the Saar. SHAEF planning did not envision anything of significance occurring via the Belfort Gap or along the upper Rhine itself. The Seventh Army was to advance *west* of the Vosges in support of the Third Army effort.[17] From the perspective of theater strategy and the need to concentrate to the north, staying out of the ground east of the Vosges made sense. As far as SHAEF was concerned, VI Corps was being committed to the wrong side of the Vosges.

On 11 September, the dashing French 2nd Armored Division (AD), a part of Patton's Third Army, linked up with the French 1AD near Dijon. French tanks entered the city against almost no opposition and continued another 40 miles to Langres. Now a continuous front of Allied troops stretched across France. Having won the race to Belfort, the 11th Panzer Division (PzD) felt confident enough to lash back southward and strike out at French I Corps's advance toward that city, causing that unit to stall in its tracks. But remnants of the German First Army and odd lots of German service troops in southern France felt considerably less sanguine. With the meeting between the Normandy and the Côte d'Azur invasion forces, the French moved quickly to cut off the last escape routes between southern France and Germany. A number of sharp firefights involving both the Free French and Maquis against German remnants broke out near Lyons and Dijon. With the escape route finally sealed, tens of thousands of German soldiers were cut off. Sixteen thousand surrendered en masse to 831D guarding Patton's formerly exposed flank.

Effective on 15 September, the 6th Army Group became operational at its headquarters at the Palais de Foire in Lyons. Devers told his chief of staff, Major David G. Barr, "I want this staff to be small, Dave, I mean small. I want it to carry out policy" and not become the day-to-day operators for which subordinate commanders are paid. "If you let the HQ get big, it won't work," Devers recalled. "We had the smallest staff, I think, that has ever done a job like that. We were absolutely organized on Leavenworth [site of the Army Command and General Staff College] lines. The things we had been taught were sound and they are sound today. What they had north of us [i.e., in the 12th Army Group headquarters], I think was most unsound and caused most of their trouble."[18] Radios were installed in the back of 6-ton tractor-trailers to keep the headquarters small, efficient, and mobile. Beetle Smith observed, "The staff of a high headquarters is always working several moves in advance."[19]

As the staff repositioned from St. Tropez, they faced many changes. Finally Devers had undisputed command authority over a specific organized entity. The 6th Army Group became a part of Eisenhower's overall command. Devers no longer reported to Wilson as deputy and no longer commanded NATOUSA and the logistics it controlled. Initially, Devers kept the French forces under Patch, but in only a few days, this proved unworkable. De Lattre's French First Army became operational under the command of the 6th Army Group. On 19 September, both the Seventh and French First Armies began reporting directly to Devers. On 22 September, Devers traveled to Eisenhower's headquarters in Granville to ask for XV Corps. The formal request followed on the 26th.

Unlike Bradley, who often got enmeshed in tactical details, especially of the First Army, or Montgomery, who expended great energy trying to influence decisions at theater-strategic level, Devers chose to run the 6th Army Group at the operational level. He set broad objectives for his armies and sometimes his corps, but he left tactics to army and corps commanders. Occasionally, Jake's directions could be a little vague. He gave Barr and his G3 (operations officer), Reuben Jenkins, enough authority to clarify his orders, so that the subordinate field armies clearly understood them, and to make corrections on the spot.[20] To handle details with the French, Devers trusted Lieutenant Colonel Henry Cabot Lodge, whose unusual background and relationship with the French belied his comparatively junior length of service. De Lattre and Lodge understood each other. Devers's manner of handling the 6th Army Group was far more consistent with army doctrine, which sought to keep army groups out of the administrative loop, than were the workings of the 12th Army Group or Clark's 15th Army Group in Italy.

The first Liberty ships to arrive at Marseilles were required to dock alongside the wharfs. Ten days later, in late September, quays that could directly offload sixteen ships were in service. An additional twenty-three ships could be offloaded by the ever-present DUKWs in the harbor. The port's potential was beginning to be realized. The Army Group G4 (supply officer) estimated that by 1 October, he could support ten divisions as far north as Dijon. That meant that he could support the Sixth Army Group reinforced by XV Corps but that he really didn't have much more to give Bradley or Patton farther north. Advances by the 6th Army Group came none too soon, as lack of supply was grounding a good part of both Montgomery's 21st Army Group up north and Bradley's 12th Army Group in the center. Bradley's southernmost army, Patton's Third, which shared a boundary with the Seventh Army, was particularly parched.

By the second week in September, Germans up and down the breadth of Europe had begun to recover their balance. Montgomery's army group halted on the outskirts of Antwerp. A little later, the First Army stalled in the Stolberg corridor just south of Aachen. Americans in the Ardennes had insufficient troops forward to consolidate their gains. Patton's Third Army wasn't able to move beyond the Moselle. The Fifth Panzer Army managed a counterattack against Patton's southern flank. As VI Corps turned west, German resistance both in the Belfort Gap and the high Vosges noticeably stiffened. Pursuing the disorganized enemy both up the Rhône Valley and across northern France and into the Low Countries was coming to an end. Inability to move supplies to the front brought Allied attacks in all sectors to an extended pause or, in military terms, to culmination, the end of the ability to continue to advance against enemy resistance.

In addition to Truscott, de Lattre also wanted to enter the Belfort Gap. But his strategic objective was quite different. The "Lost Province" of Alsace lay behind the gap. The strip of land that lay between Germany and France, the middle third of what had been Gaul, which Charlemagne had set aside for his third son at the dawn of the Middle Ages, had always been a major bone of contention between the two continental powers.

When Germany had been victorious in 1940, it absorbed Alsace, a French province since the end of World War I, back into the greater Reich. Needless to say, the French were more than sensitive about its liberation. This national objective, not the Allied theater strategic plan to defeat the Germans, was at the forefront for the French.

De Gaulle had a second worry. In its current two-part configuration, the French Army was little more than an auxiliary to either flank of the victorious Americans in southern France. Like John Pershing in World War I, de Gaulle wanted a unified French Army to become a featured entity in the recovery of French honor. Again the French worried that they would be marginalized and even shut out of the liberation of their own country. De Lattre pressured Béthouart: "It is important to hurry even more. . . . Push yourself urgently into the Gap . . . make arrangements with the U.S. 6th Army Group so that they shall not obstruct you."[21] Patch was not as determined as Truscott to enter the Belfort Gap. To meet French national objectives, de Lattre suggested that a unified French First Army enter the gap and that Truscott's VI Corps, hence the U.S. Seventh Army, move up the western face of the Vosges and then cross the mountains to enter Strasbourg. Patch understood and was sympathetic to French political sensitivities. On 3 September, he approved de Lattre's proposal. De Lattre commented, "The French Army finally acquired its tactical autonomy."[22]

Major General Friedrich von Mellenthin, chief of staff (1A) of German Army Group G, recalled that the Germans anticipated the next Allied blow would strike in the Lorraine gateway, west of the Vosges. "We had also to consider the Belfort gap . . . but we had no doubt that the main thrust would be in Lorraine, for an attack on Alsace was bound to come to a standstill on the banks of the Rhine."[23] Hitler had belatedly ordered Army Group G to leave southern France, take up defensive positions in the Vosges, and re-establish a sold link with Army Group B to the north.

The Dragoon force had sped north faster than anyone expected.[24] What, then, should be the axis of advance for the 6th Army Group north of Lyons? The French would assemble and sort out their army in front of the Belfort Gap. While not yet having command of the Dragoon force (it was still part of Wilson's MTO), Eisenhower indicated he would prefer that the Seventh Army move up the west side of the Vosges, adding its support to the Third Army's secondary campaign in Lorraine to breach the Siegfried line and threaten the industrial Saar. Both Wilson and Devers agreed.[25] But that plan did not square with Truscott, who became very focused on the Belfort Gap. With his field of vision restricted to the operating area of VI Corps, it appeared to him that the gap, with its easy access to the Rhine, was the best avenue of approach into Germany. The alternative was to march up parallel to but west of the Vosges Mountains, which Truscott viewed as a lengthy and forbidding barrier to gaining a Rhine crossing. Truscott knew little about SHAEF's grand design for the fall of 1944. At Patch's instruction, Truscott had moved around Lyons by the right flank, precipitating a tough fight at Meximieux. During the night of 2–3 September, as 11PzD covered the last Germans retreating into Belfort, Truscott sensed the German Nineteenth Army coming apart. Truscott wanted to kill Germans.

Frustrated by the less than complete success at the Gate of Montélimar on the Rhône, Truscott now wanted to again pin the Germans against a topographical barrier – this time the Vosges. Patch's initial instruction was to move almost due north up the Saone River Valley, which led to the western face of the Vosges. The Nineteenth Army, however, was retiring northeast toward Belfort. Truscott wanted to pursue what was left of it along an axis Lons-le-Saunier to Belfort, and told Patch that a move north up the west side of the Vosges wouldn't intercept the Germans struggling to get home. Chasing the Nineteenth Army would place VI Corps directly astride the gap and low ground between the Vosges and the west bank of the Rhine. Wilson personally thought Truscott had a good idea. Patch modified VI Corps orders to continue the pursuit. To keep the Germans from escaping via another major route through the High Vosges, Truscott ordered a corps reconnaissance squadron to speed up and set a roadblock at Bourg-en-Bresse. American mechanized cavalry outraced tanks from 11PzD to the town. Subsequently, a freewheeling fight ignited between panzers and armored cars. Both sides were badly bloodied before the Ghost Division continued its retreat, leaving the American roadblock intact.

Patch ordered the pair of French divisions that had advanced on the west bank of the Rhône to support Truscott's left flank by advancing from Dijon due north up the Saone Valley. While militarily useful, this

movement delayed reunion of what became the French II Corps within
the French First Army. Later the French caught up with 30th SS Division,
made up principally of Eastern Europeans with only a small German
cadre. The Ukrainians mutinied, killed their German officers, and joined
the Forces Françaises de l'Intérieur (FFI). Later, they wound up taking a
town from ethnic Russian "volunteers" in German uniforms.

Bunching up Truscott's VI Corps, and thereby the Seventh Army,
in front of Belfort was inconsistent with Eisenhower's plan, and Devers
thought of adding divisions to the Seventh Army. VI Corps had to return
to its original assignment west of the Vosges. Devers felt that the Seventh
and Third Armies had to be welded together to form a single large hammer to smash across the Rhine.

After sorting out VI Corps, the next order of business was to gain
control of Patton's southernmost unit, XV Corps. That meant that VI
Corps had to be maneuvered up close to XV Corps, which is exactly
what Eisenhower wanted. But at Truscott's behest, Patch had just issued
orders allowing Truscott to chase the Germans to Belfort. Acting on
Eisenhower's guidance, Devers countermanded Patch and redirected
VI Corps to the western face of the mountains. The ease with which
Devers changed Patch's field order says a lot about the professionalism
and good relations between the generals. In his reminiscences, Devers
repeatedly remarked that they got things done without a lot of formal
paper. This realignment was one of them. But Truscott was steamed. If
VI Corps was to move west, he wanted to get right to it, starting with
moving 45ID from his right flank to his left. But Devers had concluded
that the French could not maneuver this quickly, so he held Truscott in
place for several more days. A frustrated Truscott became even more
irritated but faithfully complied with orders.

From a corps commander's tactical perspective, what Truscott was
advocating was the right thing to do, but it was the job of Devers to insure the efforts of his subordinates were consistent with Eisenhower's
strategy. Given the lack of attention by SHAEF staff to 6th Army Group
dispositions, concentrating instead on seemingly more urgent problems,
Devers's corrections were just what an army group commander should
do. Neither the record nor the postwar interviews formally reveal Devers's motivations. They do underscore that he did fully endorse Eisen-

hower's Clausewitzian effort to destroy the Nazi's center of gravity, the Wehrmacht, in the field, as far away from the Fatherland as possible. Montgomery seemed to think a dash to Berlin would smite the evil Nazi monster. The airmen thought they could win by crushing German industry from the air. Devers unquestionably took up Eisenhower's mantra. This is exactly what General Marshall had ordered.

Miffed, Truscott took his argument one step farther. If VI Corps wasn't committed to the Belfort Gap, he would recommend that his corps be reinserted into the Italian Campaign, possibly by landing it farther north near Genoa. In the meantime, he saluted the chain of command, pushed 45ID past Besançon, and launched 31D into an assault on the ancient fortress that defended the city. Artillery pounded German vehicles fleeing the area. Patch quietly handled Truscott and got him to move to the west side of the mountains as Devers had ordered. Devers recalled, "It wasn't hard to settle because Sandy was agreeable, but it was one of those things that threatened to cause us a lot of trouble."[26] Again, Truscott saluted and complied. As it was, VI Corps had outrun the Seventh Army's supply lines. What Eisenhower wanted was a gusher of supplies flowing up the Rhône from Marseilles and feeding the parched 12th Army Group. Other than that, the order of the day was to hold the line in the south as the war would be decided in the north.

French 11D and 1AD had been moving up the west bank of the Rhône. On 1 September, de Lattre had formally recognized this group as French I Corps under General Joseph de Monsabert. They were in the process of crossing the Rhône to join up with the bulk of Free French forces to the east. Divisions already in the east were combined under General Béthouart and designated French II Corps. Béthouart had a long history of resisting the Germans that was well known to the Americans. In 1940, he had soldiered with the British-French expedition to Narvik in northern Norway. When Americans came ashore at Casablanca in November 1942, Béthouart, who commanded most of the French forces in Morocco, worked with the Americans and led a revolt a few days before the invasion against the German occupiers. When initial efforts failed, he was briefly jailed.

De Lattre also needed time to rearrange the First French Army. Units were still streaming up from the huge effort to capture and pacify the ports of Marseilles and Toulon. The French 5AD was still unloading on the quays. But there were much larger issues than logistics, issues that reached down into the soul of the French Army. Many Frenchmen from the Métropole (mainland France) did not identify with the French First Army. As an embodiment of France, it had two strikes against it. First, it grew from colonial North African roots. Second, de Lattre and his men, as occupiers of North Africa, stemmed from Vichy France. In the eyes of many a Frenchman, this affected the legitimacy of French officers, especially the senior ones. Many colonial African troops had fought for the tricolor for two or more years. They were tired of African blood being spilled while European residents stood around and watched. The obvious source of new replacements was the many youth of the FFI, the Maquis. But the French First Army was a traditional military organization manned by troops inured with discipline and officered by men with many years of military training and experience. The FFI was a loose organization with no sense of discipline led by charismatic young leaders with little field experience and almost no formal training. At first, de Lattre stated that the FFI and the French Army would not be amalgamated, implying that the Maquis did not meet a high enough professional standard. Many Frenchmen felt that the French First Army retained too much of a fascist influence left over from Vichy, and that the army should be merged into the Maquis, which contained the true values of France.

Many commanders knew of the resentment brewing within the colonial ranks and feared that many Africans would not be able to fight in the coming winter cold in the mountains. So began the policy of *le blanchissement,* literally the whitening of the French Army. The FFI was full of communists and other opponents of de Gaulle and the Committee of National Liberation. The First Army might accept company-level officers, the lieutenants and captains, who had come up among the Maquis. But higher-level organizations, battalions and regiments, were ill-trained for conventional warfare, woefully deficient in equipment and organization, and led by commanders without formal military experience. Often those leaders were ten years junior to their army counterparts. And from where were the uniforms and personal equipment for these new recruits supposed to come? The truculent Americans, already exasperated with the lack of service troops in the French organization and acutely aware of equipment shortfalls among their own troops, were not very sympathetic. Meanwhile, de Gaulle was pressing de Lattre for more combat regiments. The French First Army commander faced an enormously complex set of organizational problems.

General Devers was the American responsible for getting the French Army the best resources it could support and maintain without totally alienating an American establishment that was otherwise insensitive to problems of the French. After all, wasn't there a "war to be won"? A lesser leader would have thrown his hands in the air and said the problems were intractable. Jake combined his eternal optimism, his practical "can-do" approach, and his managerial skills to solve the problems one by one. Some issues required simple common sense and just a little bit of practical experience. No uniforms and no way to manufacture new ones in time? The Germans left a lot behind. Take their uniforms and dye them to look French. Similarly, root among the pile of discarded equipment to find what can be reissued. No modern rifles? Use what was left over from North Africa. Improvise.

When French I and II Corps were formally realigned in First French Army to the east of U.S. Seventh Army, they contained:

FRENCH I CORPS	FRENCH II CORPS
2nd Infantry Division	1st Infantry Division
4th Motorized Infantry Division	3rd Algerian Division
	9th Colonial Division
5th Armored Division	1st Armored Division

plus many smaller units.[27]

De Lattre was less interested in crossing the Rhine River than in freeing Alsace from German bondage. The question was timing. Would the French be ready to kick off in conjunction with the Seventh Army? The French Army still had many serious shortcomings, and the Germans knew it.[28] The French First Army's plan opened with a limited attack by French II Corps into the High Vosges. While it might help VI Corps a little, this maneuver was primarily a feint. Personally, de Lattre thought this effort would detract from his main operation, the recovery of Alsace, and not help VI Corps very much. The First French Army's main effort would be made by French I Corps a few days later. It would pierce the Belfort Gap and retake southern Alsace. The French attack would have to crack the German defensive line that ran through Belfort. Then the French would attack parallel to the Rhône-Rhine Canal, which flowed northeast toward Mulhouse before connecting with the Rhine. From Mulhouse, two roads led north to Colmar and Strasbourg.

While supplies were coming in over the docks at Marseilles, the railroads did not yet have the capacity to sustain an army group far to the north. More railway cars and locomotives in useable condition were found in the south of France than planners initially estimated. Still, it would take until 1 October before Thomas Larkin could support ten divisions north of Dijon. VI Corps needed time to move over to the western side of the Vosges on soggy roads broken up by the heavy military traffic.

After the Seventh and Third Armies joined up near Dijon, there was little operational purpose for the 6th Army Group, if it wasn't going to control the secondary effort, the attack into the Saar and southern Germany. Its existence rested on two factors, one political and one administrative. As Eisenhower stated in a letter to Bradley, the best way to integrate the French was to keep them within an American army group.[29] Eisenhower had more than his fill of trying to control the French. They had been trouble for him ever since North Africa in 1942. With them firmly ensconced in the 6th Army Group, he did not have to deal with French field forces directly. Second, administrative control of the 6th Army Group did not transition to the European Theater of Operations until 20 November.[30] Until then, Devers drew supplies from the Mediterranean. Much excess stock existed in the depots in North Africa. Eisenhower would have been foolish not to take advantage of this as much as possible.

SHAEF had no strategic objective to assign to the 6th Army Group, so Eisenhower gave Devers an "independent status."[31] The official 14 September 1944 order read: "[Item] 3. The mission of Sixth Army Group is: to destroy the enemy in zone west of the Rhine, secure crossings over the Rhine and breach the Siegfried Line."[32] It is important to note the position in which the order to cross the Rhine appears. This was repeated in all SHAEF general orders for the 6th Army Group through November.

Devers was assigned the usual three missions: destroy German formations in this sector, breach the West Wall, and cross the Rhine. Despite
Eisenhower's intent, those instructions can be interpreted as having the
6th Army Group form a third effort for the theater. Such an interpretation was to have damaging repercussions.

Eisenhower's decisions about the 6th Army Group demonstrate a decided lack of focus. As the eminent historian Forrest Pogue observed, "It
seemed 6th Army Group was sort of off here on the side."[33] Eisenhower
felt he was handicapped by having to keep Devers, whom he distrusted,
as a subordinate. "I told him [Forrest Pogue] I felt the same way about
Devers."[34] But he was less than forthright with Marshall about his opinion of Devers. Eisenhower didn't want much to do with the commander
of his 6th Army Group. While Beetle Smith maintained cordial relations
on the surface, he too had little use for Devers. To James Robb, deputy
chief of staff, Smith stated, "We do not have much confidence in our
friend Jakey."[35] Major General Harold "Pinky" Bull, SHAEF operations
officer, was one of Smith's closest subordinates. Late in the fall, Devers
pulled Bull aside and tried to convince him that the 6th Army Group
was a loyal team member that rarely asked for additional resources.[36]
Apparently, the pleas of the 6th Army Group commander elicited no
empathetic response anywhere within SHAEF. Eisenhower did order
Devers to send him a short daily morning "personal statement of situation in your group including air."[37] By contrast, the official historian
stated, "Eisenhower's low assessment of Devers is highly questionable.
Certainly the forces under 6th Army Group had chalked up an impressive record of military successes during the Alsace Campaign and the
reduction of Colmar. His record prior to November had been equally
impressive."[38] Devers felt that SHAEF had become too fixated on European topography at the north end of ETO. He favored a more flexible
approach.[39] Devers would be studiously ignored by Eisenhower.[40] There
was "none of the warmth of the Supreme Commander's dealings with his
friends."[41] His staff noticed the strained relationship.

Devers understood Eisenhower's two-pronged strategy. As the official history states, "A major effort in the south [i.e., the 6th Army Group
area] seemed pointless. . . . Devers's command must have seemed in-

significant despite its imposing army group designation."[42] Early on, however, Eisenhower stated that the 6th Army Group was logistically supporting "the desired secondary effort while we are going after the main business of the Ruhr."[43] Still, the group seemed up against a dead end. Eisenhower promised Bradley that the Seventh Army would always be maneuvered to support the 12th Army Group. SHAEF planners had not considered a major thrust toward Germany emanating from the Rhône Valley. Instead, the landings in the south were to open the port of Marseilles to solve theater logistical problems. Eisenhower's constant repetition at the beginning of virtually every field order that destruction of the German Army was the principal objective had a decided influence on Devers. He repeated it to his 6th Army Group subordinates: it was "the destruction of the enemy itself that counts." As Devers stated, "We must take our minds off terrain."[44]

What was the 6th Army Group supposed to do? Given September's theater strategy, Eisenhower's obvious intent was to move the Seventh Army up the northwestward side of the Vosges on Patton's flank. A Baccarat-Sarrebourg-Saarbrucken axis would have accomplished this. While the French First Army was assembling, it could hold defensive positions along the High Vosges and the Belfort Gap. Devers had but six divisions forward: three in Truscott's VI Corps and three that de Lattre had managed to move up from the fighting around the ports. Both commanders wanted to move toward the Belfort Gap. With the movement of 11PzD to defend Belfort, this avenue of approach looked much tougher. The better avenue was via the Saverne Gap, but that was in Patton's zone.

Within the 6th Army Group's area of responsibility, both Devers and Patch continued to study a more northern route through the Vosges. Devers decided to move VI Corps up into the Vosges via Saint-Dié and the Meurthe River Valley that led into the Vosges. This led northeast toward the Saverne Gap and into the area of XV Corps, currently under Patton but on which Devers had his eye to complete the Seventh Army. Movement on this axis was also consistent with Eisenhower's intent as it protected the 12th Army Group's (and therefore the Third Army's) southern flank. Both French corps were ordered to assemble on the Seventh Army's right (southern flank), thus formally creating the French

First Army with its own zone of advance under de Lattre, which in turn calmed de Gaulle. As the French gained offensive capability, a limited attack through the Belfort Gap might add to German Field Marshal Gerd von Rundstedt's headaches. Any progress through Belfort would make German positions in the High Vosges untenable, sitting on cold mountain tops between two Allied thrusts. As these German formations possessed little offensive capability, they would be far more threatened than a threat. Devers thought a fight for the Belfort Gap should last for only a few days. The larger problem was transporting supply, as the truck fleet continued to groan from overuse.

The 22 September theater strategy conference held at Shell Burst, Eisenhower's forward headquarters, concentrated on events north of the Ardennes. Operation Market Garden, Montgomery's famous "Bridge Too Far" attack toward the Arnhem Bridge across the Rhine, was in progress but going badly. Bradley's main effort was completely stalled around Aachen. Patton's secondary effort had been curtailed due to lack of supplies and was stuck in front of Metz on the Moselle. Still, SHAEF gave Devers's problems and opportunities short shrift. Patton's southernmost corps, Major General Wade Hampton "Ham" Haislip's XV, was nowhere near as heavily engaged as XX Corps at Metz and XII Corps at Nancy. Devers reiterated his need for a second U.S. corps and specified XV Corps by name. Transferring XV Corps to Devers, along with the responsibility of covering Patton's right flank, seemed to SHAEF planners to be an expedient way to shift Haislip's logistical requirements to Marseilles and away from the overloaded system emanating from Normandy, which barely supported forces in northwest Europe. They liked the switch because responsibility for covering much of the ground in Patton's southern sector went along with the troops. This, however, also opened the Saverne Gap for use by the 6th Army Group, which gave access to the Rhine just below Strasbourg. Devers and his staff seized upon this opportunity and formulated plans to advance through the gap toward the Alsatian capitol. On the Rhine's far bank, the Black Forest begins to peter out just north of that city. The conference specifically authorized Devers's attack toward Saverne. On 21 September, Devers recorded in his diary, "Had a very satisfactory conference with General

Eisenhower. The 6th Army Group is to be reinforced by 2–4 divisions. The 6th Army Group is to drive across the Rhine and through the Vosges to hold as many troops as possible in the south of Germany."

Devers felt, "with the team we have here now I feel sure we will be able to push across the Rhine in a reasonable time and in so doing to destroy much of the German Army, which after all is our objective."[45] Marshall and Eisenhower fully agreed that, in order to defeat Hitler, the combat power of the Wehrmacht had to be destroyed in the field rather than just pushing it back into Germany. In an unrelated diary entry, Devers implicitly recognized this fact. After the conference, the 6th Army Group's orders were adjusted slightly: "[The 6th Army Group] to drive across the Rhine and through the Vosges to hold as many troops as possible in the south of Germany." With these communications, Devers felt he had a green light to go to Strasbourg and beyond. Apparently, that is not what Eisenhower intended.

He saw Devers's planned advance into the Vosges and toward Strasbourg as consistent with defending the right flank of Patton's attack in Lorraine.[46] Haislip's XV Corps was fleshed out with a third division from those coming east from Brittany. An additional three divisions arriving from the United States would land in Marseilles and be added to Devers's army group. Eisenhower stated flatly that these would be the last unit reinforcements Devers should expect. Patton would continue directly toward the Saar with XX and XII Corps, which had been conducting his main attack in any event. The Third Army's zone would be narrowed by moving the boundary northward to just south of Nancy. Thus, the 6th Army Group received additional responsibility in Lorraine commensurate with a reinforced XV Corps. On 29 September, Eisenhower issued the transfer order. Devers was pleased. This gave him both the troops (XV Corps) and enough operational freedom to conduct his attack through the Saverne Gap with sufficient maneuvering room to take Strasbourg.

Although a little portly and not endowed with the figure of a fighter, Haislip had Patch's great respect as a corps commander.[47] But Haislip's troops were as exhausted as Truscott's. XV Corps was in dire need of equipment, maintenance, and supplies. Patton wanted to retain XV Corps's heavy artillery. As Devers saw no immediate need, and never particularly liked heavy artillery, those battalions were returned to the 12th Army Group. But insufficient service troops were transferred to support XV Corps. Commanders losing combat units tended to resist giving up the associated supply and maintenance units supporting a division. There simply weren't enough to go around. Already stretched by the need to provide for the undersupported French First Army, Devers's resources were being stretched again. French 2AD vehicles were badly in need of repair. Manpower and equipment shortages in 79ID resulting from more than one hundred days in continuous combat were severe. Devers estimated they would need two weeks to recover their strength.[48] These were the two divisions of XV Corps at the time of transfer. While the Seventh Army immediately provided some logistical support, it would be late October before the bulk of the deficiencies were made good.

Despite his very skillful handling of the German withdrawal from southern France, Hitler had lost all faith in Johannes Blaskowitz. On 21 September, General der Panzer Truppen (Lieutenant General) Hermann Balck, a tough commander who had led the Fourth Panzer Army on the eastern front, took charge of German Army Group G. Now that they had reached the Vosges and the Belfort Gap, the Germans stopped running. The wall of mountains and the gap would be turned into a solid defensive line that would give the Allies stubborn resistance at least until spring. The Champagne Campaign was over.

TWELVE

Into the Cold Vosges

THE 6TH ARMY GROUP COMMANDER WAS DISAPPOINTED THAT Dwight Eisenhower did not give his formation a larger role in the upcoming late September offensive.[1] Jacob Devers was anxious to stage a powerful offensive as soon as possible.[2] He applied creative thought to the mission assigned to him. Devers recognized the sterility of attacking through Belfort. Hermann Balck and his staff had come to the same conclusion. Devers also recognized that he had a much better shot at obtaining another corps, or even all of the Third Army, if he initially moved the Seventh Army up the west side of the Vosges. While he did not express it openly, Devers wanted to lead the theater's secondary attack while Omar Bradley concentrated on the theater's primary attack north of the Ardennes.

Devers produced a nonconventional campaign plan. Instead of sending his main effort into the Belfort Gap, he planned movement up the west side of the Vosges to the Saverne Gap. There he would create a strong single envelopment with the Seventh Army through the Saverne Gap to Strasbourg. Moving the Seventh Army this way also kept it close to George Patton. This facilitated a change in mission that could send it through the Lorraine Gateway at the southern rim of the Saar. The French First Army, in turn, would threaten the Belfort Gap. Germans remaining on the west bank of the upper Rhine would be pocketed by these two forces. Meanwhile, the primary mission of the First French Army was actually to regenerate itself. As an army-level formation, this unit had little offensive capability until this task was complete. Right from the beginning, the 6th Army Group Letter of Instruction No. 1

laid out the objectives that would govern movement until the 24th of November. Paragraph 2a directs the Seventh Army to seize Lunéville and Strasbourg, and then cross the Rhine. No Allied source can accuse Devers of concealing the direction of his attack from SHAEF.[3] The letter of instruction tasked the First French Army with attacking from Belfort through Mulhouse to Colmar. Devers wanted to catch as much of the Nineteenth Army as possible. A brilliant French attack up along the flat land near the river might slam against the Seventh Army in Strasbourg like a hammer against an anvil. But the Seventh Army was looking north and east of the Rhine, not south toward the French First Army. Devers's diary entry for 8 October 1944 reveals an interesting facet of his state of mind: "Also I learned that I will have to give more definite instructions to the two armies in order that their attacks bring the greatest good to the common cause. At the moment there seems to be some misunderstanding, which I will straighten out."

At first glance, the plan appears to be a double envelopment of the German Nineteenth west of the Rhine, a plan consistent with Eisenhower's first objective. But the 6th Army Group was not that strong. Effectively, the Seventh Army contained three American divisions of VI Corps, and Jean de Lattre had the equivalent of about three poorly equipped French infantry divisions assembling before Belfort. Once refitted, XV Corps would add two divisions, and new arrivals landing via Marseilles would bring Sandy Patch's army to a total of eight, but not until November. Similarly, the French First Army would increase to include two armored and five infantry divisions. Actually, Devers's plan envisioned creating a single penetration executed by the Seventh Army from Saint-Dié toward Strasbourg. At SHAEF, that appears to be how it was viewed. But Devers expected more. As XV Corps and the new divisions increased strength, an assault on the Rhine could become possible, and both the 6th Army Group and Seventh Army began looking along the Rhine downstream from Strasbourg (i.e., north) for a suitable crossing site. But this plan contravened the instruction Patch had just given. Nevertheless, the Seventh Army commander saw the logic and readily agreed. Little is said of the change in plans, which attests to the good, informal relationship between Patch and Devers. Wasn't a threatened Rhine crossing that either could envelop the defenders of

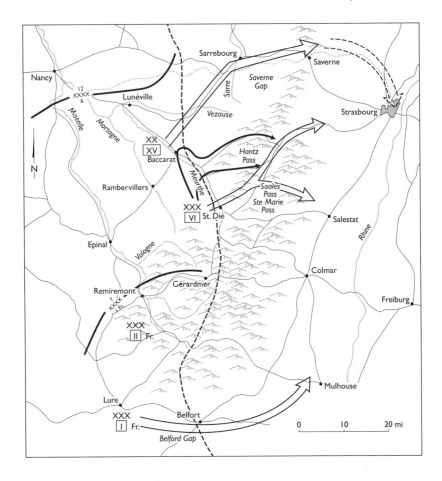

12.1. Over the Vosges to Strasbourg

the Saar or advance east of the river toward Frankfurt the best possible outcome Devers could have achieved? Napoleon's route of advance into Germany had been Frankfurt to Fulda Gap to Berlin. Was Devers very crafty or simply lucky? One thing is certain: Devers's plan was not the "safe" course of action (map 12.1).

As we have seen before, exemplary performance at a lower level of war can seldom correct a fundamental error made at a higher level. Simply put, the higher-level error usually orients the lower-level commander on the wrong objective. It seldom matters how well one advances if it is in the wrong direction. No operational plan could correct the strategic error embodied in that unfortunate selection of the 6th Army Group boundary. Perhaps Eisenhower approved the 6th Army Group's planned advance through the Vosges simply because it didn't interfere with SHAEF's primary plans.[4]

De Lattre was happy with the reshuffling, as both of his corps was united on the 6th Army Group's right side. Shooting the Belfort Gap was fine with him. Patch was disappointed that the Seventh Army was assigned to go up the road to Saint-Dié, a seemingly marginal mission. Lucian Truscott was incensed that VI Corps would not take on the Belfort Gap, which previously had been approved. He thought his new assignment was trivial. If SHAEF could not do better, then VI Corps should be withdrawn from France and make an amphibious landing near Genoa.

Devers wanted to get started into the Vosges as early as possible. He felt the resistance VI Corps ran into on 27 September was only a shell with no reserves behind it. Patch agreed. But the Seventh Army's supply situation had been termed "critical." The 6th Army Group lacked both artillery and ammunition to give proper support to sustained attacks by both the American Seventh and French First Armies. During the first two weeks of October, warfare was practically static.[5] The 6th Army Group G4 (logistics), Major General Clarence Lionel Adcock, reported that the railroads could support ten divisions as far north as Dijon, but could not provide additional lift to build up reserve stocks. The berths were being intensively worked at Marseilles, and 250 DUKWs were swimming in the harbor, offloading ships. A veteran of the Italian campaign, the 40th Engineer Combat Regiment worked at rehabilitating the railroads. In fact, the railroads did not deliver enough daily tonnage to support the Seventh Army's needs until the third week in October.

Truscott believed he could continue to chase the Germans through the smaller gaps in the High Vosges Mountains. Devers was more concerned about German resistance once VI Corps entered the mountains. He remembered Henry Wilson's admonition about the Vosges: "Don't get stuck in those mountains, you'll never get out."[6] Devers's reorientation of the Seventh Army west of the Vosges required VI Corps to shift northwestward. While Hitler approved Johannes Blaskowitz's plan to pull back and form a defense along the Moselle on 15 October, delayed movement of VI Corps due to its reorientation gave German defenders some time to prepare. During the bug-out from southern France, the German Nineteenth Army had become badly disorganized. The weakening resistance that Patch and Devers sensed in front of VI Corps was the Germans pulling back behind the river. With the Germans better set, Truscott would now have to force crossings of the Moselle instead of simply motoring across. He did so across a wide front twice that normally assigned to a three-division corps with all divisions abreast. This works only when enemy defenses are weak or badly disorganized. Despite Truscott's fears due to the pause, that still was a good description of the Nineteenth Army. Blaskowitz and Friedrich Wiese, the Nineteenth Army commander, feared that their troops would not make much of a showing along the Moselle. The Nineteenth Army was in danger of collapsing into a mob of stragglers fleeing toward the Fatherland.

The weather turned horrible. Constant cold drizzle mixed with French earth to create mud everywhere. Boots, tires, or tracks churned it up. Life for everyone in the field became even more miserable. Fog and rain severely limited operations of the small tactical air force supporting the 6th Army Group. As the 36th Infantry Division (1D) approached the river, bad memories of the bloodbath at the Rapido River in Italy haunted many veterans. It looked like the Germans were going to make a fight of it. Luckily, a retired French naval officer emerged and led them through the woods to a ford near Noir Guex, where infantrymen, shrouded by fog and pelted by cold rain, waded across against no opposition. Better to shiver in cold water than to get pierced by hot flying steel. Several sharp firefights emerged along the escarpment beyond which were delayed attempts at bridge building. Unlike at the Rapido, the Texans found solid ground on which to maneuver and forced the river. The 361D continued from Remiremont and headed toward a valley into the mountains created by the Meurthe River. The Texans were headed toward Saint-Dié and then up the N-420, which eventually ends in Strasbourg.

To reorient the corps so it would advance west of the Vosges, 451D, the Thunderbirds, had to shift from right flank to left and then cross the Moselle at Epinal against sharper resistance than they had experienced since landing in France. They then headed over relatively open ground toward Rambervillers and ultimately Baccarat. The 3rd Infantry Division on the corps's right flank tackled mountainous, wooded, muddy terrain from the get-go. Snipers and trail blocks slowed the advance to a crawl. Because of the heavy underbrush, American infantrymen could not pinpoint the source of incoming fire. But Wiese did not have enough combat power in front of Truscott to stop him. Blaskowitz reasoned that it would take the French some time to pull their army together. From the German defense facing the French, he grabbed 198ID to counterattack 45ID. The Thunderbirds were rocked back on their heels, but their attackers had insufficient combat power to seriously stall VI Corps advance. Wiese now worried that Allied troops would continue on through the Schlucht Pass from Germarder to Colmar. An attack further north via Saint-Dié in the Muerthe Valley into the Vosges was also a possibility. By the 25th, Wiese had concluded that he couldn't hold VI Corps anywhere near the Moselle. The Germans continued their withdrawal into the mountains (map 12.2).

While VI Corps entered the Vosges, XV Corps continued an attack into the Parroy Forest to the northeast, beginning on 25 September, while they were still under Patton's control. This stand of dense growth lay just south of Lunéville, where a big tank battle between the 4th Armored Division (AD) and the Fifth Panzer Army had been fought. Many European woods have been cleared of undergrowth making it easy to walk in them. Not so the Parroy in 1944. Thick underbrush limited both mobility and observation, which in turn limited the effectiveness of the attacking units. The 79th Infantry Division took on the woods with three regiments abreast. The French 2nd Artillery Division was supposed to have circled around the forest and isolated the Germans from the east, but incessant rains prevented that maneuver. Bad flying weather caused much of the air support to be canceled. American infantry clashed with their German counterparts in close combat. German commanders felt retention of the forest was essential in order to defend the Saverne Gap to the southeast. The 15th Panzer Grenadier Division was committed to hold the woods. They skillfully delayed the Americans and tormented them with artillery concentrations and small counterattacks.

Given the poor state of XV Corps, it took Wade Haislip well into the middle of October to clear the woods. The 44ID, newly arrived on the continent via Marseilles, made the final difference in the fight for the

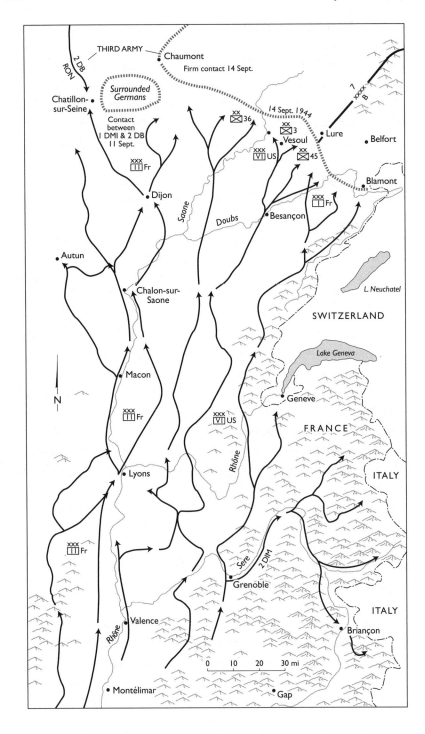

THIRD ARMY

2 DB

RON

● Chaumont

Firm contact 14 Sept.

Surrounded Germans

Chatillon-sur-Seine ●

7
XXXX
B

Contact between
1 DMI & 2 DB
11 Sept.

XX
36

14 Sept. 1944

XX
3
Vesoul

● Lure

● Belfort

XXX
III Fr

XXX
VI US

XX
45

● Dijon

Saone

Doubs

● Besançon

● Blamont

XXX
I Fr

● Autun

Chalon-sur-Saone ●

L. Neuchatel

SWITZERLAND

Lake Geneva

● Macon

XXX
III Fr

XXX
VI US

Rhône

● Geneve

FRANCE

● Lyons

ITALY

XXX
III Fr

Sere

2 DIM

N

● Grenoble

Rhône

● Valence

ITALY

● Briançon

0   10   20   30 mi

● Montélimar

● Gap

forest. At the end of the month, the French 2AD took some badly needed rest, while veteran 79ID and the green 44ID slogged through the woods to Baccarat. This attack diverted German attention from the threat that Devers and Patch were beginning to develop toward the Saverne Gap.

At the beginning of October, Devers recognized that, even if SHAEF had approved a large-scale 6th Army Group offensive across the Vosges to the Rhine, logistics couldn't support it. Devers's estimate of his logistic setup from the Mediterranean again proved to be overly optimistic. Marseilles began to work toward its potential, but forward combat divisions were three times farther away from the quays of Marseilles than preinvasion planning had assumed. While there were supplies on the docks, the railroads to the front still couldn't handle the tonnage. To conserve trucks for long hauls, horse-drawn wagons were impressed to clear the docks of supplies and restock dumps just inland. While the Seventh Army requested railroad delivery of 4,485 tons of artillery ammunition, the 6th Army Group could allocate transport for only 2,270 tons per day.[7] In addition, a theater-wide shortage of artillery ammunition created by optimists back in the United States, who had curtailed production and shipment of shells due to prognostication of early victory in Europe, limited American offensive operations. Because of shortages, actual delivery in early October dropped to 1,700 tons per day. The Seventh Army was shooting more ammunition than deliveries were replacing. Throughout the theater, artillery ammunition was short. Some forward infantry divisions were also reporting shortages in rifle ammunition, an almost unheard of condition. Supplies were indeed low. In early October, the Seventh Army had no rifle ammunition at all in its depots.[8] To maintain morale, supply officers concealed this from front-line troops. Because of the mountainous terrain and muddy conditions, three hundred mules were pressed into service hauling supplies to front-line positions.[9] From his early days out West, Devers knew about mules.

Hitler, who had never been enamored with Blaskowitz, replaced him with General der Panzer Truppen (Lieutenant General) Hermann Balck. Balck recognized the threat against the Saverne Gap that was be-

12.2. Into the Vosges

ginning to form. Once the Parroy Forest had been breached, there were few obstacles between the Americans and Saverne. If Patch penetrated through the gap to the Rhine, it would split the Nineteenth Army. Alternatively, a thrust to Sarrebourg would divide the German First from the Nineteenth Army and create a threat against the Saar. (The Fifth Panzer Army was still in a sector between them, but would be withdrawn shortly for the coming Ardennes offensive.) Operationally, the threats were about equal. Strategically, there was little comparison. Sarrebourg was the greater threat. But Eisenhower relegated both Belfort and the High Vosges to unimportance. Eisenhower's intention was to move in the direction of Sarrebourg, but the 6th Army Group's gaze went in the other direction. If Devers understood Eisenhower's intent, he was not complying fully with it. Then again, breaching the Rhine as opposed to threatening the Siegfried Line was within the scope of his orders. Better communication between the two senior officers – and past rivals – might have both exposed and resolved the issue.

German officers designated the Meurthe River, which flowed down from Saint-Dié in the High Vosges through Baccarat, as their main line of resistance. German commanders wanted time to fortify it heavily. To give themselves that time, they deployed the bulk of their forces in a 7–9-mile-wide security zone in front of the Meurthe, downslope from Saint-Dié. Balck favored creating a security zone well forward of his main line of resistance. Concealed forward outposts would call artillery on Americans exposing themselves as they advanced. When they stumbled into prearranged fields of fire, machine guns would cut them to pieces. Concealed main fighting positions sited farther back escaped American observation and the bulk of artillery preparatory fires.

Devers wanted a penetration on a relatively narrow front toward Saint-Dié. He left it up to Patch and Truscott to develop the tactical plans. Truscott was increasingly concerned that such a maneuver would expose VI Corps's northern flank to German counterattack. He looked to his boss, Patch, to insure that XV Corps made a sufficient advance to protect its sister corps. Both men, however, believed that, despite the logistical constraints, they could mount a limited offensive. While it was unlikely that they could break through to Strasbourg, they could take Saint-Dié. While there were risks to both flanks, inaction and allowing the Germans more time to solidify their defenses was the greater concern.[10] To accomplish their goals, the American generals wanted to narrow VI Corps's sector by having the French pick up the line through the High Vosges. Despite Devers's ordering the Seventh and French First Armies moved northward in mid-October, the French were slow to respond. The French wanted to concentrate on forcing the Belfort Gap despite its de-emphasis by both SHAEF and the 6th Army Group, and were loath to place more troops into the High Vosges – more headaches for Devers that would not be tolerated in an army group composed solely of American divisions.

Employing mission-type orders, Patch's two-page directive, issued on 20 September, did little more than designate the attack axis as Saint-Dié–Mosheim–Strasbourg. VI Corps would make the main effort. XV Corps would support this attack on the northern (left) flank of VI Corps. The corps commanders were left to decide the exact place and formation for the attack. The fight toward Saint-Dié during the first two weeks in October was drenched with cold rain. Foxhole life became even more miserable. Battle losses meant units were under strength, and the constant fighting while moving uphill through the woods left everyone exhausted. Broken, wooded terrain meant more troops per mile of line were needed. With XV Corps as well as VI Corps drawing on the supply line up the Rhône, supply shortages began to impact everyone. There was a noticeable falloff in the efficiency and morale among the front-line infantry of VI Corps. They had been in combat for an extended period without any rest, and now the weather was turning bad. VI Corps began rotating infantry battalions out of the line to rest the troops per Devers's admonition.

Truscott dubbed this operation "Dogface." The highest speed approach to Saint-Dié was the route up from the Moselle that passed through Bruyères. The 36th Infantry Division, reinforced by the famous "Go for Broke" 442nd Regimental Combat Team (RCT), manned primarily by Japanese Americans, would make the main effort about a week after the operation began. It was Truscott's plan to have 31D lead the attack across the remaining 12 miles from Rambervillers to Saint-Dié.

In turn, Truscott gave his divisional commanders wide latitude.[11] Command philosophy in the Seventh Army paralleled that of Patton, and was near the polar opposite of Courtney Hodges's practice in the First Army. The assault against Bruyères, spearheaded by 36ID, advanced through heavy vegetation shrouded in thick fog on the morning of 15 October. A steady drizzle added to the attacker's misery. Heavy fighting lasted four days. German machine gunners ensconced in stout buildings were difficult to dislodge. Every time the Americans made some progress, German forward observers brought down showers of artillery shells and mortar bombs through the rain. The 36th Infantry Division's enveloping force finally succeeded. The 45th Infantry Division also succeeded in capturing Rambervillers a mile and a half up the road.

"Fighting in the Vosges was characterized by the plugging advances of the infantry, the innovations of tactics of supporting troops and the desperation of the enemy," notes the Seventh Army official report.[12] Forest growth was so dense and the ground so cut up, it was like fighting in a briar patch. Often a squad leader could see only two or three of his men. It was easy to get lost and misidentify locations. Orders based on inaccurate spot reports resulted in unexpected and bitter fighting. Germans often allowed unsuspecting Americans to come in close before cutting them down, so American artillery couldn't respond. Compasses were in almost continuous use. Often skirmish lines were needed to "drag" an area bypassed by infantry attack, lest snipers begin killing GIs. During static warfare, patrolling was so extensive that it became the main combat action.[13] VI Corps veterans of the Italian campaign were not looking forward to spending another winter in the mountains.

For both sides, artillery was the biggest killer. Tree bursts from German howitzers and mortars took a heavy toll and gave the Americans a certain feeling of helplessness. It was better to stand straight up against a tree than hit the ground. Artillery adjustments were made by sound, often within 100 yards of friendly positions. Fire direction was plotted from known checkpoints in open ground and then offset into the woods. Combinations of quick and delay fusing of the artillery in dense forests proved most effective. White phosphorus was used to mark targets but was in limited supply. German troops hated "Willey Peter" as the frag-

ments burned deeply into human skin. Pour water on it and the phos-
phorous cooked you even worse. Artillery concentrations caused many
Germans to give up and surrender. The 131st Artillery Battalion said
that they could shoot up ten days of ammunition in ten minutes, so they
reduced the rate at which they serviced their pieces.[14]

With some difficulty due to the slowness of the French First Army's
occupying 31D's sector per Devers's orders, Truscott withdrew two of
its regiments and had them attack through 36ID. With this maneuver,
the corps commander concentrated five of his ten infantry regiments
(two from 36ID, one from 45ID, and two from 31D) on a 6-mile front
headed for the Meurthe River crossings at Saint-Dié. The entire maneuver was masked by a deception operation. The 3rd Infantry Division
faked an attack toward the Schlucht Pass. Radio traffic of a larger force
was simulated, and equipment with 36ID markings was "lost" in the area.
Soldiers from 31D sewed 45ID patches on their uniforms. Per the plan,
31D continued the attack toward Saint-Dié on 20–21 October. Resistance
became spotty and unorganized. The German corps commander did
not move major reinforcements against VI Corps's main effort until the
28th. Truscott had pulled off a dazzling example of concentrated infantry
attack shielded by a deception campaign. Without the help of armor or
supporting air, American mud sloggers had displayed tactical brilliance.
Despite the difficult terrain, Truscott threatened breakthrough.

To seal the impending breach, the Germans finally threw in some
infantry and what was left of the 106th Panzer Brigade, which was moved
north from in front of the French First Army. For eighteen days, the
two lead regiments of 31D fought uphill against panzer grenadiers and
troops from Austrian alpine battalions. By 3 November, 31D dogfaces
looked out on the Meurthe Valley from the heights opposite Saint-Dié.
The 45ID to the north and 36ID to the south fought hard to keep up. The
Germans torched every bit of shelter in their path, leaving the Americans
exposed to the cold rain. Much of the 16th Volksgrenadier Division and
its reinforcements had been destroyed. Over five thousand Germans
huddled in VI Corps POW enclosures. Truscott's attack to Saint-Dié
was an excellent example of the tactical use of mass on a narrow front to
effect a penetration. The infantry shined. Sometimes the fighting was in

such close quarters it was settled with bayonet and grenade. This fight showed that experienced American infantry could take on their German counterparts, even in bad weather, and beat them.

The attack to Saint-Dié was Truscott's swansong in the 6th Army Group. On 25 October, he left to take command of the Fifth Army in Italy. Major General Edward H. Brooks moved up to command VI Corps. The artillery officer, who served under Devers in Armored Force, had compiled an excellent record commanding the U.S. 2AD from Normandy to the German border. A soldier of great experience, Brooks looked the part. Quiet and unflappable, this New Englander was a highly competent leader.[15] He could move battalions better than anyone except Joe Lawton Collins. Eisenhower rated him as one of his better corps commanders and Matthew Ridgway's equal, quite an accolade. He had been Devers's choice for the job.[16]

As impressive as the advance to Saint-Dié was, the Germans were fighting in their security zone. While the bulk of its combat units were engaged, VI Corps had yet to hit the main line of resistance. This was defense in depth. From Balck's perspective at the operational level, VI Corps's advance into the Vosges was relatively unimportant.[17] Efforts of the U.S. Seventh Army from 20 September through the end of October were not operationally threatening to the German Army Group G. Only second-rate infantry and formations, burned out in the heavy combat against the Third Army around Arracourt, opposed the Seventh Army's efforts. The advance to Saint-Dié had not materialized as a threat to Sarrebourg and the Rhine.

Action by the French II Corps in the Vosges had caused the Germans to react. De Lattre was pleased but had no intention of sending more French troops into difficult terrain.[18] Instead, he pushed the French I Corps, which had not been heavily engaged, into the mountains. In order to cover the ground vacated by Truscott's westward move, Joseph de Monsabert had to extend his sector farther than he wanted. De Lattre was pushing him to make a major effort, but Monsabert had no reserves. Up in the mountains, his 31D ran into German resistance as heavy as anything they had experienced in Tunis in 1942. Casualties on both sides were high. The I Corps commander wondered if the Americans were serious about fighting in the mountains, and had left the tough job for the French. Intense cold added frostbite cases to a plethora of combat casualties. As the French ground forward, the Germans began burning mountain villages. Due to their own lack of supplies, French troops had little to offer their displaced countrymen filtering back through the lines.

Even more rain took life in the mountains to new lows. Devers requisitioned one thousand M29 weasels, jeep-sized tracked amphibians to slither supplies up the muddy trails. Dropping temperatures placed African colonial troops at a disadvantage. During October, the French actively sought to replace them with recruits from metropolitan France, but the French First Army was still a work in progress. This change-over required additional uniforms and other quartermaster equipment, and, the overstretched logistical system could not deliver these in sufficient quantities. Again the French accused the Americans of shorting them, even though French service units were completely unable to support their own troops. Nevertheless, French complaints compounded Devers's headaches; he did his best to mollify them and to meet their demands. About 19,000 FFI were organized into twenty-four light infantry battalions with no heavy weapons and much simplified training. This gave the French some troops to maintain internal security without detracting from combat force. Another 52,000 went directly into the First French Army as replacements. Devers struggled with the loss of combat troops, which the French diverted to Operation Independence, the French effort to deal with German coastal enclaves along the shore of the Bay of Biscay and the clearing of southern France.

The 6th Army Group headquarters moved to Vittel on 5 October. Marshall visited Europe in early October, precipitating a forty-five minute conference between Devers and the chief of staff. Had the disagreement between Devers and Eisenhower openly surfaced at this point, this would have been another backdoor through which to remove the 6th Army Group commander. If Eisenhower had had no confidence in Devers, and as a result was underutilizing the 6th Army Group, then he had a duty to so inform Marshall. An honest conversation between Marshall and Eisenhower might have resulted in Devers's being rotated to deputy chief of staff back in the states.

The next day, Marshall and General Thomas T. Handy, in effect Marshall's deputy chief, observed artillery batteries conducting fire missions and noted the paucity of artillery and ammunition for the Seventh Army. The 6th Army Group artillery ammunition stocks had reached their lowest level on record, impacting tactical operations both in the Vosges and in front of Belfort. Devers recorded in his diary, "I can't understand the War Department's attitude." With upcoming heavy fighting along the Rhine, a lot of ammunition would be required. At another time, he quipped, "Artillery always shot. Infantry never shot."[19] Later, Marshall's party traveled to visit General de Lattre. Upon arrival, de Lattre began to complain about inadequate receipt of supplies, blaming General Patch. Devers recalled, "Marshall straightened him out like nobody's business."[20] Marshall had such a bad taste from de Lattre's less-than-well-founded complaints that he carried his dislike over into postwar NATO assignments.

Given the Vosges before him, Devers requested the 10th Mountain Division, which ETO had previously rejected. The Pentagon denied it again as forty-nine ships would be required to move the division's animals. Devers inspected the newly arrived 100th and 103rd Divisions and liked what he saw.[21] Reuben Jenkins and Harold Bull arranged for the infantry regiments of the 42nd, 43rd, and 70th Divisions to be sent up to the front ahead of their parent organizations. The intent was to give each veteran infantry division four regiments, so three could be in place and the fourth pulled back and rested. After three weeks in the line, infantry regiments would then get a break. The units new to combat would be able to get some combat experience and guidance from a veteran division.

On 1 November, NATOUSA became MTOUSA and no longer had any control over elements in southern France. All American forces there became part of Eisenhower's ETO. Devers now wore but a single hat, commander, 6th Army Group, reporting exclusively to Eisenhower. When Eisenhower and Bradley visited Devers on the 16th, looking for supply tonnage via Marseilles for Patton's advance, Devers could promise 1,000 tons a day for the Third Army. This is about what two divisions in combat require and impressed Eisenhower not at all, even though the 6th Army Group had taken on both XV Corps and elements of the newly landed divisions. Eisenhower reorganized Thomas Larkin's logistical command, which had been part of the North African command under Devers's second hat, into an area command within John Lee's organization. In turn, Devers wasn't impressed. Lee's shortcomings were understood by all. In his diary, Devers wrote, "Larkin is probably the best line of communications commander in existence today. He belongs on our team and certainly puts out. Marked contrast to base section commanders under Lee. Our troops need a rest."

De Lattre worried that French fatigue and low morale due to the seeming insensitivity of metropolitan Frenchmen to the travails of the colonial Africans that made up most of French First Army would allow his army only limited engagement. Combat in France to date had taken a great toll on French company grade officers, and there were few replacements. In his diary, Devers mused, "This was an African Army we were fighting with and it was short of French officers." De Lattre called a halt to the French II Corps attack toward Gérardmer, which had been his main effort. The French I Corps commander thought that efforts into the mountains had been a bloody disaster. Some Maquis companies had now joined the fight, but their lack of discipline and training showed when they went up against regular German army formations. Many First Army officers worried that their troops' morale might plummet if they took heavy casualties in a grinding firefight. De Gaulle required that de Lattre detach a division to assist in law and order in the southwest of France (called Operation Independence). The 1st Allied Airborne Taskforce had been removed from the Italian border, so Devers expanded the 44th Anti-Aircraft Brigade with polyglot groups of small American units to patrol much of the otherwise vacated border. The First French Army had to patrol the remainder.

De Lattre wanted to take on Belfort with French I Corps, and Devers readily agreed. He modified the Letter of Instructions No. 2 to give the French more time to organize their assault. De Lattre advanced by slipping French I Corps along the French border, then deep into German positions. Heavy snow masked his preparations from German intelligence, who thought the French had settled into winter defensive positions. The French First Army encircled both Belfort and Mulhouse, killing perhaps ten thousand Germans in the process. But French tactical leadership wasn't very experienced, resulting in high casualty rates among attacking formations.

Eisenhower expected little of operational value would come from the 6th Army Group's attack – especially from the French First Army. But the French performance in capturing Belfort and Mulhouse established their credibility as competent combat formations. Upon tasting victory, de Lattre mused, "Terrible memories were blotted out. In this sight, our men found their surest reward."[22]

THIRTEEN

Cross the Rhine?

DWIGHT EISENHOWER WAS NOT IMPRESSED BY THE RESULTS that the 6th Army Group posted in October 1944. From 15 August to the end of September, the Seventh Army had advanced 400 miles, from St. Tropez to Rambervillers. Total advance for October and early November amounted to only 15 miles.[1] Operation Dogface, the attack into the Vosges toward Saint-Dié, was a clever tactical move. At the operational level, as far as SHAEF was concerned, it was an attack in the wrong direction, but that really didn't matter. Eisenhower wanted the Seventh Army to advance west of the Vosges from Sarrebourg north toward the Siegfried Line in close support of George Patton's attack. Thus, it is a wonder that SHAEF approved Dogface, an attack east into the Vosges Mountains. Apparently Eisenhower wrote it off as a tactical move designed to anchor the Seventh Army's right flank in the Vosges and tie down some Germans. Jacob Devers and Sandy Patch had done little to support Patton's efforts in Lorraine since clearing the Parroy Forest on the Third Army's southern flank near Baccarat. Fixated on the Rhine, Devers did not fully recognize the gap between his vision and SHAEF's limited approval. The official history states that Eisenhower doubted that Devers's command could make any major contribution to the Allied advance in November.[2] This frame of mind is important in understanding Devers's motivation in several significant, subsequent decisions.

Perhaps Eisenhower's eye was too jaundiced. The main theater effort up north around Aachen and in the Hürtgen Forest mounted by Courtney Hodges under Omar Bradley's close supervision resulted in bloody deadlock. Horrible losses were incurred there with virtually no strategic advantage to the Allies. In Lorraine, Patton wasted a lot of time and ammunition attacking the fortresses around Metz, which was little more than a large German combat outpost. After failing to clear the approaches to Antwerp in September, when they could have been had for little cost, Bernard Montgomery did little else in October save correct this mistake at great cost to the Canadians. Finally, the first Liberty ships negotiated the Scheldt and tied up alongside Belgian quays. By comparison, the Seventh Army had made spectacular improvements, allowing Marseilles to become railroad linked into the southern supply terminus behind Bradley's 12th Army Group.

Eisenhower expected that the Seventh Army would now shift its weight out of the mountains and advance west of the Vosges in support of Patton, who was looking to cross the Rhine near Mannheim. That is exactly what Hermann Balck and his staff expected. German intelligence predicted that the Americans would ignore Alsace east of the Vosges and concentrate on the historic route to the best crossing sites for the Rhine between Karlsruhe and Mannheim. The first objective on that axis was Sarrebourg, not Strasbourg. Nonetheless, the daily reports to SHAEF that Eisenhower required from the 6th Army Group clearly showed that the Seventh Army had turned east into the Vosges, heading for Strasbourg.

Lack of progress north of the Ardennes during September and October had raised the temperature of the already heated debate between the British and Americans over theater strategy. Chief of the British Imperial Staff Alan Brooke continued to insist that an Allied attack first to capture the Ruhr then Berlin was the right way, almost the only way, to win the war. Montgomery all but demanded that Bradley's two armies north of the Ardennes (the First and the Ninth) be subordinated to him, and that Patton's offensive south of the Ardennes be stopped so the field marshal could properly design a coordinated and concentrated offensive to achieve the objectives he agreed on with Brooke.

In essence, the British field marshals advocated a strategy based on geographical objectives, the Ruhr and Berlin. SHAEF's plan concentrated on destroying the German Army in the field west of the Rhine, where logistical problems would be minimized. Senior British commanders never seemed to grasp this essential point, upon which both

Eisenhower and Marshall agreed. If geography was gained but the Wehrmacht remained intact, Hitler's indomitable will would keep the war going. In order that the Germans not be allowed to pile up their forces in one narrow area to stop a single Allied thrust, Eisenhower was adamant that a primary offensive north of the Ardennes, supported by a secondary attack by Patton toward the Saar, was the best way to first destroy the German Army along the Rhine, then finish the war.[3] The Wehrmacht would have to forcefully defend their primary manufacturing area and present themselves as targets. What had been a fresh idea in late August was now a plan well-understood by the Germans and deadlocked by Wehrmacht countermoves of the last two months. Unfortunately, the Allied senior officers were as dug into their positions as the Germans.

Despite Eisenhower's initial plan to avoid becoming deadlocked on a single axis, Operation Queen, the November attack by the First and Ninth Armies near Aachen that was the theater's main November effort, repeated the previous attack against some of the toughest defenses along the Allied front. To get to the Rhine, those participating in Queen would first have to cross the Roer River. The Germans held several large dams upstream and could release a raging torrent at any time. The kick-off dates for Queen, and Patton's supporting drive across Lorraine to the Siegfried Line, had been the subject of considerable conversation. Weather played havoc with air power availability and thus the offensive's start date. SHAEF thought so little of the 6th Army Group's prospects that SGS 381, the relevant plan, didn't list a start date for the 6th Army Group's effort. SHAEF thought the 6th Army Group was little more than a subordinate sideshow to the supporting attack. Allied intelligence officers had observed that, at the operational level, it took the Germans about two full days to react to a major Allied attack. In November, the Allies wanted to time the three pending attacks about two days apart. That way, the Germans would be just getting their operational reserves moving when yet another threat appeared.

In November, Eisenhower was calling the same play that had already been stopped for no gain. Maybe it was time for a new campaign plan. Devers thought he could provide just that opportunity – if only he was allowed to get in the game. SHAEF's directive did contemplate a Rhine crossing for the 6th Army Group. Dated 28 October, it stated,

10. The mission of the Southern Group of Armies [6th Army Group] during the
first and second phase is:
   a. to advance in zone, secure crossings and deploy in strength across the
   Rhine.
   b. to protect the southern flank of the Central Group of Armies [i.e.,
   those of Bradley, Hodges, and Patton]. Initially this will involve
   denying Lunéville [near the Parroy Forest, west of the Vosges] to the
   enemy.[4]

Lunéville, just southeast from Nancy, was the base of Patton's southern-most XII Corps, which was making the main effort in the Third Army's upcoming westward attack toward Sarreguemines. The implication, but not the literal order, was that Devers would stay on the west side of the Vosges in order to deny Lunéville to the Germans. Paragraph 10(a) seems to be something of an afterthought or maybe simple inertia from orders that dated back to 15 September. But it did list a Rhine crossing supporting Patton's secondary attack. That is far more expansive than Eisenhower's early September guidance to Devers to perhaps attack into the Vosges in order to pin down the maximum number of Germans.

At a Brussels meeting of 18 October, Eisenhower's theater strategy emphasized the now-familiar main attack toward the Ruhr with a secondary attack by the Third Army toward the Saar. Brooke and Montgomery objected to Eisenhower's proposal of a secondary attack. They demanded concentration north of the Ardennes to the exclusion of all else. A major thrust farther south from the 6th Army Group was, literally, the furthest development from their minds. Of necessity, Eisenhower needed to address the intense arguments, which threatened to burst the seams of a combined British and American strategy. He regarded what was happening in the 6th Army Group sector as subsidiary, noncontroversial, and settled.

Devers's principal effort was to protect the flank of the Third Army and attack northward toward Karlsruhe, then northeast toward Nuremberg. No mention was made of an eastward advance via Strasbourg and across the Rhine. Montgomery and Bradley had continued to discount any possibility of a serious contribution from the 6th Army Group. Paragraph 6 of the SHAEF order states, "maintenance resources available from the Mediterranean" would be used for "overwhelming the enemy west of the Rhine and, later, of advancing into Germany."[5] Eisenhower

wanted Devers to hold the upper Rhine opposite the Black Forest, eliminate any Germans found west of the Rhine, and support the right flank
of Patton's November attack. But that is not what Devers took from his
orders. He still sought the Rhine, and it was toward the Rhine that Devers began to move.

On 23 October, Eisenhower wrote Jake a letter with very specific
guidance.[6] While Devers had not suggested that the Third Army become part of the 6th Army Group or that his army group take over the
role of secondary attack, he had suggested a more expansive thrust into
Germany to justify the 6th being a larger army group. While there is no
written evidence to document it, Eisenhower and Devers may have had a
less-than-conclusive conversation about an eastward attack at their face-
to-face meeting on 18 October. In his letter of 23 October, Eisenhower
made it clear that he was "shifting the center of gravity [of the 6th Army
Group] further to the north.... [To] advance to Munich is a subsidiary
role.... Protect Third Army flank.... Cross the Rhine in general area
Karlsruhe-Mannheim." While he did not expressly say so, Eisenhower
did not see any need to advance through the Belfort Gap or attack east
of the formidable Vosges Mountains. He intended the Seventh Army to
remain west of the mountains close to the Third Army's right wing in
order to provide support for the theater secondary attack spearheaded
by Patton and passing directly from Lorraine (not Alsace) due east into
Germany. Lest there be any confusion, Eisenhower directed Devers to
orient the 6th Army Group on Nuremberg via a Rhine crossing in the
vicinity of Mannheim, which had been Patton's focus since landing in
France. In the same letter, Eisenhower indicated that the Third Army
would advance on a more northeastern route via Frankfurt toward Kassel as part of the encirclement of the Ruhr after capturing the Saar. The
principle mission of the 6th Army Group was to protect the 12th Army
Group's southern flank, which would be in the vicinity of the axis laid out
for the Third Army. Eisenhower further stated that the 6th Army Group
might not have the logistical resources to make it as far as Nuremberg.
Any movement into southern Germany toward Munich would be "a
subsidiary role to be subsequently carried out only if resources permit."

General Friedrich Wiese's Nineteenth Army, the German defenders
of Alsace, had lost its principal mobile reserve. The 11th Panzer Divi-

sion, which had bedeviled the 6th Army Group's advance from Marseilles since the beginning of the campaign, had been shifted over to oppose Patton. The Fifth Panzer Army and its subordinate units, XLVII and LVII Panzer Corps, had been withdrawn to prepare for the German Ardennes offensive. The Nineteenth Army had been reduced to less than fifty thousand effectives, about half of what opposed Patton's Third Army. Balck reasoned that the blank wall of the Black Forest on the upper Rhine and the difficulties of the French First Army, with its internal disorganization and lack of training, made this sector the one on which to economize. Despite the departure of German mobile formations to ready themselves for the upcoming Ardennes attack, commanders in Army Group G were feeling fairly confident in their positions. The retirement from southern France had ended, and both the First and Nineteenth Armies were regaining some of their balance. Devers's rapid advance up the Rhône and across the Moselle had been slowed to a crawl. German defenses along the Vosges and blocking the Belfort Gap were coagulating. Fortification of the Winter Line in those mountains was not as advanced as had been planned. On 3 November, Gerd von Rundstedt submitted a report stating that the two field armies of Army Group G had recovered some defensive power and were fighting well. Its staff was concerned about the reduction in armored reserves but felt that winter weather in the mountains would slow the Americans to a manageable pace.[7]

Weather in the Vosges continued to be miserable. It rained almost every day. Frequent high winds whipped stinging cold droplets onto exposed flesh, and snow appeared at higher elevations. Actual temperatures were not unbearable, but they made anyone living outdoors miserable. Temperatures ranged from 38–68° Fahrenheit in October and 25–60° in November. In the latter half of October, only one day was suitable for air operations. No ground support missions were flown from 5 to 19 November.

Like Patton entering Lorraine in late August, Devers and virtually every other senior officer in the 6th Army Group wanted to be something more than minor supporting actors in the upcoming offensive. The staff understood their primary mission was to provide "protection of the southern flank of the Central Group of Armies" (that is, Bradley's

12th Army Group). They were aware of the formal order, SGS 381, of 28 October, which is somewhat ambiguous. None of the principal staff officers interviewed, however, mentioned the more specific letter from Eisenhower to Devers of 23 October, and given its specific singular addressee, was there any reason that they should? But there was a lot of debate among the staff as to what would be most helpful. Should they closely follow Patton along the western side of the Vosges? Or would it be better to cross the Rhine and then move north, thereby unhinging the defenses in front of Patton, allowing him to rapidly advance to the Rhine? "This was essentially a choice between close in support on one hand and indirect support by wide envelopment on the other."[8] The officers asked themselves, Would Eisenhower approve a Rhine crossing in the south while the rest of SHAEF's forces were so far away? The 6th Army Group's written record contains a lot of rationalization and self-justification. No one asked these questions of Bradley or his staff. It is easy to guess where Devers came down in this debate. The tone of the 6th Army Group record suggests an attempt to justify grabbing onto a technicality in the order. The staff concluded that taking an opportunity to seize a bridgehead across the Rhine was consistent with Eisenhower's directive for the first phase. Literally, exploitation of that opportunity – a major advance east of the Rhine – was properly a part of Eisenhower's second phase.

The Saverne Gap, a wide swath of lower ground that separates High Vosges from its lower but more rugged counterpart to the north, runs east from the Moselle to the Rhine. Topography in the gap is low enough to have allowed the Marne-Rhine Canal to be constructed there. It is a natural avenue of advance, wide enough to allow an army to pass. Devers and Patch agreed that the Seventh Army would attack either through the gap or via the minor passes just to the south. Devers remembered Henry Wilson's advice not to get caught up in combat in the mountains; he admonished Patch to heed it as well. Army group long-range planners began making studies of a Rhine River crossing near Rastatt, about 30 miles north of Strasbourg. This would be a logical extension of the push through the mountains to Strasbourg. Instead of turning south toward Colmar and Belfort, however, this move swept north along the river. If the Seventh Army could blow through the Saverne Gap, a Rhine crossing appeared to be within reach. Devers underscored, "we must concentrate on a narrow front when attacking."[9] This was in marked contrast to the 12th Army Group's attacks in the fall of 1944, which could be roundly criticized for their lack of concentration.

Devers was itching to leap the Rhine. He and his staff recognized that a crossing north of Strasbourg would avoid the Black Forest and instead open onto ground that lead to Karlsruhe. From there they could advance either north, deeper into Germany near Frankfurt, or west, enveloping German defenses blocking Patton. The 6th Army Group's operations order clearly stated the objective was to cross the Vosges and break out to the south to seize Strasbourg. This move, and the attack up from the Belfort Gap described below, appeared to be a double envelopment meant to destroy the Nineteenth Army west of the Rhine. The order did not specify the Seventh Army's subsequent mission. But the Seventh Army had identified Rastatt as the best place to cross the Rhine. That town was selected because it dominates the road net east of the river, especially those leading in the general direction of Nuremburg.[10] Planners understood that the big Kehl Bridge at Strasbourg led only into dense growth and steep slopes. Special river crossing schools to train troops to deal with the Rhine's strong current were established at Valskhomer and Dole on the Dobbs River. The veteran 40th Engineer Combat Group stockpiled assault boats, DUKWs, and bridging equipment. Quartermasters and transportation officers began planning for the supply buildup a crossing would require.

Devers planned to move the Seventh Army via the Saverne and gaps through the mountains to gain both Strasbourg and access to Rhine crossing sites. Initially, Wade Haislip's XV Corps would move in the direction of Sarrebourg. This maneuver would be consistent with what both SHAEF and the Germans expected of an attack staying west of the Vosges. Devers shifted the Seventh Army's main effort about 30 miles to the north. Instead of cutting through the Vosges at Saint-Dié south of Strasbourg, it now would emerge north of the city and closer to the northern limit of the Black Forest on the Rhine's far bank. Given the way the Nineteenth Army was deployed, this became the move General Balck most feared from Devers. Instead of continuing north, along the western face of the Vosges, Devers, and Patch would turn Haislip's

XV Corps east and push through the main entrance to the Saverne Gap. VI Corps would continue through the minor gaps to the south, still headed toward Strasbourg. Initially, the Seventh Army designated VI Corps as the main effort. As the start date approached, the army staff adopted a more flexible plan that could shift weight between the two corps depending on their relative success.

According to General Jean de Lattre, Devers was aware of the organizational trouble within and the extended front of the French First Army. As a result, his initial thoughts were to task the French with generating only a supporting attack that might draw off some German strength. De Lattre and his I Corps commander, General Antoine Béthouart, however, created a plan that would break into the Belfort Gap at Dobbs and advance as far as Mulhouse. I Corps had presented a plan on 16 October that was the basis of de Lattre's Personal and Secret Instruction No. 4 to Béthouart on 24 October. When de Lattre presented this to Devers for approval, he readily agreed to this more aggressive plan.[11] In the meantime, the French created a deception plan to mask evidence of their planned strike at the Doubs River.

Devers's operations officer, General Reuben Jenkins, recalled, "I felt that General Devers gave the French and Seventh Army all the guidance they needed to close to the Rhine, and his own concepts for this operation were completely sound. Devers asked me the chances for the November attack. He had two plans. In one, armor led; in the other, infantry preceded the tanks, but he favored the first. If XV Corps led, Devers envisioned [Jacques-Philippe] Leclerc [French 2nd Armored Division (AD)] would advance through 79th Infantry Division."[12] He worried that weather would stall the attack. Devers's "main effort was to break through and go straight to the Rhine and Strasbourg. Devers said, 'Rube, nobody but an utter fool would do what I'm about to do. That's the reason why we'll take them by surprise. They won't be expecting us. We are going with the alternate plan to lead with the infantry. Say your prayers.' The old man was almost in tears. This attack was going to enable Patton. If he was under Ike pressure I didn't know it."[13]

The 6th Army Group directive of 24 October governing the upcoming attack to Strasbourg was consistent with and authorized by Supreme Council of the Armed Forces (SCAF) message No. 114.[14] But it swung wide of Eisenhower's intent. From his actions and those of his staff, it is possible to infer that Devers knew he was coloring outside of SHAEF's prescribed lines. It wasn't that SHAEF staff had no idea. Recalled Jenkins, "I was on awfully good terms, I thought, with General [Harold] Bull, who was [SHAEF] G3 [chief of staff for operations], and General Jock Whiteley who was Deputy G3, on Eisenhower's staff. They were both very helpful and cooperative on this thing. They wanted us to *go.* They *wanted* us to succeed. I don't think there was any question about it."[15]

Devers estimated that Patch would need about two weeks to break through the Saverne Gap and advance onto the Alsacian Plain. The French would need about the same time to break through at Belfort.[16] Beyond these first objectives, Devers projected a Rhine crossing above Strasbourg. With his troops on the east side of the Rhine, the German First Army would be trapped in Lorraine between Patch and Patton. That was quite a dream. At least Devers was thinking in the right dimension – destroy the Wehrmacht. But he knew that the 6th Army Group did not have enough troops to fully exploit what he was starting. Jenkins acknowledged that later: "I think he fully realized that. He said so more than once."[17] Fixing this problem would be Devers's job.

An assistant G4 (logistics) in the 6th Army Group believed that "There is no doubt that we could have supported Seventh Army beyond the Rhine. There wasn't any great opposition on the other side of the Rhine. . . . General Devers was a great army group commander. There was no equivocation on what he wanted; he was a moral individual of the highest order." Devers was a "tremendously intelligent [man] who went to the root of the problem." Few leaders "had the guts to do what he did – namely to go in with what he had into the unknown and maybe get whipped. He was well liked by his people."[18]

A preliminary attack by French II Corps to gain the Rochesson Heights south of Germeter commenced on 3 November. Despite heavy French artillery preparation, German resistance was fierce. French II Corps reached its objective on the 5th and held on despite heavy German counterattacks.[19] On the same day, Devers flew up to Patton's headquarters to coordinate his attack date with the Third Army.

Resistance and obstacles in front of the Third Army were formidable. Water coming down the rivers that flowed from the Vosges guaranteed that Patton would be in a lot of mud. Devers advised his classmate that runoff currently was heavy, and he would do better in about a week. That would also better synchronize with the 6th Army Group's build-up. "We'll go faster and accomplish more."[20] Patton was adamant, though, about starting on the 7th. Devers flew on to Bradley's headquarters.

German intelligence officers did not have to be clairvoyant to discern what the Americans were likely to do. SHAEF's principal campaign design hadn't changed much since mid-September. After talking with Patton and Bradley, Devers became more convinced than ever that the Third Army should be in the 6th Army Group and oriented on an envelopment of the German First Army by crossing the Rhine at Rastatt.[21] Devers was confident that Patch had the Seventh Army under control. On 7 November, Devers met with de Lattre. De Gaulle wanted some French First Army troops diverted to Paris to assist in keeping law and order. Recognizing that a major eastward attack was about to develop, de Gaulle apparently canceled the move.

The Seventh Army attack order of 5 November states, "Seventh Army attacks on D-Day and destroys enemy in zone west of the Rhine; captures Strasbourg and maintains contact with right flank of Twelfth Army Group. VI Corps attack D+2 on axis St. Die-Strasbourg. XV Corps attack on D Day toward Sarrebourg, forces the Saverne Gap, captures Strasbourg and is prepared to exploit east of Vosges."[22] At the beginning of the effort to break through the Saverne Gap, the Seventh Army contained,

VI CORPS	XV CORPS
14th Armored Division (Combat Command A)	French 2nd Armored Division
3rd Infantry Division	44th Infantry Division
36th Infantry Division	79th Infantry Division
100th Infantry Division	
103rd Infantry Division	
117th Cavalry Group	106th Cavalry Group

Terrain in the Vosges Mountains was far more difficult than that which the U.S. First Army fought through up north in the Stolberg Cor-

ridor and Hürtgen Forest. But the result was far different. The Seventh
Army did not face the best German field formations. Then, again, the
defenders in the Hürtgen were not Rundstedt's best either. In the VI
Corps's area to the south, 45ID was refitting after hard fighting near
Saint-Dié. Both the 3rd and 36th Divisions could have used a similar
respite. The 79ID had just finished sixteen days of rest and training after
the bloody fight in the Parroy Forest. The 14AD, 100ID, and 103ID were
formations fresh off the boat from the United States. They were to have
disembarked in western France, but because of the shipping back-up
along the Channel coast, they were unloaded in Marseilles and assigned
to Devers per Eisenhower's earlier promise. VI Corps was opposed by
three Volks divisions (the 16th, 708th, and 716th) of LXIV Corps under
Wiese's Nineteenth Army. The 708th Division was in good shape after
having been sent to Czechoslovakia for reorganization and training. The
16th Volksgrenadier Division (VGD) had been badly damaged in earlier
fighting. The 716VGD was marginal at best. The 361VGD and 553VGD of
the First Army's LXXXIX Corps defended north and south of Sarrebourg respectively. Neither of these outfits was up to intended strength.

A small attack by 100ID preceded the main VI Corps attack. It was
to pull Germans into the northern sector of VI Corps and away from its
intended route of advance, which was along highway N-420 to N-392
and onto Strasbourg. Then XV Corps would begin its attack. Initially,
Haislip's forces would advance to Baccarat then Sarrebourg. This would
threaten a move northward into the southeastern portion of the Lorraine Gateway. Instead, XV Corps would then turn east and make for
the Saverne Gap. A subsequent advance by French armor from near
Saverne southeast toward Strasbourg was indicated. VI Corps would
commence its main effort toward Strasbourg two days after XV Corps.
Its primary thrust was to be up route N-392 and then into Strasbourg
from the southwest.

Patch did an excellent job of coordinating the efforts of both his
corps. In turn, the efforts within those two formations were well-syn-
chronized. Balck had set his interarmy group boundary just south of the
Saverne Gap. American intelligence picked this up. Patch wanted to tear
that open with XV Corps. The 100ID's preliminary attack was designed
to do this by dislocating the northernmost division in the Nineteenth

Army. As the Germans reacted, both of Patch's corps would begin their main efforts. Depending on what happened, either corps could then lead the advance to Strasbourg. Both corps commanders insured their main assaults were narrow penetrations, not broad frontal attacks. Instead of battering away at prepared German defenses, American infantry would slice through the four defensive belts on narrow fronts. Once through, follow-on units would envelop the defenders from the rear, widen the breach, and shatter the defense. As a recent historian has observed, American forces would be used as "scalpels carving holes in the defenses . . . rather than battering rams."[23] Here the corps commanders were correct both according to the situation and the "book": Field Manual 100-5 Operations.

General Edward Brooks recognized that the German defenses facing VI Corps were also weak and lacked depth.[24] He was concerned that 31D would be too punched out if it made an opposed assault river crossing over the Meurthe, and their flanks too exposed to continue the exploitation. Instead, he decided to lead off with his two new divisions attacking north and south of his intended point of main effort. The Century Division began its supporting attack four days before the main effort, and would penetrate on a 2-mile front and then turn southeast to envelop 716VGD. Brooks wanted the bridges and road junction at Raon l'Étape secured. This would prevent a gap from opening between VI and XV Corps to the north. The 103rd would then take Saint-Dié, which was south of the intended Meurthe crossing. After a few days catching its breath as corps reserve, 31D would make the corps's main effort. If 103ID was able, it would parallel 31D to the south. The 36ID stood on the high ground overlooking Saint-Dié and the Taintrux Valley 4 miles from the Meurthe. It would cover the southern half of the corps sector and maintain contact with II French Corps of de Lattre's army to the south. The 36th would get a small breather at the beginning of the operation. It did not have a mission to attack but would be prepared to join the corps attack on order.

Preliminary movements of 103ID allowed it to clear a triangular hill mass between Taintrux and Saint-Dié. Raon l'Étape would be 100ID's first big fight. Instead of making a frontal assault there, the division commander, with Brooks's concurrence, decided to move north to Baccarat and cross the river on bridges already held by French 2AD, and then to attack Raon l'Étape from the rear. On 12 November, two regiments made this enveloping maneuver while the third demonstrated across the river directly before Raon l'Étape. Unfortunately for 100ID, the Germans, survivors of 708VGD, had used the pause to construct new positions to defend to the north – the direction from which 100ID's two regiments attacked. On the 14th, 100ID began a series of battalion-size attacks to penetrate these freshly constructed positions. They took several successive ridges that ran perpendicular to their axis of advance. This was tough, wooded country, and the dogfaces fought in very bad weather. The ridges presented far worse obstacles than anything in the Hürtgen. But the untried 100th broke through. By the 16th, they had gained key high ground that dominated Raon l'Étape and the Plaine River Valley. The 708VGD counterattacked, but they didn't have the strength to beat the Century Division. By the 18th, 100ID had captured Raon l'Étape. The Winter Line that was to have held until April had been ruptured in a few days. While 708VGD had already been beaten up in the fighting southwest of the Saverne Gap, the Century Division had put in a good first performance. Its third regiment crossed the river and advanced another 1.5 miles. Now 100ID's attack was running out of punch. Elements of 716VGD occupied positions blocking further forward movement. For a while Brooks considered deploying 14AD to exploit a breakthrough made by 100ID. The 716VGD's intact position dissuaded him. The 100ID had accomplished its mission, however. It moved German focus from Saint-Dié and to the north, away from the main effort.

The Saverne Gap was a wide avenue of approach. The 44ID was facing down elements of three German divisions and had to hold the corridor open. Devers's biggest worry was that the Germans would come up the Sarre and cut Patch's communications via the gap.[25] Reuben Jenkins felt it was critical to get VI Corps elements facing Colmar to turn north and defend against a possible counterattack. "We didn't have the troops for an operation this size," he said.[26] The Germans missed an opportunity to cut into Patch's left flank and penetrate 44ID, because they had neither the command agility nor the troop strength. This demonstrates the importance of the modern emphasis on getting inside the enemy's decision loop. Put another way, audacity prevented the Americans from getting hit.

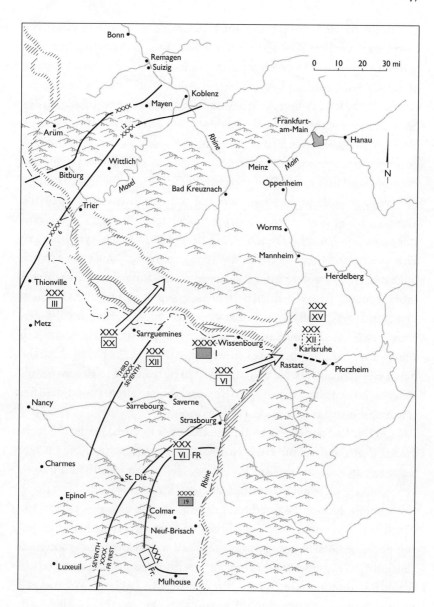

13.1. Plan of Possible Advance East of the Rhine

To the north, Haislip estimated that German strength opposite XV Corps was insufficient to man the several continuous lines that had been laid out. Instead, he expected to find individual strong points, placed in great depth, holding key ground. The defenders had few mobile reserves. If the lead American divisions could get beyond the defensive belts, Patch thought they would be able to move quickly. Haislip ordered his division commanders to stand ready to bypass defenders in order to keep up the momentum of the attack.[27] XV Corps led with 44ID attacking from west and north. The 79th would then attack the town through French 2AD south and east, enveloping 553VGD. This would allow the French a little time to ready a deep exploitation through the forward infantry divisions. The French would head east 10 miles on the road to Phalsbourg, and then turn off on the road to Saverne.[28] XV Corps struck out for Sarrebourg, two infantry divisions attacking abreast. The roads into the mountains were lined with dense evergreens. French 2AD coiled up behind them, ready to exploit any breakthrough. Leclerc and his men were on a holy mission. Early on, he had sworn an oath to liberate both Metz and Strasbourg, principal cities of the two Lost Provinces, from the hated Germans. While he was supposed to be readying to sweep toward Saverne, he really was planning to leap past the gap altogether and slither into Strasbourg, another twenty miles away.

Leclerc had done something like this once before. During the large sweep after the breakout from Normandy, the Americans gave Leclerc leave to run ahead and enter Paris first. He turned permission into license and ran all over the top of advancing Third Army units to get there. Fortunately, he was assigned to Haislip's corps, which was part of the Third Army during the incident. Fluent in French, Haislip had attended the École de Guerre between the wars and was sympathetic to French sensibilities. He smoothed things over with higher ups. Later, Haislip would say that he never issued direct orders to Leclerc. "Whenever I wanted him to do something, I would say: Leclerc, this is what I am planning to do. It looks to me as though you could do this."[29]

Heavy rain gave way to a blizzard. The entire XV Corps sector was covered. Despite the weather, Germans had dug several antitank ditches across the main highway at Phalsbourg. Many streams overfilled their banks, and some roads and bridges disappeared into the turgid water.

The 791D penetrated the lines of 708VGD. German troops began to melt away and 791D could advance as it pleased. Americans walked into Halloville and continued on in the direction of Sarrebourg. After some unorthodox maneuvers, 44ID also made progress. By the 16th, German commanders recognized that their situation had become critical. The 553VGD retained a cohesive defense, but the 708th was not faring well. Timing the armored advance was critical. On that day, Haislip began to push the French 2AD forward.

Haislip's two most forward infantry divisions rotated northward, creating a shield along the Moder River. While each German formation initially defended well, they began to come apart when Americans got behind them. Battalion by battalion, German morale began to fail. These makeshift units, many with Austrian fillers, did not have the cohesion for which the German Army had been famous. Large bodies of Germans began to surrender. Each American division took thousands of prisoners, but Leclerc moved too fast to bother with them.

Despite local counterattacks, Haislip sensed the impending break-through. So did Devers. He said, "We'll take them by surprise. They won't be expecting us to go straight at them."[30] On 18 November, 44ID began to break into the tactical depth of 553VGD. Under assault from the 79th, 708VGD, the new boy on the line, began to collapse. The 791D began to pick up speed. Leclerc's armor made ready to advance south of Sarrebourg and then turn right and into the Saverne Gap. The following day, 31D of VI Corps began its attack by attempting to infiltrate across the Meurthe. The swift current of the flooded river, rather than enemy activity, frustrated this effort. Rapid water swamped the infantry's rubber rafts. That evening, larger engineer boats were used for infantry platoons crossings, which the Germans didn't oppose. With security in place, engineers assembled a pair of foot bridges and a light vehicle bridge. By first light, 31D had five infantry battalions on the far bank. By 21 November, both 100ID and 31D were making substantial progress.

To reinforce 31D's successful crossing, Brooks altered his plan. Instead of a separate assault, he fed two regiments of 103ID into the 31D bridgehead. Continually rising waters took out one of the foot bridges and made the vehicular bridge impassable. These two Cactus Division regiments sought to envelop the defenders in the Foothill Line in front of their sister regiment near Saint-Dié. The Germans had the choice of running or being surrounded, so they pulled back from the town. Brooks's offensive had splintered the line of reinforced bunkers with a few well-directed blows. "The rapid advance of VI Corps is due to the personal leadership of Ted Brooks," said Devers. "He has a marvelous personality and exceptionally fine battle sense. . . . Commanders of armored units must be bold, aggressive men who waste not a minute."[31]

The 31D stumbled into something more – something that had been just a rumor. At Natzviller, the Allies for the first time liberated four thousand people from a Nazi concentration camp. The Americans moved so quickly that the Nazis didn't have time to blow up the camp. Vichy complicity in these crimes against humanity was exposed.

On 19 November, Haislip indicated that this was a good time for French 2AD to spring through holes created by the infantry and seize the Saverne Gap. He planned an advance of combined arms, American infantry, and French armor. To that end, 44ID and French 2AD were to assemble near Hemming. Typically, Leclerc had his own plans. His division did not enter the gap itself. By following small side roads and trails, French units snuck past German roadblocks on the larger highways and debouched onto the relatively flat Alsacian Plain. Leclerc had far outdistanced his American infantry support. French tanks broke onto the Plain of Alsace from the Birkenwald on 21 November. Having cleared the Saverne Gap, the French 2nd Armored Division was in good position to take Strasbourg.

Like XV Corps, VI Corps had already broken through the main German defenses but had not cleared the mountain range. Brooks was on the verge of committing his exploitation force. But he had only a single combat command of the inexperienced 14th Armored Division to fill the job. Devers had not been very happy with the early performance of 14AD.[32] Sensing the enemy's complete withdrawal, Brooks ordered his corps to change over from attack to pursuit on 21 November. Ever the tanker, he wanted to begin exploitation as soon as he saw an opening. Despite maddening delays, VI Corps advanced 15 miles by the 24th. Americans captured another line of partially finished defensive positions and stockpiles of ammunition, barbed wire, and other construction materials.

XV Corps was now in a better position to strike for Strasbourg than VI Corps back in the mountains. Reversing the initial plan, Patch ordered Haislip to have French 2AD seize the Alsatian capital. By doing so, he avoided a major inter-Allied problem as the French wanted to control Strasbourg. With or without orders, Leclerc was about to travel the final 20 miles and take Strasbourg. Devers worried that poor weather would prevent sufficient armor support for the infantry divisions that would have to follow lead French elements that were already through the Saverne Gap.

The 100ID was switched from VI to XV Corps. French 2AD advanced on two axes along minor approaches north of the Saverne Gap. Leclerc's men searched for every path and mountain trail. His instincts were correct. By 22 November, French armor was cleanly through the gap. Haislip authorized French patrols to scout toward the Alsatian capital. Knowing how Leclerc slipped the leash on the road to Paris, the American general knew that restraining Leclerc was a hopeless cause. So French tanks roared off. Devers was with Haislip when he ordered Leclerc to take Strasbourg on the 22nd. He was involved in developments and understood both the ever-present risks and the great potential rewards of breaking through the Nineteenth Army and attaining the Rhine.

Both Patch and Devers worried that a separation was opening between XV Corps and XII Corps, Patton's southernmost formation. This could provide the Germans with an opportunity to slice off XV Corps by exploiting that gap west of the Vosges. While it might be interpreted as a lack of attention to the specific mission of protecting the 12th Army Group's southern flank, the Germans had no force from which the 12th Army Group needed protection. While Jenkins felt the Americans didn't have sufficient troops to pull off even the first phase of the offensive, the German bench was even emptier.

Neither 6th Army Group nor Seventh Army headquarters required clearance for a specific route of advance to Strasbourg. This gave Leclerc a great deal of latitude. The French avoided the German defenses at Phalsbourg in order to gain speed. American infantry would subsequently attack and seize the town. American-made but French-driven vehicles careened all over the light-duty roads they traveled to Strasbourg. Leclerc's lead unit made for Pont de Hehl, the major bridge across the Rhine, but manned blockhouses on the far bank prevented a crossing. French armor raced into the city from the north and west, and the city fell on 23 November. The capital of Alsace was again in French hands. Devers recalled that hardly had Haislip given the order to advance into Strasbourg than the French reported that the city had already had been captured. Devers and an aide jumped into a jeep and hightailed it toward Strasbourg.

In ten days, XV Corps had advanced 50 miles. The French 2nd Armored covered the last 20 from Saverne to Strasbourg in a little over three hours. By comparison, the Seventh Army had advanced only 12 miles in the forty-five days prior to the November offensive. Reporting the win to de Gaulle, Leclerc's cable stated, "We will not rest until the flag of France also flies over Paris and Strasbourg." While it had entered Strasbourg, French 2AD's hold on the city was tenuous. The French could not take the western side of the bridge over the Rhine because blockhouses on the German side of the Rhine set down intense direct fire over the river. German artillery shelled the city. Strasbourg's main power plant was hit by German 240mm howitzers on the far bank. French 2AD spent 24 and 25 November cleaning out pockets of resistance and forts east of the Ruhr.

After the war, Jenkins stated that SHAEF staff were incensed that Strasbourg had been captured, a development they had not expected. "And I don't blame them," commented Jenkins.[33] To the east lay the Rhine. A single armored division did not have the strength to cross it and hold Strasbourg. But the Pont du Kehl beckoned.

Senior American commanders expected trouble when the Free French came in contact with the many residents of Strasbourg who did not consider themselves French. Having been citizens of Germany for four years, many Alsatians of German descent acted like loyal Germans, defending their birthright from the Gallic interlopers. General Devers organized a special unit, "T Force," to enter the city, monitor the change of governance, and prevent chaos. Thousands of collaborators who had aided the Nazis or openly participated in the Vichy government had already been thrown into prison. Communist elements of the resistance were ready to fight the de Gaullists. On 29 November, American troops reported the city to be in great turmoil. Leclerc ordered that civilians shooting at his troops be shot on sight, and five "hostages" be summarily executed for every man he lost to such treachery. This violation of international law shocked Devers. He immediately ordered Strasbourg to be plastered with posters proclaiming that the Allies would comply with the Geneva Convention, thereby negating a French general's orders as to what should happen on French soil. Through backchannels, Devers let both Leclerc and the military governor of Strasbourg know, in no uncertain terms, that improper Free French behavior would result in immediate cessation of all American support for the French Army.

Far to the south, the French faced the Germans blocking the Belfort Gap. Devers recalled that he couldn't get a commitment from Jean de Lattre to attack into the gap on 17 November in coordination with the Seventh Army's assault toward Saverne. Then, at Charles de Gaulle's invitation, Winston Churchill showed up to visit French First Army. Devers dispatched Henry Lodge to represent the 6th Army Group during that occasion. Devers was furious that de Lattre had refused to attack on time, apparently because of Churchill's visit. Admittedly, however, the weather was so bad that Churchill had asked, "You're not going on with your attack in this weather?"[34] Jake confronted the French general: "You gave me your word that you would attack on schedule." De Lattre responded, "Yes, but I did not say 'on my honor.'"[35]

Tasking the French with crossing the Rhine that far south simply made no sense. First, there was nothing but a wall of rugged, tree-covered ground on the far side from the Swiss border to Strasbourg. The French had nowhere to go. Second, the French First Army didn't have the amphibious assault equipment to cross the Rhine. Patch's engineers strained to assemble the required rafting and bridging to support the impending crossing at Rastatt and had nothing to spare. Stocking French magazines with sufficient ammunition was a Herculean task. They began their assault toward Belfort with a terrific cannonade, which, as Devers recalled, was "the way the French always got started."[36]

To almost everyone's surprise, the French First Army threw back the Germans defending Belfort. De Lattre sidestepped Belfort to the south and struck out for Mulhouse, about 20 miles to the north. The untried First Division Blindée (1AD), the spearhead for the attack by I Corps, clanked into Mulhouse on the 20th, forcing Wiese's army headquarters to flee. As the chief of staff of German Army Group G stated, "The French armor attacked with extraordinary dash and élan, reflecting the temperament of the army commanded by General de Lattre de Tassigny."[37] Apparently Wiese thought the action around Belfort was a raid and that the main threat was in the High Vosges. French II Corps did everything it could to reinforce that notion. Back in Belfort, the thick walls of Fortress Salbert were scaled in a surprise attack by the Commandos d'Afrique. The German division commander defending the city was killed, and the division's retreat poorly handled. The Germans counterattacked, but de Lattre sprung a trap near Burnhaupt snaring several thousand Germans. The French First Army demonstrated aplomb with which most outside observers, including Wiese, had not previously credited them.

By 16 November, the tanks of French 1AD were everywhere. German defenses along the Doubs River were repeatedly ruptured. Semi-trained new recruits from the FFI took a lot of casualties but showed panache in their attacks. Some Germans broke and ran for cover in the defensive bastions around Belfort. On the 17th, the French 1st Armored moved to exploit the widening breaches in German defenses. Devers recalled, "The French just went through that pass like nobody's business. They were in Mulhouse before you could turn around, and they were so enthusiastic about it that they didn't prepare themselves so the Germans counterattacked."[38] But the counterattack failed to dislodge them.

French 1AD of I Corps then went on to liberate Mulhouse on the afternoon of 20 November. Yet pockets of German resistance held out until follow-up forces and the Maquis could deal with them. In the mountains, French II Corps did not begin significant eastward movement until the 19th. By that date, German defenders were anxious to withdraw before the French advance lest they become trapped between two pincers. Both French corps linked up in Burnhaupt, west of Mulhouse. Wiese combined three divisions into the 63rd Attack Corps and punched south with the intent to cut off the French incursion to Mulhouse by counterattacking all the way to the French border. In its first employment as a massed unit, the First French Army defeated this German attack. But northward French movement toward Colmar had been stopped. Despite de Lattre's exhortation to move northward, fighting in and around the suburbs of Mulhouse continued. The two French corps finally linked up on the 28th by which time a good deal of Alsace had been liberated. Fighting had been heavy. Sixty charred panzer hulks littered the battlefields. Some of the destroyed Panthers contained documentation that said they had left the factory on 11 November. The French took seventeen thousand prisoners and estimated that they had killed another ten thousand. But the Free French lost ten thousand men and were no longer able to move north. Plans to clear additional ground along the Rhine going north to Colmar could not be accomplished.

Now de Lattre wanted to cross the Rhine into purely German territory near Neuf-Brisach. Instead, Devers pleaded with them to finish the job west of the Rhine by heading north all the way to Strasbourg where the U.S. XV Corps, led by French 2AD awaited. De Lattre directed the French I Corps to Colmar. But the Germans held. On 28 November, the French 1st Division entrained to reinforce efforts to clear Germans along France's west coast on the Bay of Biscay. The German LXIII Corps reverted to defense and prevented de Lattre from immediately collapsing what became the Colmar pocket. It was during this fight on 25 November that Eisenhower traveled to the French First Army to meet with de Lattre and his corps commanders.

Harth Forest was outflanked on its north. "In the mind of the 6th Army Group commander, the junction of his two armies and the complete liberation of Alsace was only a matter of days," wrote de Lattre, "and that was the hope in all the echelons."[39] It was all the French First Army could do to close up on Burnhaupt. French 5AD had the honor of closing the pincers on LXIII Corps. De Lattre's General Operations Order No. 174 of 30 November stressed the need to defend against further German counterattacks: "The wear and tear of our means was decidedly too serious to allow us to drive against an enemy now holding shorter lines."[40] In other words, the First French Army had reached its culmination. It was a spent force, incapable of closing the final 60 miles to Strasbourg. Devers had a big problem.

The 6th Army Group continued its offensive toward the Rhine. Reasoned analysis allowed Haislip and Patch to ignore their open flank and achieve a major breakthrough at Strasbourg. While both antagonists had weak points, only the Americans could continue to develop the situation. If only Joe Lawton Collins and Courtney Hodges had reached a similar conclusion about the Hürtgen Forest in September! The Seventh Army had no reason to genuflect to the U.S. First Army. The eminent commonwealth historian Chester Wilmot described the assault as a "brilliant stroke at Strasbourg [that] split the Germans in two. The Germans could not repair the breach."[41] Furious, Hitler declared that the Colmar Pocket, the last Alsatian soil in German hands, was to be held at all costs.

Both Rundstedt and Balck realized the danger of the penetration created by the Seventh Army.[42] Left unsealed, it opened a major breach between the German First and Nineteenth Armies. Patton's attack with XII Corps in the southern portion of the Third Army's sector added to the gravity of the situation. The thin German defensive line attempting to impede the Seventh Army's advance might be enveloped and destroyed, leaving an open road over the Rhine and into the Reich. German intelligence probably didn't know that Patch was already assembling DUKW amphibians to support a forced Rhine crossing. Jenkins recalled, "General Devers rode hard on both the Seventh Army and the French Army, particularly on the French, in those two operations."[43]

Only a major counterattack to regain Saverne would end Balck's crisis. But no German armored reserve worthy of mention existed. Rundstedt pleaded for headquarters to release Panzer Lehr, a German armored division, which was near Münster preparing for the Ardennes attack. Hitler acceded. It would have to move 300 miles in two days. The upcoming Ardennes offensive now marginally aided the 6th Army Group's attack into Alsace. Hitler would not release additional troops, so Balck scraped together what he could to add to his comparatively small force. Rundstedt ordered Balck to commit it en masse in an attack from north to south to seal off the American penetration at its base.

On Thanksgiving Day 1944, Division Panzer Lehr clanked southward in two columns. It moved toward the opening gap between the U.S. Third and Seventh Armies, seeking to hit the exposed northern flank of XV Corps. Boundaries are notorious weak spots. More than likely, German intelligence had identified the seam. With great boldness, the panzer division attacked down the western face of the Vosges. Exploiting a gap in Allied forces was what Eisenhower and his staff feared most. Balck, the Army Group G commander, had not lost his nerve. But he did not have the troop strength to back up his audacious maneuver. Both of Balck's army commanders, having a better grasp on the real situation, had little faith in his plan. First Army commander, General Otto von Knobelsdorff, who controlled the actions of Panzer Lehr, estimated that the division would do well to hold what was left of his Saar Valley position.

Upon learning about the counterattack, Haislip stopped additional units from coming through the Saverne Gap toward Strasbourg. En route east to create part of the "northern shield," 441D backstopped the 106th Cavalry Group, which was guarding XV Corps' northern flank. But Haislip did not recall his other divisions east of the Vosges. Panzer Lehr forced one of 441D's regiments back. The divisional commander moved his other forward regiment back so as not to give the panzers the opportunity to flank either of them. But Panzer Lehr of November 1944 was not the same quality division the Allies had fought in France during the summer. Many of its fighters were semi-trained recruits. The Germans did not have enough counterattack power to turn back Devers's bid for the Rhine.

Panzer Lehr wasn't the only armored division looking for an open flank. XII Corps, the southern wing of Patton's Third Army, was located northwest of the attacking Germans. General Manton Eddy's forces were making steady if unspectacular progress advancing toward the Sarre River. General Eddy, XII Corps commander, was concerned that his 4th Armored Division would become bogged in a move across soggy open ground. To facilitate their advance, he received permission to move 4AD through XV Corps's zone. On the eve of Panzer Lehr's attack, this placed the American armor in a fortuitous position. The 4th Armored saw an opportunity to bite Panzer Lehr in the flank. Lehr's offensive action became an opportunity to pulverize a panzer division in the open. Brushing aside grenadiers from 361VGD, the 4th Armored tore into the western column of Lehr's attack. Mud kept most German and American tanks road-bound. Seasoned American armored infantry proved more than a match for newly inducted panzer grenadiers. Aside from presenting lucrative targets, the German attack against XV Corps had no significant impact on the Seventh Army's offensive. Patch and Haislip were ready to resume their advance to the Rhine.[44]

In both the Seventh and French First Army areas, German defenses were falling apart. The German command structure was incapable of keeping pace with the maneuvers of the 6th Army Group and was breaking down.[45] This was an attacker's dream. Balck did not know the status of troops supposed to be countering the 6th Army Group pincers closing around the Nineteenth Army. At the theater level, Rundstedt thought that the French attack down south was the major threat, and was not aware of the gap opening between his First and Nineteenth Armies. He thought Panzer Lehr could deal with the problem. As the official history states, "Devers's 6th Army Group had shattered Wiese's Nineteenth Army in a series of hammering blows."[46] A fifteen-mile gap opened. This was large enough to allow a multidivisional-sized force to blow through and reach the Rhine. Wiese knew that his forces were once again close to collapse.[47] He had exhausted his meager reserves, and higher headquarters said no more should be expected. Between Patch and de Lattre, the Nineteenth Army faced being cut off in a double envelopment. Hitler was furious and blamed his local commanders. By early December, both the army and army group commanders were relieved of command.

In the First and Ninth Armies' attack north of the Ardennes, Operation Queen, Omar Bradley halted the Ninth Army repeatedly because the First Army was having so much trouble. What should have been two penetrations on a narrow front like the Seventh Army's attack through the mountains to Strasbourg became two blunt frontal attacks. The German players were getting two moves to one against the Americans. The contrast in both army and army group commanders is revealing.

Balck agreed with Wiese's assessment that the Nineteenth Army was about to be surrounded and destroyed. But because of vague information at his higher headquarters, Balck had trouble convincing Rundstedt of the seriousness of the risk. The field marshal hesitated and then began reconsidering the situation as more reports filtered in. Finally, Rundstedt reached Balck's conclusion. The Nineteenth Army would have to retreat across the Rhine.

From top to bottom, U.S. Seventh Army commanders were full of vigor and ready to continue into Germany. The twin barriers of the Rhine and the Siegfried Line were both within range of immediate assault, and General Patch was confident of the ability of his Seventh Army to breach them. From the beginning of the "Champagne Campaign," 6th Army Group planners had thought to cross the Rhine.[48] The mighty river flows in a contained 700–750-foot channel and moves about 4 miles per hour at Karlsruhe and 6 at Basel. These speeds are at the upper limits of what 1944 river-crossing technology could handle, and were about the maximum current in which pontoon bridges could be erected. Several dams on the upper Rhine could flood the river so care had to be taken by the Allies.

The army group engineer, Brigadier General Henry C. Wole, who had extensive experience from combat landings in Italy and Dragoon, began studying the problems with the use of a hydrological laboratory found intact at a hydroelectric equipment manufacturer in Grenoble. Over 300 assault boats, 150 DUKWs, and a pile of 25-ton pontoon bridging were assembled.[49] The 6th Army Group was planning ahead. In comparison, the 12th Army Group headquarters had specific objectives assigned on the Rhine near Cologne as part of the theater main effort but did little planning. In fact, that HQ was so busy looking after tactical details that it failed to prepare to handle the problems of crossing the much smaller Roer River, which was an intermediate obstacle not successfully crossed for many months to come. Devers knew what he was supposed to do.

Based on preliminary plans and the speed with which the Saverne Gap had been penetrated, Patch and Haislip remained convinced that XV Corps could easily seize a bridgehead across the Rhine at Rastatt.[50] As early as 21 November, Patch directed the Seventh Army engineer to alert the veteran and very capable 40th Engineer Combat Regiment (40th Combat Engineer Group) to prepare to support a Rhine crossing.[51] That was just about the time both of his corps had broken through the initial German defenses. DUKWs, bridges, ferries, and other specialized equipment were ordered forward. The Seventh Army engineer declared that he was ready to support a two-division assault crossing.

Initially, Devers and Patch looked for a crossing to commence between 10 and 20 December.[52] The Seventh Army was on a roll. Preparations were coming together so quickly that both generals agreed they could advance the crossing into the first week in December – a little more than a week ahead of schedule. XV Corps reconnoitered the Rhine between Strasbourg and Soufflenheim and prepared to take advantage of any quick opportunity to cross.[53] Patton's fast-working staff would need a week a month later to swing III Corps from east to north to rescue

Bastogne. While no one on the Allied side could have known at the time, this would have created a major assault across the Rhine about ten days before Hitler's Ardennes offensive. If the Americans had established a multidivisional bridgehead that threatened to surround both the German First and Nineteenth Armies, it is hard to imagine their ever beginning the Battle of the Bulge. The eminent Napoleonic strategist Carl von Clausewitz had considered the situation of two opposing armies mounting offensives on separated fronts almost simultaneously. His unequivocal conclusion was that the army that pushed first and hardest would win.

The concept of operations assigned the crossing itself to Haislip. XV Corps controlled four infantry divisions. The more experienced units, 45ID and 79ID, were closest to the river and would have made the assault crossing. The 40th Engineer Group had marshaled its equipment to support a two-regimental assault crossing as early as 0600 on 25 November. VI Corps was ready to advance through a XV Corps bridgehead and exploit up the east bank of the river.[54] Brooks maneuvered VI Corps north away from Strasbourg and toward the gaping hole in the German lines. His corps contained 3ID, 36ID, and 103ID, elements of 14AD, and the French 2AD. The 36ID, the southernmost division, was to have been withdrawn from Colmar containment operations by 30 November and coiled up for offensive action. By early December, the 12th Armored Division became available to the 6th Army Group. Of course, the French First Army would have to slide north to cover the northern arc of the Colmar pocket covered by VI Corps. That move should have eliminated what was beginning to form as the Colmar Pocket.

The 6th Army Group and SHAEF staffs were in communication about Devers's plans. "[Ken] Strong and [J. F. M.] Whiteley were also an inspiration. They see our problem from an impersonal point of view."[55]

On 11 December 1944, Devers wrote to Marshall: "De Lattre is in one of his temperamental modes at the moment and it always takes us some time to get him started again. . . . I shall have trouble clearing up the pocket in the Alsatian plain, for the French at the moment have an inferiority complex. However it is my opinion that we can keep the drive to the north going and possibly get set for a quick crossing of the Rhine."

FOURTEEN

Throw Down at Vittel
and Its Aftermath

GEORGE MARSHALL'S COUNTERPART, CHIEF OF THE BRITISH
Imperial Staff Sir Alan Brooke, was almost beside himself. He felt that
Eisenhower had splattered scarce combat resources up and down the line
without concentrating sufficient combat power to win on the decisive
front north of the Ardennes. Brooke confided in Bernard Montgomery,
"You have always told me, and I have agreed with you, that Ike was no
commander, that he had no strategic vision, was incapable of making a
plan or of running operations when started."[1] The two British field marshals communicated almost every night. Since late August, Montgomery
had been grinding on Eisenhower to shift the First and maybe the Ninth
Armies to Montgomery's army group and place the British marshal in
sole control of a single "full-blooded thrust," while everyone else stood
down so support could be concentrated.

Marshall and Brooke almost never agreed on anything. But the pressure coming from the British, and the lack of any real results since early
September, set Eisenhower's teeth on edge. In turn, his list of perceived
shortfalls committed by Jacob Devers was long. In his estimation, Devers had shot wide of the mark several times. Neither Eisenhower nor
his chief of staff, "Beetle" Smith, thought Devers had done a decent job
since assuming command of the 6th Army Group. Eisenhower had told
Devers to stay west of the Vosges. Now he was about to attempt a Rhine
crossing on the east side, and he hadn't told his boss.

The attitude around SHAEF did not favor Devers. Smith and Eisenhower had been particularly unhappy with Devers's management of the
Alsace campaign in October and early November. They felt he had not

acted aggressively enough to exploit his numerical advantage against the Germans.[2] Given the achievements of the 6th Army Group, especially when compared to that of Omar Bradley, this hardly seems an objective conclusion.

Devers's operations officer (G3), Reuben Jenkins remembered, "I noticed General Devers sometimes felt that General Eisenhower should have given him much greater latitude. I don't believe General Eisenhower was guilty of favoritism to anybody. He was too cold-blooded to favor anybody for anything. He was not that kind of guy in my opinion."[3] Jenkins thought that the problem started when Devers criticized Eisenhower's management of North Africa upon taking up as deputy commander in the Mediterranean. "There was not the warmth between those two men that you normally expect," Jenkins continued.[4] Eugene Harrison concurred. "I felt that General Devers and General Eisenhower did not get along."[5] Eisenhower had come to dislike face-to-face meetings with Devers almost as much as meetings with Montgomery. By the time he gained command of the 6th Army Group, Devers had learned not to try to influence the supreme commander and to stay out of his way.[6]

While Devers, Sandy Patch, and their staffs feverously worked on plans to cross the Rhine, Bradley and Eisenhower began a tour in November of the southern half of ETO. First, they met with George Patton in Nancy. Horrible weather and river flooding had bogged his attempt at breakout through Lorraine. The Third Army's offensive was crawling through the mud before strong, triple-layered defenses. It was clear that Patton was nowhere near breakthrough. While Eisenhower and Bradley differed in the details, both agreed that Patton needed major assistance in order to get moving. Before the two men, Patton asked that XV Corps be returned to the Third Army. He had a study prepared for his two seniors. Patton pointed out "that between Luneville and Thionville there was room for only one army, and there was just one natural corridor."[7] While Eisenhower tended to agree, Bradley thought the change would take too much time. But he saw that with six divisions to cover 70 miles of front, Patton could not concentrate for a significant attack. Instead, the 12th Army Group commander proposed to narrow the Third Army's sector by moving the army group boundary north. XV Corps, still under Patch's control, would have to take up the ground vacated by the Third

Army. Patton would then be able to better concentrate XII Corps for attack from east of Nancy and into the Saar via Saarbrucken.

Neither Eisenhower nor Bradley expected much from the 6th Army Group for the remainder of the year. After speaking with Patton, the two senior officers had one critical item on their agenda for their upcoming meeting with Devers. They wanted to take a couple of divisions from the 6th Army Group and give them to Patton. Eisenhower saw nothing east of the Vosges Mountain he wanted. The French could guard whatever part of France they held. While Eisenhower knew that the Seventh Army had thrust through the Saverne Gap and gotten to Strasbourg, it is not evident that he appreciated the implications of this move. Still concentrated on his theater strategy, which placed the main effort north of the Ardennes on Operation Queen, with Patton attacking on a secondary axis toward the Saar, Eisenhower considered Strasbourg extraneous.

After leaving Patton's HQ at Nancy, Eisenhower and Bradley planned first to visit the Seventh Army's two corps headquarters, XV Corps (commanded by Wade Haislip) at Sarrebourg and VI Corps (commanded by Edward Brooks) at Saint-Dié. Then they would have dinner and remain overnight with Devers at the 6th Army Group HQ in Vittel.

Patch and Devers, "looking happy and boyish as usual" according to Bradley's aide, joined the traveling party at Lunéville on the way to Sarrebourg.[8] When the heavy brass arrived there on the 24th, Panzer Lehr, advancing to the attack, was only a handful of miles away. The panzers and the 4th Armored Division (AD) were tangling, but the Americans had yet to attain ascendancy. XV Corps headquarters troops were digging defensive positions. Haislip tried to wave the senior generals along and out of danger. In response to his pleadings, Eisenhower laughed and scolded, "Dammit, Ham, you invited me for lunch and I'm not going to leave until I get it."[9]

Patton's earlier presentation and Bradley's influence appear to have reaffirmed Eisenhower's opinion of what XV Corps should do. In his 5 November diary entry, Patton noted that Devers "would push XV Corps along on our right" in order to support the Third Army's offensive.[10] While he had not done that, Devers believed he had complied with the overall intent of Eisenhower's instructions. There was, however, the little matter of the gap that had opened between XII and XV Corps. The official historian suggests that, while dismissing the threat posed by Panzer Lehr, its recent attack, though unsuccessful, may have struck a note of caution with Eisenhower.

He found Haislip and his staff busily preparing for an impending crossing of the Rhine. Surprised and displeased, he immediately issued verbal instructions to cease all efforts to cross the Rhine and to reorient XV Corps northward into the widening gap. They were to advance on the west side of the Vosges in close proximity to, and supporting, Patton's attack.[11]

At the time of this order, loaded DUKWs were already moving to forward assembly areas to prepare for their entry into the Rhine's swift-flowing waters.[12] Sixth Army Group officers in attendance were stunned at Eisenhower's reaction but said nothing. Since daily situation reports and copies of all formal orders had been routinely forwarded to SHAEF, they were surprised that he seemed to know nothing of their preparations. Apparently, this was the first Eisenhower had heard about a Rhine crossing.

Even before he arrived at XV Corps HQ, Eisenhower already had a head of steam up because Patton was stalled. Devers had much of his army group on the wrong side of the Vosges, that is, on the eastern side, not on the western one helping Patton to execute SHAEF's theater strategy. The great Queen offensive was stalled at the Roer River, 25 miles short of the Rhine. American intelligence had identified one of the two panzer armies coiled to crush any 12th Army Group crossing force over the Roer. Queen was a great disappointment.

From Sarrebourg, the group traveled on to VI Corps HQ ensconced in the ruins of Saint-Dié. General Brooks, elated at the progress his corps was making, also was preparing for a Rhine crossing. Again, Eisenhower halted further efforts. On the way to Vittel, the atmosphere between Eisenhower and Devers must have been unbelievably tense. Eisenhower had just halted his 6th Army Group commander's preparations for crossing the Rhine. Instead of reinforcing the Seventh Army, Eisenhower had arrived looking for two divisions and was ready to take them from the 6th Army Group. Devers was about to make the sales pitch of his career to the supreme commander; Eisenhower was getting ready to spank Devers.

With VI Corps on the Rhine north of Strasbourg, and the First French Army advancing up the eastern face of the Vosges toward Strasbourg, the 6th Army Group had an exhilarating opportunity to perform the feat that had eluded all of the Allied armies since September: leap the Rhine! But with that advance came a problem. South of Strasbourg, the Germans retained a bridgehead across the river centered on Colmar. What became known as the Colmar Pocket might prove a significant risk to any Rhine crossing. Devers and Eisenhower had diametrically opposed opinions about the relationship of opportunity to risk of Devers's proposed offensive.

One cannot understand the Rhine crossing opportunity without also evaluating the risk at Colmar. Eisenhower was deeply concerned about the Germans who remained west of the Rhine from just south of Strasbourg to just north of Mulhouse, centered on Colmar. Devers argued that remnants in the Colmar Pocket had no offensive capability and would be cleaned up shortly by the French First Army, while VI Corps was turned north to follow XV Corps across the Rhine. Devers may have appeared to be shooting from the hip, but he did have good staff work and an intelligence summary to back up his judgment. He had swung the Seventh Army northward only because Jean de Lattre promised that the French would swiftly clear the Rhine's west bank.[13]

Devers knew a German panzer army was to the northeast and that it was possible a segment of it could be used to cut off VI Corps.[14] SHAEF intelligence was aware of the Sixth Panzer Army but believed the bulk of it was just north of the Ardennes, waiting to deal with Bradley if he succeeded in crossing the Roer, 150 miles north of the Vosges. That boded ill for the chances of the main effort. What no one knew was that the panzer army was massing for the Ardennes attack. When interviewed twenty-five years after the war, Devers was still dismissive of the threat: "The Colmar Pocket wouldn't have amounted to anything if SHAEF had given me two extra divisions. They really weren't needed north of me [between Strasbourg and Rastatt] as there was nothing but mud and water up there. I would have had the Colmar Pocket cleared up in two or three days. . . . However I [was] responsible for the Colmar Pocket."[15]

Devers had a totally different perspective than Eisenhower's. What a breathtaking set of events had just occurred in the Saverne Gap! Devers recalled, "I was poised to cross the Rhine. Eisenhower didn't know it, and I wasn't telling anybody, but I was poised in the forest near the Rhine."[16] After months of deadlock up and down the entire Western front, the seemingly unimportant 6th Army Group had created a tremendous opportunity, a "clean breakthrough to the river."[17] Patch had amphibious assault equipment for six battalions and was confident his troops were capable of getting across the river.[18] Both Patch and Devers were ready to move.

Devers was determined to change Eisenhower's mind.[19] His staff had prepared a detailed presentation of the opportunity to cross the Rhine and capture the German First Army. With such a hole in the German lines, the Third and Seventh Armies could destroy the bulk of Hermann Balck's forces. That was consistent with Eisenhower's first strategic objective, destroying the German Army west of the Rhine. With the two U.S. armies victoriously astride the Rhine, they could then move in whatever manner that best executed theater strategy to finish destruction of the Wehrmacht, penetrate into the innards of Germany, and win the war.

After dinner at 6th Army Group HQ in Vittel, Bradley, Devers, and Eisenhower retired to Devers's office to discuss strategy. Only the three generals were in the room, and the door was closed. Devers readied to make his pitch. He had the maps and material his chief strategic planner had prepared, which laid out current German defenses, a scheme of maneuver, and the terrain and corridors to be used. Devers presented a map with overlays highlighting the railroads, mountains, terrain, rivers, and approaches down the Rhine Valley (see map 13.1).

Later, General Eugene Harrison recalled the concept for the attack. With all of the commotion around Aachen and Metz, "the Germans would be incapable of bringing any forces to stop an attack down the Rhine Valley."[20] Two armies, Third and Seventh, would attack along the ancient line of conquest, the plains of the upper Rhine Valley. The 6th Army Group had two railways, one east and another west of the Rhone River, and a pipeline and two railroad lines stood ready to bring supplies north. A second pipeline was almost completed. This provided more supply tonnage than the 12th Army Group could provide to Patton's effort.

In retirement, Devers recalled saying at the Vittel meeting,

Well, Ike, I'm on the Haguenau River, moving north. I've got everything in the woods there to cross the Rhine. On the other side, there are a lot of pillboxes, but they are not occupied. I want to cross the Rhine and go up the other side and come back behind their defenses. They've got some defenses up there. We've been up and seen some of them. We got close up. In that way, I will force the Germans to lighten up Patton's front, and I think I've got enough that I can hold this corridor. Patton can then move, and then I can move. If he can get moving and get across [the Rhine] and [keep] going, he's got nothing ahead of him but to keep going ahead. All I've got to do is hang on.[21]

Eisenhower didn't seem interested. He responded, "Well, I'm thinking of taking two divisions from you. I wouldn't think of you crossing the Rhine."

At times, the discussion became quite heated. People outside of the room heard a lot of yelling. Bradley opined that an assault against fixed fortifications on the east bank of the Rhine was foolhardy and would fail. He was guessing. Devers recalled, "Bradley said, 'You can't cross the Rhine because those pillboxes are like hedgerows.'"

Devers responded, "Well, there is nobody in those pillboxes."

"How do you know it?" responded Bradley.

"Because I've been down, and I talked to some patrols I found along the river that have just come back from over there. Also, my intelligence tells me that."

Ike began to respond. "Well . . ."

Devers cut him off. "Ike, before you make a decision about this, and I feel very strongly about it as you can see. I am really worked up about this. I've always been taught that you always reinforce strength. You never reinforce weakness. This is a basic thing of an aggressive commander. Patch is successful. His divisions are all in good strength. I know Patton's divisions are under strength. They've had casualties. But we are up to strength."[22]

Devers knew Patton had endured fifty thousand casualties in the fall campaign. Trench foot was rampant in the Third Army. The roads in Lorraine had been torn to pieces from the rain, heavy traffic, and artillery fire. Patton had barely slithered his way to the West Wall through mud created by the worst rains in fifty years. The runoff from the Vosges

Mountains added to his misery. Devers had warned him about this and suggested he start later in November, after the ground had a chance to absorb the water. But Patton refused the advice. Bradley's two-army assault barely lurched to the Roer and had no chance of reaching the Rhine. "The Allied offensive, except in 6th Army Group, was stopped cold with no prospects in sight. When Marshall visited in October and was shown the plans for Queen, his private opinion was, I didn't see how [Bradley] was going to do it [cross the Rhine], myself."[23]

Devers inferred that Eisenhower was ordering him to pull back into the Vosges. "Ike, that doesn't make sense. The only way you are going to shorten my line is to pull back into the mountains. By that you increase my line because I have no field of fire in these Vosges Mountains where I have a field of fire up here in the fortified places. It doesn't take any troops to hold them." Eisenhower continued to insist that the 6th Army Group be weakened in order to reinforce Patton's stalled attack in Lorraine. Devers made a counteroffer: "Why don't you shorten Patton's front and give me more of Patton's sector? I can do that. I can sideslip a little bit because there isn't too much in those mountains. This will help you out with what you're working on."[24] Devers reasoned that, by taking on a larger sector, he could avoid losing the divisions Eisenhower was looking for but still contribute to solving the problem.

When Devers countered that he could take over part of the Third Army's sector *and* cross the Rhine, he was out of his depth, which must have been obvious to the other two generals in the room. The 6th Army Group could not go it alone. Such rashness must have made Eisenhower even less eager to allow Devers and his men to cross the Rhine. Having Germans west of the Rhine around Colmar only added to the risk, and that finally overwhelmed Devers's proposal. Rearranging troops along hundreds of miles of front was difficult and time-consuming; this had been Bradley's reason for leaving XV Corps with the Seventh Army instead of returning it to the Third.

When he saw that Eisenhower was not budging, Devers backed up a little and argued that the Seventh Army's advancing on the far side of the Rhine would do more to break the Third Army free than simply supporting Patton's right flank west of the river. Bradley strongly disagreed. The debate lasted until 2 A M. Devers continued to argue for permission to make a major effort over the Rhine. He repeated that the Seventh Army, not the Third, should be reinforced. After all, Patton's effort had yet to bear fruit. Devers did not directly bring up the notion of transferring the Third Army to the 6th Army Group, but his plans officer, Reuben Jenkins, had discussed this with Eisenhower's operations officer, Harold Bull. Many are the paths that consensus builders tread upon, but virtually no one begins the journey by surprising a superior with a course to which he or she is diametrically opposed and starting from the doghouse raises the difficulty exponentially.

Without question, Eisenhower took a careful look at Devers's presentation and the Seventh Army plans. And, as commander, Eisenhower had the final word. "You won't cross the Rhine and you won't send two divisions to Bradley."[25] He halted all further preparations to cross the Rhine. Columns of engineers and bridging equipment on their way to the crossing sites were turned around. He issued direct orders for XV Corps to travel back over the Vosges and support Patton's attack by paralleling it in the southern portion of Lorraine.

Eisenhower left the meeting very angry. He had taken Devers's criticism personally. Devers also was angry. He wondered if he would ever be included in Eisenhower's inner circle. Many years into his retirement, he maintained that he was always loyal to Eisenhower: "Maybe I was a little too aggressive with Beetle [Smith] in 1943."[26] Devers felt that Eisenhower's decision not to press a Rhine crossing was a major error.[27] The already poor relationship between Eisenhower and Devers became much worse, and Devers began to openly disparage Eisenhower around headquarters, which sealed his fate.

Devers, and later Patch, were stunned by Eisenhower's decision, having understood that his instructions to Devers on 23 October had been to seek a Rhine crossing and to deploy in strength.[28] Furthermore, SHAEF's 28 October directive stated that the Allies would take "any opportunity" to gain a bridgehead over the Rhine.[29] Instead of aggressively attacking, Eisenhower was concerned about remaining German units west of the Rhine wedged in between Patch and the French First Army in the Colmar Pocket, fearing that this German force might advance north into the flank of the Seventh Army as Patch attempted to attack northeast. The truth was that what was left of Friedrich Wiese's Nineteenth Army wasn't about to bite anyone. Pressed from north and south, separated from their First Army, Germans in the pocket were more worried about saving their own hides, as Devers had said.

After all of the snarling among the British and American chiefs and all of the acrimony between Eisenhower and his northern and central army group commanders, it was probably too much to expect him to designate a new main effort on the spot. Besides, Eisenhower had repeatedly endorsed the concept all the way up to the combined chiefs, and he and his staff had consistently underscored the need for a strong secondary attack. What Devers was proposing did not have to stray from the established theater strategy or the location of the main effort. The Devers plan still contained a primary attack in the north and a secondary attack in the south toward the Saar, with operations designed to destroy German combat power along the Rhine. Rather, Devers's proposal was a new operational concept to execute that strategy by redirecting the secondary effort.

An intermediate objective less than 100 miles further south than Patton's current objective, Rastatt was a tremendous opportunity. The operational focus, crossing the Rhine in Patton's area near Mannheim, remained unchanged. Rastatt was a means to the end, forcing a fight to seize the Saar and creating further penetration of the Frankfurt-Fulda Gap. A shift of the attack to be mounted by Patton to the south to follow the Seventh Army either over the Rhine or to an envelopment of German First Army was a far less radical and risky maneuver than attempting to capture a series of four bridges with airborne troops *before* "a bridge too far" at Arnhem. As Patton was later to demonstrate in response to the German Ardennes offensive, the Third Army could turn a corps ninety degrees and begin to fight in a new direction in only a few days. What better way to surprise the Germans and present them with huge American columns racing through a major rupture in German defenses? In this way, the Allies might have regained the initiative instead of having to wrench it from freezing German hands in the Ardennes. After destroying major German forces in the south, the Allied main effort on the north German plain could rev up and pick its way through German resistance that had been thinned to meet the southern emergency. This alternative would have been far better than battering the 12th Army Group against existing defenses in some second iteration of Operation Queen.

But Eisenhower wasn't in the frame of mind to entertain a new operational perspective, and that was the end of the Devers's proposal. As the 6th Army Group history records, "General Devers was anxious to make a crossing of the Rhine on the Seventh Army front but his basic mission of assisting Twelfth Army Group was a controlling factor and General Bradley preferred the maximum of close in support west of the Rhine. [Eisenhower's] apparent decision was to continue operations for decisive defeat of the enemy west of the Rhine and to await a more favorable opportunity for opening the SECOND PHASE involving the capture of bridgehead over the Rhine and deployment on the East Bank."[30]

What was behind Eisenhower's intransigence? At the end of August, Bernard Montgomery had sidestepped Eisenhower's clear intention to take Antwerp in order to follow his own agenda toward the Rhine. Even Omar Bradley had ignored Eisenhower's directive to concentrate two corps in the Aachen Gap in early September and instead sent V Corps on a fruitless expedition into the Ardennes.[31] Why was Eisenhower now putting his foot down on subordinates who freelanced away from the established SHAEF plan? Eisenhower's principal biographer suggests that, "by November 20, he was becoming discouraged."[32] For over two months, nothing had gone right. Market Garden had been a failure. Courtney Hodges had been bloodily unsuccessful both at Aachen and in the Hürtgen Forest. Patton was stalled in front of Metz on the Moselle in the sector north of Patch's. Was it the months of argument from Field Marshals Brooke and Montgomery that the Ruhr and north German plain were the only objectives that mattered? Was it the memory of the way Montgomery had burned him in that conversation aboard Eisenhower's B-25 at Brussels airport when Market Garden had been both presented and approved? Or was it that he simply did not trust either Devers's presentation or his ability to lead a group across the Rhine?

What Devers was pitching at Vittel was something the SHAEF planning staff had never considered, an envelopment of the forces west of the Rhine that barred the Third Army's advance by cutting them off with a major sweep east of the Rhine.[33] Even if Eisenhower didn't trust what he was hearing, he could have brought in key members of SHAEF and Third Army staff. Bradley and Devers could have met them at Devers's HQ the next morning to get the facts straight and review plans in more detail. A similar meeting on short notice under much more dire circumstances would be held to deal with the German Ardennes offensive at Verdun on 19 December. Patton had already thought about the major alternative and concluded a stab across the Rhine at Rastatt had merit. In a 24 November letter to his wife, Patton wrote, "I personally believe the VI Corps should have crossed the Rhine."[34] Patton also disagreed with Eisenhower's leashing of Devers. Bradley couldn't figure out how to get over the Roer, let alone the Rhine. Patton was more than willing to serve in Devers's 6th Army Group.

Devers was proposing a creative extension of the basic two-pronged SHAEF plan, retaining the primary attack in the north but redirecting the secondary attack over the Rhine at Rastatt and then onto the Saar by a less direct route than the one on which Patton had been unable to advance. Under Devers's alternative, the subordinate attack, after eliminating the German First Army, could then follow the old Napoleonic route to Berlin via the Fulda Corridor. Eisenhower's plan had deadlocked for the better part of two months. Many knowledgeable officers expected a static campaign to emerge with little progress until spring.[35]

As events were about to demonstrate, Eisenhower was in grave danger of losing the initiative. Devers had in front of him an opportunity to tear a big hole and get Patton across the Rhine and on his way into the Saar. As the official history states, "Instead Eisenhower and his major subordinates remained preoccupied with their existing plans." The official historians labeled their section describing that "a dubious decision."[36]

After the Vittel meeting, Eisenhower cabled Marshall: "As you know, the French made very fine advances in the extreme south against relative weak resistance and Seventh Army had broken through the Vosges. All the current operations in that region are, of course, merely for the purpose of cleaning up that flank as a preliminary to turning the bulk of the Seventh Army north to make, along with Patton, a converging attack upon the great salient in the Siegfried line west of the Rhine," and "so that Devers can hurriedly throw his strength north [i.e., in support of

Patton]."[37] Only a few days later, Eisenhower made the same point to the combined chiefs: the reason for continuing to concentrate on the north is that "the great bulk of the German Army is located there." Thus, "the cheapest way of protecting our flanks and rear [was] the 'Dragoon' force." Recent success by the 6th Army Group had created "a very healthy flank condition that will permit greater concentration further north for future attacks."[38]

Eisenhower's book *Crusade in Europe* was his sincere effort to recount the campaign in Western Europe and spread the credit. In light of this, his comments on the "throw down in Vittel" are rather sharp: "I particularly cautioned Devers not to start this northward movement, on east of the Vosges Mountains, until he had cleaned out all enemy formations in his rear." Leaving such a pocket "would be certain to cause us later embarrassment." He believed that Devers's estimate of the French First Army's immediate effectiveness was overly optimistic, while at the same time, he probably underrated the defensive power of the German units. "Colmar always bothered me."[39]

In fairness to the defensive oriented argument, the Colmar Pocket threatened to badly stretch an already undersized 6th Army Group. On Thanksgiving Day, Devers was confident that the French First Army could take care of this salient: "The German Nineteenth Army has ceased to exist as a tactical force."[40] Failing to deliver on that estimate would become a major bone of contention between the two senior American generals well past 1945. A German counterattack at the base of the Vosges threatened to cut off Devers's attack. On the other hand, Eisenhower had a taste of Balck's best shot: the attack by the 21st Panzers backed by what was left of the 25th Panzer Grenadier Division. Eisenhower wouldn't even let that effort disturb his lunch! Uprooting Patton's attack, which had already ground his infantrymen into Lorraine's mud, and sending his men off gallivanting through Alsace was also a risk that Bradley in particular was unwilling to shoulder.

A larger risk of Devers's proposal was the need for additional troops. The 6th Army Group had enough combat power to leap the Rhine, but at best it could move up the far side of the Rhine with but a single corps. While this was more than the paltry force Montgomery's plan provided for, had it linked to an Arnhem crossing, such a maneuver would need at least another corps from the Third Army. Eisenhower should have been aware that his staff had already concluded from a theoretical exercise that it could release a corps to reinforce another sector.[41] But removing another corps from the 12th Army Group would effectively shut down Patton's upcoming offensive plans. Rather, it would move that offensive 60 miles to the east. More importantly, it would transfer overall command of the secondary attack from Bradley, a general Eisenhower held in great esteem, and entrust it to the man he considered ".22 caliber."

In his study *Eisenhower's Lieutenants*, Russell Weigley observes, "General Eisenhower's decision against crossing the Rhine had also ensured that the advance of 6th Army Group would no longer be spectacular." Weigley also states categorically, "Devers was wrong."[42] The French First Army had "shot its bolt" and was unable to collapse the Colmar Pocket on its own. True. The Nineteenth Army elements within the pocket repeatedly rebuffed French attacks, but it was in no shape to threaten Patch. And Patch was ready to cross the Rhine. Writing twelve years after Weigley, the official Army historians, Jeffrey Clarke and Ross Smith, took a different view: "Eisenhower's decision not to exploit in some way the Belfort and Saverne penetrations to the Rhine is difficult to understand."[43]

The most unbiased contemporary evidence is the 6th Army Group Intelligence Summary 10, released the day that Devers and Eisenhower had their confrontation:

> The combined attack of the First French and the Seventh Army has completely disorganized the enemy's resistance. The swift advance resulted in the annihilation of two German divisions, the capture of 15,000 prisoners, including several generals and members of Nineteenth Army headquarters, and considerable equipment. The present disposition of the enemy remains chaotic. With both his flanks dangerously threatened, he cannot have any hope of reestablishing the required balance west of the Rhine. Even the commitment of one or two fresh major [German] units could not materially change his situation, particularly if the weather permits constant air bombardment of the crossings.[44]

But intelligence (G2) also estimated that several days after the Germans identified the specific crossing sites, they could mass three infantry and two armored divisions to oppose a Rhine bridgehead. G2 concluded, "Subsequent buildup of enemy strength might well require support from outside Sixth Army Group to exploit the breakthrough," and the orientation of the army group needed to switch from south toward Colmar to north to move into Germany.[45] In other words, at least an additional Third Army corps would be needed to develop a decisive maneuver. If Eisenhower judged the opportunity insufficient to redirect Patton's offensive, then he was correct in shutting Devers down. In an obtuse way, General Jenkins came to a similar conclusion: "I don't believe there was really a golden opportunity to jump the Rhine at all. We simply did not have the strength to do it."[46] As Devers admitted, "He [Eisenhower] had a hell of a difficult problem and I was taking a chance. There is no doubt about that."[47]

By this point in the campaign, Eisenhower had learned the lesson about retaining reserves. In a later communication, he related to Marshall, "Flexibility requires reserves."[48] If he went over the Rhine, Devers had none. Eisenhower had wanted to retain flexibility to reinforce success if Bradley could produce one.

On 5 December, Devers wrote in his diary: "Had quite a long talk with George Patton at his headquarters. George has the right idea and I believe that between us we can crack this front and get on to the Rhine, probably faster than they can get north. I wish he were under my command. Then I would be sure."[49]

In a candid moment with Colonel Thomas Griess many years later, Devers's innermost thoughts had not changed from those heady days in late 1944: "They should have given me the Third Army and then directed our efforts toward the Rhine. All we had to do was drive up the west side of the Rhine and cut them off before they crossed the Rhine. We could have done this if we had had the proper organization. Actually I could have crossed over with a detachment going up the east bank, but not turn inland, then cut back across the Rhine again and unleash Third Army so it could run."[50] Devers further speculated, "We wouldn't have had the Bulge, really, because they would have had to pull some [of the striking power] from Fifth and Six Panzer Armies and come down and strike us. But they would have found us well prepared for this. That was my belief then and it is now. I think we could have shortened the war." Devers felt the Marseilles-Rhone railroad link could have supplied Patton as well

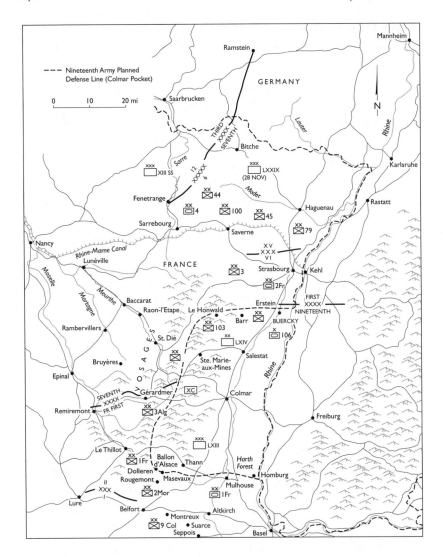

14.1. 6th Army Group, 26 November 1944

as the 6th Army Group.[51] While his operations officer had brought this alternative up with SHAEF staff, Devers never formally discussed it with Eisenhower (map 14.1).

Devers's G2, Eugene Harrison, came to similar conclusions. In his words, "The Battle of the Bulge would never have occurred. It is quite possible that the German [First] Army would have been cut off and would have surrendered. By hindsight now we know that this attack probably would have succeeded. . . . But the attack was risky."[52]

During a conversation after the war, Field Marshal Gerd von Rundstedt asked Sandy Patch why the Americans didn't cross the Rhine north of Strasbourg when the Germans "had nothing to defend with." When Patch replied that he had moved the assault boats forward, but that Eisenhower had directed him north instead of east. Rundstedt replied, "for a young fellow, you are all right."[53]

Would a multicorps crossing of the Rhine have prevented the Battle of the Bulge? The Germans had little to oppose such a major offensive and undoubtedly would have had to react. Troops taken from the German Ardennes offensive to meet a Rhine crossing at Rastatt would have taken a great deal of punch out of that attack. A major crossing south of the Ardennes would have materially affected operations north of those wooded ravines. It might have precipitated a major battle close to the Rhine. Perhaps the decisive battle to destroy the Wehrmacht would have taken place just east of the Rhine instead of just west, where Eisenhower would have preferred it. But it would have occurred before Christmas instead of over several campaigns that extended into the spring of 1945. On 19 December 1944, three days after the start of the Battle of the Bulge, Devers wrote in his diary, "Events at this moment prove the maneuver [crossing the Rhine at Rastatt] would have been successful."

While grumbling over the loss of the argument, Devers immediately ordered maneuvers to comply with the supreme commander's intent. He issued these in written form in Letter of Instructions No. 3 dated 26 November 1944, directing the Seventh Army to deploy west of the Vosges and "attack North with least possible delay," to "assist Third Army in breaching the Siegfried Line," and to "destroy enemy in zone West of the Rhine." Devers sent a cable to Eisenhower, with a copy to Bradley, confirming his orders but holding out for some promise about a subsequent operation. The mission was "to breach the Siegfried line west of the line, destroy the enemy in zone and deploy in strength across the Rhine." The 6th Army Group was to "launch a strong attack *west* of the Vosges."[54]

Significant threat or not, the Colmar Pocket was still a thorn in Devers's side for which the French would need to provide relief. After the

meeting at Vittel, Eisenhower, Bradley, and Devers went on to French
II Corps HQ where they met with Jean de Lattre. Then they moved onto
French I Corps. In his diary, Devers recorded, "Had a great day with the
French. General de Lattre was at his best. Never have I seen such traffic
jams. Feel sure the French are going to bag the five German divisions
which are on their front. . . . Our whole attitude is to accomplish the
impossible, and it goes down to the last GI. Plans for regrouping and
continuing the push and at the same time rounding up the German force
west of the Rhine go along with vigor."

Despite this enthusiasm, Devers was far off the mark on the French
and their ability to reduce the Colmar Pocket. Why? Floods and troubles
among both the metropolitan French and the French colonials.

French 2AD was in Strasbourg at the north end of the pocket. The
French First Army, two corps strong, had just steamrollered the Germans from Belfort to Mulhouse. It stood on the southern rim of the
pocket about 60 miles away from Jacques-Philippe Leclerc's division.
After the stellar combat performance of both French 2AD from the north
and the French First Army from the south, it is reasonable to expect that
they would quickly eradicate the disorganized last infestation in Alsace.
The 6th Army Group staff thought so, and that is what Devers had told
Eisenhower. German resistance up the Rhine was practically nonexistent. The French First Army had captured the German VXII Corps
commander, and Germans were fleeing north.[55] "Devers planned for the
French First Army to wipe out the pocket. VI Corps wiped their hands
of the matter. We were very surprised when French couldn't handle it,"
stated a 6th Army Group staffer.[56] Despite direct orders, neither French
formation advanced to Colmar. They shot all the artillery ammunition
they could get but could not move German infantry from their positions.

General Harrison never thought the Germans in the Colmar Pocket
were much of a threat. Initially, there were about five thousand defenders. The road leading north was poor, which meant it would be difficult
to support an attack in that direction.[57] Before the throw-down at Vittel, the chief of staff of the Seventh Army stated, "To clean up Colmar,
I must not weaken the Seventh Army's rapid advance into Germany in
the north." His statement reflected the thinking up and down the chain
of command of the 6th Army Group at the time.

In retirement, Devers mused, "Perhaps I turned Brooks north too soon."[58] That is, he might have turned American troops away from clearing Germans from the ground south of Strasbourg in favor of reinforcing the flank toward Germany proper and Rastatt. So there was some concern in his mind about the risk at Colmar at the time. But the principal staff officers thought it was far more important to move north and supported the action taken. The north flank of the Seventh Army lay completely exposed. Recalled Jenkins, "He [Patch and the Seventh Army] was stretched like a piece of tissue paper. . . . [On the northern flank] we had a gap of tremendous width. The 44th Infantry Division (1D) was facing three divisions down the Bleis valley. . . . Moving Brooks north was right decision." Jenkins was concerned that Germany should counterattack down the valley and cut off Patch after he got through the Saverne Gap. "That was one reason why it so important, in my opinion that we get Brooks out of the Colmar Pocket as fast as we could and to the north to reinforce that flank. Germans had a wonderful opportunity to counterattack and they missed it. Had they cut behind the Saverne Gap, Patch would have been in deep trouble." Furthermore, "Germans had some mobility. That's why Brooks had to turn north." When Brooks moved up, "that tightened the line-up for us to be safe with the Seventh Army. At time of Vittel conference, Brooks hadn't moved, but you knew he was going to be moved."[59] General Isaac White, chief of staff of the Seventh Army, agreed with Jenkins's assessment about turning Brooks north.

Everyone, including Eisenhower, was concerned that the Seventh Army was stretched too thin. But the Germans were stretched even thinner. If it became a contest of switching troops to a new front, the advantage was distinctly with the Americans. Not only did they have the trucks with which to move; they had the aircraft with which to prevent German movement.

Prior to the Vittel meeting, Devers had gone to Strasbourg to meet with Leclerc. The ground south of town is low and flat with several large streams, including the Ille River, running through it. The rains had flooded the area. Leclerc did not want to take his armor into this mess. In addition to the mud, the Germans were moving fifteen self-propelled artillery pieces around and shelling Allied units that showed any aggressiveness. The former French tanker said that southward movement into this sloppy mess was a job for an infantry division. Devers agreed. But, he said, he didn't have one. Leclerc would have to take it on by dismounting his armored infantry and inching his tanks southward. Still, Leclerc wouldn't move. One reason for his failure to act may have been that Leclerc had an aversion to the senior officers of the French First Army because they had served under Vichy for a period. As far as Leclerc was concerned, that was treason. "We would have closed it off in 24 hours if we had gone down there," recalled Devers. "I just could not get Leclerc to do it." He added, "Leclerc's inability, or refusal, to drive south caused the Colmar Pocket."[60] This is probably the most factual assessment of the proximate cause of the failure. Initially there wasn't much there, and Leclerc had just provided a 20-mile example of what his trips could do. Had the Frenchmen done as requested, the relationship of the two senior most American generals might have been a lot more cordial.

If Leclerc wouldn't move, could not the seven divisions of the French First Army have made short work of Colmar? But the colonial troops, the Senegalese and the Berbers, had reached their limit. De Lattre felt the Americans overlooked "the fatigue which, after two weeks of incessant and violent fighting, in almost continuous icy rain began to weigh heavily on all of our units."[61] They had already taken ten thousand prisoners. "The wear and tear of our means was decidedly too serious to allow us to drive against an enemy now holding shorter lines." De Lattre opined that French I Corps "was not unwilling but just unable to do more."[62] De Lattre hoped that Brooks would "turn down [south] between Colmar and the river and clean that area out. It was absolutely flooded and Brooks would have been ineffective." Jenkins felt that "de Lattre needed another corps and SHAEF should reinforce them."[63]

At the time, Harrison got up at a morning briefing and said, "There are 5,000 Germans surrounded by 125,000 Frenchmen and the French won't fight. [Devers's chief of staff, General David] Barr would agree with me."[64] This attitude on the part of his staff got under Devers's skin. He called them in and pounded the table: "Now, I want you to know that I am in command of First French Army. I want you to know if there is any cussing or derogatory remarks about the First French Army, I am going to make them. So we quit criticizing the French." Harrison continued,

"Ike wanted us to clean Colmar up and justly so I think. It wasn't a major threat. I did not consider it too much of a serious threat to our flank."[65]

Devers was aware that schisms existed within the French camp, but initially, he didn't understand their depth. In early December, he communicated to de Lattre, "The extent of your forces exhaustion cannot, in my opinion, be notably different from that of the division at present engaged with the German on the other sectors of the front. I find, meanwhile, that Allied gains are taking place elsewhere. There should be no more delay. You will take steps . . . to make certain that the Germans are driven east of the Rhine."[66]

Despite the tone of his letter, de Lattre felt Devers "showed a little impatience . . . [but] Devers better understood the difficulties of our sector than they did at SHAEF." Devers anticipated trouble as the Battle of the Bulge progressed.[67] While not abandoning his confident approach to the situation, Devers was critical of the First French Army commander. In a communiqué to George Marshall, Devers wrote, "De Lattre's army, after a slow start, made a magnificent advance in the Alsatian plain where they are again slowed up. De Lattre is in one of his temperamental moods. And it always takes us some time to get him started again. . . . I shall have trouble clearing up the pocket as the French at the moment have an inferiority complex." Patch, Haislip, and Brooks "performed the impossible and are moving forward . . . possibly to get set for a quick crossing of the Rhine."[68] Undoubtedly Devers recalled the way Marshall had blown up at de Lattre during their meeting in October. Note also that Devers indirectly appealed Eisenhower's decision to cancel the Rhine crossing at Rastatt by bringing it up with his old mentor, the only man that could overrule Eisenhower.

The problem within the ranks of the colonial French went much deeper than just being wet and tired. The First French Army was basically an African army (Berbers as well as blacks), and the colonial troops had lost their fighting spirit. German propaganda had had an impact. De Lattre explained, "The fighting man who has come from North Africa sees his comrades falling around him without even one Frenchman from France coming to fill the gaps caused by the battle." The colonial troops suffered from "malaise and abandonment."[69] A lot of colonials fell in the very hard fighting in the two-week slugfest up from Belfort. Many a colonial wondered why he should continue to do so for metropolitan French-men who disdained from even dirtying their hands in this tough fight. The troops no longer were willing to pick up the attack. Senior French officers, recalling the rebellion that occurred in the ranks in 1917, were very worried. Perhaps this wasn't the time to push the men. No replace-ments were arriving from North Africa. De Gaulle recalled, "[Antoine] Bethouart [I Corps commander] explained to me that, given the morale of his men, he was paralyzed along his entire front." The 2nd Moroccan and 1st Armored commanders "both informed me that their means were insufficient for them to advance." The people were vehement in their expressions of faith, which made it impossible to forget how severely the war had chastened every Alsatian heart.[70]

Devers was beside himself. Instead of attacking along the low open ground of the Alsatian Plain near the banks of the Rhine, the French seemed to be fumbling in the wooded foot hills of the Vosges and not at-tacking directly into Colmar. At first he saw the pocket as an opportunity to kill more Germans, rather than as a festering sore. He confided in his diary, "Having a great deal of trouble keeping the French at their job of closing the pocket and cleaning up the German here west of the Rhine. All they have to do is avoid the forests and push with their strength down the center, forgetting the mountains. It they don't do this immediately, a great many of these Germans will escape across the river."[71] To bolster both French combat power and French prestige, Devers subordinated U.S. 36 ID to de Lattre's command to clean out the Colmar Pocket. Ini-tially the Texans were to follow French 2 AD across the Ille River and be the infantry Leclerc so badly wanted.

During its drive up from Belfort, the French First Army suffered heavy officer casualties. They simply could not replace their losses. De-vers felt a lack of junior officers able to inspire the colonial troops was a major factor in the loss of morale and offensive capability.[72] Jenkins concurred in that assessment: "If they had had the leadership in the junior grades, noncommissioned officers, platoon and company com-manders that they should have had, I don't think there would have been any question but that they would have gone [and attacked]."[73] If the French First Army had attacked against only five thousand defenders, they should have prevailed, and the Colmar Pocket would never have existed. Jenkins estimated that the French could have held the Rhine from the Swiss border to Strasbourg with two divisions, leaving another five French divisions to support operations at a crossing site to the north. If there was no pocket, then what would have been the odds of the Rastatt crossing being successful? Jenkins summarized, "Colmar was lack of leadership at the lower levels on part of the French Army; there was nothing we could do about it."[74]

Not only was there division between metropolitan Frenchmen and their colonial French counterparts; there was great enmity between those French who immediately rallied to the Free French cause upon the fall of their country to the Germans in 1940 and those who went to North Africa and served under the German-controlled Vichy government. The two forces were quite different. The French 2nd Armored was made up of men from metropolitan France. The French First Army contained a lot of colonial troops and French men from North Africa. In Leclerc's view, de Lattre was stained from his cooperation with the Vichy French, the people who cooperated with the Germans, and would have nothing to do with him. Finally, Leclerc presented Devers with a letter, apparently with the acquiescence of the defense minister, André Diethelm. He and officers of French 2AD wanted to serve with the American army and not with the Vichy-contaminated First French Army.

Devers was shocked. No American senior officer would dare exhibit such behavior. Devers said, "Leclerc was a fighter. Leclerc didn't want to work under de Lattre, and told me he wouldn't work under him. I tried to make Leclerc do that. It was a mistake. If I ever commanded troops again where I had that resistance, I would never try to do that. I just don't think you can do it."[75] Belatedly recognizing the problem, he kept French 2AD with the Seventh Army for the remainder of its service with the 6th Army Group.

They were Free French and didn't want to fight with First French Army, which they viewed as tainted from their pre 1943 association with Vichy. As Devers stated, "Leclerc had a great division, they fought well, but they were difficult when they weren't permitted to do just what they wanted to do."

The Germans weren't idle during the morale-induced pause on the part of the French. Hitler was adamant about retaining his toehold in

Alsace. He appointed Heinrich Himmler, as commander of the Home
Army to insure the bridgehead to Colmar was held at all costs. The 6th
Army Group Summary Intelligence of 2 December estimated that the
Colmar Pocket contained 13,000 German soldiers, only 4,500 of them
in organized infantry formations. Under the cover of darkness and fog,
the French estimated the Germans poured into the pocket an additional
thirty battalions of reinforcements from Germany.[76]

In December, 4AD returned back into the Third Army's zone by
attacking toward Sarre-Union. Patch, perhaps hedging his bets, had a
contingency outline to attack northward west of the Rhine, and his army
reacted quickly. The four infantry divisions of XV Corps turned north
and advanced first to the Moder River and then onto the Maginot Line
including the forts around Bitche. To XV Corps's right, VI Corps advanced northward through the Haguenau Forest ant just over the Lauter
River, which defined the old border between pre–World War I France
and Germany. On the way, the 117th Cavalry Recon Squadron (mechanized) on VI Corps's extreme right flank crossed over the road that led
due east to the bridge at Rastatt.

In his 4 December diary entry, Devers wrote, "Time to concentrate
Seventh Army west of the Vosges and attack northward per Eisenhower's
instructions." The 361D was attached to the French to reduce the Colmar
Pocket with a completion date of 15 December. That attitude continued
right until the eve of the Battle of the Bulge. In a 14 December conference
with Patch, Brooks, and Haislip, Devers emphasized the advance west of
the Rhine to destroy German formations and loosen German defenses
resisting Patton's advance.

Devers had turned the entire Seventh Army (less 361D and Leclerc's
2AD, both of which were attached to French II Corps) northward to
support Patton. Unfortunately, de Lattre lost French 11D to Operation
Independence, the effort to establish normalized French rule in southwest France. He fully expected that de Lattre would make short work of
the pocket.[77] A major French assault by French II Corps on the pocket
had been scheduled for 5 December 5but was delayed two days because
of horrible weather. Before this attack could get started, Himmler and
his reinforcements struck first. The Germans were highly motivated.

French 21D "reached the limit of its strength and artillery ammunition shortage."[78] Even 361D lost several towns to the spirited Nazi attack. Devers personally inspected 361D and felt it was so run down from constant combat since landing on the beach during the first day of the campaign that it needed extended rest, reinforcement, and retraining to integrate the new replacements.

Both Devers and de Lattre initially expected that the Germans would hollow out the Colmar Packet and withdraw most troops east of the Rhine. Certainly they had many uses for them in shoring up their hard-pressed defenses along the entire front. Instead, the Germans reinforced the salient, bringing it up to ten divisions. Friedrich Wiese scrapped up replacements from every corner to bring these anemic units into at least defensive combat shape. Still they proved to be far more than the French First Army could handle. Hitler was so determined to retain his west bank enclave in Alsace that he ultimately transferred control of its defense to a new formation, Army Group Oberrhein, controlled by Himmler. Subsequently, he would sack Wiese, replacing him with General Siegfried Rasp. Himmler and his Home Army did not report to Rundstedt but directly to Hitler.

On 5 December, Devers had received a call from Eisenhower, who wanted to know how his subordinate was doing and that he was complying with instructions. Devers was doing his best. Both corps of the Seventh Army rotated from east to north to face what was left of the German First Army. Weather created as much resistance as did General Otto von Knobelsdorff's First Army. Foggy drizzle kept American airpower grounded. Cold rain made the GIs living outdoors miserable and sick, but wasn't cold enough to freeze the mud retarding American vehicles. Within the 6th Army Group, rain had become a way of life. Among the Germans, Balck shuffled worn out stubs of once-proud German divisions into the First Army to create an east-west line of resistance that could impede the U.S. Seventh Army. East of the Vosges, VI Corps slogged through the dank Haguenau Forest and attempted to dislodge Germans from their holes. Civilians in traditional black Alsatian garb franticly waved at their liberators as GIs advanced over rain-swollen streams against limited German resistance. Americans again closed on the Rhine to the east. Edward Brooks admonished his division commanders to "go rugged" right up until halted by the Ardennes attack with little lasting effect. On the western face of the mountains, XV Corps advanced north toward the Maginot Line. Attacks there stalled before the old French fortifications, within 10 miles of the German border.

On 12 December, Antoine Béthouart asked for a pause so French I Corps could recover from its efforts. De Lattre approved. On the 13th, General Joseph de Monsabert, commanding general, French II Corps, told Devers he was optimistic about the upcoming renewal of his attack. Monsabert stated that, recently, his intelligence staff estimated that an additional five thousand Germans had been added to the pocket. A series of strong German counterattacks had pummeled French II Corps, which included the U.S. 361D. De Lattre informed de Gaulle of the "depression that prevailed among his subordinates and a feeling of isolation from the French nation. The general impression is that the nation had neglected and abandoned us. Especially among the officers. Some have even gone so far as to believe that the regular overseas army is being deliberately sacrificed. The real source of the problem is the nation's non participation in the war."[79]

Devers related in his diary that, "At a conference with Army and corps commanders this morning, all expressed supreme confidence in their ability to breach the Siegfried line with their currently available troops within a very short time.... I have utmost confidence that we will break through the Siegfried line on the front of Seventh Army shortly."[80] All divisions in VI Corps crossed into Germany. General Brooks encouraged his commanders to "go rugged" in their advance. VI Corps 791D put assault bridging across the Lauter River, and Patch called Brooks with the news of the German Ardennes assault. Rather than advising caution, Patch encouraged Brooks, "Now we want you to go as fast as humanly possible."[81]

De Lattre had informed Devers on 12 December that he could not reduce the pocket "in the immediate future."[82] He sought an additional two American infantry divisions to bolster his efforts against the Colmar Pocket. Devers, responding crisply, ordered the First French Army to eliminate all German forces west of the Rhine no later than 1 January and to do so with their existing forces, which really was not in keeping with growing German strength within the pocket. On the 14th, Eisenhower needled Devers by reminding him that eight Allied divisions were now engaged at Colmar. The Seventh Army as well was experiencing increased German resistance. XV Corps, advancing on Bitche, ran into several tough fights that stalled the advance. On the 17th, VI Corps reported increasing resistance at the Siegfried Line. Assaulting troops were stopped cold before the concrete of the Ensemble de Bitche. Meanwhile, XXI Corps HQ, newly arrived on the continent, got ready to integrate into the Seventh Army.

Throughout this period, additional German reinforcements were rapidly changing the correlation of forces south of Strasbourg. Devers recorded in his diary, "As it is now it is very doubtful whether we will be able to sustain our rapid advance for no effort has been made by SHAEF to reinforce us in any way whatsoever. It would seem to me that strength should be reinforced, not weakness." Supposedly southwest France was under Devers's jurisdiction. In fact, this quadrant was left almost entirely under French control. The Provisional Government deemed only French troops would be used to reduce the coastal pockets, and had been withdrawing elements of the French First Army in order to reassert its sovereignty and combat Germans held up in fortress ports like Lorient. Given de Lattre's inability to reduce Colmar, SHAEF now deferred reduction of Atlantic pockets until Colmar Pocket was reduced.[83]

As early as 14 December, the 6th Army Group reported to SHAEF that the French First Army was badly weakened from its drive from Belfort to Colmar. The French 11D had to be withdrawn to be reconstituted and retrained. But Devers was optimistic that the Seventh Army's advance northward was making good progress and could breach the Siegfried Line if given perhaps two divisions of fresh troops.[84] It is clear where Jake's gaze lay. Not surprisingly, perhaps, his estimate proved wide of the mark. A memo that same day from Harold Bull to Beetle Smith summarized German reinforcement in Colmar but stated that there was no evidence that they had any intention of striking from that pocket.[85] The enemy's plan, Bull declared, was "to remain in West of the Rhine as long as he can." Bull underscored that the moving of the bulk of the

Seventh Army to support Patton had weakened the Allies around Colmar, and that Colmar should take priority instead. Nothing was done at SHAEF to follow up on Bull's recommendation.

Devers now ordered that U.S. 31D join 361D in support of the northern flank of the French. "Reinforced with these 2 major units, I think I can say that the reduction of the German pocket will be quickly secured."[86] After being reinforced by 31D, de Lattre launched a double envelopment of the pocket. On 15 December, French II Corps headed directly south from near Strasbourg toward Colmar, while French I Corps came up from the south. Neither attack in the increasingly inclement weather did more than dent the reinvigorated German defenses. Dogfaces of 31D did no better than their French counterparts. Allied vehicles, mired in the flooded and rain-soaked ground, were all but immobilized. After a week of little progress and under the strain of reacting to the Ardennes offensive, Devers called the attempt off. SHAEF was so overloaded by the German offensive, they hardly objected. Eisenhower had ordered all Allied offensive action to desist while they dealt with the Bulge.

Devers was less than pleased with the halt. He issued a warning order to the First French Army to be prepared to resume on 5 January. By then, Jake reasoned, the Ardennes attack should have shot its bolt. But as General Charles Palmer said, "The Colmar pocket remained because the French didn't have enough strength to wipe it out," given its reinforcement.[87] Later Devers stated, "This is the one case where I failed as commander of foreign troops. We got the Colmar Pocket because I had no reserves to put in there. I thought Leclerc could handle the Germans to the south. He couldn't."[88] "I am responsible. Nobody else."[89]

Instead of being in the supreme commander's good graces, Devers had sunk to a new low. According to Eisenhower, Devers's "failure to eliminate the Colmar Pocket later exerted a profound and adverse effect on our operations."[90] No real progress at reducing the pocket was made until late January, well after both the Ardennes and Nordwind. This left additional grit in the gears when a major inter-Allied crisis occurred in late December.

It was not as though Devers was a pariah. Following the meeting at Vittel, communication with Eisenhower was very cordial, with no reference to the Vittel discussion. At times, Eisenhower continued to support Devers, despite his personal opinion. It was akin to observing the furrows on his face as a record of the burdens of his office. When Montgomery was campaigning for Bradley to become overall ground commander, Eisenhower designated Montgomery as northern army group and Devers as southern. Still, it was the case that Devers had not seen the larger problem at Anzio, had exaggerated the initial logistical support he could give Bradley from Marseilles, and had underestimated the trouble the French would have to close the Colmar Pocket.

It was also the case that, as Forrest Pogue would note fifty years later in the official history, "The 6th Army Group, cast only for a supporting role in November, gained several of the month's most important victories."[91]

FIFTEEN

Nordwind Strikes Devers

ON 19 DECEMBER 1944, SENIOR COMMANDERS GATHERED IN Verdun to attend Dwight Eisenhower's emergency conference to react to the German attack in the Ardennes, the clash known as the Battle of the Bulge.

"Jake, how soon can you take over Patton's front?" Eisenhower asked.

"What with?" Jacob Devers responded.

"With what you have."

"The whole front?"

"Yes."

"Well," Devers replied, "It isn't a question of how soon I can take over his front; it is a question of how soon Patton can get out of there so I can get in. His front is a quagmire."

Eisenhower turned to George Patton. "How soon can you do it?"

"Forty-eight hours," responded the confident Third Army commander.[1]

By 20 December, Devers had written confirmation of the orders to his army group to reorganize and move into the Third Army area. Before the Verdun meeting, Devers had agreed to take over part of the front as requested by Patton. The 6th Army Group had already begun northward movement of the 12th Armored Division (AD). The Seventh Army did a good job of shuffling divisions north to cover 30 miles of ground vacated by XII and XX Corps. The 103rd Infantry Division (ID) moved 100 miles back across the Vosges and occupied some of the vacated ground. Devers exhorted, "We shall pursue our new mission with all our energy." Later he said, "Seventh Army did a terrific job. We had to sideswipe one division over the front."[2] He added, "The means are meager and the front long. . . . It was really a hazardous job, but we did it."[3]

"Patton and Patch – sort of blood brothers, you know, they worked together extremely well," recalled Reuben Jenkins. "The passage of lines was a rough period. Seventh Army and 6th Army Group histories understate the problems."[4] Third Army logistical installations were left in place under command of the Third Army even though they were now in the Seventh Army's area of operations. The 12AD and 36ID were disengaged and moved near Sarrebourg to reconstitute a SHAEF reserve. Now they were also positioned to move to cross the Rhine. Devers's forward HQ was moved back to Phalsbourg.

In just forty-eight hours, Patton rotated III Corps 90 degrees from attacking east to attacking north, slammed into the German flank, and ultimately pushed through to relieve Bastogne. It was a tremendous operational maneuver. Less has been said of the Seventh Army's operational maneuver to cover the front vacated by Patton.[5] In his diary, Devers sarcastically recorded, "On that occasion [the Vittel Conference] the Sixth Army Group had to go to the rescue of the Third Army to its left; now it was necessary to go to the rescue again of the Twelfth Army Group."

Eugene Harrison remembered that Devers called "[Sandy] Patch about continuing [his attack toward the Siegfried Line versus] pulling back as we had ordered him to and as we had been ordered by SHAEF. But General Devers just finally ordered him to do it and he complied." Harrison continued, "I saw absolutely no hesitation or sign of stress in Devers. We did not think at any time that the German attack would succeed. I suppose that's why we did not feel too badly about it."[6] In a meeting with Devers, Patch felt it was a difficult proposition to give up a strong position when he felt confident he could hold it. Both American generals agreed that giving up Strasbourg would be a political disaster for France.

On 19 December, Patch had informed Devers that VI Corps could no longer hold its forward-most positions east of the Vosges. Devers authorized the withdrawal of VI Corps into the previously planned defensive line behind the Moder River, but to withdraw only under severe German pressure. Devers had always been aware of the risk of being in the northeastern tip of France east of the Vosges extending into Germany:

"I didn't put logistical units on the Strasbourg plain" for just this reason, he later recalled.[7] The potential withdrawal gave up a significant but sparsely populated slice of Alsace 10–20 miles wide and about 30 miles long. Strasbourg remained well protected.

Eisenhower had already ordered withdrawal from the area. General Edward Brooks, commander of VI Corps, which occupied most ground east of the Vosges held by the 6th Army Group, recommended a delaying action forward of the defensive line east of the mountains, but not a retreat into the Vosges. "He didn't see any necessity of giving up more territory. . . . [We] were all pretty confident we could handle the situation on the ground."[8] Devers's Letter of Instruction No. 5, dated 21 December, ordered the Seventh Army to abandon present offensive operations at once and defend against any major hostile penetration. He ordered a "stand in zone," which is almost the opposite of "no retreat."[9] The letter further ordered Seventh Army commanders to be prepared to yield ground rather than endanger the integrity of their commands. Devers had confidence in his subordinate commanders. He instructed Patch to create a reserve force of a regimental combat team plus additional armor and designated it the 6th Army Group reserve. In this manner, Devers took out a small hedge against his own optimism.

Devers had not completely given up hope of crossing the Rhine in the near future. Letter of Instruction No. 5 also said, "Disposition of troops along the West bank of the Rhine and of bridging material will be such that they can be readily employed in an attack across the Rhine north of Strasbourg." Guessing that the Bulge would be over or at least contained shortly, he issued Letter of Instruction No. 6 on 22 December warning Jean de Lattre that the French Army should prepare to resume its Colmar offensive by 5 January. Devers decided to allow the French First Army to retain control of the U.S. 31D. To solve the continuing problem of Jacques-Philippe Leclerc, French 2AD was moved back to the Seventh Army, replacing 12AD as the Seventh Army reserve.

Like much of nonurban France in 1944, most roads in the 6th Army Group area were light-duty and did not bear up to heavy military traffic. In Lorraine, the road net was sparse, causing a great deal of difficulty for both the Third and Seventh Armies as they repositioned. Devers remembered that despite the difficulties, "we did it because we worked together like nobody's business."

By 21 December, it was becoming apparent to the German High Command that the Ardennes offensive was bogging down. They looked at their operational alternatives. The Oberkommando der Wehrmacht (OKW) and Hitler himself eyed the thinning lines of the Third and Seventh Armies as Patton rushed troops north to strike toward Bastogne. Both von Rundstedt and Hitler concluded that a fresh offensive in this sector offered great opportunity.[10] At first, they looked to envelop the Third Army with a strike through Lorraine, perhaps toward Metz, which might be matched by a drive south from the Ardennes to cut off Patton. Both German staffs concluded that German forces simply did not have the strength to pull this off. As an alternative, they looked toward American weaknesses to the south that might allow German attackers to reach the Saverne Gap. Here the staffs differed slightly. OKW detected the weakness at the boundary between XV and VI Corps, where 100ID met Taskforce Hudelson (built around the 106th Cavalry Group reinforced by part of a 14AD combat command less its tank battalion).

Thus was born "Nordwind," the plan for the second German winter offensive on the Western Front. (American GIs sometimes referred to it as the "January Attack.") The goal of the offensive was to split the two corps of the Seventh Army in order to cut off VI Corps east of the Vosges and allow for deep penetration south toward Saverne, where the Seventh Army had first crossed the Vosges.

At this stage, Eisenhower was very worried about the risk to VI Corps east of the Vosges. Devers felt he could keep VI Corps essentially in place and handle any German thrust with 6th Army Group resources. Both American generals continued to be concerned about the Colmar Pocket, though Eisenhower more than Devers. Eisenhower worried that a German offensive was taking shape that would pound VI Corps to pieces by smashing it against the pocket. Devers's intelligence staff believed that the Germans would attack to cut off Americans east of the Vosges. SHAEF also recognized this potential risk. Devers summarized, "[The Germans would] cut me off at Sarrebourg which was my real dread. I would be in a fix because I had only one pass [the Saverne]. I had the Colmar Pocket behind me. I didn't have any supplies or support units on the Alsatian Plain. I had most of my tanks and artillery back in the mountains. I guess he [Eisenhower] was going to order me back into the Vosges in order to shorten my lines. I said, Ike that doesn't make sense."[11]

Devers wasn't as concerned about the risk to VI Corps as he was determined to boost the performance of the French First Army so that he wouldn't be further embarrassed by a German-held pocket west of the Rhine. Despite the shock of the German Ardennes offensive, Jake retained his offensive stance.

On 22 December, de Lattre arrived for dinner at 6th Army Group headquarters in a very bad temper. In response to what he thought was a defeatist attitude that had crept into the language of recent orders from French HQ, Devers had written a sharp letter to de Lattre "in an effort to stiffen French leadership."[12] The fastest way for an army to lose spirit was for it to believe that things topside were not well. De Lattre agreed. Devers went over the problems division by division. Both mentioned that Leclerc's actions had not helped matters. Devers promised better artillery and air support, and additional artillery ammunition. Letter of Instruction No. 6 issued that day gave the First French Army more ammunition and two artillery groups. Devers reiterated his confidence in de Lattre, who responded, "There is certainly a much better understanding." De Lattre promised to reduce the Colmar Pocket by New Year's, nine days away. Devers accepted that de Lattre would deliver on his promise, and this became the underpinning for his continued optimistic representations to SHAEF. Later de Lattre recorded, "Devers' even temper never deserts him."[13]

Although reports from the Ardennes began to look better, SHAEF did not consider the Bulge won by any means. "Bedell Smith called me and said that Eisenhower said I hadn't carried out his orders," said Devers. "I pointed out [that] I carried out his orders with energy. Smith released SHAEF reserve to me which gave me an additional feeling of confidence. But I felt compelled to give up Strasbourg," something to which Jake was vehemently opposed. To insure he had a clear directive, Devers sent his chief of staff, David Barr, to SHAEF headquarters in Versailles.

As usual, Eisenhower was miffed with Devers. In the fall, Eisenhower had directed the 6th Army Group to "get us an easily defended flank," that is, a line up against the Rhine that could be contained with a minimum number of troops.[14] Instead, Devers had punched through the Vosges and captured Strasbourg but had left the Colmar Pocket to the south. Now a German counterattack threatened to open a seam in the Seventh Army front, which left the southernmost army group in a situation that, in Eisenhower's estimation, was "inherently weak from a defensive standpoint."[15] In order to pull VI Corps from its "awkward situation" east of the Vosges where it might be cut off and to create something of a reserve, Eisenhower ordered Devers to pull it back into a more easily defended positions in the mountains. While reconnaissance elements would remain, a withdrawal would expose Strasbourg to recapture by the Germans.

By 26 December, the worst of the Bulge crisis had passed. The gray clouds over Bastogne had broken, allowing both air drops and close air support. Patton's tanks were well on their way to that beleaguered town. In the north, U.S. 2AD had bloodied its counterpart, the 2nd Panzer Division (PzD), thereby blunting the Nazi's westernmost spearhead toward the Meuse.

To reduce the risk and allow for XXI Corps and two divisions to be coiled up as SHAEF reserve, Devers had ordered VI Corps elements east of the Vosges to withdraw back into the mountains, leaving only light security forces in place. In this manner, Devers did not expose Strasbourg to a raid unless the Germans committed enough forces to move what amounted to flank guards.

Still, Eisenhower worried over the 6th Army Group's exposure east of the Vosges. Calling in his G3 (operations officer), General Harold R. Bull, Eisenhower said, "Pink, you better go and see Devers today.... This is not where I told Devers to put his weight [indicating on a map an area east of the Vosges at Haguenau Forest up to the Lauter River]. I think the best line is this [a pull back into the Vosges]."[16] General Bull traveled to Lunéville to meet with Generals Barr and Jenkins and to deliver written orders with accompanying maps. The 6th Army Group main line of resistance was to be the Vosges. The intent was to reduce VI Corps's exposure. Perhaps Bull didn't focus on the fact that a full VI Corps retreat into the mountains also exposed Strasbourg and its population. Prewar Alsace had been French but had been annexed by Germany in 1940. Some residents remained loyal Frenchmen; others felt their loyalty was owed to Germany. Reoccupation by German forces would expose civilians to reprisals.

Devers called de Lattre to Vittel and informed him of Eisenhower's orders. Eisenhower could not have picked a worse day to announce that Strasbourg was to be put at risk. De Gaulle had just delivered a rousing speech there stating that the city would not fall into German hands again. Having been just reabsorbed into France, it was second only to Paris as a symbol of a resurgent France.

De Lattre assigned the U.S. 3ID to bolster Joseph de Monsabert's II Corps. Monsabert said the fighting up from Belfort toward Strasbourg for the last fifteen days had been harder than anything he had previously seen. He admitted that colonial troops were complaining about the leadership of their white officers.[17] De Lattre understood the order from Eisenhower. But as a French soldier, how could he leave a major population center exposed without putting up a fight? The commander of the French First Army was being pulled in opposite directions by his superiors on two different chains of command. For purely Allied reasons regarding the Germans, he understood the need to protect VI Corps. On the other hand, de Gaulle, as head of the French state, had to be concerned about defending the people of Strasbourg. A pullback would endanger the citizens he was sworn to protect. Thinking in those terms and realizing the risk to VI Corps was not overwhelming, how could SHAEF put an ally in such a dilemma?

Because of the danger to the military solidarity of the alliance, de Lattre understood that he needed a total plan adopted by agreement with the American command. He cabled Devers that the decision to withdraw American forces "leads me to earnestly ask you to obtain above all else, SHAEF's agreement that the 7th Army's withdrawal might be limited to the Strasbourg canal, so as to give the French 1st Army time to take responsibility for part of the defense of this line."[18] Via a courier, he sent a letter to de Gaulle: "I earnestly ask you to intervene personally with SHAEF so that an agreement be effected quickly. . . . This agreement would make it possible for me to reconcile my duty as a French General to my country, to the honor of my army and to you, my political and military leader – a duty which I will put above everything with my duty as a soldier, my duty of discipline in relation to the Supreme command of the Allied Armies, among which the French 1st Army holds a strategically vital place."[19]

Devers met with Eisenhower in Paris on 28 December to plead his case not to withdraw from Strasbourg, but Eisenhower could not be moved. He pointed to a map and demonstrated how withdrawing VI Corps into the Vosges would shorten the 6th Army Group's line and allow Eisenhower to create a reserve with which to meet a German attack. Desire for that reserve seemed to blind him to the French national perspective. He was concerned that the Germans would attack both down the western face of the Vosges and from the Colmar Pocket, brushing aside the forward elements of VI Corps.[20] In private, the deputy supreme commander, Air Chief Marshal Sir Arthur W. Tedder, asked Eisenhower if opening so much of Alsace to reoccupation by the Germans was a wise move. Eisenhower replied that the need to create some operational reserve to restore some Allied flexibility was paramount.[21]

Devers came away from that meeting even more convinced he had to protect Strasbourg and the French people of Alsace. He felt that Eisenhower's orders did not recognize local conditions or accurately balance alternative threats. "It was [a] very tense time, and Ike, where he was, always saw things much worse than I saw them where I was fighting."[22] On the Alsace Plain, the Americans had good long-range fields of fire. Pulling back into the mountains, American units would have to mount a defense from many small valleys and draws, which would actually increase, not decrease, the amount of infantry needed to defend the line. And, of course, the 6th Army Group would have to leave Strasbourg unprotected.[23]

In Devers's estimation, the immediate threat was to the Sarre River Valley, which XV Corps amply protected. Withdrawal of VI Corps units was not immediately necessary. East of the Vosges, the Seventh Army had another defensive position in mind, the Rhone-Marne Canal, which was a barrier on the plains to a German movement southward. Besides, Patch also knew the French would not tolerate a withdrawal that exposed a large portion of the Alsatian populace to the Germans. Devers sent his chief of staff, David Barr, back to SHAEF to argue the case with Eisenhower's chief of staff but to no avail.

As Devers and Patch both predicted, the second major German offensive came down the Sarre River to cut off the Seventh Army, not down near Strasbourg.[24] Still, right after Christmas, Devers met with his staff and Patch at Phalsbourg to work out the details of carrying out their orders. The group decided to tap 12AD, which was not engaged, and 36ID, which was refitting under the newly arrived XXI Corps HQ, to meet Eisenhower's requirement for establishing a reserve. Composed of untested and of tired troops, it nonetheless met Eisenhower's size requirement.

Via Patch, Devers instructed VI Corps, in defense of Strasbourg, to construct three intermediary defensive lines but to fall back only when heavily pressured by a large German attack. The first line followed the Maginot Line, the second ran along the Moder River, and the third stretched from around Bitche to Strasbourg. Devers made it clear to his staff and subordinates that, in order to accumulate reserves and create a more solid defense, he was willing to give up the entire Alsatian Plain in order to defend the city.[25]

As General Eugene Harrison, 6th Army Group G2 (intelligence), said after the war, "If the Germans drove southwest down the western face of the Vosges, which is what they attempted to do, the roads [over which the exposed Americans would have to either be supplied or withdraw] could have been very easily cut off and captured: That is, the corps that was to the east [VI Corps] could have been very easily cut off." He confided to his boss, "Jakie Devers, you have your neck stuck out over there if they attack. . . . It was the first time during the war that I was actually frightened as to what might happen."[26] Eisenhower and the SHAEF staff weren't entirely wrong. General Harrison went on to make an essential point: "If the Germans came back in, there would have been a lot of Frenchmen executed. . . . General Devers had the courage to leave [VI] Corps over there exposed, and he got away with it. This took a great deal of courage. With this act alone General Devers won the eternal gratitude of all the French."[27] Subsequently, atrocities were committed in many villages recaptured by Germans.

Colonel Reuben Jenkins, Army Group G3, agreed with Eisenhower. To cover Patton, "We had stretched so blooming thin, we were badly exposed. Tactically I think the signal was right because we were running too big a risk of being caught. We pulled back across the Moder [River]. Haislip had a plan to move all the way to the Maginot Line if necessary and then strike back."[28] This pullback removed the bulk of

U.S. forces from the Haguenau Forest, which had been the staging area for the Rhine crossing at Rastatt, and placed the Americans a good 10 miles southwest of that site.

Devers again flew to SHAEF to meet with Eisenhower, Smith, and Bull in Versailles. Eisenhower pointed out that the 6th Army Group would definitely be threatened in the Sarre Valley, and it would have to stop the German attack on its own. Devers responded that he wasn't interested in holding territory but was concerned about protecting French citizens from Nazi wrath. Eisenhower was very definite that VI Corps must move its troops back into the Vosges and hang on. The 6th Army Group would not be reinforced or receive any more ammunition. But he also wanted to hold Strasbourg and Mulhouse if at all possible. Devers had an indication that de Lattre would take this matter up to the senior political level and appeared happy the Frenchman was doing so. Given the orders to withdraw into the Vosges, Devers was concerned about French attempts to hold the city on their own. On 26 December, 31D replaced French 2AD, ostensibly so it could go into reserve. The division was badly in need of refitting. On the 31st, Devers informed SHAEF of the inadequate preparation of the French divisions that were supposed to defend Strasbourg. Quick inspection of these ersatz divisions showed little combat capability.

Devers underscored that XXI Corps was SHAEF reserve and not to be touched until released by SHAEF.[29] Letter of Instruction No. 7 issued on 28 December stated, "Seventh army will continue defense and will be prepared to give ground to prepare the integrity of its defense. Defend west of Bitche-Maginot line, east of Bitche then continuing down the east side of the Vosges." The weekly intelligence summary issued on 30 December estimated that in the Colmar Pocket, eight divisional formations controlled fifteen thousand combat effectives; the Seventh Army's northern front faced nine divisions and thirteen thousand combat infantry.

On New Year's Eve, the day before the Nordwind attack, Devers forwarded to SHAEF a summary of the threats facing the 6th Army Group and its ability to resist German assaults.[30] He continued to point to the threat down the Sarre Valley against XV Corps, not the VI Corps positions east of the Vosges, as the principal risk. Of course, a successful

German attack down the Sarre would threaten to cut off VI Corps. In his daily summary to SHAEF, Devers estimated 35,000 infantry effectives manned the Colmar Pocket, a significant increase from earlier estimates. He noted that the most likely attack from Colmar would be on an axis Homburg-Sarrebourg. Weaknesses in French training and morale were candidly recounted. Devers estimated that it would take six weeks to bring the French up to training standard. Devers also recommended that everything east of the Moselle be placed under a single command – by implication, the 6th Army Group. At that time, virtually all of the Third Army was northeast of the river. Eisenhower did not respond to this suggestion.

Patch was certain he would be attacked during the night. The intelligence indicators were unmistakable. The Seventh Army defended 84 miles of front. Just before the Nordwind attack, Devers visited every corps and division HQ to insure "there were no slips." The army group commander wanted every penetration to be sealed off because the Germans didn't have much in reserve behind this attack.[31] As to Nordwind, Eugene Harrison recalled, "We knew when this attack was coming, who was going to make it, and where it was going to be made. So that didn't bother us at all."[32] In retirement, Devers claimed that he was never worried about the German thrust, and that even before the attack, the Sixth Army Group G2 had a good handle on the movements of the principal German formations. Nor was Devers concerned about a threat from the Colmar Pocket. Only Eisenhower and the SHAEF staff were.[33] Devers positioned XXI Corps in secondary defensive positions behind XV Corps to cover the Sarre Valley rather than to backstop VI Corps (map 15.1).

Once German intelligence documented the thinning of Seventh Army lines to cover the Third Army's pre-Christmas left wheel to relieve Bastogne, Hermann Balck's Army Group G was ordered to take advantage of this new American weakness. In formulating Nordwind, German planners sought to achieve what both Eisenhower and Devers feared most: to cut off Seventh Army forces east of the Vosges by penetrating west of the Vosges Mountains with an advance along the Sarre Valley to Phalsbourg and the Saverne Gap.[34] VI Corps (from west to east: Taskforce [TF] Hudelson, 45ID, 79ID) held the ground east of the

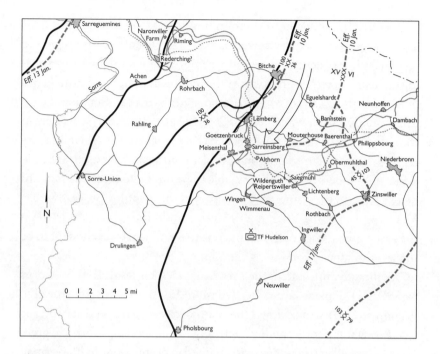

15.1. Nordwind

Vosges through the mountains and up to the Maginot fortress of Bitche. XV Corps (from east to west: 100ID, 44ID, 103D) continued the line from there to past Saregemines and the Sarre River. The first intermediate objective of the German attack was the juncture between 100ID and TF Hudelson. The second prong of the attack struck the boundary between 44ID and the other flank of the Century Division with the intent to surround and destroy the latter. Then German reserves could enter the resulting hole and exploit toward Puberg, overrunning the weak TF Hudelson in the process. The area of attack had a poor road net, which the Germans deemed helpful in blunting the American advantage in mechanization. All in all, it was a competent plan taken on by a somewhat depleted array of German forces.

Unlike at the Ardennes, Ultra gave significant warning of Nordwind. Divisional and regimental journals of the time show ample evidence of the estimated time of German attack. The two attacks were to meet in

Sarrebourg. In addition to surrounding 100ID, this would cut off VI Corps, which is what Eisenhower feared.[35] The Seventh Army prepared a secondary line of defense 10–11 miles behind the forward divisions' existing main line of retreat. This was a sensible precaution. The two divisions of XXI Corps (12AD, 36ID), then designated as SHAEF reserve, and two-thirds of 14AD were available to back up the line. Three divisions were in the process of assembling after just arriving in Marseilles. Their infantry regiments, formed into taskforces under their respective assistant division commanders, were also available to be integrated into the forward defense (42ID, 63ID, and 70ID). As part of the thinning process within VI Corps east of the Vosges, TFs Herren and Linden were inserted on the easternmost edge of the corps zone to guard what was thought to be the less threatened zone along the Rhine.

Although anticipated, the German attack hit hard. XIII SS Corps (17SSPzGD [Panzer Grenadier Division], 19VGD [Volksgrenadier Division], 36VGD) struck down the seam between 44ID and 100ID. The 17SSPzGD was poorly handled tactically, but its schnapps-fortified grenadiers attacked with great ferocity. Bathed in bright moonlight, German 36VGD, just to the east of the SS grenadiers, stumbled into a killing zone set up by the "Jersey Blues" (44ID) and left behind so many dead that GIs dubbed the ground "Morgue Valley." After intense fighting, 44ID backed up toward Singling, while 100ID tenaciously held onto Rimling.

On 100ID's right flank, Johannes Blaskowitz's main effort containing four volksgrenadier divisions plus 6SS Mountain Division – well trained, at full strength, and fresh from Scandinavia – struck at TF Hudelson and ran up against the rightmost regiment of the Century Division. German infantry penetrated Hudelson's outposts and roadblocks by moving cross-country. The German First Army held back 25PzGD and 21 PzD so as to be positioned to exploit any breakthrough. TF Hudelson's mechanized cavalry reconnaissance squadrons, composed mainly of machine gun jeeps and scout cars, were not designed to withstand a heavy attack. Armored infantrymen from a battalion of 14AD made a stouter block but also were soon overwhelmed. Due to the heavy snow and paucity of roads, most of the vehicles were left behind.

The pullback of TF Hudelson caused 100ID's right flank to bend backward, but the division's primary defensive positions held. Sandy

Patch and Wade Haislip fed two of the green reinforcing infantry regiments into 100ID to solidify its hold. A phone conversation between a Century Division operations officer and one from a cavalry squadron that was part of TF Hudelson typifies the stress and confusion created by the attack:

> "We are falling back a little."
> "How far is a little?" asked the 100ID major.
> "About 2,000 yards."
> The Century officer swore. "Do you have to fall back so far all at once?"
> All he heard was a click from the phone at the other end of the line.[36]

The Century Division was in danger of double envelopment, a fate that destroyed 106ID during the opening moves of the Bulge. But skillful placement of all five regiments under the command of General Withers Burress into a defense with great depth allowed them to hold the division in place, disrupting any chance of success Blaskowitz's attackers might have had.

Previously, in the run up the Rhône Valley and the assaults into the Vosges, Patch had stayed out of the tactical affairs of his single U.S. corps. Nordwind required active tactical management of the two corps then under his command, as Balck strove to split them and penetrate deeply. Patch quickly shifted gears, regrouped, and concentrated forces as necessary to counter German thrusts. He kept current on the latest intelligence and conditions on the battlefields without overly crowding his corps commanders. De Lattre kept a tight rein on his commanders and closely orchestrated tactical developments in the French First Army. Patch could handle his own logistics. Always deficient in this department, the French First Army required much more support from 6th Army Group staff.

At daybreak on New Year's Day 1945, Haislip was at an artillery observation post with a good overview of the battlefield, just where he needed to be. Against all that white snow, XV Corps artillery cut three German divisions to pieces.[37] While battle reports describing the German attack on the west side of the Vosges were still unclear, Eisenhower called Devers and ordered him to *immediately* withdraw the bulk of VI Corps back from the Lauter River east of the Vosges and into defensive positions in the mountains. Eisenhower wanted withdrawal to free XXI

Corps as a SHAEF reserve, but he gave Devers leeway to use the corps if necessary to maintain the integrity of his army group. Devers transmitted the instructions to the Seventh Army, stating that Eisenhower gave them no choice: Patch and Brooks must retreat into the Vosges. But he said that outposts and security patrols were to continue to remain east of the mountains and provide some resistance to immediate German attempts at occupation. "These light forces were in no sense to be considered sacrifice troops," said Devers to his staff, and would retreat rather than face destruction. Devers summarized the situation, enjoining the Seventh Army to accept the loss of "Strasbourg and territory east of the Vosges rather than in any way impair its ability to release SHAEF reserve organizations."[38]

The 45ID was not badly hit by the German attack that smashed TF Hudelson on New Year's Day. To compensate for the developing hole, the division commander, Major General Robert T. Frederick of 1st Allied Airborne Taskforce fame, moved his easternmost (right flank) regiment, which had to move back anyway per orders, and inserted it on the left flank of 45ID. Under the direction of Brooks, who was busily reshuffling his entire corps, a regiment from 70ID, not yet committed to combat, and most of the infantry of 79ID, which also had to pull back to comply with Eisenhower's instructions, reinforced Frederick's swelling Thunderbird. As troop density increased, the heavy fighting devolved to bitter struggles to control the area's small villages with their comparatively warm cellars. Again the balancing hand of Patch is evident. He quietly combed his service and support units to cull out additional infantry replacements.

Later, Devers visited the 45th Division, which was supposed to be pulling back to the mountains. Instead of finding American troops on the trucks headed west, he found French civilians. Devers queried a sergeant, who responded, "Well, General, these people will get killed if we leave them back there and we have got to get them out." Observed Devers, "When you have sergeants like that, no Germans are going to lick them."[39]

Two days before the start of the German offensive, General Alphonse Juin, de Gaulle's chief of staff, had raised the issue of defending Strasbourg with SHAEF. If the Americans weren't going to defend it, the

French offered Beetle Smith three semi-formed and untrained divisions composed primarily of former FFI to defend the capital of Alsace. These willing troops were neither properly trained nor equipped for combat. General Thomas Larkin stated that he could not support them logistically. Instead, Smith directed Devers to take the best French units and concentrate all available equipment there.

Eisenhower had told Devers to pull back and be prepared to lose ground east of the Vosges. Soon after, he accused Devers of dragging his heels. The Germans were fighting to penetrate XV Corps with an eye toward isolating the bulk of VI Corps east of the Vosges, and senior commanders were worried. In the first days of the Battle of the Bulge, 106ID had been cut off and virtually destroyed; most of its men would wind up in POW cages. On New Year's Day, Eisenhower met with Smith and told him, "Call up Devers and tell him he is not doing what he is told. Get VI Corps back."[40] Devers's orders were to hold the Alsace Plain with reconnaissance units that could warn of a major attack. On the 2nd, he ordered XXI Corps as SHAEF reserve to be committed only by the supreme commander's order. Devers altered the interarmy boundary to transfer ground immediately north of Strasbourg to the First French Army. Without disclosing his intentions, Devers was making room should the French have to defend Strasbourg on their own per de Gaulle's instructions.

Eisenhower had ordered troops supporting Operation Independence, the pacification of southwestern France, to be recalled. Something of a hole developed in the French lines as French 2AD pulled out to go into the Seventh Army reserve. French 11D, returning from duty in southwestern France and stiffened by some armor from French 5AD, entered the area just as the Germans struck. Because Patch had needed to pull 103ID completely west of the Vosges to backstop the defenses astride the intercorps boundary, VI Corps elements defending east of the mountains had been thinned to little more than a force with a guard mission. In effect, they complied with Eisenhower's new, stricter order.

Devers did not catch up with Patch until the early hours of 2 January. Patch was attempting to fend off the beginnings of a major German offensive. Reluctantly complying with Eisenhower's order, Devers had the Seventh Army pull the exposed divisions back into the Vosges in stages along three phase lines over three days, finishing on the last defensive line north to south from Bitche to Strasbourg. That final line was to be occupied only on Devers's direct order. Devers told Patch these moves would be made as necessary regardless of French political repercussions. As was his style, Devers set the critical controls in place then let his capable subordinates run their own fight, even though the combat was intense.

On New Year's Day, Eisenhower had informed Juin's senior liaison officer at SHAEF that he had ordered the 6th Army Group into the mountains, a move that would cede control of Strasbourg to the Germans. De Gaulle immediately ordered de Lattre to defend Strasbourg even if VI Corps pulled out. The Seventh Army history records that the instructions from Devers were to withdraw "regardless of the political repercussions and the evacuation of the Strasbourg area."

At de Gaulle's instruction, Juin met with Smith on the 2nd of January. Juin stated that Strasbourg constituted a symbol of French resistance and greatness. The liberation of this city was the final sign of French national rebirth. Its abandonment would lead France to doubt in victory; moreover, it could have repercussions throughout the world.[41] De Gaulle had also written Franklin Roosevelt on this matter and had the French ambassador request an audience to deliver it. The French government could not accept a retreat in Alsace without fighting. De Gaulle confidentially requested the president to intervene in this affair. Roosevelt declined to see the ambassador, stating that the matter was "purely strategical and tactical" and should be presented to Eisenhower.[42] Eisenhower was not unaware of the problem of French people returning to German control. On 2 January, he wrote to de Gaulle, "I know you appreciate my great concern for the French inhabitants who will suffer greatly should it be necessary to effect a withdrawal of that area. I am, also grateful to you for indicating that you share my views from the military point of view."[43] Eisenhower also returned XXI Corps to SHAEF reserve and control. The 6th Army Group was not to endanger the integrity of U.S. units east of the Vosges.

Eisenhower's response enraged the French leader. On 3 January, de Gaulle replied to Eisenhower asking for an appointment. He also ordered the military governor of Metz to hold the Meuse crossings and French territory, even if the Americans withdrew. De Gaulle ordered the French

First Army to defend Strasbourg and Alsace: "I order you to take matters into your own hands and to assure the defense of Strasbourg."[44] In response, de Lattre ordered the 2nd Algerian Division into Strasbourg to defend the city alone if the Americans pulled out. Devers was in the city at the time. De Lattre ordered the Algerian commander, Major General Augustin-Leon Guillaume, to "make a Stalingrad out of Strasbourg." Devers recalled Guillaume "was a great soldier" with a good sense of humor. He responded emotionally, "you mean I sacrifice my whole division?" He and the men under him were ready to carry out their order. Devers recalled, "If I ordered the French out of Strasbourg, the French commander wouldn't obey."[45] A letter from the military governor of Strasbourg, General Schwartz, to General Patch poured gasoline on this incandescent issue. The governor said departure of Allied forces would result in a wholesale massacre of the civilian population.

Besides the French, Eisenhower had his hands full dealing with senior British leadership. Bernard Montgomery was again pushing to become the overall Allied land commander, and Alan Brooke was openly disparaging Eisenhower's handling of the Bulge. Eisenhower confided in de Gaulle, "I am having a lot of trouble with Montgomery, a general of great ability but a bitter critic and a mistrustful subordinate."[46]

On 3 January, after a meeting of Eisenhower, Brooke, and Churchill to discuss Montgomery's situation regarding command of American armies and the north face of the Bulge, de Gaulle burst into Eisenhower's office. Churchill was still there. De Gaulle said that French public opinion would not tolerate a lack of defense of Strasbourg. Strasbourg had been liberated scarcely a month before, and de Gaulle stated that it would be fatal if it was abandoned without a fight. The French population would rise up at such an outrage. Eisenhower pulled out a map and began his military explanation for the order to withdraw. Responded de Gaulle, "If we were at kriegspiel [war game] I should say you are right. But I must consider the matter from another point of view. Retreat in Alsace would be a national disaster."[47]

After the war, de Gaulle would write, "That the French Army should abandon one of its provinces, and this province in particular, without even engaging in a battle to defend it; that the German troops, followed by Himmler and his Gestapo, should return in triumph to Strasbourg, to Mulhouse, to Sélestat would be a terrible wound inflicted on the honor of our country and its soldiers, I did not consent to it." Furthermore, "If the French government could entrust its forces to the command of a foreign leader, it was on the formal condition that the use made of those forces be in accord of the nation's interest. If not the French government was obliged to resume command of its forces. This is what I determined to do, with all the less scruple since Allied headquarters had not even deigned to inform me of a matter which touched France to the quick."[48]

He threatened to pull French troops from the Allied effort. Eisenhower responded by threatening to withdraw all American logistical support from the French, which would essentially eliminate it as an organized military force. De Gaulle responded, "The outraged French people forbid the use of its railroads. And communications."[49]

De Gaulle became so agitated that Eisenhower feared the French forces would lose control of the population and anarchy would result. De Gaulle agreed that defenders in Strasbourg might have to conduct a fighting withdrawal, but a voluntary pullout could not be tolerated. If the Allies would not defend Strasbourg, de Gaulle would order French forces under French command to defend the city. Eisenhower began to understand that de Gaulle truly feared that the nascent French government would lose all control of the French population, "and that we would have a state bordering on anarchy in the whole country." If that happened, logistics to American units would also be completely disrupted. Eisenhower concluded that holding Strasbourg had become a military necessity. He picked up the phone and ordered Devers to cancel the withdrawal. Juin would accompany Smith to Devers's HQ to insure the defense orders were properly issued.[50]

Eisenhower had decided to modify his orders to the 6th Army Group to "the extent of merely swinging Sixth Corps from its sharp salient [to Lautenberg to the east] with its left resting on the Vosges and its right extending generally towards Strasbourg."[51] This was essentially the last defense line Devers had already outlined. After de Gaulle left, Churchill confided to Eisenhower, "I think you have done the wise and proper thing."[52] De Gaulle recounted, "We parted good friends at the door of the Hotel Trianon. Yesterday the defeat before Colmar had shaken the First Army's morale; today satisfaction at having saved Strasbourg rekindled every heart. General de Lattre's in particular."[53]

Arriving at Seventh Army headquarters in Lunéville on 3 January, Devers had instructed Patch to withdraw from Strasbourg and pay no attention to political pressure to continue to hold the city. While still at Patch's headquarters, the new SHAEF order came over the wire. Devers immediately ordered VI Corps to stop its pullback into the Vosges and along the Rothbach River.[54] Eisenhower again released XXI Corps, probably with the thought of reinforcing VI Corps. Devers didn't see that need but used them temporarily to restore XV Corps positions.

Valid military logic underpinned Eisenhower's original orders. But there were two key questions. How serious was the threat from the Nordwind offensive? And would a pullback substantially reduce Allied risk? Devers argued that, upon closer analysis, the 6th Army Group did not have a lot to worry about and that, in the abstract, a retreat was not justified. Add the intense French desire not to expose her population to German occupation again, and for Devers there was no question but that the 6th Army Group should stay put.

Eisenhower did not lose his starch while communicating with de Gaulle. In his January 5th cable to the French leader, he recounted the sacrifices Allied dispositions had had to make to defend Alsace and then dressed down de Gaulle: "I must urge again the over-riding necessity of maintaining the infantry strength of the French First Army."[55]

Perhaps as a statement of public policy, SHAEF could have maintained that it would only respond to strictly military affairs. But one cannot change the reality of the political implications of military decisions simply by willing them away. In his written explanation to George Marshall concerning the decision to abandon Strasbourg, Eisenhower noted, "I looked at the matter merely as a conflict between military and political considerations and felt completely justified in handling the matter on a purely military basis."[56]

Eisenhower's initial move was faulted because he was blinded by his own unrealistic assumption. He was highly irritated that Devers had placed him in this predicament by pushing VI Corps east of the mountains and then failing to get the First French Army to eliminate the Colmar Pocket. But on 1 January, Devers was proved correct and Eisenhower caught off base. Still, Devers admired Eisenhower: "He was wrong on all of those decisions, and he had to give in on them and that always makes it hard for a man. He gave, too. He was flexible. That is the reason why he was big in my mind. . . . I flew up there and told them personally. I did what I ought to do and it proved to be right."[57]

With Allied resistance stiffening, local German commanders of the assaults on the Seventh Army kept expecting to be reinforced by the armored exploitation force, 21 PzD and 25 PzGD. But American commanders reacted faster than the Germans thought possible. German spearheads had not reached the Saverne Gap, and, without this objective in hand, Hitler refused to release the panzers.[58] As a result, Americans maintained a lateral mobility advantage by using arterials such as N-419 to shuttle reinforcements to needed areas. Sensing that the German advance was ebbing, and given the exhausted troops of TF Hudelson, Patch maneuvered the lightly engaged 103ID, along with some engineers fighting as infantry, laterally more than 25 miles and plowed right into the path of the faltering German attack. The 103ID had hopscotched past the 44th, 100th, and 45th IDs, all heavily engaged, and the intercorps boundary to deliver the coup de grace against the primary Nordwind attack. It was a brilliant achievement that established Patch as a first-rate battlefield commander. A regiment from 36ID backfilled the hole left behind by the soldiers of 103ID, who immediately busied themselves with attempts to chew off the base of the German spearhead. By 5 January, the German attack from the north against the VI–XV Corps boundary had pretty much played itself out. The 6th SS Mountain Division was still pressing an attack into Wingen, a 10-mile penetration at its deepest. There they were contained with little of strategic value lost by the Americans.

But the Germans were far from finished. German intelligence had identified weak spots among former 79ID positions, which had been thinned. As the Cross of Lorraine Division had maneuvered to the west, some of the extended positions along 31 miles of the Lauter River in the most exposed easternmost sector of VI Corps were thinly guarded by newly arrived infantry regiments from 42ID. The training record of these regiments was poor, and senior commanders hoped that these troops would be shielded from heavy combat. Germans from 553ID crossed the Lauter virtually unopposed during the morning and tore into the sparse clumps of green troops. With few antitank weapons, the Americans couldn't deal with the German assault guns that soon led the advance.

General Blaskowitz had finally wheedled approval from Hitler to release the armored reserves to bolster the Nordwind attack.[59] XXXIX Panzer Corps, which controlled 21PzD, 25PzGD, and 245VGD, struck at the very vulnerable eastern tip of VI Corps at Lauterbourg. Only a few scattered elements of 45ID and 79ID were able to mount anything of a defense. Kampfgruppes from 21PzD joined the volksgrenadiers chasing the inexperienced Americans toward the small Landsgraben Canal.[60] Brooks told the 79ID commander, Ira White, to clean out the German incursion. Reinforced by a handful of 14AD tanks, veteran 79ID infantry regained a foothold in the village of Gambsheim. German counterattacks threw them back to the canal. There was too much ground and too few defenders to form a solid defensive position. But the GIs and some Algerians to their east slowed the German thrust, which had been launched with insufficient reconnaissance of the ground. Blaskowitz was so incensed at the poor handling of the panzers that he threatened to court-martial their leaders for lack of aggressiveness.

Between 5 and 25 January, the Germans mounted five division-sized attacks, most directed at VI Corps east of the Vosges and the French positions just north of Strasbourg. Nordwind had been controlled down through channels from de Rundstedt's OKW. Attacks emanating around Strasbourg and the Colmar Pocket were directed from Heinrich Himmler's Army Group Oberhein. Having been hastily planned, these attacks were poorly executed. While most of Norwind's operational objectives had not been obtained, Himmler was determined to present the Führer with Strasbourg.[61] On 7 January, the Nineteenth Army, a part of Himmler's army group, launched an attack from Colmar northward toward Strasbourg, paralleling the Rhine-Rhône Canal with the tough 198th VGD reinforced by about forty tanks. Had the Allies withdrawn completely from the city, Himmler might have had his present for Hitler. Had the French been forced to fight with untrained FFI divisions, there might have been a large bloodbath. De Gaulle did have something to worry about besides pride.

On 9 January, elements of 21PzD and 25PzGD resumed their attack against remnants of 42ID near Hatten on the northern outskirts of the Haguenau Forest. German use of flame-thrower tanks caused some members of the Rainbow Division (42ID) to surrender. Perhaps made of sterner stuff, their battalion commander radioed his company commanders to hold their positions, let the German armor pass, and fire at the enemy infantry. South of Hatten, Sherman tanks from 14AD ambushed and blasted the German tanks. Covered by supporting artillery fire, the Shermans counterattacked into the infantry as both sides desperately fought for dominance in town. A 14AD attack on Rittershofen was less successful. For several days, the enemies deadlocked. Other VI Corps elements tried to counterattack the Germans, but German armor ferried across the Rhine stopped these weak efforts. Between this assault and one mounted by 6SS Mountain Division in Wingen, VI Corps found itself threatened on both its flanks. Eisenhower and SHAEF had feared this eventuality.

But Devers and Patch had events well in hand. With 36ID from XXI Corps and 103ID entering the northern front of the Seventh Army, they relieved 14AD and joined a very busy General Brooks. He needed more. Devers released his final army group reserve, 12AD. He hadn't been impressed with the performance of either 12AD or 14AD. In his diary, he wrote, "When I see their men they are not alert or on the job. I am not impressed with their leadership."[62]

The 79ID had not been successful in clearing up the German bridgehead around Gambsheim, just above Strasbourg. Moving toward the town of Herrlisheim to restore American lines east of the Vosges where VI Corps had had to yield ground, 12AD expected to meet with only small remnants of German infantry, perhaps six hundred in all. Instead, 12AD met with disaster in Herrlisheim. The lead infantry battalion lost contact with, and therefore control of, all of its companies. They were cut off and sliced up. Soldiers running from the town said other Americans had been surrounded. A tank company sent in to find them came out with only four of its seventeen tanks. The combat command gave mixed orders. A battalion headquarters surrendered to the Germans. Another tank battalion lost all of its tanks.[63] Two American battalions were essentially destroyed. Survivors of 12AD withdrew from Herrlisheim on the night of the 10th. It was not an impressive demonstration of the Armored Force.

Meanwhile, panzers moving south had finally broken through thinly held VI Corps lines east of the Vosges, driving the Americans back into the Haguenau Forest. Division and regimental staffs lost control of their units as the mixture of constant reinforcements and retreats made the jumble unmanageable. Fierce fighting devolved into a series of sharp company- and platoon-sized firefights. Each side attempted to cut the other off with little success. The greenness of both new American and rebuilt German units was evident to all. German reinforcements were perceptively tipping the balance of power around Rittershoffen and Hatten. On the opposite flank, a 45ID counterattack resulted in a reinforced battalion being cut off. After several days of effort to relieve them in the face of cold, blowing snow and artillery ammunition shortages, the American remnants surrendered. It had been a tough fight by desperate men on both sides.

Perhaps because of the confused nature of VI Corps's positions east of the Vosges, and the reports of German Rhine crossings both north and south of Strasbourg, Eisenhower put in a call to Devers. Jake recorded it in his 10 January diary entry: "I received a telephone call. General Eisenhower is getting a little nervous about my front. There is no need for that. What we need down here is a little help in the form of simple support. If we get it, we can continue to destroy the German Army west of the Rhine. If we don't get it, we can still withdraw without too much trouble to ourselves. His tone is unmistakable."

For the next several days, 21 PzD, now joined by 10SS PzD, 11PzD, and the 7th Parachute Division, moved south through the Haguenau Forest, pushing delaying elements of VI Corps back across the Moder. Some German spearheads made it across that stream. To the east, combat swirled around Herrlisheim near 553rd PzGD's initial Rhine bridgehead. The 10th SS Panzer Division rolled south toward this embattled town. The German High Command rearranged their paltry reserves. On 16 January, 10SS PzD, the 7th Parachute Division, and some ancillary units organized as XXXIX Corps but now subordinated under Himmler's army group attacked southward from Lauterbourg down the west bank of the Rhine, pushing aside the remaining defenders from 70ID and infantry from the newly arrived American divisions. Soldats linked up with Himmler's forces that had attacked across the Rhine north of Strasbourg. Patch and Brooks had been expecting such a move. The attack also ground against what was left of 12AD, which had launched another attack to regain Herrlisheim that very same day.

VI Corps had lined up most of four infantry divisions in defensive positions along the Moder. What was left of 12AD and 14AD coiled up behind the infantry as a reserve. Still concerned, Eisenhower released the 101st Airborne Division from SHAEF reserve to buttress Devers's defenses. Normally this division would have stayed to support the planned offensive north of the Ardennes. French II Corps had also stiffened French 31D defenses north of Strasbourg and west of the Rhine.

The final German attacks came out of a blinding snowstorm on the night of 24 January. Attackers attempted to cross the Moder north of Strasbourg where it traverses the Alsatian Plain east of the Vosges. The Seventh Army was still in a defensive posture.[64] The 103ID was under extreme pressure, especially around Rothbach. The 6th SS Mountain Division managed to eke out three small penetrations. In fierce, sometimes see-saw fighting, the breaches were sealed. Realizing Nordwind attacks had shot their bolt, Hitler withdrew all the mobile divisions on the 25th. The last wisps of Nordwind dissipated in the cold air.

On 12 January 1945, the Soviets began the greatest threat to the Third Reich to date, their winter offensive. Over 175 Soviet divisions, most of them in East Prussia and Poland, threatened to crush what remained of the Eastern Front. In the presence of this gathering whirlwind, continuing unsuccessful German attacks in the West made no sense. Unhappy with the results of the ill-conceived attacks against the U.S. Seventh Army and the provincial capital of Alsace, Hitler sacked Blaskowitz and allowed Himmler to relinquish command around Strasbourg. Then he suspended further German offensive action. The remnants of divisions in the best condition were shuffled east to stem the flow of the communist hordes. German casualties amounted to some 23,000 versus 13,000 American dead and wounded.[65] Nordwind and related attacks around Strasbourg mangled the last German mobile reserves and gained nothing.

SIXTEEN

The Colmar Pocket
Finally Collapses

IN A SERIES OF COMMUNICATIONS TO GEORGE MARSHALL AND
his senior commanders from 10 to 20 January 1945, Dwight Eisenhower
summarized the recent German attacks and laid out his specific plans for
the final phases of the war in Europe.[1] He broke the final operation into
three phases: destroying German forces west of the Rhine, crossing the
Rhine with a concentration in the North, and a final offensive to the East
through central Germany. Above all, the German armed forces had to be
crippled so that the Nazi monster, regardless of its will, would be unable
to resist the Allies as they brought about the end of Hitler's rule. Eisenhower intended to do this by assembling "the greatest possible eventual
concentration in the north."[2] Bernard Montgomery would command
the main effort north of the Ruhr with Omar Bradley prosecuting a secondary effort south of the Ruhr but north of the Ardennes. With the
elimination of the Bulge at the beginning of February, Eisenhower had
formed a general reserve of about twenty divisions with which to finish
the Wehrmacht. In order to achieve these concentrations, he wanted a
defendable line right up against the Rhine everywhere to the south.

For the 6th Army Group, this meant eliminating the Colmar Pocket
and holding the upper Rhine with a minimum of force, that is, with
the semi-trained and semi-organized French Army. If there was enough
combat power left over, the 6th Army Group might advance east of the
Rhine. That advance would be on one or both of two axes: from Mainz to
Frankfurt or from the lower Rhine south of the Ruhr. A thrust across the
south of Germany was explicitly ruled out. Thus, the 6th Army Group
was again cast in a supporting role guarding a less-active southern front.

During the southern advance to the Rhine, Jacob Devers felt "the only sound thing to do was to give the Third Army to the 6th Army Group and grant us a boundary line. I am sure the staff recommended it up there [at SHAEF]."[3] In turn, it was hard for the First French Army to accept a strictly defensive mission. "Since my policy was unable to accept this strategy," wrote Charles de Gaulle, "I made my own decisions. Our troops would have to cross the border. They would do so, if possible within the inter-Allied framework. If this was not possible, then they would do so on their own account."[4]

The Colmar Pocket, still to be dealt with, covered some 850 square miles on the west bank of the Rhine between Strasbourg and Mulhouse. On a map, its perimeter appeared as a 70-mile lopsided semicircle. On the ground, it wound along flooded areas and mountainous terrain for 130 miles of battle line. After the failure of the Bulge and Nordwind attacks, the Germans could hardly consider additional major offensive action. They viewed the pocket as a means to draw off Allied strength to a sector that could not possibly be decisive. The Germans lacked the strength to go west, and the Black Forest was a major impediment to the Allies going east. Nevertheless, Eisenhower became increasingly irritated at the existence of the Colmar Pocket. In his mind, its reduction was a precondition for any major movement east of the Rhine. A cable to Marshall records Eisenhower's perspective: "At the moment, the most worrisome area is the south. . . . The great danger is that Devers will be caught out of position and some of his troops manhandled. . . . He was badly mistaken in the ability of the French to finish off the Colmar pocket."[5] As late as 7 January, Germans pushed Frenchmen back south toward Strasbourg in a limited attack between the Rhône Canal and the Rhine (map 16.1).

"The Colmar Pocket episode had not enhanced Jake Devers's already middling standing in my eyes or Ike's," wrote Bradley. He continued, "After taking Strasbourg in November, the French had lazily and ill-advisedly failed to clear about 50,000 Germans west of the Rhine in a thirty by fifty area we called the 'Colmar Pocket.' . . . Because of the ineptitude he had shown in the so-called Colmar Pocket operation, I had little faith in Devers and even less in de Tassigny's French First Army. I foresaw a long bloody campaign going nowhere at great cost to us."[6] Finally, he

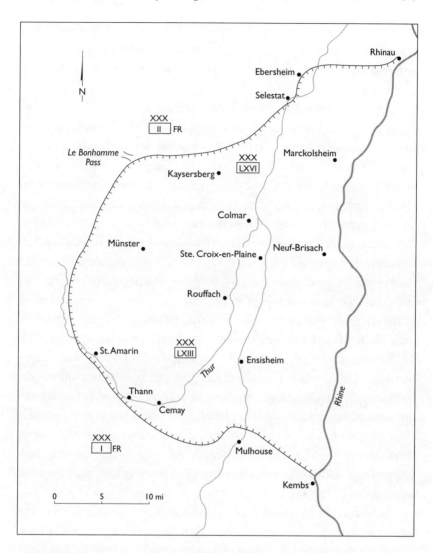

16.1. Colmar Pocket

added, "It affected Eisenhower like a burr under his saddle. Eisenhower had begun to openly talk about replacing Devers with Patch."[7] Bradley's words reflected thinking at SHAEF headquarters at the time.

Devers acutely understood he had to eliminate the Colmar Pocket posthaste. While he believed it was but a small exposure as elsewhere the

Germans were in full retreat, he recognized the priority Eisenhower had placed on Colmar. If Devers concentrated on eliminating the pocket, he knew Patch could advance the Seventh Army to the Rhine under his own power.

Even before the fight through the Ardennes and the Nordwind attacks, Devers had planned for an offensive to reduce Colmar. His optimism remained irrepressible. Ultra intelligence had indicated that the German armor withdrawing from the Bulge was not going to be reinserted into Nordwind and that Jean de Lattre was overestimating German strength in the pocket.[8] In the past, Devers had been trying to do too much with too little. Given the morale crisis and then the need to deploy the French 3rd Infantry Division (1D) to defend Strasbourg, the French First Army had not been ready to attack on 5 January. To resolve the French internal organizational problem, many colonial troops had been replaced with metropolitan French who had only recently rallied to the Tricolor. For example, 91D, which had been manned primarily with black African soldiers, underwent almost complete *blanchement.* The newly raised 101D, which suffered from similar training and equipment shortages, was full of unruly and ill-disciplined FFI volunteers from around Paris, and it was nowhere near an attack formation. Renewing their junior leadership – sergeants, lieutenants, and captains – was their most acute need. As both of these divisions were in French I Corps, this formation was less than attack-ready. Allegations that the 6th Army Group was draining the French of logistical support were prevalent but not accurate.

In his earlier efforts to gain Eisenhower's permission to cross the Rhine at Rastatt, Devers had overstated the combat power the First French Army retained after their remarkable attack up from Belfort. General Reuben Jenkins observed, "The French just got the fight knocked out of them."[9] Jenkins felt that white-haired Antoine Béthouart, commanding general of French I Corps, had become too timid. In Jenkins's opinion, the corps had to instill leadership from the front, and it had to lean forward. In return, Béthouart's staff burned Jenkins in effigy.[10]

If Jenkins was overly hard on Béthouart, the French general was not about to oversell the offensive capability of his depleted corps. In addition to the teething troubles of 91D and the rawness of 101D, a very shot up 31D had been sent north to defend Strasbourg. In French I Corps, only the 1st Armored Division (AD) and 21D were capable of serious offensive action.

On the positive side, the relationship between the senior leaders of the First French Army and the 6th Army Group had reached a new level of compatibility. De Lattre recognized how far Devers had gone to facilitate the French need to defend Strasbourg during Nordwind and he had extended himself to keep de Lattre from receiving directly opposing orders from the Allies and the French government. "Our friendliness [was] cemented in the difficult days at Strasbourg. . . . They were more than Allies; they were a part of ourselves. . . . I rather reckoned on the friendly understanding of General Devers, and on the easygoing cunning of General Guillaume," wrote de Lattre after the war.[11] Still, de Gaulle chafed at having to listen to the Allies giving the principal units of the French Army orders within the boundaries of their own country. Through Alphonse Juin, he kept pushing de Lattre to begin a major invasion of Germany. Differing sets of directions from his two superiors continued to compound the stress on de Lattre.

On the 11th, de Lattre traveled to Vittel to present to Devers a plan to resume pressure on Colmar. The French commander understood that the viability of his army as a combat force was in jeopardy. If he could not clean up the pocket, any attempt to restore French honor would come to naught. Devers entered into his diary, "General de Lattre told me of his many sleepless nights and troubled days; said he wanted to attack, the only way to get out of his dilemma. This is what I have wanted to do for some time. If the French will fight and take aggressive action, I feel sure there is no reason to lose Strasbourg."[12] He was happy in the spirit he found in the French general. De Lattre "seems to rise to real heights of leadership when necessary." Devers told de Lattre that the First French Army had insufficient combat power to close the pocket, and that he would seek additional forces from Eisenhower. The army group commander was worried about French 11D's commander (part of Béthouart's I Corps). He seemed to lack the drive to carry a division and had been losing ground to an inferior force for two days. De Lattre defended him, saying 11D had to insure Strasbourg's safety as well and was not in a position to take risks. Devers promised to give the French some additional support to close the pocket, although he was not sure from where he would get it. De Lattre seemed reassured after the meeting. Later he wrote, "Not only did Devers adopt my way of looking at things, but he made haste to satisfy my needs."[13]

Two days later, on 13 January, "Beetle" Smith came down to visit both the French First Army and 6th Army Group. Eisenhower frequently sent Smith when there was a problem or a subordinate needed a stiff talking to. Jake still had concerns about the ability of VI Corps to hold the positions into which they had been pushed back. Devers impressed Eisenhower's chief of staff with his desire to clean up the pocket and conduct an immediate offensive against it. He wheedled Smith that the 6th Army Group would need an additional armored and infantry division to reinforce 3ID on the northern edge of the pocket held by French I Corps. Devers must have impressed Smith. On the 14th, Smith cabled that 10AD and 28ID would be attached to the 6th Army Group. Smith cautioned that 28ID was very beat up from its ordeal in the Ardennes; in fact, it did not figure large in subsequent operations. On 17 January, Haislip initiated limited attacks to straighten his line. The 70th ID especially made progress penetrating the Siegfried Line, seizing high ground overlooking Saarbrucken.

As Devers had not been able to eliminate the Colmar abscess, Eisenhower knew he would have to reinforce the 6th Army Group further, believing as he did that French divisions "have a low combat value."[14] Both Eisenhower and his chief of staff remained unhappy with Devers's stewardship of the 6th Army Group. To date, despite his assurances, Devers had not eliminated the Colmar Pocket. Smith remarked, "[We] don't have much confidence in our friend Jakey."[15] Eisenhower wanted theater reserves all up in the north. Instead, because Devers had not reduced the pocket and instead had maneuvered north of Strasbourg, precipitating a series of fights, the supreme commander would have to send a portion of his precious reserves south to clean up the mess.

On 24 January, Major General John "Jock" Whiteley, an able British officer on Smith's staff, telephoned Bradley. Eisenhower wanted him to loan Devers a couple of divisions for an attack in Alsace to clean up the pocket. George Patton, who was in Bradley's HQ at the time, said the 12th Army Group would be giving up a sure thing for a sideshow. In response to Eisenhower, Bradley said, "I trust you do not think I am angry. But I want to impress on you I am goddamned well incensed." Then he in effect told Eisenhower he could take every corps in the 12th Army Group and send them somewhere else. Patton chimed in, "Tell them to go to hell and all of us will resign. I will lead the procession." Bradley slammed down the receiver.[16] Eisenhower relented, but again he was not happy with Devers for having placed him in that position.

The recently arrived XXI Corps headquarters, which had earlier been used to control the SHAEF reserve, would be retained by the 6th Army Group as its third U.S. corps. Devers attached this formation to de Lattre's army. After feeling pigeonholed as commander of an army of inferior soldiers, de Lattre was deeply honored at what his friend Devers had decreed. Devers directed his staff to create a plan to eliminate the pocket. Almost every tactician's gaze focused on the last major span standing across the Rhine and into the pocket, the railroad bridge at Neuf Brisach. That town, which is built within an old Vauban fortress, lies about 7 miles east of Colmar and 2 miles from the town of Brisach on the east bank of the Rhine. French I Corps was tasked to drive north from Mulhouse to the bridge, a distance of about 17 miles. Germans remaining in the pocket would then be cut off and vulnerable to destruction.

Not wanting to overcommit French II Corps, de Lattre proposed attacking just the south side of the pocket with French I Corps. Instead, Devers suggested reinforcing this effort with American forces from the north to provide the combat power necessary to squeeze the pocket shut with pincers from north and south along the Rhine. Textbook thinking recommended pinching off a salient at its base in order to bag the greatest number of enemy. The "base" of the salient in this case was centered on the largest surviving bridge over the Rhine.

Colmar was situated on soggy ground crisscrossed by many watercourses. The 6th Army Group plan was to employ French I Corps and an American corps of three divisions to capture Neuf Brisach from the north.[17] This attack would be preceded by a strike by French II Corps from the south, with a primary attack toward the Neuf Brisach Bridge and a secondary attack on a more westward path to fix the Germans in place. Then, assisted by an airdrop, French II Corps would take Colmar itself. Planners thought the southern attacks would draw German reserves away from the path of the subsequent northern attack. French I Corps would attack from the north, but at less depth than the Americans, and capture the city of Colmar. Devers planned to use XXI Corps, Major General Frank W. Milburn commanding, containing the 28th, 35th, and 75th Divisions. French II Corps was buttressed by the veteran U.S. 3ID. Devers described Milburn as a lean man with the muscular look of a fighter. De Lattre liked and accepted the American plan.

The 6th Army Group planners had set the attack for early February to get better flying weather. Devers liked the plan but rejected the timing out of hand. Ostensibly, he wanted a 20 January start to insure the ground would be frozen, and the large number of streams and canals that cross the area would be at their winter lowest. Given Eisenhower's well-founded impatience, it is possible this was the real reason for Devers's haste. The pressure from Eisenhower bore down on Jake, who was already in the doghouse. Up north, Montgomery was preparing Operation Grenade, a multi-army effort to gain the Rhine. But Eisenhower would not let Montgomery commence unless the situation in Colmar was well in hand.

XXI Corps would not be in place for a 22 January kickoff, so Joseph de Monsabert's French II Corps would begin the attack from the south, initially bypassing Colmar in a drive for the bridge at Neuf Brisach. When the operation reached its full stride perhaps a week later, Milburn's corps would provide the hammer blow. Both Devers and de Lattre accepted the change. Jenkins estimated that the Rhine from Strasbourg to the Swiss border could be held with three French divisions.

In keeping with his philosophy that a commander should be where the trouble is, Devers and a small group went up to the Colmar Pocket and stayed there for about ten days. In one case, he gave a direct order to a French division commander. While this routinely happened between British and Americans, the French could be very sensitive. Devers believed that a foreign commander must be persuaded, not simply ordered, to be firm. Unless an American commander has confidence in the professional qualifications of his foreign subordinate commander, Devers believed he should give him detailed, specific instructions. If he has confidence in that subordinate, he can give him considerable latitude. When a conflict arises, the American commander must take a broad view. "What a mistake it is, at the higher levels of command," wrote Devers, "to try to draw a sharp dividing line between military factors and civilian political concerns."[18] Such an artificial distinction nearly led Eisenhower to make a serious mistake with the French about the defense of Strasbourg. The historian Forrest Pogue once asked General Marshall about the issue of distinguishing between military and political objectives. Marshall replied that he never gave his subordinates guidance to attempt to separate these two critical issues. Moreover, in this instance, the French needed to regain their self-confidence. Devers wanted them to be successful. Henry Cabot Lodge observed that "Devers was wise in giving his [French] subordinates great latitude. The general wanted to receive a lot of information but did not give a lot of detailed instructions in return."[19]

While much reduced in ferocity, Nordwind was still blowing the Seventh Army southward to the east of the Vosges. As late as the 16th of January, Devers was concerned about the ability of the hard-pressed VI Corps to hold its defensive line. The 12AD went into reserve on the 19th as it was judged in unsatisfactory condition to re-enter combat. But he would not slow the Colmar preparations. SHAEF nixed the idea of an airborne assault but continued to task the 101st Airborne Division with buttressing Devers. He used the paratroopers to pull 36ID back to continue its rebuilding. The 6th Army Group Intelligence Summary of 20 January stated that the Germans no longer had any offensive capability left in the Colmar Pocket.

Reducing the pocket was as much about logistics as tactics. After dealing with the Ardennes and Nordwind, virtually all Allied units were far below authorized strength. Given the paucity of French service troops, the French First Army was in particularly bad shape. For example, French 5AD had only 61 percent of authorized fighting vehicles operational. To help deal with the situation, the 6th Army Group opened its spare parts bins and replacement stocks, providing much-needed assistance.[20] As a result, French 5AD were in a position to make an effective contribution to the upcoming battle. But the drain retarded 6th Army Group efforts to regenerate many American units, such as 28 and 36ID, which had been badly shot up and were of limited combat value in mid-January.

Letter of Instruction No. 8 from the 6th Army Group issued on the 18 January set the 20th as the date French I Corps would begin their assault from the south, with the attack by II Corps from the north commencing on the 22nd. Béthouart planned to strike deep into the German positions near Cernay with two divisions on a narrow front, with the objective of cutting the road net in the Cernay-Guebiller area and attacking toward the Brisach Bridge. A secondary one-division diversionary attack would emanate from around Mulhouse. Jenkins communicated to Béthouart via a liaison officer: "If you lean forward you will go forward because he just doesn't have anybody in front of him."[21] The American officer proved too optimistic. Even so, the German presence in the pocket wasn't massive, about fifteen thousand combat effectives controlled by eight divisional HQs. By 1945, most German formations were regimental-sized affairs with a divisional flag. Many soldiers available for duty were ill-trained or not ethnic Germans.

De Lattre would support the effort by sending out false communications that French 1AD was to be detached from II Corps and sent up north. While the two French corps drove toward each other, the raw French 101D (I Corps) contained the remaining Germans in the Vosges until they could be cut off by the twin advancing French pincers north and south. In his 19 January diary entry, Devers found de Lattre aggressive, driving, and determined. Devers estimated that the French would have a tough four or five days, but that they would be able to outlast the Germans.

A German commander said, "Whoever wins the winter wins the war." And it wasn't the French that were winning the winter. Without the constant exhortation and encouragement from Devers, de Lattre would have postponed. Remarked de Lattre, "Personally, I would rather have waited."[22] Both logistical problems and the weather looked awful. But the American appealed to the Frenchman's sense of honor. Devers's impact cannot be underestimated.

From the beginning of the French attack into the pocket, the weather was atrocious. De Lattre referred to it as "a Siberian winter."[23] Wind whipped snow that already stood 3 feet in the fields. Troops attempting to advance in the frozen weather quickly became exhausted. "Not a mule succeeded in following. As for vehicles, they were out of the question," said de Lattre. French troops had greater difficulty fighting the snow storm than the Germans. "They had visibly lost faith."[24] Nonetheless, because the Germans could not imagine the Allies' attacking in such atrocious weather, Béthouart's troops achieved tactical surprise. On 20 January, 102 batteries fired in support. (During the eradication of the Colmar Pocket, American and French forces fired 24,000 long tons of artillery and mortar ammunition.) German reaction was everywhere brisk and successfully parried I Corps. The French, moving up the Ill and from west of Mulhouse toward Ensisheim then into the dense Harth Forest along the Rhône-Rhine Canal, were met by strong resistance. While the Germans did pull some panzer reserves south, neither Heinrich Himmler nor his commanders took the I Corps effort seriously.[25] On the 22nd, de Lattre said he needed more infantry to reduce the Colmar Pocket.

Initial gains by II Corps fared only a little better. By the end of the first day's assault, II Corps's objectives had been reached only in the southern portion of its sector. The Ill River had been reached, but enemy fire on the bridges kept French armor from crossing. The German commander held positions west of the Ill with outposts and delaying detachments. Initially as part of French II Corps, John "Iron Mike" O'Daniel, a warrior whose features looked as though they had been carved with a chisel, and his top-notch 31D moved its regiments one after another, first east then south, in order to open a path for French 5AD to advance toward the Neuf Brisach Bridge. O'Daniel hoped that the Germans would misinterpret his maneuvers as an attempt to encircle Colmar. French II Corps planned to advance from Illhausern to Neuf Brisach and seize control of the Colmar Canal crossings. When the U.S. 31D and French 5AD firmly had control of the Rhône-Rhine Canal, French 11D would then strike out for the Rhine.[26]

Despite the weather, the men of 31D moved rapidly and gained a wooden span over the Ill River, at that spot about 60 feet wide with steep banks. Pushing south they then ran into trouble when tangling with the main German defensive positions. An attempt to move tanks across the bridge resulted in a Sherman falling along with splintering timbers straight down into the middle of the river. Then the Germans attacked with heavy jagdpanzers in the lead, sending American infantry back across the cold stream in something of a panic. A division wag penned,

> But we had our weaker moments
> Even when success is Huge
> 'cause the outfit took a licken
> At the bridge at Maison rouge.[27]

But 31D held. To their north, French 11D attacked across the Ill and gained several small bridges capable of supporting light vehicles. A stiff fight for the town of Selestat broke out. German counterattacks drove the French from many of their initial gains.

Jake wrote in his diary, "Germans have gone into towns we relinquished and killed many of the inhabitants. Hard for a US soldier to withdraw and leave people unprotected. General de Lattre gave me a fighting talk; stated he was never discouraged."[28] The French retook the towns from the Germans at bayonet point. The fight swirled back and forth for several days. Despite the failure in the Ardennes and with Nordwind, there was still a lot of fight left in the Germans. Opposing the French were the skeletons of twenty-five German battalions with weary but battle-hardened noncoms leading a lot of raw recruits. At first the Germans intended to restore their prestige in the "lost province" of Alsace by executing converging attacks on it. But that didn't go far. Now II Corps was to push south to Neuf Brisach.

Progress in the first week had been disappointing for the Allies. VI Corps north of Strasbourg was still beating back Nordwind swirls. Devers agreed with de Lattre that French soldiers lacked "the punch or the willingness to go all out," even though their mission was to liberate French territory that had been incorporated into the Reich.[29] His diary entry for 26 January said, "Situation does not look good. We are not making the progress we should toward the elimination of the Colmar pocket."[30] He knew he would have to depend on XXI Corps to carry the day. SHAEF allotted another two divisions, 75ID and 35ID, to the 6th Army Group. Taking over the central portion of the French First Army's front, including 31D's sector, Milburn's corps attacked with three U.S. infantry divisions abreast and 12AD held in reserve. Instead of holding it for later exploitation, de Lattre transferred the French 5AD to XXI

Corps, which immediately used it to reinforce 31D. Devers told Patch that 35ID needed a rest and to relieve it.

It wasn't until 27 January that serious advance resumed. After heavy fighting, 31D cleared the junction of the Ill River and the Colmar Canal. By the 29th, the Germans were evacuating, leaving tough rearguards to prevent rapid Allied advance. On the 24th and 25th, Eisenhower and General Juin, de Gaulle's chief of staff, had exchanged several sharp letters in which Juin admonished Eisenhower, "I told you, in my opinion [winning the battle of Alsace] should be your sole preoccupation of the moment."[31] While O'Daniel's men fought tenaciously to maintain their positions along the Ill, Eisenhower met with Devers in his Vittel headquarters on the 27th. In no uncertain terms, Eisenhower demanded that the 6th Army Group clean up the Colmar Pocket immediately. Patton had crossed the Moselle on 24 January.

Devers swung the Seventh Army around to the right, which pinched out Milburn's XXI Corps. Despite the dressing down he received, Jake became optimistic as he saw the developments. In his diary, he wrote, "The feeling I have had for several days is now beginning to crystallize. The Germans are not as strong as we think."[32] Amazing the difference a day makes. On 28 January, XXI Corps formally joined the fight under control of de Lattre.

The two senior American commanders could not have known, but the fighting along the Ill caused the gears on the German side to shift. As early as the 25th, Army Group G staff had concluded that the Colmar Pocket was of no further military use except as a delaying position to tie down Allied forces, and they prepared to withdraw their most exposed units. On the 28th, even Hitler agreed to partial withdrawal but wanted to hold something of his foothold west of the Rhine in Alsace. On this point, von Rundstedt agreed, as he thought Patton's eastward lunge was about to begin, and the pocket would slow down Allied efforts to support that advance.[33] On the next day, Hitler sent Himmler off to the Eastern Front and reassigned all of the forces around Colmar to Army Group G, now under the command of SS General Paul Hauser.

Unfortunately, Eisenhower's attempt to help matters along in late January had the reverse affect at the inter-Allied level. He reminded General de Gaulle of the need to keep French infantry replacements flowing and of the need for additional French service troops. On 23 January, he met with General Juin, expressing the hope that the French soldiers would be inspired to attack. Informed of the meeting, de Gaulle expressed surprise at "the severity of a judgment" about the French performance. Eisenhower responded that he only meant to underscore the importance of eliminating the pocket.[34]

Allied pressure on the pocket caused German units to shift and become terribly intermingled. German intelligence had not picked up the movement of the U.S. XXI Corps until its divisions entered combat, adding further confusion and German loss of tactical control. They didn't recognize that the U.S. 3ID was striking for the Neuf Brisach Bridge until the 30th. On the other hand, they concluded that the French were attempting to seize the Neuenburg Bridge over the Rhine at Chalampe. Army Group G ordered General Siegfried Rasp to prevent the destruction of his remaining forces in the pocket and to pull back all of his men that remained in the Vosges. But he was not given the authority to move any of them back across the Rhine.

The German withdrawal from the mountains toward Colmar led to a second surge by both French and American units under de Lattre. Buttressed by elements of French 5AD, the U.S. 3ID approached the Neuf Brisach Bridge. Reuben Jenkins remarked that Milburn's troops did a superb job, which heartened the French.[35] German defenses in Colmar collapsed, and the French, with 3ID's assistance, took the town. To avoid further damage or French civilian casualties, little artillery was used in or near Colmar. The U.S. 75ID advanced toward the Rhône-Rhine Canal, allowing 3ID to move over it and then south down the east side of that waterway. Stubborn German resistance around Neuf Brisach led to the decision to send a refurbished U.S. 12AD south and link up with the French 2nd Moroccan Division advancing north at Rouffach on 5 February.[36] This split the pocket north-south. Remaining German defenses crumbled into uncoordinated fragments. The 6th Army Group Weekly Intelligence Report No. 9 issued at the end of January stated, "The offensive power of the enemy had definitely diminished along the front. The Germans retired in good order into the Siegfried line."

On 2 February, the French First Army's offensive began to yield significant results. Two divisions broke through the main German defensive belt the next day. By day's end, I Corps held the Ill River from Mulhouse to Ensisheim and the Thur River from Cernay to Ensisheim. After two weeks of tough fighting, the corps had taken its primary objective. Now it could pivot on Ensisheim and head for the Rhine. Germans still clinging to the Vosges were completely cut off. I Corps continued on to the Rhine at Chalampe. Jenkins recalled, "Béthouart's final attack went extremely well."[37]

U.S. forces began redeploying northward while the French cleaned out scattered German remnants. Devers, suggesting that moving these divisions north was a large and unnecessary effort, proposed retaining them to create a major offensive into Germany south of the Ruhr. But Eisenhower and his SHAEF staff were firmly focused on an offensive north of the Ardennes.

North of the pocket, French II Corps lost contact with mainline German defenders on the 31st and reached the Rhine the next day. In ten days, the corps had lost 347 killed, 1,843 wounded, and 608 missing. Many young men from metropolitan ranks rallied to the colors, but only 60 percent of authorized equipment was available. By 9 February, French I Corps reached the last standing bridge over the Rhine at Chalampe, which the Germans promptly dropped into the river. The Colmar Pocket was closed. De Lattre proudly recorded, "Four American Divisions acquired the right to bear, like our own, the insignia of the French 1st Army."[38] Franco-American relationships within the 6th Army Group could not have been better. Jake received "an exceptional message of confidence and loyalty from General de Lattre. It was a message that touched me deeply and which I shall always remember for it came from the heart." He also received the eternal gratitude of the French for defending Strasbourg.[39] In this part of France, many avenues are named "Devers."

After regular French forces swept up the remnants of the Wehrmacht west of the Rhine, they were replaced by FFI who manned outposts along the Rhine. This allowed the bulk of de Lattre's army time to repair badly worn equipment, absorb new recruits, and give many tired units some rest. The number of French casualties overwhelmed French hospitals near the front as there was insufficient means to evacuate them. Devers noted in his diary that de Gaulle wanted to elevate

Jacques-Philippe Leclerc to corps command, but the mercurial French general refused as he still would not serve under de Lattre or anyone who had been associated with the Vichy.[40]

The *Seventh Army Report of Operations* stated that, "after the poor performance at Colmar, Devers assigned First French Army to guarding the Rhine." French 1 A D might be capable to take offensive action in two or three weeks, but "the remainder of the First French Army is incapable of offensive action until it undergoes a thorough retraining and refitting program for a minimum of 6 weeks."[41]

At the Seventh Army, most of the U.S. VI Corps remained in place along the Moder River, but Edward Brooks mounted limited attacks to redress the German bridgehead at Gambshiem. Lack of ammunition for U.S. artillery made this an infantry slugfest over the soggy, flooded ground that continued into mid-February. Still, VI Corps regained its original main line of resistance on 26 January.[42] Limited attacks were also mounted along the XV Corps front, but for the most part, the Seventh Army used the downtime to bring itself back up to strength and conduct refresher training. Artillery ammunition remained in short supply, and Devers worked to improve matters. A number of divisions that had been sent to handle Colmar and other 6th Army Group needs were released back north to the 12th Army Group.

Even before the Bulge, cleaning up the Colmar Pocket was a lower-level requirement. There was nothing near Strasburg that had the military importance of Antwerp. Eisenhower continued to harangue Devers for not cleaning it up, and later dipped into theater reserves long after there was any real threat from Colmar. With no offensive capability, Colmar could have easily been bottled up like the fortress cities on the Bay of Biscay or the isolated islands of the Pacific that were bypassed by island hopping.

The Colmar Pocket induced operational mistakes on both sides. Hitler wanted to retain a Rhine bridgehead to provide a perimeter from which offensive action might be rekindled. The Ardennes offensive had demonstrated that the Germans were still capable of offensive action. But expecting two separate offensives to be successful was unrealistic. The German Nineteenth Army, badly needed for defense of the Reich, was lost for no gain. The official history states that creation of the Colmar Pocket was "a product of two factors, Eisenhower's eagerness to have Patch's Seventh Army turn north, and Hitler's determination to hold onto a portion of Alsace at all costs." The inability of the 6th Army Group "to eliminate the pocket in December was perhaps inevitable . . . because of the lack of trained French manpower. . . . It would have been better to leave a defensive holding force around Colmar and turn the bulk of First French Army north."[43] The history goes on to say that the Germans were in about the same shape: "Army Group G has only one capability: to defend itself."

Eisenhower blamed Devers for the judgment that the French were strong enough to eliminate German forces south of Strasbourg. But looking back to the Vittel throw-down, Devers had the larger issue right: it was better to ignore these German troops in the first place. As the 6th Army Group history records, "The attrition in supplies and equipment at a time when the entire Army Group was attempting to conserve supplies so that the offensive [over the Rhine] might be resumed, was out of proportion to the forces supposed and the mission at hand."[44]

After cleaning up the Colmar Pocket, the First French Army took a break. Rest and regeneration was badly needed. As it rebuilt itself, it also created the framework for the postwar French Army. Most of the remaining Africans returned to home shores and were replaced by new metropolitan recruits and former members of FFI. The French First Army also lost another division to the French Army of the Alps, commanded by General Droyen, who reported to Devers, and which guarded the Franco-Italian frontier in the mountains. In addition to the French First Army, Jake had to monitor a brace of French divisions guarding the Italian border and trying to bring some semblance of order to southwestern France. French 21D returned to the 12th Army Group. Almost unfettered opportunities to pursue and destroy the Wehrmacht seem to lie before the Allies.

By this time in the campaign for Western Europe, "Units like the 3rd Infantry Division had almost unconsciously perfected their combined arms teamwork to a fine art."[45] Devers could reflect on what he had wrought at Fort Knox in 1941–1942. Devers had been a major engine of change from the bifurcated notion of heavily armored but slow "infantry accompanying tanks and lightly armed and armored but fast cavalry tanks that could rampage through the enemy's disorganized rear." In its place, Devers had championed the main battle tank, in this case the M4 Sherman, which could perform both roles. When enemy tanks were present, commanders yelled for 76mm-armed "Easy 8s." In the summer of 1944, Patton had told Jake that the sight he had developed for the 76mm "is a wonderful thing."[46] When the fighting was house to house, close in and nasty, the heavier armored "jumbo" M4s were in demand.

In Europe, dogfaces rarely advanced against heavy resistance without tanks smashing down the machine gun nests and fortified houses and bunkers. Unlike the British system, tanks and infantry worked in closely integrated formations. Infantry carefully probed forward, noting where Germans were and where they weren't so that the tanks didn't get ambushed. They picked out the Germans brave enough to sneak forward in an attempt to fire a panzerfaust antitank weapon at close range. When machine guns kept the infantry from moving, tanks sent the German machine gunners into kingdom come. When things got a little tougher, good fire direction procedures rapidly called in mortars or artillery. Engineers came in behind, clearing the way for something less versatile than a tank, spanning obstacles and dynamiting anything bigger. Infantry searched holes or houses to insure nothing capable of hurting a tank was hiding. Without Devers's energetic leadership back at Fort Knox, neither the equipment nor the doctrine would have existed to create such a smoothly running, all-purpose combat organization.

The tank-infantry combined arms team that 31D brought to near perfection began to create a new idea – "overwatch." Infantry would precede tanks to clear out ambushing antitank weapons, especially in towns. The relative uselessness of the towed 57mm antitank gun, and the relative ineffectiveness of the tank destroyer as compared with the tank as an antitank weapon,[47] relegated the once-popular notion of the dominance of antitank guns without ability or armor plate to move in the face of the enemy to the dust bin.[48] In the clash of ideas, Devers had first transformed his own thinking to the armored combined arms team and then caused the creation of the units that turned these ideas into lethal action.

The fighting in Alsace also revealed that heavy tanks were not the be-all. "Tiger!" brought fear to anyone within sight of one. They were hard to kill and carried incredible firepower. But soggy Alsace demonstrated that Tigers and their kind were not invincible. Their heavy weight and relative lack of power hindered their off-road mobility. Roads leading into the mountains often proved too steep for these underpowered monsters, and their engines frequently broke down.

The real Achilles heel of combined arms formations was their supply lines. As Patton once explained, "My men can eat their belts. But the tanks have to have gas!" In his 16 January 1945 diary entry Devers recounted how his old colleague in North Carolina highway crime, Brehon Somervell, had expressed his pleasure at how well Tom Larkin managed the logistical system that facilitated everything that happened. That was also due in large part to the attention Devers had paid to transporting huge tonnages on a daily basis. Not only did that require transportation equipment but the operation of roads, rails, and bridges, which Devers insured were rehabilitated in time to allow the flow of materiel to go forward. Jake just didn't think up ways of how to do this. He streamlined the original ideas and made them happen, both on the battlefield and along the main supply routes. Not many senior leaders could cite such accomplishments on so many fronts.

SEVENTEEN

Undertone to Austria

IN MID-JANUARY 1945, DWIGHT EISENHOWER CHANGED THE focus of his final drive. Instead of Berlin, which he said had no military value and in any case was far closer to Soviet forces, the SHAEF commander shifted his gaze southward to Leipzig and the remaining Nazi forces in southern Germany. As part of this adjustment, the long-held notion that the Allies would concentrate not only north of the Ardennes but north of the Ruhr relaxed. Given the preference of both Eisenhower and his staff for a two-fisted effort, Eisenhower kept Bernard Montgomery and three armies advancing north of the Ruhr with Berlin as a possible terminus, but tasked Omar Bradley with pushing the Third Army south of the Ruhr but north of the Moselle, focused on Bonn with Leipzig as a possible final destination. The First Army would advance just north of that industrial area, completing its encirclement where a major portion of the German Army could be trapped and destroyed.

The British immediately protested and requested the combined chiefs of staff review his decision. A number of high-level communications were exchanged, but Eisenhower's message to George Marshall on 15 January best summarizes the situation.[1] Eisenhower reiterated his commitment to focus the main effort north of the Ruhr with an attack commanded by Montgomery and consisting of First Canadian, Second British, and Ninth U.S. Armies. The secondary attack moved north from George Patton's Lorraine campaign to a thrust under Bradley south of the Ruhr to Bonn. South of the Moselle would be strictly defensive along the easily held Rhine. "I required Devers's army group, for the first two acts, to remain essentially on the defensive," wrote Eisenhower after the war.[2] He also cabled Marshall that he knew Jacob Devers would have trouble with Charles de Gaulle about the proper objective for the French Army. French divisions "had a low combat value," and his biggest worry was that "Devers will be caught out of position and some of his troops manhandled."[3] This was yet another indirect slap at Devers's attempt to cross the Rhine at Rastatt before Eisenhower was ready for that as a follow-up attack.

In mid-February, the Seventh Army continued its limited offensive to straighten its lines and retake ground lost during Nordwind. Sandy Patch gained a foothold on German territory near Saarbrucken, the area where the Seventh and Third Armies converged. Like the French, the Seventh Army took time to absorb new reinforcements, repair equipment, and conduct refresher training. Care had to be taken lest military traffic tear up the light French road network. Cold, nasty weather persisted, and efforts were made to get most troops under the roofs of warm buildings. Railroads were rehabilitated all the way up to field army dumps, easing logistical problems. But artillery ammunition shortages continued to inhibit operations. During a limited attack, one division's artillery was limited to shooting only eleven rounds per gun per day, making the attack an infantry brawl. Dogfaces still went on patrol, sometimes precipitating sharp firefights. American assessment of the status of German forces continued to decline.

To the north of the 6th Army Group, the Third Army in early February breached the Siegfried Line and advanced toward Prum. The 4th Armored Division (AD) rolled into Bitburg, while the Ninth Army, fighting under the direction of Montgomery's 21st Army Group, approached the Rhine south of Dusseldorf during the first days of March. The First Army finally waddled across the Roer River, turned angry by German flooding, and closed on the Rhine near the southern edge of the Ruhr (map 17.1).

The opportunity of the L-shaped frontline near the boundary of the 12th and 6th Army Groups led Eisenhower on 13 February to instruct Bradley and Devers to begin planning a joint offensive there. In response, the Seventh Army drafted a plan of attack, Undertone, which advanced all three corps abreast to the Rhine. Armored divisions with each corps were positioned in depth and readied to exploit whichever breakthrough looked most promising. The Seventh Army's main effort was to be made

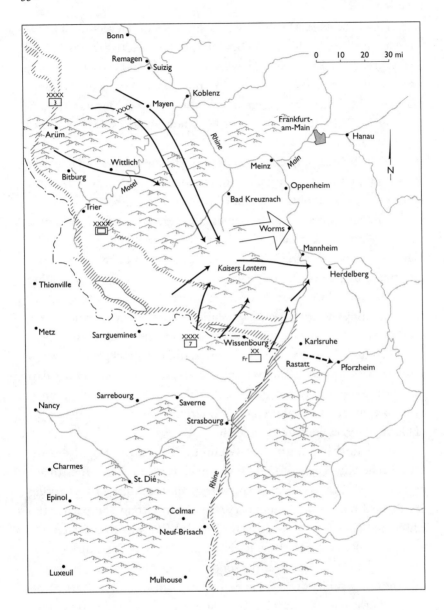

17.1. Third and Seventh Armies Surround Elements of Army Group G

by XV Corps's advancing up the break in the wooded mountains near Homburg, known as the Kaiserslautern Corridor.[4] The 6th Army Group intelligence reported, "The collapse of German forces in the north has left Army Group G only the higher echelon with units on the west bank of the Rhine River. Army Group G [now commanded by SS General Colonel Paul Hauser] had a strictly defensive capability."[5] Against a hardened enemy defense, a commander would normally want to concentrate maximum combat power on the narrowest front, but against weak resistance, a rapid sweep forward made sense. As Undertone was consistent with Eisenhower's orders to close to the Rhine and destroy German forces, Devers readily approved it and sent it up to SHAEF.

Patton wasn't idle. After ejecting the German Seventh Army from the Vianden Bulge and the rapid capture of Bitburg, he wanted to continue to pursue the enemy across the Moselle. He envisioned his XX and XII Corps surrounding the remnants of the German Seventh Army. A deep Third Army penetration southeast to Kaiserslautern and then a turn due south would encircle a lot of Germans as well as attack from the rear the West Wall positions defending against Patch's Seventh Army. This move would close off the L and add much of the German First Army to the American bag of prisoners. The maneuver was far more sophisticated than his simple bashing ahead at what had amounted to a German combat outpost at Metz the previous fall, as had characterized American operational planning.[6] Patton told his corps commanders that the logical extension of that operation would be an assault crossing of the Rhine in the area of Mainz or Worms, both ideal sites. He did little to conceal his disdain for Montgomery's extensive and time-consuming preparations for a set-piece Rhine crossing north of the Ruhr. Bradley saw the logic of Patton's plan and also forwarded it to Eisenhower.

Eisenhower approved the plans but created deeper objectives: over the Rhine between Mainz and Mannheim, just as Patton hoped. But he designated the Seventh Army as the main effort for that maneuver with the Third Army providing a supporting attack across the Moselle.[7] This made good military sense as the Third Army retained flexibility to assist other 12th Army Group efforts, such as the upcoming encirclement of the Ruhr to the north. It also gave a starring role to the Seventh Army and 6th Army Group, which is the opposite of displaying any animus toward those organizations. As Eisenhower reiterated to Marshall, "I have ignored the personal ambitions of any individual."[8] Selecting the Seventh Army certainly was *not* a vote of "no confidence" in Devers or his army group.

Under the new plan, the Third Army was to sweep south of the Moselle through the low Hunsrück Mountains and onward to the Rhine. Bradley liked Patton's plan as it minimized the chances that the 12th Army Group would lose further troop strength to either Montgomery or Devers.[9] At first, Devers was concerned that the Third Army would be poaching on his zone of advance, especially if it operated up to the Kaiserslautern corridor. He legitimately worried about potential fratricide resulting from the two armies' colliding on an active battlefield. But in the spirit of team effort, and knowing which way the wind blew at SHAEF, Devers went along with this change. He authorized Patch and Patton to talk directly, thereby easing the bureaucracy of interarmy coordination.

Eisenhower was painting on an even larger canvas than his army and army group commanders. He kept his theater plan of a main attack north of the Ruhr firmly in the center of his vision. Devers's mission was to mount a secondary attack to draw German strength away from Montgomery's main Rhine crossing (codenamed "Plunder") and Bradley's supporting attack (codenamed "Lumberjack").[10] As with earlier SHAEF-planned offensives, the secondary attack in the south provided insurance against deadlock in the north. SHAEF transferred four divisions from the Third to the Seventh Army in recognition of the 6th Army Group's designation as the main effort.[11] Eisenhower's closest friend, Bradley, was less than happy, but the decision was based on military considerations, not favoritism.

While the Saar was Germany's second most important industrial region (after the Ruhr), this concentration of economic resources was not the primary strategic objective of the offensive. As Eisenhower had consistently stated and Devers understood, the overarching objective was to destroy the Wehrmacht. With the armed forces destroyed, the Nazi regime would be helpless to resist the imposition of unconditional surrender. Eisenhower smelled the opportunity to surround a good portion of Army Group G.

All senior British and American commanders recognized that possession of the triangle of territory bordered on the northwest by the Moselle River, the southwest by the Siegfried Line, and the east by the Rhine known as the Saar-Palatine would uncover important Rhine crossing sites. Seizing those sites would lead to yet more opportunities to inflict damage on the Wehrmacht. Much of the terrain was hilly or mountainous, rising to 3,000 feet with few steep valleys like the Saar Gap, but containing good roads that would support heavy military traffic. A lot of the ground was covered by either dense industrial development or forest, both favoring a defender whose primary forces were infantry defending behind thick minefields. Operationally, the Allies wanted to pass through this area as quickly as possible while capturing the largest number of prisoners – or inflicting the greatest number of German casualties – possible.

In addition to three strong U.S. corps, the Seventh Army had operational control of the French 3rd Infantry Division (1D), which was to clear a strip along the Rhine up to the Franco-German border at Lautenberg. The attack was to commence on 15 March with the Seventh Army, now containing fourteen divisions, as main effort. The French First Army would hold the Rhine. Undertone was timed to commence after Lumberjack but before Plunder. There were no signs of immediate German withdrawal. Most senior commanders expected that, given remaining German strength, the Seventh Army was in for a tough fight along the Siegfried Line. Even at this time, German defenders manning the Siegfried pill boxes were in comparatively good shape. The Third Army, already with a head start beyond the West Wall, initiated its attack on 12 March. Patton's tank columns attacked southeast. He issued verbal orders to his corps commanders that the interarmy boundary was no constraint.[12] He pointed to the same Rhine crossing sites along fairly flat terrain near Mannheim that he had identified during the summer of 1944 pursuit. They were now in the 6th Army Group's zone. A collision around Kaiserslautern loomed.

In a surprise move six days before Undertone was to commence, the First Army's 9A D seized a bridge across the Rhine at Remagen. To say the least, as Patton put it, "I was just a little envious."[13] Part of Eisenhower's plan was to close up to the Rhine all along the front. Despite his desire to hold to the defensive at the Rhine south of the Moselle, his field commanders wanted to cross this great river as soon as possible. But first the Saar-Palatinate.

By not pausing in their pursuit of Germans retreating across the Moselle, Patton's forces struck first. His infantry broke through the bluffs and hills lining the river, and his tanks exploited at rapid speed. German defenders were sparse. Every German soldier who could find an excuse drifted backward toward the Rhine. Russell Weigley writes that "Patton's brief impatience had been partly provoked by fear that Patch's Seventh Army might yet reach the middle Rhine before him."[14] German intelligence expected Patton to strike north toward the Remagen bridgehead. Instead, Manton Eddy's XII Corps, which led Patton's attack, headed south. Immediately, Eddy's corps picked up steam. Attacking southeast, it appeared that XII Corps would reach Kaiserslautern before the Seventh Army. By doing so, Eddy would trap most of the German defenders in a pocket.

Hitler railed at the antics of that "American cowboy general" and demanded an immediate counterstroke. But the German unit flags on his operations map represented nothing in the actual world. There were no divisions capable of counterattack. Still, there were pockets of loyal Nazi troops that had fight left in them, even if they had little ability to maneuver. Charging headlong into one of those hornet's nests could get a GI killed just before everyone went home. While leading their troops forward, American leaders had to deal with this hesitation.

When the interarmy group offensive got started, the 6th Army Group did not anticipate that the Third Army would wind up crossing in front of the Seventh Army. Patton, no fool, issued verbal orders for his lead troops to cross into the 6th Army Group's zone. British Major General Jock Whiteley, acting as peacemaker, called the 6th Army Group to try to keep the two American armies from crashing into each other. It was a delicate situation. Reuben Jenkins recalled Jake's reply: "You call Whiteley and tell him we don't give a damn who wins this war."[15] Whiteley responded that Patton had trapped von Rundstedt, the cagey field commander of all German troops, on the Western Front, with his pincer attack. The SHAEF assistant G3 (operations) continued, "Rundstedt is not going to get out of this."[16] Patton's troops continued to the Rhine, and the Seventh Army adapted.

It was as much as 20 miles from the Siegfried Line when it began its offensive on 15 March. Withholding the timing of D-Day and H-Hour from division commanders until the last possible moment, Patch attacked during hours of darkness with no artillery preparation.[17] Patrols from 70ID probing two days before had found nothing between them and the outskirts of Saarbrucken along the river, and got a 2-mile jump on the rest of XXI Corps in the wee hours of the 15th. Nevertheless, Frank Milburn's exploitation force, 12AD, was taken from him and attached to the Third Army's XX Corps, reinforcing their exploitation, which was already in progress. Good relationships built over time and constant telephone calls between Patton and Patch speeded this useful adjustment. The 63ID attacked on schedule and fought its way through two bands of the Siegfried Line south of Saarbrucken.

In XV Corps, 45ID executed a passing of lines through the sector of 44ID while 3ID maneuvered to the right of the 44th. These attacks easily swept away delaying German forces until the Americans directly confronted the Siegfried Line. There, 3ID met a sharp German counterattack that temporarily held up the procession. While some divisions faced tough local fights to break through, just to the north, the Third Army made a German withdrawal only a matter of time. The German division in best shape, the 6th SS Mountain – a former Nordwind spearhead – had already departed to stem the flow of Patton's advancing troops. The 100ID easily took their longtime nemesis, Bitche, in the Maginot Line on the 16th, but ran into a pack of Tigers and Jagdpanthers east of town; the heavy German armor was dispatched only by the valor of good infantry and some bazookas. After observing the 100th's assault on Bitche, Devers felt sure his troops would successfully breach the Siegfried Line. Wade Haislip had wanted to simply bypass Bitche as it would quickly fall far behind the advancing American spearheads, but he complied with Patch's orders.[18] Devers did not interfere.

Up and down the line, the Germans were conducting a delaying operation. Despite Hitler's "no retreat" order, local German commanders shepherded their embattled troops into relative safety behind Siegfried Line concrete. VI Corps, attacking four divisions abreast across the Rothbach and Moder Rivers, achieved complete tactical surprise. The 42ID, using mules to haul supplies over the remaining rough terrain of the Vosges, outflanked Germans defending roadblocks and sent the entire defense back into Germany. Seeking high ground instead of advancing over easier terrain, 103ID captured Baerenthal, which unhinged German defenders attempting to impede the division's advance. Given mission type orders, subordinate commanders in the Seventh Army came up with many creative tactical solutions. On the extreme left flank of the Seventh Army, German units in danger of becoming encircled were authorized to fall back. American operations officers expected the hammer of the Third Army at their back, and that a steadily advancing U.S. Seventh Army would unhinge the whole front.

Units ignored the roads on valley floors, which proved to be heavily mined, and advanced along the ridges as they had been trained. Dogfaces were learning. On Patch's right flank, the 36th and 103rd Divisions of VI Corps, after overcoming a tough "crust" of an initial defense, began moving northeast and had achieved a breakthrough into the Hardt Mountains where they were blocked with nowhere to go. Operating under VI Corps control, the French 3rd Algerian Division more than kept up despite early tough German resistance. Like their leaders, they were determined to avenge themselves on German soil. Jean de Lattre had attached tanks from French 5AD to the Algerians to speed what he hoped would be his opening to a Rhine crossing north of the Black Forest.

To VI Corps's left, XV Corps, the army's main effort with orders to go all the way to Kaiserslautern, was stalled by a stout German defense. At first, XXI Corps's sole attacking formation, 63ID, hit tough resistance from the concrete fortifications of the Siegfried Line. Then the entire German right wing in front of XXI Corps began to peel back. Patch maneuvered elements of 6AD through the easternmost portion of XXI Corps's zone to break free. About the same time, 45ID broke free of the last Siegfried pillboxes. Patch guided his now-unleashed main effort into the race toward Kaiserslautern. When that town fell, the remainder of the German First Army had only difficult roads through the Hardt Mountains on which to make good their escape to the Rhine. Troops penetrating the Palatinate found the cities chaotic. Patch gave each corps commander the greatest possible latitude to manage their own pursuit. Each corps conducted aggressive and highly mobile reconnaissance, and retained a strong reserve.[19]

The meeting that Eisenhower orchestrated on 17 March in Lunéville to coordinate the movements of the Seventh and Third Armies was somewhat anticlimactic, given the earlier phone call between Whiteley and Jenkins. The upshot was that the Seventh Army, instead of being the main effort, would become a support to the Third Army. Patch voiced no objection. The goal was to destroy the German Army. Said Patch, "We are all in the in the same army."[20] Eisenhower recalled that in the past, poor interarmy communication had allowed otherwise trapped Germans to escape. Perhaps he was thinking of the Falaise Gap debacle where fears of boundary incursions had led to delays on the part of both Montgomery and Bradley and allowed tens of thousands of Germans to escape.[21]

Eisenhower suggested that the Third and Seventh Armies co-locate their headquarters. Patch responded that he could reach Patton by phone as easily as he could raise his corps commanders.[22] If there ever was tacit admission by the supreme commander that the Third and Seventh Armies should have been under the same group commander, this was it. Later, Eisenhower said that their operation in March 1945 "was one of the most magnificent things that we did during the whole war – Patton due east, Devers due north."[23]

The two American army commanders drew their own boundary, which designated the area from Kaiserslautern to Worms just across the Rhine as 6th Army Group territory. Even then, Patton sent a brace of divisions south into Seventh Army area (with Patch's concurrence) to lock down Germans attempting to escape. Eisenhower asked Patch where and when he expected breakthrough. Patch replied that he expected it in XV Corps's zone and perhaps to the right of XXI Corps, and that it would take three days. On 20 March, 63ID and 45ID all breached the line. The next day, XXI Corps broke through as well.[24] French 3ID, facing some flat, open terrain swept by German automatic weapons, had a tougher time advancing.

The action represents a great deal of operational maturity on the part of Devers and Patch. General R. W. Grow, commander of 6A D, designated boundary lines as "stop, look and listen lines. . . . When properly employed they become aids not restraints."[25] In other words, they are highly useful control tools, but they don't have to be treated as unquestioned absolutes, an admonition to commanders to effect careful coordination and reappraisal whenever a control tool appears about to inhibit an important maneuver or attack. Many historians argue that at Falaise, Bradley used the boundary situation to hide his reticence to execute an advance that Patton was willing to risk.[26]

Devers could have complained, like Montgomery did during the run up through northern France and Belgium, that Bradley was impinging on 6th Army Groups lines. Instead, Devers focused on the ultimate objective, destroying the Wehrmacht, and subordinated everything else (including ego) to achieving that objective. In this case, he stands above his peers. Eisenhower was worried about Germans' escaping a huge trap. It was Devers who had to take the supine position in order to prevent an enormous error. He did it without question. If anything should have raised his reputation in Eisenhower's eyes, it was this and the subsequent exploitation all the way down into Austria. It was exemplary operational execution. Perhaps Marshall hadn't been all wrong in his initial staffing plan in 1942, when he slotted Devers for army group and Bradley for army command.

By 20 March, the 6th Army Group had breached the Siegfried Line and was now threatening the Rhine. Spearheads had advanced as much as 80 miles in nine days, so fast that Germans had to retreat by day and night on the few good roads that traversed the wooded hills. American fighter bomber pilots could not believe their luck. Soon the forested mountain roads were littered with discarded, smashed equipment and broken bodies, both human and equine. Artillery of various 6th Army Group formations added to the din. In desperation, the Luftwaffe scraped together what it could find to interfere with the carnage. Three hundred machines marked with swastikas took to the air. Some of them were jets. Anti-aircraft gunners, with a rare opportunity to demonstrate their skills claimed twenty-five planes. Marauding fighter bombers downed another eight.

Between the artillery shelling and the P-47s run amuck, the Seventh Army officially reported, "it was difficult to describe the destruction."[27] Unfortunate German towns along the Siegfried Line were little more than dusty rubble piles. Fires burned out of control as there were no longer fire departments extant to fight them. In a letter to his wife, Patch said, "The carnage on our front is even worse than it was around Montélimar."[28] XV Corps had to extricate itself from some Third Army columns that were still in the Seventh Army's area. The 6th Armored, recently transferred to Patch from Patton, rejoined its old stable-mate, the 4th Armored, on the outskirts of Worms. In doing so, it crossed the supply road to the 12th Armored and 94th Divisions looking across the Rhine at Mannheim. Patton's 10th and 11th ADs were intermixed in Patch's columns clanking across the Palatinate. Instead of stopping to regroup, the pursuit accelerated: blitzkrieg had returned to the American army. Seventh Army staff estimated that the Germans lost 75 percent of their infantry that had opposed the Americans at the beginning of the fight. Patch's men herded 22,000 into POW cages. Patton's haul was more than 68,000.[29] As Germans accelerated their retreat, logistics became more of a constraint on the Allied advance than German resistance. Devers marshaled some assets of the 6th Army Group to feed the need.

Still, no withdrawal orders reached German ears. Without permission, a steady stream of vehicles, some pulling field pieces, trundled east across the last bridge spanning the Rhine at Germersheim, 19 miles south of Mannheim. As tanks from Patch's 14th Armored approached the outskirts of town, the bridge went up with a roar. U.S. Seventh Army intelligence estimated that the German Seventh and First Armies lost 75 percent of their infantry on the west bank. That is the way Eisenhower had always said it should be – destroy the Wehrmacht on the west side of the Rhine. The official history declared that the pincers "provided a remarkable example of offensive maneuver."[30]

The Seventh Army Intelligence summary of 17 March noted that "Army Group G has the unenviable task of supervising two faltering armies, the German Seventh and First. Nineteenth German Army no longer poses the threat of an offensive action."[31] Just as Undertone began, Eisenhower sent communications to Devers indicating that both the U.S. Seventh and Third Armies might be placed in his army group for the drive south with the goal of advancing on Kassel. Ultimately, 6AG would be responsible for area south of the Main River.[32] Devers must have said under his breath, "finally." But it did not come to pass.

By the 21st, the entire Seventh Army was in motion. Both 6AD and 14AD exploited beyond the infantry and met only spotty resistance. Rioting broke out in several towns as civilians, released from any civil control, got out of hand. American troops began reaching the Rhine; Montgomery's big river show was set to go off on the 22nd. Therefore, Patton simply had to cross any way he could on the 21st.[33] Being out in the lead of the Third-Seventh Army offensive, he was just into the most unorganized of positions to do so in the nick of time. The 51D, veteran of many river crossings big and small, put boats into the water at the little town of Nierstein, near St. Goar, just into the Third Army zone about 8 miles north of Worms.

By 21 March, Third Army divisions stood before Mannheim, Worms, and Mainz, the three cities Patton had identified the previous summer as his primary Rhine crossing sites. Relatively flat land extended as much as 15 miles on the west side of the river and for several miles on the east, making transit easy for attackers and their engineers. The Rhine was about 1,000 feet wide and 17 feet deep there, flowing swiftly between reverted banks. There was some concern that the Germans would release water from dams upstream to flood the area. The Swiss pledged to guard the rivers between Lake Constance and Basel. The Seventh Army G2 (intelligence) opined that the Germans would not prematurely open the dams because they needed the hydro-power associated with them.[34]

Patton didn't pause at the Rhine. While Montgomery readied a huge set-piece invasion across the river, 51D boarded some rubber assault boats and paddled across on the night of the 22nd. Patton had beaten Montgomery again, by a few hours. In the air, Allied forces executed Operation Clarion to paralyze what remained of the German transportation system. Three days later, the 6th Army Group put a corps across the river at Worms. A drop by the entire 13th Airborne Division had been planned by the 6th Army Group to cross the Rhine. It would have been the only combat drop by the full 13th Airborne Division. Patton and Patch had moved so fast that the air drop was canceled.

With Americans across the Rhine at Remagen and St. Goar, and with Montgomery about to launch a major offensive over the Rhine north of the Ardennes, Hitler decided to replace Von Rundstedt for the final time. Field Marshal "Smiling Albert" Kesselring, the German commander that so badly stalled the Allies at Anzio and Monte Casino when Devers was deputy commander for the Mediterranean, would command all German defenses in the West for the final months of the war. The Allies moved a Canadian corps and British division from Italy to reinforce Montgomery. These forces landed on the quays of Marseilles and took the railroad north – another Operation Dragoon benefit.

From Montgomery's Rhine crossing, the U.S. Ninth Army advanced across the north face of the Ruhr. The U.S. First Army looped northward from the Remagen bridgehead and met William H. Simpson's army at Lippstadt on April Fool's Day. The day before, Eisenhower had appealed to the German nation. He asked the soldiers to surrender and the civilians to begin planting crops. It was time to move past this war. The end was in sight.

The 24 March Intelligence Summary stated, "Army Group G has been reduced to merely an expression. . . . The enemy is completely restricted to a single capability: to withdraw into the interior of Germany before our advancing forces."[35] American operations maps displayed fewer and fewer red symbols, as there were fewer and fewer organized German units remaining. The Rhine was now a challenge only to the engineers. Railheads along its east bank supported each attacking army. For once, transportation and fuel would not impede swift and deep Allied advance. Along the road, "GI Diners" exchanged cold rations for hot. Engineers readied what was to become the huge Roosevelt Memorial Bridge at Mainz.

By the 25th, the Seventh Army was in its sector along the length of the river. SHAEF planners had always focused on Worms as a crossing sight, since the topography on the east side of the river there facilitated a protected airborne drop. Now Devers's troops were entering the town without aid of paratroopers. The Seventh Army actually preferred a flatter plateau at Speyer south.[36] Patch, liking the proximity to the Third Army's successful crossing at Oppenheim, overruled the proposed change and directed the columns carrying the landing craft to proceed in the vicinity of Worms. No one believed that German remnants could emplace a coherent defense against a river crossing.

In the last days of March, the Seventh Army no longer faced a continuous and coordinated German defensive line. Assembling the crossing force rather than German opposition paced its preparations. After the aborted crossing near Rastatt, the 6th Army Group engineer had carefully stored away the river crossing equipment and plans. Now Patch ordered his two most experienced divisions to force the river. The 3rd and 45th Divisions, veterans of the invasion of the Côte d'Azur, readied for yet another landing – on the Rhine's far bank. Instead of the pneumatic craft and oars slapping the water that characterized many river crossings, assault boats powered by 50-horsepower engines carried the dogfaces against the river's strong current. As predicted, Germans did not release water from dams upstream, fearing interruption of electricity for the factories downstream.

Like the 15 March kickoff, the Rhine crossing operation began at 0230. Heavy German anti-aircraft guns leveled at American engineers as they moved their equipment into the water was the most difficult impediment. XV Corps artillery fired ten thousand rounds in the early morning of the 26th, turning the night sky over the crossing crimson. At the 45ID's sector, where artillery held its fire, a sharp fight developed at water's edge. Unlike in Normandy, most of the amphibious dual-drive tanks made it out of the water and immediately began shooting up pockets of Germans still willing to fight.

As they moved east, Americans found only isolated pockets of resistance in villages where Germans had taken refuge. Infantry trudged their way through 2 miles of woods until they reached the autobahn heading east. Haislip ordered 12AD to cross and begin exploitation. VI and XXI Corps had stayed behind near Speyer, ready to make another crossing. With so many bridges now emplaced by American engineers, these corps made administrative crossings on bridges erected by other units.

Given the strength of his army and the disintegration of German forces as he advanced, Patch planned to sweep his army eastward with all three corps abreast, XXI Corps in the center and in the lead with XV

Corps on the left and VI Corps on the right. XV Corps crossed the Rhine at Aschaffenburg on a bridge previously captured by 4AD of the Third Army. Germans put up stiff defense, and 45ID had to fight hard for it. On 27 March, XXI Corps looped northward into the center of the Seventh Army sector, crossed the Rhine at Worms, and, led by 12AD, chased the remnants of German XIII Corps through the Odenwald. By the 30th, it had reached open country. Just south of Wurzburg, they had a bitter fight with an 88mm battalion at Konigshoffen to the south. The 42ID had a three-day fight to capture Wurzburg, and then joined 12AD, which was already fighting for Schweinfurt. One of the few instances where German civilians in large numbers joined their soldiers in defending against the Americans was in Aschaffenburg on the Seventh Army's left in XV Corps zone. Haislip didn't hesitate to use massed artillery and air strikes to reduce the defenders' position to rubble. The 45th ID cleared what was left, house by ruined house. This raised the risk of nonresisting civilians falling victim to American fire.[37]

At the beginning of post-Colmar planning, yet another major difference between Allied and purely French objectives had surfaced. In initial planning, SHAEF envisioned only a limited role for the French in the advance deeper into Germany. They assigned the French First Army to hold the upper Rhine, a mission for which the limited French offensive capability was well suited. This made strictly military sense. The French First Army would defensively hold 155 miles of the front from good defensive positions while the Allies concentrated five other armies on sub-segments of the remaining 255 miles.

Devers wanted the French to pick up responsibility for holding the Rhine north of Strasbourg as the Seventh Army moved into the Palatinate, but saw no military reason for French forces to cross the Rhine, especially into the wasteland of the Black Forest. Needless to say, that did not sit well with the French. De Lattre echoed de Gaulle when he said, "Invasion of Germany was for our country a duty and a RIGHT. Yet the plans of the Supreme Allied Commander did not answer to our wishes in the least."[38] De Gaulle gave de Lattre secret instructions to be liberal in his interpretation of the location of the boundary so that French forces would have a direct avenue into the Reich north of the Black Forest. Initially, Devers and Patch had welcomed the addition of French 3ID to the initial Seventh Army attack of 15 March. For de Lattre, it was his wedge to get French troops moving north along the Rhine until they were clear of the Black Forest on the opposite bank.

At first, Devers did not pick up that de Gaulle wanted to establish a postwar French zone of occupation in Germany east of the Rhine. On 29 March, the French national leader telegraphed de Lattre, "My Dear General, you must cross the Rhine, even if the Americans do not agree and even if you have to cross it in rowboats. It is a matter of the greatest national interest."[39] De Lattre was a step ahead of de Gaulle. Three days prior, de Lattre, feeling confident of his deep camaraderie with Devers, approached the army group commander. "I rushed to Devers at Phals-bourg. With perfect confidence, I told him what was at the back of my mind. Our friendliness, cemented in the difficult days at Strasbourg, justified me in so doing." The French needed access to the Rhine north of Karlsruhe so they would have decent ground east of the Rhine on which to advance.[40] De Lattre continued,

> The official reason for excluding the French from a Rhine crossing was insuf-
> ficient bridging to allow First French Army to cross. De Lattre felt that the
> Americans were preventing the French from crossing the Rhine and used the
> bridging argument as an excuse. ["That isn't so," Devers would later state.[41]] Yet
> 6th Army Group issued an order on 12 March to send 2 French divisional bridg-
> ing companies to U.S. Seventh Army to replace units Patch was ordered to send
> to Montgomery [which] further incensed the French. To cross the Rhine and
> carry the war to the interior of Germany appeared to be a Utopian dream as far
> as we were concerned.[42]

For Americans crossing at Worms, Speyer was of no use. Why not give it to the French?

Jake was nothing if not savvy. Throughout his entire career, he had empathy for another's point of view. The direction from Eisenhower was to treat the French like just another army. Where he could be, however, Devers was more elastic. As long as he was sure that the French did a reasonably good job of attaining the Allied objective, he would allow the French some leeway. He did not want to be party to a major inci-dent, such as almost happened when Jacques-Philippe Leclerc's division bolted Bradley's army group and raced for Paris in August. He took it upon himself to satisfy de Lattre's request.[43] Devers's Letter of Instruc-tions No. 12 dated 27 March read,

3.b. First French Army

Regroup rapidly so as to provide a corps of at least one armored and two infantry divisions for a crossing of the Rhine in the Germersheim area to seize Karlsruhe, Pforzheim, and Stuttgart.

By doing so on his own responsibility, Devers did both the French and the United States a major service. But Eisenhower added this to his list of Devers's deficiencies. After the war, de Gaulle, referring to the incident, said, "General Devers, a good ally, and a good comrade, sympathized with General de Lattre's desire."[44]

When the 3rd Algerian Division reached the planned crossing site at Speyer where VI Corps had earlier planned to cross, however, they found a single rubber assault boat! After sending several solitary boatloads across, someone came up with another four. German sentries finally detected the French, and a small counterattack ensued. But the French with their mighty armada were not to be denied. At Germersheim, the 2nd Moroccan crossing the Rhine with twenty boats were hit hard by German fire. Many boats sank, and only a handful of Moroccans clung to the east bank. French artillery encased them with protective fires. The bridgehead grew to a brace of battalions by night fall, and the French never looked back. General Edward Brooks, looking at the plight of the French, allowed them to come north to Mannheim and use his already overcrowded bridges. French reconnaissance men motored 20 miles east in short order. There they found American armor poaching on their zone, just like Patton had done to Patch. Such is "fluid" warfare. De Lattre was happy his troops had not waited even another hour to stake their claim. If he had waited one more day, he felt that the French would have believed themselves frozen out of their proper place in the occupation of Germany.[45]

The creation of a French zone of occupation in southwestern German had been decided at the intergovernmental level at the Yalta Conference. But its borders were not settled until days before war's end in May.[46] Right up until the end, the French worried lest their Allies not give them their due. Bridges made of sections just recently manufactured in French factories and from other sections hidden during the occupation were erected. General Brooks lent additional boats and heavy bridging, which arrived after 31 March. French engineers constructed a 20-ton bridge at Speyer. By 4 April, 130,000 French troops and 20,000 vehicles were already on the right bank.

After the war, Eisenhower would observe, "Military plans, I believe, should be devised with the single aim of speeding victory."[47] If only a single country's armed forces are involved, this can be easy to achieve. The senior officer has the clout to maintain discipline and should do nothing but achieve his country's objectives. But the situation changes dramatically when several sovereign countries ally. Carl von Clausewitz wrote that war is but an extension of politics. The wise allied leader determines where the allies share common interests and where an ally has another objective. American commanders often found the French difficult because they mistakenly assumed that the French shared a common objective with them. Roosevelt's guidance was not to get involved in another county's diverging objectives. By this time, however, the U.S. government had finally joined the British in recognizing de Gaulle as the head of a provisional French government.

Acting as if France had no other legitimate war goals might have been a good public position for an Allied leader, but it was certainly naive to think those goals would remain subordinate forever. In the spring of 1945, the Americans thought of the French as supplicants that should be willing to participate in the overall defeat of Germany. Not wanting to become the new French kingmaker, Roosevelt refused to recognize de Gaulle, or anyone else, as the legitimate and anointed leader of France in exile with whom Eisenhower was to deal. Many may have assumed that the bifurcation of military from political considerations was well-established U.S. policy, but in a 1956 interview, General Marshall, responding to a question from Forrest Pogue said, "I never told planners not to consider political questions."[48] Eisenhower was familiar with the writings of Clausewitz, and it is clear that Marshall agreed with Clausewitz on this point. Devers's approach had solid grounding in both the history of military strategy and Marshall's actions.

Even in his otherwise conciliatory book, *Crusade in Europe,* Eisenhower wrote, "When inspired, the French are great fighters. I personally liked General de Gaulle. We felt, however that these qualities were marred by hypersensitiveness and an extraordinary stubbornness in matters which appeared inconsequential to us."[49] And though Eisenhower made positive mention of other French officers, including Alphonse Juin, conspicuous by his absence from Eisenhower's volume was de Lattre. By contrast, Devers told Forrest Pogue, "I had [de Lattre's] confidence and he had mine. He was a fighter."[50]

On 31 March, the 6th Army Group G2, Eugene Harrison, made the observation that the Germans could not contain the Allied bridgeheads over the southern Rhine. They were too badly damaged to form a redoubt. The German Seventh Army was foundering; the German First Army was in need of complete overhaul. Since its losses around Colmar, the Nineteenth Army was no more than a small collection of training cadres that could do little but withdraw or become enveloped. The German army was having great difficulty re-establishing a continuous front. Meanwhile, Hitler babbled that if the army could hold out for another four weeks, hordes of Me262 jets would tip the balance in the air.

Upon clearing the Rhine, the 6th Army Group continued its pursuit of what was left of Army Group B. Always attuned to the logistical needs of getting an army group to gallop, Devers insured that a well-developed rail and depot system stretched from Marseilles to the German border, including an operational gasoline pipeline connecting Marseilles with the Saar. In order to relieve congestion on the Rhine bridges, laying additional pipe across the river became a major construction priority. While fuel consumption would exceed the amount flowing forward toward the end of April, stocks were sufficient to prevent repetition of the shortages of the previous August. Reduced ammunition consumption associated with pursuit warfare prevented another artillery ammunition shortage. In March, over 575,000 tons of cargo landed in the ports of southern France, principally Marseilles, making the 6th Army Group independent of the still-strained logistical complex in northwest Europe and contributing as much as half the tonnage required for the 12th Army Group. But every mile moved east or south of the Rhine increased the strain on the trucking system and forward supply depots.

Theater-wide, Eisenhower's first concern was to encircle the Ruhr and destroy the German forces thus trapped. The U.S. Ninth Army was returned to the 12th Army Group and became the northern arm of the encirclement. Past Kassel, Patton's Third Army changed its axis almost due north to meet up with the Ninth at Paderborn. The 6th Army Group again was relegated to protecting the Third's open flank and becoming responsible for ultimately occupying southern Germany, including Bavaria. Its eastward advance would continue to the hills that formed the southeastern wall of the Fulda Gap of Cold War fame.

Just south of Aschuffenburg, 451D encountered the toughest resistance the entire corps had seen east of the Rhine, which took several days to eliminate.[51] Moving from that city, XV Corps, as the army group's northernmost force, raced up the Frankishe Salle River, past Schweinfurt and toward Bamburg. Heidelberg fell with little struggle. A few days later, the 6th Army Group forward headquarters (TAC) moved in. XXI Corps, after moving northward behind VI Corps on 27 March to become the center corps, made a parallel advance from Worms to the vicinity of Würzburg. This took the corps through the rough wooded terrain of the Odenwald. While infantry normally leads in such terrain, German resistance was so light that 12AD led the pursuit. Sixty miles of German territory east of the Rhine rapidly passed under their treads.

VI Corps, now the Seventh Army's right flank, broke a path through Worms and advanced southeastward toward the Neckar Valley. The 10AD sped through the Kraichgau Gate that led to the Neckar River near Heilbronn. The Tiger Division was moving a couple of days behind its sister units to the north. Americans began hitting what German civilians called 61-minute road blocks: the GIs laugh for 60 minutes and then dismantle them in 1. Unlike along the Rhine, many of the smaller towns showed few scars of war. As they advanced away from the Rhine and deeper into Germany, buildings in many of the smaller villages seemed to be intact and habitable. A surprising number of glass window panes remained unbroken. Where there had been no bombing, artillery, or firefights, the inhabitants prayed the war would pass them by quickly and leave few discernible traces. For the most part, German civilians remained indoors. Remarked one dogface, "Some places we kicked Germans out of their house with food on the table and the beds made. Here in Germany sullen looking civilians well dressed and fed would stare at us, never speaking unless spoken to." American soldiers marveled at the well-built German houses they passed and wondered why the Germans started the war in the first place. Discarded German uniforms were everywhere. Much of the remaining Wehrmacht transport was horse-drawn. In places, carcasses of dead horses lined the roads. At times, columns of GIs passed gaunt displaced people from all over Europe now released from the camps but not knowing where to go.[52]

The Seventh Army advanced on a 100-mile front. For the most part, German resistance was only coordinated locally, but the chances of an individual American division running into trouble were increasing. Eisenhower had directed the 6th Army Group toward Nurnberg, 120 miles due east of Mannheim. There was a sharp firefight for control of that town. Devers, aware of Bavaria to his south, began thinking about a turn to the southeast to cover this territory without jeopardizing the right flank of the 12th Army Group. Jake's initial concept was to rapidly advance the Seventh Army south through Germany and into Austria, trapping what was left of the German Nineteenth Army in the Black Forest and then tasking the French with finishing the kill. However, in his 4 April diary entry, Devers acknowledged that he had insufficient strength to both secure this arc and advance his troops, with the exception of XV Corps to the northeast.[53]

There was concern over a final Nazi stand in a fortress in Germany's southern mountains adjoining the Alps in an area that became known as the National Redoubt. Many intelligence officers had looked at this possibility and discounted it. But all remembered the number of Germans after World War I who maintained that the Kaiser's army had not been beaten in the field but been sold out by politicians. What if the Nazis retreated into the mountains and then disbanded without ever formally surrendering? Would a similar argument be made now?

Devers understood SHAEF's concern about rumors of a last-ditch stand in the southern mountains. The Seventh Army G2 was also worried. But Devers's chief intelligence officer, Eugene Harrison, discounted the rumors. What few resources the Germans could scrape up were being thrown into the desperate Battle of the Ruhr.[54] While not too worried about a Nazi redoubt, on 31 March, Devers sent his G3, Reuben Jenkins, to brief SHAEF staff on a 6th Army Group plan to send the right wing of the Seventh Army behind the rear of the German First and Nineteenth Armies. This maneuver would cut off any withdrawal into the redoubt. Then the French First Army would drive along the east bank of the Rhine to clean up. Devers recognized that this would also solve de Lattre's problem with his orders from de Gaulle.

The next day, General Harold Bull read the report from Seventh Army intelligence about the possibility of the redoubt. Bull thought it best that the 6th Army Group extend its southward operations into the

Alps. When the Allied commander in Italy, Field Marshal Harold Alexander, concurred, Eisenhower considered an increase in Devers's mission. "The trouble with Devers's plan," observed Russell Weigley in his study of Eisenhower's lieutenants, "was that this fear [of a Nazi redoubt] was insufficient to persuade Eisenhower that Devers merited a role possibly approaching Bradley's in its conspicuousness."[55] SHAEF rejected Devers's plan. The Seventh Army would continue to parallel the 12th Army Group's drive across Central Europe (map 17.2).

But it was time to stop heading east. On 2 April, Eisenhower ordered both the Third Army and 6th Army Group to begin a giant right-wheel maneuver southeastward to sweep from Nuremberg down the Danube Valley to Linz, Austria. Bull drafted Eisenhower's operation Order Fwd18475 of 2 April 1945. After the Ruhr, the main effort would be by the 12th Army Group due east on an axis from Kassel to Leipzig. The 6th Army Group, said Devers's operation order, "will protect the right flank of the Central Group of Armies [12th Army Group] ... be prepared to launch a thrust on the axis: Nurnberg-Regensburg-Linz, to prevent consolidation of German resistance in the south." But this thrust to the south would occur only if the 12th Army Group's flank was secure. The army groups' boundary ran just south of Frankfurt. Devers and Patch, "accommodating as usual," stretched the Seventh Army to cover a 120-mile front and was so dispersed that concentrations of highly motivated Germans could still cause trouble.[56] Russell Weigley summarizes the environment in which General Devers had to lead:

> So much did Eisenhower's strategy in early April emphasize the favored Central
> Group of Armies [Bradley's 12th Army Group] rather than any help Devers
> could offer against the threat of the Redoubt, that Devers' army group received
> territorial responsibilities considerably disproportionate with its numbers.
> Because none of the Anglo American commanders believed they could count on
> the French First Army as equivalent to an equal number of American divisions,
> SHAEF's and Devers' planners alike would impose the work of any offensive on
> Patch ... [which stretched the] Seventh Army front to 190 kilometers, more than
> twice the frontage of any of Bradley's armies.[57]

This is not to say that Eisenhower was unjustified in weighing his main effort more heavily than a secondary effort. But Devers had to make do with a limited force to get the job done.

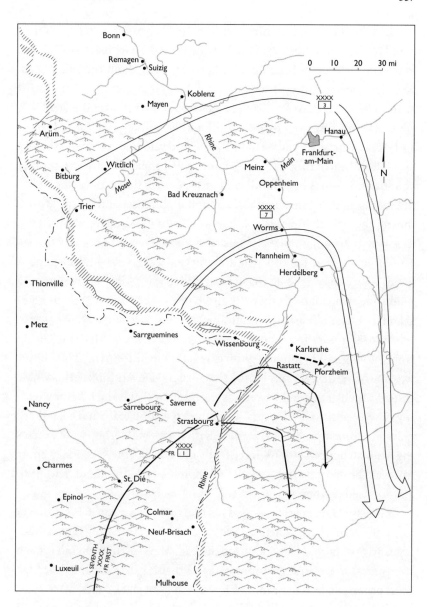

17.2. Third and Seventh Armies Sweep South

Devers continued to think that the Third Army should be subordinated to the 6th Army Group, especially for the final push to the south.
Patton and Devers wound up talking face to face about the sharp turn.
Recalled Devers, "They drew my [boundary] line short and kept Third
Army with the 12th Army Group, and it was spread all over the devil. We
were making quite an angle turn. From Nuremberg [we turned south
and] took Munich. I had been to Patton and said 'Now George, the rivers all flow [north to south]. . . . You just push ahead and we will protect
your flank. We may be behind you a little because the turn is difficult.'"[58]
There was no question about rigid boundary lines separating the armies
during the Bavaria operations. "George Patton and I agreed, so I said,
'George, go through there and bust this,'" said Devers.[59]

After the war, Jenkins would observe, "Devers was more adept at
handling troops on the go than in a stabilized situation. He really was a
mobile fighting man."[60] This was also true of successive VI Corps commanders Lucian Truscott and Edward Brooks. "Devers was just as mobile thinking as Patton thought he was! . . . Reorienting 6th Army Group
from moving east to moving south in reaction to Third Army's maneuver
was one of the best actions I think that General Devers took in this whole
thing." Much of that maneuver was executed by Patch and his team herd-
ing the Seventh Army. Devers "assemble[d] a good team and then [had]
enough self-restraint not to meddle with them while [they were executing his instructions]." Jenkins ruefully observed, "The secondary effort
is never the color bearer. It is the whipping boy. Commanders want to
stay focused on their main effort."[61]

General Devers was awarded his fourth star on 3 April. Eisenhower
had not initially recommended the promotion, nominating Omar Bradley, Carl Spaatz, and George Patton instead. Marshall himself intervened
to insure that Devers was promoted and that his date of rank preceded
most others, including Bradley's. Even at this late date, Marshall showed
by his actions that he still held Devers in high regard. Jake briefly thanked
his superior and the staff around him for their continued hard work and
support. A lot was going on, and everyone quickly returned to the needs
of an army group that was about to make almost a ninety-degree turn.
XV and XXI Corps had advanced deep into Germany, fulfilling the Seventh Army's mission of protecting the 12th Army Group's southern flank.

On 12 April, Roosevelt died. While many were aware of the president's frail health, everyone was shocked by his death. Just three days later, SHAEF intelligence would report that it was only a matter of time before "organized resistance in Hitlerite Germany collapses completely."[62] For such a valiant leader not to see the end of his difficult struggle was a bitter pill.

The Ruhr Pocket had collapsed completely, thereby freeing much of the theater's effort. Eisenhower decided not to waste a lot of American lives racing the Russians to Berlin.[63] Turning Patton and Patch south in tandem was a logical choice. In fact, the two armies would have collided with each other if the Seventh Army had not turned. The move would also realize Devers's longtime wish to harness these two strong horses in a single army group. He had no objection with making the big turn toward Austria via Nuremburg.

As the 6th Army Group's northernmost formation, XV Corps cleared the Hou Rhoen Forest on the 12th Army Group's southern flank. The 14th Armored got into a small, sharp fight at the confluence of the Fraenkische and Main Rivers. P-47s took the starch out of the resistance. Then to the east, the tankers stumbled into the horror of the Hammelburg concentration camp. To the south, XXI Corps jumped the Main River at Wurzburg before the Germans could emplace a coherent defense. Lead American elements paddled across in a couple of canoes they found along the west bank. Emerging from the Odenwald, 12AD fought a sharp engagement to gain bridges over the Main just west of Wurzburg. The 42ID had a short, intense firefight there, and the city never did formally surrender. The GIs of 42ID just crushed the fight out of those who resisted, including the police and fire departments, repelling a final close-in attack by two hundred Germans. With Wurzburg clear, XXI Corps had a virtually unopposed run to Schweinfurt, which was about the limit of its northeasterly advance. Devers placed restrictions on further eastward movement lest the 6th Army Group get strung out all over Germany. There was enough territory in the army group area to be cleared of Germans.

The XXI Corps boundary now made a right angle at the far outskirts of Schweinfurt. Quick capture of intact bridges allowed tanks to get into the fight for the city, which fell on 5 April. From there, XXI Corps turned ninety degrees and advanced south in the general direction of Ansbach. To the north, XV Corps, as the outside corps in the Seventh Army's giant turn, headed south from the Hohe Rhoen hills toward Bamberg. Only occasional delaying detachments from LXXXII Corps interfered with their southward road race – and the Germans slowed them but little. The boundary between the two armies, hence between the two army groups, continued to slide back and forth with the ebb and flow of the herd thundering south. For a while, Devers assigned the hapless 13th Airborne Division to make an assault on Nuremberg.

De Gaulle, who felt Devers's turn southward was designed to hem in the French Army, instructed de Lattre to take Stuttgart. De Lattre felt he must clear the Black Forest of Germans. He responded to de Gaulle, "I must warn you against a premature advance of the First French Army."[64] The French engaged in heavy fighting for several weeks and took 110,000 prisoners in the Black Forest. Later, Devers entered into his diary, "The trouble with the French is they seem to feel they should be consulted on everything. I am the only officer who could want this army group."[65]

On 4 April, to maintain control, Devers put in a phase line temporarily restraining advance beyond Karlsruhe-Heilbronn-Kitzingten-Schweinfurt to prevent further uncoordinated advance. He was concerned that de Lattre's force pushing eastward into Germany would overextend French resources that were still needed to guard the upper Rhine south of Strasbourg as well as the Italian border. Despite the mighty American logistical support machine, forward units were beginning to outrun their supplies. As Devers recalled, "You can't just be running around the country galloping. That is a wonderful thing, that mobility and that drive . . . but somebody had to throw the caution flag."[66]

However concerned Devers was about control, German problems were far worse. On 3 April, Army Group G lost contact with the German Seventh Army and no longer even pretended to issue orders to it. The army group headquarters focused attention on the German First Army and appended Nineteenth Army, which had lost contact with Kesselring at OKW. Hitler ordered the completely disorganized army group to counterattack, an instruction that was simply ignored.

In an attempt to cut off the Nineteenth Army in the south and destroy it, VI Corps advanced southeastward, paralleling the Neckar

River Valley, as the inside corps of the formation. As part of the main VI Corps effort, 10AD drove straight from Heidelberg toward Heilbronn. The main effort was to advance southeast up the Neckar River, cross the Jagst River, and take Stuttgart. Once VI Corps had that, French divisions already across the Rhine would turn south to envelop the German Nineteenth Army.[67] Initially, 10AD was to make a hasty crossing of the Neckar at Heilbronn and continue south. American radio intercepts identified no major formation defending the city. There was none. But there was strong organized resistance. Local Nazi commanders amalgamated a large contingent of Hitler Youth, several school battalions of highly motivated noncommissioned officers candidates, and assorted slivers of other units into a force several thousand strong, well-supplied with artillery. To demonstrate his determination, the SS commander hanged six of Heilbronn's most influential citizens after accusing them of defeatism.[68] When 10AD initially ran into resistance, Brooks ordered an infantry battalion attached to the tankers to make a hasty crossing and guard engineers that would emplace a pontoon bridge. But resistance increased. Given the fluid nature of previous advances, he ordered the armor to make a wide envelopment east of the city and told the follow-on force, 100ID, to take over the mission of crossing into and capturing Heilbronn. When a battalion of the Century Division using assault boats slipped across the Neckar in the early morning hours of 4 April, they were counterattacked by a determined force of much larger size. The Nazis drove the GIs back into a handful of industrial buildings along the river. German artillery directed by observers with a panoramic view from some hills to the east prevented all attempts at bridging or even raft-building. After a second battalion paddled across in rubber assault boats, little else could cross the water due to intense German artillery fire.

The 10th Armored attempted to make quick work of encircling Heilbronn. But the 17th SS Panzer Grenadier Division (SS PzGD) had other ideas. American armor ran up against some formidable resistance where the Jagst River joins the Neckar north of Heilbronn. Brooks reacted by attempting a wide double envelopment of Heilbronn. Combat Command A (CCA), 10th Armored, looped north to Crailsheim. Combat Command B (CCB) was to move south of Heilbronn, cross the river, and become the right-hand pincer. At first CCA kept up a good pace against stiff resistance. On the third day, the 6th CCA clanked 30 miles down a narrow road through the woods and entered Crailsheim. CCA's progress worried the Germans as it threatened to penetrate and destroy the First Army. A stray German Alpine regiment was in the area. Still full of fight, these mountain troopers infiltrated to the narrow road and then established a solid block, which neither the much-extended armored combat command nor 63ID could dislodge. Of all things, some twin engine ME-110's bombed Tiger Division soldiers in town. CCB, which had failed to find a crossing site south of Heilbronn, moved north to rescue its stable-mate but precipitated a heavy fire fight along the road and could not get through. VI Corps had not anticipated a major delay at the Neckar and Jagst Rivers.[69]

Now the Centurymen on the east bank of the Neckar were fighting for their lives and part of 10AD was cut off. Given the intense, bitter fighting, it didn't remotely look like the Wehrmacht was twitching on its last legs. Inside Heilbronn, two American platoons were cut off and captured. The remaining riverhead flattened against the Neckar. German artillery broke up any attempts at bridging. General Patch sent 100ID's third regiment, which had been guarding anti-aircraft units moving through less than fully secure countryside, to help. Century Division had created a second riverhead into Heilbronn, but both were now pinned down by German artillery. The 100ID attempted to loop its third regiment around to the north in a much closer envelopment of the city than the wider sweep by 10AD, but it could not complete even this less ambitious effort in time to affect the battle. The situation was getting serious. Every morning before dawn from 4–8 April, Germans counterattacked 100ID inside Heilbronn. For a time the Nazi-indoctrinated teenagers fought savagely. After five days of heavy fighting, the Hitler Youth began to crack. Steady GIs and intense mortar fire became their undoing. Defying pistol shots from their own officers, they began to scamper into American lines close by, some of them crying. Century Division ferried some heavy weapons across the river. VI Corps artillery on the west bank repeatedly sent the city's rubble high into the air. A bridge was finally completed into the southernmost riverhead, and a tank company crossed before German gunners found the range, dropping the pontoons into the water.

In Crailsheim, sixty C-47s flew into a captured Germen airfield and provided supply for CCA. Apparently concluding that there was no reason not to employ its last strength in defense of the Fatherland, the Luftwaffe continued to strafe the transports on the ground, but with little effect. Germans attacked the stranded armor. Who said the war was over? With its tail between its legs, Tiger Division no longer attacked west toward Heilbronn but northeast toward 63 ID.[70] The Century Division was on its own and under heavy fire in Heilbronn. After nine days of building-to-building fighting, 100ID finally cleared the city. Division commander Withers Burress had pulled 100ID to its feet. Although none of the combatants knew it, less than thirty days of hostilities remained.

Just prior to the Heilbronn fight and motivated by a desire to expand the postwar French area of occupation within Germany, Charles de Galle pressured de Lattre to obtain Stuttgart as an approved Allied objective. To accommodate de Lattre, back on 28 March, Devers had included this provision in his Letter of Instruction No. 12. The French advance, however, was limited to 20 miles, and the French maneuver was to cover the flank of VI Corps's advance. Devers implored de Lattre to delay his advance until VI Corps had moved far enough along the Neckar to be in position to trap the remaining Germans. He had every intention of taking the city with American troops. But the Heilbronn-Crailsheim fight, combined with de Gaulle's secret orders for de Lattre to seize the city, derailed these plans. Devers wasn't surprised when he found de Lattre had his own campaign plans to take Stuttgart by double envelopment. French 5AD sliced ahead into the Seventh Army's zone to capture Tubingen.

Despite de Lattre's warning about the forest's difficult terrain, and Devers's orders not to cross and enter the forest, on 16 April, de Gaulle ordered French I Corps to cross the Rhine at Strasbourg and enter the Black Forest. Nine French divisions squeezed over the Rhine, mostly into the forest. A lot of this was militarily unnecessary, but de Gaulle insisted that de Lattre's forces establish a presence for postwar political purposes. Later, de Lattre stated, "Eisenhower gave me an order to stop but I refused."[71] Devers then directed VI Corps to complete encirclement of the Nineteenth Army by advancing south on an axis past

Stuttgart to Tubingen, Lake Constance, and the Swiss border. Despite Devers's admonition to carefully time an approach on Stuttgart, on 17 April, de Lattre ordered French II Corps to enter the zone reserved for the Seventh Army and begin to envelop Stuttgart while I Corps cleared the Black Forest. Near Stuttgart, initial German resistance was quite strong. To the north, the U.S. 10AD finally broke free and advanced 30 miles, placing it east of Stuttgart on the 19th. Tiger Division entered the foothills of the Schwabian Alps and cut the main road from Stuttgart to Ulm. This rapid advance canceled yet another planned drop of the 13th Airborne Division.

After 18 April, resistance to 100ID decreased as Germans fled from Stuttgart. But 103ID ran into bitter fighting along the autobahn leading south. The French took Stuttgart and continued to mop up in the Black Forest. Bowing to the fact that the French were in Stuttgart, Devers relented on the 20th and later adjusted the interarmy boundary, legitimizing de Lattre's movement into that town. Down in the Schwartzwald, French I Corps actually made good progress and trapped the bulk of German LXIV Corps, capturing 28,000.

Devers was aware of the secret German nuclear research facility at Hechingen, 50 miles southwest of Stuttgart. Allied knowledge of work on a German atomic bomb was a closely guarded secret known to only a few. Devers's orders to get there quickly morphed into a version of "do what was needed to retrieve the German scientific effort, even though the entire area was occupied by truculent French troops." A detachment of engineers drove into the scientific compound, captured the German scientists, and then bluffed their way past the unsuspecting French. Mission accomplished without creating an inter-Allied brouhaha.

But another incident could not be overlooked. Press reports of French colonial troops raping and pillaging in Stuttgart alarmed everyone. After fighting its way through Heilbronn, VI Corps moved south toward Stuttgart. Shocking initial reports from 100ID's commander confirmed lawless behavior on the part of some troops. American correspondents came back from Stuttgart with stories of wholesale rape and of German civilians' being held in a cave against their will. Devers, accompanied by Henry Lodge, personally set out for Stuttgart to resolve what was becoming a major incident. Upon entering the city, Jake met up with the colonial French division commander and said to him, "Look, I didn't come here to accuse you or your troops of raping here. I came to protect you. Do you want it spread all over the [press] that this great and glorious division did all these things in the town of Stuttgart?" Devers recalled, "That sobered him up. Clean it up. You know what is wrong here. He [the French commander] did it. He shot an officer and a couple of enlisted men and that stopped all the foolishness."[72]

But the situation was just too volatile. Devers ordered Stuttgart to be occupied by Americans. On 24 April, Devers ordered de Lattre out of Stuttgart. Learning of this, de Gaulle ordered the French First Army to keep possession of Stuttgart so that the city could become the kernel of a French zone of occupation in Germany. The order would create many headaches for Devers. De Lattre immediately informed Devers of the communication but also told him that "Stuttgart is entirely open to the requirements of the 6AG for all passage of troops, supplies, implantations, and services common and necessary to the two Armies."[73] To attempt to accommodate the French so that they wouldn't openly defy SHAEF orders, Devers carefully drew the interarmy boundary to give the French a corridor into Austria. Eisenhower finally relented, and on 28 April, accepted with regret maintenance of French troops in Stuttgart.[74]

The 10th AD cut the Stuttgart-Ulm autobahn at Kircheim. Much of LXXX Corps escaped, though LXIV Corps was smashed in the jaws of the pincers. But de Lattre wasn't done seeking French national objectives. First, he wanted to enter Sigmaringen, about 45 miles south of Stuttgart on the Danube, to capture Philippe Pétain and a group of Vichy officials who had fled France. Second, he wanted to cross the Seventh Army zone and take Ulm, the site of Napoleon's great victory over the Austrians in 1805. Ulm would present a special problem for Devers as it was a primary transportation hub well within the Seventh Army's zone. The 44th ID had been tasked to capture it. Remaining Germans were trying to escape what had become a pocket around Stuttgart. Ulm appeared to be the next point of concentration for a stand against the marauding Allies. The 10AD ran hard, refueling mostly by air with transports landing at airfields closest to the thirsty tanks. De Lattre drove past the zonal boundary "stop sign" with no intention of even slowing down. Fortunately, French and American forces recognized each other, and a nasty episode was avoided. Still, Devers was furious and immediately demanded the French withdraw into their sector.[75]

As they passed the River Main, the Seventh Army's advance began to converge with the Third Army after Patton shifted to the southeast upon capturing Kassel. Sandy Patch wheeled his army south and headed toward Munich. This move essentially roped off the French First Army into an area extending south from Stuttgart to the German border. Patch advanced on a 120-mile front, twice the width of the armies in Bradley's group. Several French divisions had been diverted to their national interior or the Italian border, or remained on guard duty along the upper Rhine. Only six divisions were left to clear the Black Forest. To keep them from interfering with the U.S. Seventh Army, Devers also turned the French First Army south to the Danube. But the French were determined to repeat Napoleon's triumph at Ulm. Although the city was deep within the Seventh Army zone, de Lattre proceeded anyway. Advances were hindered less by German resistance than by the massive traffic jams that had resulted from the Allied advance. Devers altered boundaries to avoid an inter-Allied jam and to keep the French legal. Then he carefully maneuvered the two armies to minimize the confusion and led the French south rather than east. After an ad hoc Franco-American force liberated Ulm, the French quietly withdrew.

President Harry Truman was shocked at French zonal violations and their disregard of Allied orders. He sent de Gaulle a stern letter, intimating that the French might again be cut off by the Americans. Rather coolly, de Gaulle responded that there would be no more incidents of this nature if the Allies recognized and made accommodations for French interests. By 20 or 22 April, the French had lost their punch.[76] After Ulm was sorted out, Edward Brooks headed straight for the Alps. Devers strongly felt that Ulm should not be transferred to the French. Later he learned that General Joseph de Monsabert, French I Corps commander, hadn't wanted to extend to Ulm either.[77] As the tricolor snapped in the breeze atop the city's old fort, Devers was beside himself. While tactically not the best move, Devers accommodated the French by again shifting the boundaries to legitimize the French maneuver. "Ulm was another Napoleonic thing de Lattre had to take," Devers decided. "Monsabert didn't want to do it."[78] De Lattre ignored the order from de

Gaulle and cheered the French soldiers in Ulm. French officers did not call him "Roi [King] Jean" for nothing.

The Seventh and Third Armies were free to run south because organized resistance in the Ruhr Pocket up north had also collapsed. With ever-diminishing Wehrmacht capability left intact, Eisenhower felt confident to release his reserves. Thousands of German soldiers trudged into POW camps without even having to be monitored by escort guards. Their commander, Field Marshal Walther von Model, dubbed "Hitler's fireman" for all of the disasters he held together over the last years of the war, walked into the woods and shot himself. With the reduced threat, the newly formed U.S. Fifteenth Army took over rear-area security duty in western portions of Germany. For the 6th Army Group, that released the 3rd and 36th Divisions to rejoin the exploitation. It didn't take 31D long to find another fight.

The Seventh Army's last big conflagration was in Nuremberg. In two days, the 3rd and 45th Divisions of Frank Milburn's XXI Corps had raced 30 miles from Bamburg to the outskirts of the city that was something of a Nazi shrine. Mesmerizing annual pageants had been staged there in the prewar days. Filling in for a heavier armored unit, the 106th Cavalry Group encircled the town as dogfaces began their assault on the 16th. About 35 miles from Nuremberg, panzers clanking forth from factories and repair depots fought 14AD northeast of the city. That division also bailed out one of the cavalry squadrons that Germans had tried to rout, virtually annihilating those who made the attempt. The 88mm anti-aircraft guns, which had defended the city from B-17s and Lancasters, now pounded the American soldiers that penetrated their defensive ring. Once in the city, GIs cleared out ardent defenders from the rubble of building after building. It was a bloody business. American artillery kept regrinding the broken masonry, and dogfaces, smelling the end was near, were happy to sit back and have the big guns do the dirty work. By the 19th, John O'Daniels's veterans scrambled over what was left of the medieval walls of the old town. A five-day fight brought about the destruction of an old nemesis, the 17th SS PzGD. With the loss of Nuremberg, the German First Army's right wing essentially collapsed. XV and XXI Corps rumbled south 50 miles to the Danube. The 12th Armored won the race and crossed over on a more-or-less-intact 600-foot-long bridge at Dillingen. Two infantry divisions of XXI Corps followed several days later. On the 16th, Devers met with Bradley and Patton at Wiesbaden, again to sort out boundaries. In their haste to go south, units tended to confiscate roads as needed, and the resulting unanticipated traffic snarls were a constant menace. Boundaries can be good things.

With Americans crossing the Danube virtually anywhere they pleased, centralized Wehrmacht control of defenses in southern Germany all but ceased. Here and there, bands of the most dedicated German soldiers offered resistance, some of it as fierce as it was futile. The Seventh Army history later picked up a phrase from someone at SHAEF: "the disarming, by battle, of the German armies."[79] Hitler's birthday on 20 April also marked the end of organized resistance. The remainder of the military campaign was anticlimactic. Still, a careless or unlucky GI could get himself killed. Each corps adopted basically the same exploiting formation, an armored division in the lead under instructions *not* to mop up but to keep going, with infantry divisions following to insure no German with fight in him had a weapon. Ahead lay Augsburg, Munich, and the Austrian border. VI, XXI, and XV Corps advanced abreast with each division running toward the final stop lines along the Inn River and Salzburg. The road net was sparse. A blown bridge became a serious obstacle as the rapidly flowing streams coming down from the mountains were unbridgeable with pontoons. Some troops passed ME-262 jets parked in the trees just off the autobahn they were using as a runway. Bucking up his men, General Brooks said, "I want speed today." Whenever armor was stopped by a fire-covered roadblock, infantry quickly dismounted and enveloped the defenders, allowing the advance to resume. Armor sped 100 miles in less than five days.

Spring was in the air, and even the most grizzled American GIs were beginning to think they were going to survive the war. Picturesque "Hansel and Gretel" Bavarian villages hung out white sheets. Germans mostly stayed indoors as American armor rumbled past. Americans were in no mood for dealing with dangerous resistance – except in front of XV Corps. American firepower splintered buildings that harbored the few that did shoot. In order to minimize the killing, 10AD adopted the procedure of sending burgomasters of towns that had already surrendered into towns the division was about to approach. Often this worked and lives were spared. Long-suppressed German anti-Nazi organizations began to surface. The German general in command at Augsburg wanted to fight. Germans identifying themselves as the Freedom Party of Augsburg came out to meet the approaching Americans and escorted them to the wavering German general. Given five minutes to surrender, the general stiffly did so and stepped out onto a street already bedecked with white bed sheets gently rolling with the breeze. At Landsberg concentration camp, about one hundred Hungarian troops assigned there drew themselves up in parade ground formation and formally surrendered. Perhaps it was the safest way to avoid newly liberated people that had survived the horrors of the camp. On the way to Munich, members of 42ID and 45ID stumbled into one of the most horrible places in a very sad country – Dachau. Some prisoners were so excited they charged an electrified fence and died at their moment of liberation. Other prisoners hunted down guards who had attempted to hide and bludgeoned the life out of them. Americans had to fire over the former prisoners' heads to stop the brawl.[80] Over thirty thousand wretched souls clung to life within the camp of horrors. Many thousands of Allied prisoners began clogging the roads. The Allies received word that German authorities no longer attempted to move them away from the American advance. This released some tension from the advance.

The 20AD put in its brief combat appearance with XV Corps. Patch altered corps boundaries and directed 31D into Munich. Within the city, civilians pleading with authorities to surrender broke into revolt. Street fighting between German troops and the civilians they had sworn to defend broke out, extinguishing lives during the two days American troops took to relieve them. The 45ID had to fight from room to room to subdue an SS barracks on the north side of the city. By darkness on 30 April, it was over.

Eisenhower designated the final 6th Army Group objective: linking with U.S. Fifth Army elements coming through the passes in the Italian Alps. First contact on the Italian border was made in the Brenner Pass with 88ID of the U.S. Fifth Army on 4 May. Contact with the 10th Mountain Division in the Resin Pass was made on the 7th. The French continued south into Austria and along the shore of Lake Constance on the Swiss border. De Lattre's army pinned the remnants of XLIV Panzer Corps against Lake Constance and herded its bedraggled survivors into POW cages. Moving south, the French linked up with other 15th Army Group forces emerging from the Italian mountains. Again there were Franco-American squabbles as de Lattre insisted on extending his authority over several mountain passes to which American troops had beaten their French allies by a day or two.

Patton, who had entered Austria from Germany to the east of the 6th Army Group, paused before Salzburg for lack of infantry. Recognizing the almost complete breakdown of the Wehrmacht, Devers understood that speed was more important at this late date than communications security. Using nonsecure radio and telephone, he negotiated with Eisenhower, who, with Patton's concurrence, changed the army group boundary. It was classic Devers. Seeing the immediate need, he ascertained the sensible objective despite the printed rules and sprang immediately to action. This was the kind of decision that caused Marshall to take notice and advance Devers from his early days at Fort Bragg. As the official history records, "So swiftly did XV and XXI Corps advance, Bavaria seemed to be one endless array of white banners."[81] Any chance of a final Nazi mountain redoubt disappeared in that sea of white flags. Elements of 31D were first into Berchtesgaden. Soon the roads were filled with units that wanted to say "me too" recorded the Seventh Army history.[82] Despite the rumors, no formal Nazi retreat into the mountains had been planned. But Hitler did intend to leave Berlin on his birthday to continue the war from Bavaria. Many ministries had already made the trip.[83]

Everyone knew German surrender was imminent. On 3 May, Jake first learned that Kesselring was looking to surrender his command, having asked Admiral Karl Doenitz for the authority to surrender. But fighting at reduced levels continued in Austria. Patch was still advancing toward Innsbruck; Patton toward Linz. As might be expected, there was some confusion about who had authority to make – or accept – surrender and who should surrender to whom. Of course, the French had their own ideas. De Lattre insisted that the German Twenty-Fourth Army surrender only to him. At first, Devers thought Kesselring would surrender all troops in southern Germany to the 6th Army Group commander. But the post-Hitler government granted the field marshal authority only to surrender Army Group G; he was granted no surrender authority for units still fighting the Soviets.

On the night of 4 May, Devers expected Field Marshal Kesselring to appear at an estate near Munich for the formal surrender. But Kesselring was still not sure of his authority to do so. Instead, he sent General Friedrich Schulz, commander in chief of Army Group G. The negotiations, such as they were, commenced on the rainy 5th of May. No French representative attended.

Devers specifically stated that this was no armistice. General Friedrich Foertsch, the German commander in apparent local control, made no objection. He pointed out that German communications were almost nonexistent, and that many German units might not receive orders of surrender. Then he asked if the Americans were going to turn prisoners over to the Soviets. De Lattre later complained that, as the official French representative, he had not signed, therefore the French were still at war. And some SS units claimed that Kesselring, a Wehrmacht officer, had no authority to surrender for them. In one instance, the SS attacked Woergl Castle, where some prominent officials of Vichy France had been imprisoned by the German Army, which had now surrendered. German troops joined dogfaces from 361D in fighting off the SS. Field Marshal Kesselring proposed to General Devers that organizations of German technical troops not be disbanded and be used to repair telecommunications and the railroads. Devers thought this was a good idea, but SHAEF turned it down.[84]

From St. Tropez to Innsbruck, the 6th Army Group had suffered 23,303 dead and 107,583 wounded. Approximately half of those had worn the tricolor. Devers issued an order of the day: "The enemy has been vanquished."[85]

On 7 May, Eisenhower cabled the combined chiefs of staff: "The mission of this Allied force was fulfilled at 0231 local time, May 7th 1945."

EIGHTEEN

Postwar

IN A LETTER TO GEORGE MARSHALL IN FEBRUARY 1945, DWIGHT Eisenhower rated his top thirty-eight officers. This was serious business in which a commander was expected to be brutally honest. As might be expected, Eisenhower rated Omar Bradley first, tied with Carl Spaatz, the air commander. Walter Bedell "Beetle" Smith was third, George Patton was fourth, Mark Clark fourteenth. Jake Devers was twenty-fourth. Every army commander in Europe and six corps commanders came in ahead of him. Eisenhower placed Sandy Patch, Lucian Truscott, and Alan Brooke above Devers. Damning with faint praise is something of an understatement. Devers was the only ranking officer that was asterisked. Eisenhower wrote, "The proper position of this officer is not yet fully determined in my own mind. The overall results he and his organization produce are generally good, sometimes outstanding. But he has not, so far, produced among the seniors at the American organization here that feeling of trust and confidence that is so necessary to continued success."[1]

When it came to promotion, Patton, an army commander, got Eisenhower's nod for four stars but not Devers, an army group commander. When officers are of equal rank, the one with the earliest date of rank is senior, making that date extremely important. When the promotions were actually made by Marshall, Devers received his fourth star with a date of rank ahead of Bradley and Smith, both of whom had been junior to Devers in 1942. Patton, Devers's classmate, had to wait just a little longer. Obviously, Marshall and Eisenhower still did not see eye to eye about Devers. Right after the end of hostilities in Europe, Marshall moved Devers into General Lesley McNair's old position as commander, Army Ground Forces (AGF). From 1940 to 1943, this had been one of the most influential offices in the army. McNair had first designed the tactical units, the divisions; he had organized them out of raw manpower and new equipment, and trained them for war. Devers said, "I was the trainer of the Army."[2]

In June 1945, the first atomic bomb had yet to be exploded. An invasion of Japan, while increasingly unlikely, was still a distinct possibility. Jake's new assignment, replacing his lifelong friend "Vinegar Joe" Stilwell, who was retiring due to deteriorating health, was of operational importance. But Hiroshima and Nagasaki ushered in a new reality. It is possible to infer that moving Devers to AGF was Marshall's way of retaining Devers's experience and using it to influence the army's future direction (as he had at Armored Force) without placing him directly in Eisenhower's face, as he would have been had he been given one of the major operational commands in Europe. But as the record shows, an incident had lowered Jake in his mentor's eyes. As everyone expected, Eisenhower replaced Marshall as chief of staff.

Devers was aware that he was not viewed favorably by Eisenhower. He was going to cut Devers down to size.[3] One general officer recalled Eisenhower saying, "Wait until I get back to Washington. I'll put him his place."[4] Jake later told Colonel Thomas Griess, "I think Eisenhower wanted to get me out of Washington."[5] Eisenhower didn't consult with Devers when AGF was moved in October 1946 from Washington to Fort Monroe, Virginia, an old coast artillery post at the mouth of Hampton Roads. In March 1948, the command would be renamed Army Field Forces.

Jake liked the posting to Fort Monroe where he could be close to his friend and mutual rascal Pete Quesada, who was based with the tactical air forces just up the road at Langley Field. Wartime provider of air cover to General Patton, Quesada was a champion of close air support. Devers had been impressed with the way he "got things done in an unorthodox way."[6] Bur at the time, the air force, newly separated from the army, was primarily interested in strategic bombing with atomic weapons. As part of the air force reorganization, Quesada's post was made subordinate to the Continental Air Command and stripped of all aircraft. Quesada was bitter that his efforts had come to so little.

Devers also spent time with the intelligent and knowledgeable Admiral William H. P. "Spike" Blandy, one of the most brilliant men in the navy. Jake liked him immensely; he felt Blandy possessed good judgment and should have been a much higher admiral.[7] The three got together for lunch once in a while to discuss developments. As senior officers of the three services, they facilitated thinking on joint issues, a benefit Fort Monroe provided into the twenty-first century. Jake was glad to be out of the Pentagon so he could concentrate on developments in the field rather than army politics. As usual, he immediately became embroiled with current issues at Fort Monroe. He wanted them to keep the old Point Comfort Hotel, which still sits waterside at Fort Monroe after providing accomodations to generations of soldiers, sailors, and their families.

In addition to being the army's trainer, Army Ground Forces oversaw formulation of army combat doctrine at the various branch schools around the country. Service forces, such as Quartermaster and Engineer, retained their own schools and continued to develop their own doctrine. After the war, there was a lot of effort to encode the tough lessons combat had taught into the field manuals and current army thinking about future warfare. Many outside of the army, however, thought ground forces would become much smaller and less used now that America had the nuclear bomb. Most eyes were focused on the air force, with its new jets and wonder weapon. Devers coordinated doctrinal developments through his G3 (operations officer) at Fort Monroe. Perhaps emulating his experience at Armored Force back in 1941–1942, Devers wanted to combine doctrine and weapons development. He thought especially that Ordnance at Aberdeen Proving Ground ought to be within his command, and he established contacts there.

Jake wasn't satisfied with the Infantry School at Fort Benning. "I sent the finest combat commander I knew, rough and tough Mike O'Daniel."[8] John "Iron Mike" O'Daniel had commanded America's most decorated division, the 3rd Infantry, which had served well from North Africa through southern France to the German-Austrian border. Others worried about O'Daniel's administrative skills. Devers sent him his former deputy chief of staff, Colonel Shepard, who had worked for O'Daniel at the 3rd Infantry Division.

Next, Devers felt that the Armored School did not have the drive it needed to generate a first-class arm. To stir them up, he sent an outstanding tanker, General Bruce Clarke. A leader in the crack 4th Armored Division (AD) and then leader of 7AD that held the German onslaught in the Bulge before the Belgian town of St. Vith, Clarke picked up the Armored School portfolio.

General Clarke remembered his summons to the office of the commander, Army Ground Forces, in 1948. Getting right to the point, Devers said, "I don't like the way the Armored School is being run. Go down there and fix it." Clarke recalled, "General Devers brought to the Armored Force an appreciation that it is a much larger part of the army than the old Cavalry."[9] Devers told Clarke to look to engineers, artillery, and infantrymen as potential armored division commanders, as well as tankers. Soon both of these veteran leaders began producing the quality of officers and trained soldiers for which Devers was looking.

Reflecting the opinion he had held since his time as a senior instructor at Fort Sill back in World War I, Devers maintained that army schools were too theoretical and not sufficiently grounded in fundamental instruction in arms and the services. Solid leaders with proven combat records were needed to establish the practical approach that Devers wanted. Jake always emphasized practical "how-to" instruction over more generalized education. Some senior officers favored this; others felt this short changed the educational development of important leadership skills.

Devers felt much of the curriculum in the senior staff colleges was redundant. "We over educate our senior officers," commented Devers.[10] He felt the military didn't need both the Army and the National War Colleges, and favored creating a common officers' school at Fort Riley that second lieutenants from both USMA and Reserve Officers' Training Corps (ROTC) would attend, regardless of branch. He wanted to send both ROTC and West Pointers to Riley and "to mix them up under a senior ROTC general." Jake recognized that, in the future, most officers would commission through ROTC, and that the favoritism often shown USMA graduates should not become a barrier within the officer corps. Devers did not have direct control over the Army War College, and his views did not prevail. Neither did he have much influence over the Armed Forces Staff College, a Marshall creation.

Jake hated "ticket punching," the habit that ambitious officers used to make their service records look promotable, instead of staying in a job long enough to absorb its lessons. He preferred a three- or four-year tour so that the officer became fully proficient at the task assigned. In training, he thought "zero defects," setting a standard of no mistakes, was a ridiculous method that instilled timidity in future combat leaders. "Give an officer a chance to make an honest mistake," he argued.[11] Devers installed General Manton Eddy, who had the reputation of thinking deeply about tactics, at Leavenworth and made him senior fellow to coordinate the combat and combat service support schools, so they had common doctrine and were not teaching at cross purposes. Eddy had full responsibility despite Jake's urges to kibitz on this subject. He would have liked to put in David Barr, his 6th Army Group chief of staff, but he was a two star and the slot called for three.

To supply experience and brain power to continue to develop doctrine, Devers formed boards that met at Fort Monroe under the direction of his G3. Devers wanted to make sure the United States got all of the benefits of America's many commanders with combat experience. After being staffed at Fort Monroe, major equipment or doctrinal questions were sent to the relevant schools. Devers ran close herd on his Field Force boards, the organs that set the requirements for weapons and equipment to be developed. Under General Charles Bolte, Jake appointed a board to see that reserve field grade and general officers were capable commanders with war experience. Devers felt that all divisions should follow the World War II armored division approach, with a variable mix of battalions and companies at the combat command level. After a Pentagon misstep in the late 1950s that was supposed to create atomic armed divisions but which many thought did not have enough conventional firepower to punch their way out of a wet paper bag, the army created the reorganization of army division (ROAD) concept with brigades that could be tailored to the mission in a manner very similar to combat commands.

Devers told prospective division commanders to get a great chief of staff, use him to assemble a good staff that could work long hours together, plan training carefully, insure that it was realistic and relevant, and stress teamwork throughout the division. While personally shy of the press, Devers understood its power.

Devers had always been a proponent of artillery forward observers in light aircraft. Postwar, he had a hand in selecting light planes for the army. A school to train army pilots in light aircraft was set up at Fort Sill, home of the Artillery School. "I had a lot to say about the equipment," said Jake.[12] He always understood the tremendous advantage artillery observers in light aircraft had in spotting for artillery fire, and said it was time "to get the Army into the air." He favored Piper machines, citing their stability, which aided observers in giving accurate firing data.

Some people also credit Devers with being the father of army helicopter aviation. That is quite an accomplishment for an officer who started out with horse-drawn artillery. Devers recalled, "At the same time I was getting into the helicopter business [in the late 1940s] ... I presented [the concept of helicopters] personally to Vandenberg. He agreed but never followed up."[13] In the late 1940s, a staff officer had looked at a Sikorsky machine located at a coast guard base in New York Harbor. Based on his report, Devers took a ride. He commented on the high level of vibration that would interfere with an observer's ability to accurately report positions of enemy sightings. Then he took a more satisfactory ride in an early Marine Piasecki. Now he was interested.

Larry Bell, the founder of Bell Helicopters, had a decent fledgling helicopter but was about to close his business for lack of orders. He had none, and his tiny company was trying to survive on motorized lawn equipment. At the time, Bruce Clarke was a member of Devers's direct staff. In a small world, Bell was a patient of Clarke's brother, a physician, and they had gotten to know each other. Bell asked Bruce if he could get him an appointment with Devers. Jake, being already interested in the helicopter, invited both of them for lunch on his boat. Bell told Devers of his small company's precarious financial state and asked him to buy fifty machines for the army. After the flying demonstration, Bell wanted $35,000 per machine. Devers insisted on the initial quote of $25,000.[14] There might not have been a formal RFP (request for proposal) and competitive bidding, but none of that extensive paperwork was necessary or required. America's money was being closely guarded by a Pennsylvania

Dutchman. Bell indicated his agreement. Now Jake had to figure out how to get his hands on a couple of million dollars. That afternoon, Devers wrote to Eisenhower that he wanted to buy fifty helicopters. Within three days, Eisenhower wrote back approving the purchase but said there was no budget for them. If Devers could find the money, go ahead.

That was all he needed to hear. In his inimitable way, he thought something must be done. Once committed, he never took no for an answer. With all the charm he could muster, he approached the Aviation Board. The only funds they could scare up were from a maneuver and field exercise account. They funneled the funding through the Aviation Board at Fort Bragg to cover the purchase. That was the beginning of Bell OH13 (47G), the bubble-shaped helicopter that, when not spotting for the artillery, carried two stretchers, one each over its two landing skids. They saved many lives in Korea and became famous on the television show *M.A.S.H.* The contract also saved Bell Helicopter from financial ruin. The company went on to create the UH1 "Huey," the Vietnam workhorse.

In a similar manner, Devers boosted the struggling Army missile program. At the time, Wernher von Braun was incarcerated at forlorn Fort Bliss, Texas. Devers established a guided missile center, and moved it to the site that had been recommended, Redstone Arsenal, and the surprising amenities of nearby Huntsville. The rest is history.

As in his prewar days, descriptions of Devers and his command style in his final assignment demonstrate how much his subordinates liked serving under him. When interviewed, General Charles Bolte recalled, "I never served with a more satisfying commander. . . . His simple forthright and direct method of operation is something that I admire. . . . He wants to go direct to the point . . . [and] gets thing done. . . . [H]e is not a theoretical man.[15] Just before his retirement, Jake was under consideration to head the Weapons System Evaluation Group. Devers was particularly interested in developing the equipment that experience demonstrated was needed, and that new science could make available. He wanted to enlist industry in the design of new equipment, especially tanks, an area in which the U.S. Army needed a lot of development. He had shown quite a knack for this type of work back at Fort Knox, and was familiar with both artillery and armor. "I knew what was needed was a low silhouette, more gun power, less weight and I knew some methods of doing that."[16] But he didn't get the position. Instead it went to General John E. Hull, a man Devers thought capable but with no drive. Ordnance wasted millions on tank development. Jake thought Omar Bradley had a hand in preventing his appointment but was not sure.[17]

Devers was big on army bands. "If you go up there with music, everybody followed you and you had plenty of people on your team."[18] Devers searched around his large command for the best musicians and took steps to insure that the Army Field Forces Band shined when it performed. Their quality placed pressure on the various Washington, D.C., area military bands to improve markedly. The Army Field Forces Band traveled to every state and in every country behind the Iron Curtain.

Even though he reported directly to the chief of staff, Devers saw Eisenhower only a few times. He met with Eisenhower before a hearing on relief of the 7AD commanding officer. "From his demeanor I had an indication that he had something – a chip on his shoulder – with reference to me. So I was careful after this in everything I had to deal with him."[19] Later, Eisenhower told him he was on his way to Columbia University (where he served as president from 1948 to 1953) and was only holding down his current job for Bradley. Devers responded, "I am glad to know that. I know I am getting older and on the way to retirement so I'm not in competition with Bradley for anything."[20] Jake mentioned that President Harry Truman hailed from Missouri as did Bradley.

After forty-four years of commissioned service, General Devers retired in September 1949 at the age of sixty-two. That same year, Henry Cabot Lodge, then the senator from Massachusetts who had performed so spectacularly as Devers's liaison to General Jean de Lattre, rose on the Senate floor to be recognized. After reiterating the high points of General Devers's service to his country, Lodge continued,

> While the positions which General Devers held were of high responsibility, it is not of these I wish to speak but rather of his personal qualities.... General Devers was 100% the military professional in the very finest sense.... A man of boundless energy, he demanded much of others and drove everyone hard, but no harder than himself. He had no favorites, no stable companion or crony to relieve the loneliness of high command.... He was the very opposite of self centered and he avoided publicity for himself. Because he was deeply interested in other men and had spent his life in studying them . . . he could draw on the

experience of a life time in selecting those who were to help him. . . . He gave his whole trust to the people in whom he once expressed his faith. He did not harass. He made each one of his subordinates feel that he was actually "in business for himself." Although a man of boldness, he had great common sense and a keen realization of what was possible. [He had] a very marked ability to make a little a long way. . . . He had imagination and a rare ability to understand the factors which were important. . . . [He] never made the mistake – which, alas, was too often made – of thinking that at the high level of command the military and the political are entirely separate. . . . He had the knack of taking men who had not always been successful and by making them understand that he expected the best of them, thereupon getting their best. When he assumed command of the French troops, he made the simple declaration, "I want the French to be successful." A favorite phrase of General Devers, "Rather than sit still and be shot at it was better to do something – even at the risk of making a few mistakes, because you can make mistakes and evolve." He was a man so fundamentally optimistic that it was impossible for him to take counsel of his fears.[21]

At the end, Jake made a serious mistake of his own.

Jake liked to say, "Coincidences shape history. . . . Luck and serendipity are two of life's most important attributes." Had not McNair had a good recollection of Devers, or had Marshall not have been willing to give stars to a man he did not know well but came with high recommendations, Jake might have finished the war as one of many crackerjack artillery officers. That he became bitter from a career that saw him rise to become the four-star commander of one of only three U.S. army groups is a measure of his enormous ambition.

General Marshall could not have missed Eisenhower's less than glowing opinion of Devers for much of World War II. Marshall said Devers "did good work in Europe" on top of his sterling record during the early years in the United States. Then an incident occurred that "changed my view of him," recalled General Marshall. "He was on a board which listed generals in order that they should be promoted. He moved his own name up two. Members of the board wanted me to move it back. I didn't touch it, but it changed my view of him. He got into the ambitious class . . . got the personal ambition thing too much. . . . Devers [retired] pretty much embittered."[22] Clearly, Jake felt that Eisenhower had treated him unfairly. Was that the proximate cause of the incident to which Marshall refers? After all of the accolades as to his integrity, this was a lapse. Perhaps he was too ambitious.

There were some who felt Devers's principal strength was Marshall's patronage. When that waned, so did Devers. Given Jake's extensive, consistent record, it is hard to support this premise. Right up until his retirement date, Jake remained a high energy igniter of improvement for the army. Devers was bright, empathetic to other people, incredibly optimistic, and boundlessly energetic. When all the talk was completed, he got things done, faster and better than all but the very best of his contemporaries. But Marshall's support had been crucial.

Georgie Devers's family had land down in Virginia. After retirement, the Deverses settled into a cattle farm in Herndon. For a while, Jake carried on as a good Pennsylvania farmer should, running a clean spread, keeping careful records of what worked well, and watching expenses closely. Initially, a single bank had a branch in the Pentagon. In order to secure the benefits for service people and Department of Defense employees there, Jake, at the behest of some of his Washington, D.C., friends, became a director of a competitor, the First National Bank of Arlington. Jake worked hard to straighten out senior management and get the bank started.

Other high-level job offers came in over the transom. After the war, every corporation wanted heavy brass on their boards or among their senior executive staffs. Devers would not take such a position if the company only wanted to exploit his name, so he leaned heavily toward the nonprofit sector. There were several organizations with different slants on safety. The trustees of the American Automobile Association (AAA), a consumer advocate, approached him because of his experience with the major car manufacturers in Detroit during tank development. This made some sense to Jake. His job was fundraising, and he didn't like it, but the people within the organization were pleasant. Fundraising for AAA was difficult because the auto industry had its own safety organization and saw no reason to contribute. Besides, Devers recognized the conflict of interest between AAA and the auto manufacturers. "You can't take money from big manufacturers, because you are supposed to be their watchdog."[23] After a short and relatively unproductive stint in 1950 as managing director of the AAA Foundation for Traffic Safety, he resigned, stating that he could add nothing to the organization.

Fairchild Corporation was a much better fit. The corporation had begun as a first-rate camera manufacturer with an association with IBM. Then airframe manufacturers saw an opportunity in aligning a precision camera company with their observation aircraft. This led to Fairchild's becoming a supplier to Douglas DC-3 production. Toward the end of the war, Fairchild had a very large all-aluminum glider under development. When the war ended, gliders fell out of favor, so Fairchild added two piston engines to their prototype glider. The result was a very agile, small, rough airfield cargo aircraft with a rear ramp that facilitated rapid unloading even of jeeps. It became the Vietnam War workhorse, the C-123, and is still prized for its ability to get into unimproved clearings.

Born and raised in the south in the "Good Old Boy" tradition, Fairchild's president, Richard Boutelle, was bright, ambitious, aggressive, and imaginative. The profits from the DC-3 contracts convinced him that he wanted to get into the airplane business. The stature, connections, and expertise of General Devers were a perfect opportunity for Fairchild. Jake, always wanting to "get the army into the air," seeking another challenge and desiring to employ his expertise to the development of military equipment, was intrigued.

Boutelle knew of Devers's association with army aviation, recognized both Jake's knowledge in developing systems and his reputation in the military, and hired him to develop depth in the military air transport business. Jake became technical adviser to the president of Fairchild Engineer & Airplane Company with an office in Washington. When interviewing for the position, Devers said that, at sixty-four, he didn't want a 9-to-5 position. Instead, he wanted to contribute his expertise to engineers working on improving military equipment. From his Armored Force experience, Devers recognized the primary objective in solving transportation problems was to lighten army equipment.[24]

Recognizing the C-123's potential to transport forces, Devers convinced James Gavin, the former commander of the 82nd Airborne Division and a deep thinker about the future of "brushfire wars" and the value of airborne and air landing mobility, to get away from Fort Bragg and inspect the Hagerstown facilities and developments of Fairchild Engineering. Jake would never recommend a product because it was manufactured by his employer. But he always supported an innovative piece of equipment that showed promise with his characteristic high-energy enthusiasm.

The C-123's problems revolved around the same issues Devers had wrestled with back in Armored Force, weight and power plants. Jake provided technical suggestions that improved the plane. He also came up with some modifications to one of Fairchild's most famous airplanes, the C-119 "Boxcar," at that time the standard deliverer of paratroopers. Because of problems with that aircraft's aerodynamics (small wing, high wing loading, drag), the engineers initially doubted the Boxcar would fly. Fairchild literally overpowered the problems with huge engines that rattled the plane unmercifully during takeoff. Fairchild's designers weren't the best, but their products gained wide acceptance.

Boutelle was a good hunter with knowledge of firearms and perhaps too much of a lady's man for Jake's taste. Over the years, Devers didn't appreciate his employer's lifestyle of heavy drinking and womanizing. Needless to say, Boutelle coveted Jake's ability to open door throughout the army. Devers retained this essentially part-time position until 1959, when he was in his early seventies. He enjoyed being associated with the technical development of aircraft and weapons systems, and the freedom of coming and going as he pleased.

Following his retirement from the army, however, Devers was almost immediately recalled to public service. In June 1951, Devers became chief military adviser to Dr. Frank P. Graham, head of the United Nations Mission to Pakistan, India, and Kashmir, and president of the University of North Carolina. Chester Nimitz had already been appointed to be the operational head of what was expected to become the UN operation that would oversee a referendum in Kashmir and then the disentanglement of Indian and Pakistani forces that had entered Kashmir to enforce their government's respective claims. When the British withdrew from the subcontinent, their former colony was separated into principally Muslim Pakistan and Hindu India. But a dispute over the allocation of the northern state of Kashmir led to open warfare. Graham had asked General Marshall to recommend an individual to become chief military advisor. Marshall selected Devers, who would serve under Nimitz.

The last thing Jake wanted was a ceremonial or figurehead position. If he engaged an issue, he wanted to be a major player with the power to get things done. With Graham, he negotiated the right to be present at every important meeting or conference. To assure Graham that he would not usurp the latter's authority, he promised to remain quiet in every conference unless Graham asked a direct question of him. Graham agreed. Devers spent June through September of that year on the ground in South Asia attending negotiating sessions. December found the general in Paris attending Security Council meetings on the problem. Devers recalled that neither country really wanted combat to break out over the strongly held differences. Each of the many small states was supposed to vote for the country they wanted to be integrated into. Many local Hindu leaders of predominately Muslim regions, however, simply joined India without holding elections. When tribes revolted and marched on India, Jawaharlal Nehru, prime minister of India, coaxed the UN to step in, arrange a ceasefire, and establish a committee to decide the issue. Twenty years later, Devers recalled how Nehru was a major thorn in everyone's side.

In his trademark high-energy way, Devers rode the rough terrain of the ceasefire line in the rainy season. Devers knew both the chief of staff of the Indian Army, General Kodandera Madappa Cariappa, and the chief of staff of the Pakistani Army, General Ayub Kahn, who later would become prime minister. These two officers knew each other well from prior service with the British and admired each other. Both armies were deeply nationalistic and would do whatever their governments asked. From the detailed information he gained during his extensive time on the ground, Devers could see that neither army wanted to fight the other. If Nimitz could conduct an honest plebiscite, most of Kashmir would join Pakistan. The Pakistanis agreed to elections. Nehru, probably recognizing the likely election results, said he didn't believe in the commission. Thereafter, the Pakistanis, recognizing they had no negotiating leverage, would not agree to anything. Nehru was to set the date for elections but studiously avoided doing so. He was an avowed socialist who was openly hostile to the British and American capitalist ways, and publicly tilted toward the Soviets at a time when the Western powers were fighting communists in Korea, a war many thought was a preamble to a larger communist military adventure to upset or even overthrow the West. Devers intimated that Nehru's actions prevented a real solution, and that the problem would continue to fester for decades.[25] Devers went on to state that failure could be traced back to the unwillingness of Graham to push Nehru until he would agree.

In January 1957, the Infantry Board began talks with the Armalite Corporation, a division of Fairchild, about a rifle capable of firing a lighter round than the one that had been around since the beginning of the century, the .30 caliber. The board was in the process of standardizing on the 7.62mm round used in the M14 rifle, which was a .30 caliber round shortened to reflect the smaller space current gunpowder required. All NATO members except the United States wanted a round lighter than the 7.62mm. Armalite had been working on the AR15 rifle since 1955, designing it around the .223 "hornet" round that small game hunters had begun to favor. Fairchild spent a lot of energy attempting to get the army to look more closely at the AR15. Tests at Fort Benning found that the AR15 gave superior performance over M14s, with ammunition at half the weight of the 7.62mm. While the rifle offered less range, it had much less recoil, which allowed recruits to take to it more easily. Yet because of its muzzle velocity, the AR15 retained a surprising amount of combat power. Devers, knowing the importance of reducing the infantryman's load and the compound power of muzzle velocity, saw the immense value of the weapon and the benefit to both the army and to Fairchild if it was adopted. Jake had always felt that, at 9.5 lbs, the M1 should have been lighter.[26]

Boutelle, being a hunter, understood the issues involved and went out to the coast where his people were working on the project. He found three people at work developing the rifle. Then he went to infantry boards and found what they wanted. There was support for the project, but the boards weren't getting anywhere. Boutelle then went to Devers to get an understanding of what was happening. Jake instantly recognized the problem. Ordnance developed rifles, not the Infantry.

Unfortunately, the light rifle ran into an almost impenetrable wall of "not invented here" at Devers's old nemesis, Army Ordnance. The Massachusetts congressional delegation, home of the M14-producing Springfield Arsenal, was another problem. The AR15's inability to mount a bayonet despite its infrequent use in twentieth-century combat was used as an excuse to hold it back. The marines were particularly troublesome. Rising to the challenge, Jake enthusiastically supported the AR15 and used his recognition factor and reputation among senior officers. He called on the Infantry School's commandant with an AR15 in his kit, and wrote to the famed airborne commander Maxwell Taylor, then chief of staff, figuring the weight and size would appeal to the former paratrooper. To his surprise, Taylor responded that he thought the 7.62mm weapon was the way to go. Not wanting to come to a conclusion given all the prior data, he mandated another series of tests. They added a raft of additional specifications to which Devers objected. "This really got ridiculous," Devers recalled. "[Ordnance] required a lot of minor changes."[27] After much time and effort, the army awarded Fairchild a small contract. It wasn't enough to keep the project alive.

Devers understood how the world worked. Instead of going to his army friends, "I should have gone to the senators from Massachusetts."[28] But at least the less-hidebound air force recognized the value of the light weapon, especially on their tactical transports, and bought enough weapons to keep the project alive. Fairchild really did not have the engineering and production acumen to support large-scale production, so the company sold its patents to Colt. The AR15 morphed into one of the most successful and long-lived infantry firearms since the Brown Bess, the M16.

Part of Devers's portfolio of activities was serving as a member of various public commissions within the United States. Pennsylvania had not forgotten one of its most illustrious sons. While at Fairchild, Devers received a call from Governor John S. Fine of Pennsylvania. Ugly rioting had broken out in the prison system, and the governor was forming a new commission to institute fundamental reform. He had good penologists and several Pennsylvanians who knew the type of people incarcerated. Jake was a little surprised when the governor made him chairman. The commission contained a penologist from the hardest prison in America, Joliet in Illinois, and one from New York State who was credited with humanizing that large prison system. Under Jake's leadership, the Pennsylvania Special Commission made thirty-two recommendations.

Governor Fine steered all of them through the legislature in a matter of months.

After yet another serious prison riot, the governor appointed Devers to the permanent Pennsylvania Crime Commission. With extensive experience in motivating reluctant participants, Jake was something of a moderating force on the commission. Devers had earned the reputation for giving a man who had make a bad mistake a second chance, and was compassionate about the downtrodden. He maintained his lifelong belief that you "don't put anybody in jail if you can help it."[29]

The governor was impressed with Jake's acumen, his compassion, and the energy he displayed despite his years. He asked Devers to serve on the Inspection Board of Pennsylvania Prisons. Jake took the post most seriously and continued his careful oversight. He became a resource for the Commonwealth of Pennsylvania and served in a number of capacities over the years. As he did his entire adult life, Jake sought to maintain a close association with his hometown of York. He was particularly proud then his home city named a public school after him.

For many years, General Marshall, continuing in the tradition of his commanding officer in the Great War, General John "Blackjack" Pershing, served on the Battle Monuments Commission. This was the organization that Pershing had started after World War I to preserve the overseas cemeteries that were the resting place of so many fallen Americans. Pershing felt the efforts to maintain the overseas monuments and cemeteries was an excellent way to maintain warm relations among wartime allies. No one had actually appointed Marshall to the commission; he had simply carried on after Pershing died. After this great man passed, on the recommendation of Admiral Thomas Kincaid of Pacific war fame, Eisenhower appointed Devers as chairman of the monuments commission. From 1959 to 1969, Devers served without pay. It was only fitting that one of General Marshall's closest associates, who had seen extensive combat, succeeded him in that endeavor. When Devers stepped down in his late eighties, General Bruce Clarke, a decorated hero and by then a four-star officer, replaced him. Given that the commission was nonpolitical, Jake had stayed through several administrations. He had always steered clear of the more traditional veterans' organizations, as they almost always became involved in issues that some found partisan. He made an exception for the National Association for the Uniformed Services, an organization that looked out for the status of military retirees. Of course, that included Jake himself and the hundreds of thousands of veterans that had served under him. Over the years, Jake was invited to give speeches to veterans and concerned citizens groups about military affairs. While at Fairchild, Devers also served on the U.S. Military Academy's Thayer Award Committee. In conjunction with this endeavor, he had the opportunity to call on Dwight Eisenhower. As he recalled, his reception was superficial. When he asked for an autographed photo, all he got was a stock, mass-reproduced facsimile.

In 1964, Devers took notice of one of the last freewheeling maneuvers, Desert Strike, that ranged across several southwestern desert states and southern California. Mechanization was undergoing something of a renaissance. Mechanized and armored divisions maneuvered against each other in a manner a little reminiscent of the Louisiana maneuvers.

Back when Jake commanded AGF right after the war, the Devers had sought a farm near his new duty station, but they could not find a decent spread near Fort Monroe. They moved instead to some acreage that Georgie's family had near Herndon, Virginia, and later decided that something closer to Washington would better fit with their lives. Georgie designed a beautiful home, which they built 20 miles from the District of Columbia. They had come a long way from boiling grass from their front yard in Wyoming. Georgie now had a staff to maintain their household.

When Georgie's father died, leaving her mother alone, the Devers finally moved into the home they owned in Georgetown. Devers's daughter also lived in Georgetown. Once upon a time, to occupy young Jakie, grandfather Loucks had given him piles of old letters to play with, from which he soaked off the old stamps and put them in books. This became Jake's stamp collection. Having ignored it for thirty years when he went off to West Point, Jake picked it up again; it was a good way to become reacquainted with geography. It was a hobby he could share with his daughter, who also collected stamps.[30] After retiring from Fairchild, Jake took up photography as well.

Not long after moving to Georgetown, Jake's beloved Georgie passed on. After his wife's death, the general's sister, Katy, came to live in his household, maintaining the woman's touch that Georgie had provided for so many years.

The tumult of the Vietnam War occurred late in Devers's very long life. He felt that the United States should have never gotten involved. Like many of his generation, however, he believed that once the country became involved, it had an obligation to clean it up and exit the war a winner.[31] In the Richard Nixon era, Devers was involved in Americans for Winning the Peace, a pro-administration organization to which a number of his banker associates belonged. Devers was a vociferous opponent of the all-volunteer army. He thought it would create a real danger to America. The program would be too expensive. Without the draft, the army would not get a large enough cohort from the best and brightest of American youth. He felt the quality of army manpower would suffer, and the American people would become divorced from the army. Jake went a step further and was a strong supporter of universal military training, that is, military training for all healthy males of draft age. He did not live long enough to see the success the all-volunteer force became.

Jacob Loucks Devers passed away on 15 October 1979 at Walter Reed Army Hospital at the age of ninety-two.

Epilogue

BEFORE D-DAY, DWIGHT EISENHOWER APPEARS TO HAVE concluded that Jacob Devers was not steady or reliable enough to become a senior member of his innermost team. In a confidential personnel evaluation to George Marshall, Eisenhower raised questions about "trust and confidence" in Devers, stating that while his performance could be brilliant, Eisenhower had some reservations.

Up until that time, Marshall's experience with Devers had been quite different. He had found the man from York to be a star performer with exceptional talent and productivity. Marshall did not want to sacrifice the good work he was getting from either of these two senior commanders. In an attempt at being a good team player, Eisenhower had minimized to Marshall the friction he had with Devers. Up until the 6th Army Group reached the Vosges Mountains, Eisenhower had retained Devers, who proved to be his most creative army group commander in a method that Eisenhower apparently found acceptable.

Then the crevice that existed between SHAEF and the 6th Army Group leadership began to surface. Communications problems had already appeared in September 1944 between SHAEF and the commanders of both the 21st and 12th Army Groups. Bernard Montgomery failed to take advantage of an opportunity to easily seize Antwerp and its all-important waterway to the sea and instead launched his own run on a bridge too far. Omar Bradley did not concentrate sufficient available resources in the Aachen Gap, as Eisenhower had advised him, and therefore did not reach the Rhine by early October as he should have. While it is possible to entertain a range of "what-ifs" with the 6th Army Group, that would only be playing Monday morning quarterback. A lesson that can be drawn is that more objective communication could have avoided command surprise, as long as SHAEF staff was willing to forcibly present to their boss information he did not want to hear. Other authors have previously identified how SHAEF tended not to pay attention to the 6th Army Group, and this work strongly reinforces that observation. Had a senior staffer more closely monitored developments in the Southern Group of Armies and communicated those discordant notes to Eisenhower, perhaps the most fundamental error, command surprise, could have been avoided. Certainly, "Beetle" Smith repeatedly proved he was not a shy chief of staff.

Both subordinate commanders and staffers liked working for Devers. He was bright, quickly identified the essential points of most problems, and used all of his skills to demolish bureaucratic roadblocks that might impede mission accomplishment. This last point always improves an organization's morale, probably more than most senior leaders recognize. Jake's entire career was filled with shining examples of successful application of mission-type orders. Devers repeatedly showed great restraint from interfering with the work of subordinates, which became his secret method for accomplishing more in a short period of time. As he said, it was far better to have to occasionally live with a subordinate's mistake in return for overall increased performance from the whole team. But he monitored developments and maintained control. When the 6th Army Group began to career out of control in its rampage through southern Germany, Devers did not hesitate to pull in on the reins. His interactions with the French contain many examples of how holding the reins loosely could avoid conflicts over legitimate differences that arise among national governments while showing good judgment about when to apply control to improve overall performance. It was a tricky business that required a great deal of flexibility, adaptability, and good judgment. Marshall never counseled his subordinates to ignore the important international political implications of alternative military courses of action, an observation still relevant to modern-day issues. In this regard, a towering world leader echoes Clausewitz's observation that war is an

extension of politics. In his handling of the French (and the Poles), Devers provided a record of useful practical application.

Yes, Devers was ambitious. So are most senior leaders, though many
try not to wear their ambition on their sleeves. Devers did make mistakes. He was a good-hearted man, not a vindictive one. There is much
to admire about Devers, and much to learn from his stellar career.

In the end, a character flaw combined with his many creative talents
to send him, despite his accomplishments, into relative obscurity with a
bitter taste in his mouth:

> Many are the talented people who know the frustration
> of almost triumphing but for a small flaw.
> Few are the people who stand in the winner's circle
> to receive the accolades of the crowd.

So, what had happened at Vittel? Devers and his staff had come
up with a good idea, which was under resourced but still showed great
promise. Jake's larger idea incorporated the Third Army into a major
secondary attack, which could have drawn a corps from the First Army
south of the Ardennes, a contingency S H A E F planners already had studied. A shift of this magnitude would have taken advantage of Allied mobility, logistics, and air strength. It had the promise of being a winner,
especially if the Nazi monster clung to life. Jake's decision to spring it
as a surprise to Eisenhower may have been a major mistake. Ike arrived
at Vittel in no mood to entertain a major strategic change. His staff had
done the workup. But Ike came preconditioned to discipline a truculent
subordinate, to "stick to the script."

As was his style, Eisenhower listened and looked carefully at the
6th Army Group plans. Despite a couple of stumbles, Devers was an
excellent leader. And as subsequent events, such as the reaction to the
Bulge and the 3–7 January 1945 Nordwind offensive demonstrated, he
knew his trade well and was an excellent practitioner, derisive comments
from the British notwithstanding. Even Patton liked Jake's plan. It beat
anything the unimaginative Bradley had produced, and it was less risky
than Market Garden. Unlike September 1944, however, when Eisenhower had altered strategy in the face of his marshal's competing plans,
in December, he stuck to his plan and carried it forward to win the war.

The Devers plan might have won it faster or with fewer casualties. We will never know.

Certainly Eisenhower's decision was within the scope of sound judgment. Had the risk of failure loomed larger, the penalty of not being more aggressive would have tipped the scales, and Devers might have prevailed. In his memoirs, Eisenhower states flatly that he did not allow personal likes or dislikes to cause him to favor one subordinate over another. A careful review of the historical record suggests that there is no reason not to take Eisenhower at his word.

Notes

1. Early Years

1. This and all subsequent unidentified quotations in this chapter are from Thomas Griess interviews with Jacob Devers, tapes 2 or 5, Griess Research Collection, York County Heritage Trust (hereafter Griess/Devers).

2. Thomas Griess interview with Walter Bond, 7 August 1970, p. 2, Griess Research Collection, York County Heritage Trust.

3. Thomas Griess interview with Catherine Devers, 20–21 September 1971, Griess Research Collection, York County Heritage Trust.

4. "I did belong to a gang, but not a belligerent one, the Park Street Gang. We did have knives but we never used them for anything but whittling wood." It was a far more innocent age.

5. Jerry D. Lewis, "Everything for Jake," *Colliers,* 26 June 1943.

6. Griess/Devers, tape 25, 25 March 1969, p. 3; Forrest Pogue interview with Jacob Devers interview, p. 74, Marshall Library (hereafter Pogue/Devers).

7. Pogue/Devers, pp. 74–75.

8. Griess/Devers, 5 October 1975.

9. Griess/Devers, 17–20 August 1970.

10. Griess/Devers, tape 20, p. 3.

11. Griess/Devers, tape 45, p. 255.

12. Thomas Griess interview with Williston B. Palmer, tape 53, 11 July 1972, p. 1, Griess Research Collection, York County Heritage Trust.

13. Griess/Devers, tape 36, p. 43.

14. Griess/Devers, tape 36, pp. 43–44.

15. Griess/Devers, tape 36, pp. 10–12.

16. Griess/Devers, tape 18, p. 25.

17. Thomas Griess interview with David G. Ershine, 13 August 1971, tape 46, box 93, p. 3.

18. Thomas Griess interview with Edward H. Brooks, Griess Research Collection, York County Heritage Trust.

19. Griess/Devers, tape 19, December 1969, p. 32; Griess/Devers, July 1959, set of questions.

20. Griess/Devers, tape 37, p. 39.

21. Thomas Griess interview with Catherine Devers.

2. The Interwar Years

1. Thomas Griess interview with Jacob Devers, tape 19, p. 32, Griess Research Collection, York County Heritage Trust (hereafter Griess/Devers).

2. Thomas Griess interview with Eugene L. Harrison, tape 70, pp. 45–46, Griess Research Collection, York County Heritage Trust.

3. Griess/Devers, tape 69.

4. Griess/Devers, tape 4, p. 6.

5. Griess/Devers, tape 41, p. 101.

6. When he was chief of staff, MacArthur pigeonholed Marshall into what might have been a career-ending assignment with the Illinois National Guard.

7. Griess/Devers, tape 26, p. 9.

8. Griess/Devers, tape 37, p. 8.

9. Griess/Devers, tape 32, p. 19.

10. Thomas Griess interview with Charles D. Palmer, 30 May 1974, pp. 31–33, Griess Research Collection, York County Heritage Trust.

11. Griess/Devers, tape 41, 11–12 August 1971. See also chapter 1.

12. Devers typed notes, box 4, Griess Research Collection, York County Heritage Trust.

13. Senator Henry Lodge Address, pp. 21, 22, Additional Resources, Devers Papers, York County Heritage Trust.

14. Griess/Devers, tape 27, p. 29.

15. Thomas Griess interview with Edward H. Brooks, tape 64, Griess Research Collection, York County Heritage Trust.

16. Griess interview with Harrison, 27 December 1974, pp. 69–70.

17. Griess/Devers, tape 38, pp. 8–11.

18. Unnumbered typed page, box 7, Griess Research Collection, York County Heritage Trust.

19. Griess/Devers, tape 37, p. 39.

20. Griess/Devers, tape 19, p. 32.

21. Forrest Pogue interview with Jacob Devers, Fairchild Aircraft Corp., Alexandria, Va., 12 August 1958, p. 5, Marshall Library.

22. Griess interview with Harrison, 27 December 1974, pp. 69–70.

23. Griess/Devers, tape 2, p. 7. Subsequent stories about construction at USMA are from the same interview.

24. George Marshall to Daniel Van Voorhis, 24 January 1941, Bland and Stevens, eds., *Papers of George Marshall*.

3. Marshall Recognizes Devers

1. Forrest Pogue interview with Jacob Devers, Fairchild Aircraft Corp., Alexandria, Va., 12 August 1958, p. 24, Marshall Library (hereafter Pogue/Devers, Fairchild).

2. Pogue/Devers, Fairchild, p. 4.

3. *Harper's*, p. 474.

4. Pogue/Devers, Fairchild, p. 14.

5. Thomas Griess interview with Anthony McAuliffe, 11 July 1972, Griess Research Collection, York County Heritage Trust.

6. Forrest Pogue interview with Jacob Devers interview, p. 6, Marshall Library (hereafter Pogue/Devers).

7. Thomas Griess interview with Jacob Devers, tape 2, p. 5, Griess Research Collection, York County Heritage Trust (hereafter Griess/Devers).

8. Thomas Griess interview with Eugene L. Harrison, tape 69, 27 December 1974, p. 23, Griess Research Collection, York County Heritage Trust.

9. Pogue/Devers, p. 7; George Marshall to E. L. Daley, 13 September 1940, Bland and Stevens, eds., *Papers of George Marshall*, 2:305.

10. Pogue/Devers.

11. Thomas Griess interview with Eugene L. Harrison, p. 16.

12. Griess/Devers, tape 41, 12 August 1971, p. 11; Pogue/Devers, Fairchild, 12 August 1958.

13. Pogue/Devers, p. 156.

14. Pogue/Devers, p. 11; Griess/Devers, tape 40, p. 10; tape 41, 12 August 1971, p. 11.

15. Thomas Griess interview with Eugene L. Harrison, tapes 69–70, 27 December 1974, p. 16.

16. *Washington Post*, 24 July 1941.

17. Frank B. Watson, 23 July 1941.

18. Griess/Devers, tape 39, p. 12.

19. Senator Henry Lodge Address, p. 17, Additional Resources, Devers Papers, York County Heritage Trust.

20. *History of Armored Force,* 9, York County Heritage Trust.

21. Pogue/Devers, p. 14.

22. Thomas Griess interview with Charles D. Palmer, 30 May 1974, p 35, Griess Research Collection, York County Heritage Trust.

23. Griess/Devers, tape 44, p. 240.

24. Pogue/Devers, p. 12.

25. Groves went on to construct the Pentagon and then oversee the Manhattan Project that built the atomic bomb.

26. Griess/Devers, tape 44, p. 244.

27. Griess/Devers, tape 44.

28. Thomas Griess interview with Eugene L. Harrison, box 91, tape 69, p.13.

29. George Marshall to QMG Gregory, 20 March 1941, Bland and Stevens, eds., *Papers of George Marshall,* 2:446.

30. Pogue/Devers.

31. Pogue/Devers, pp. 128–129, 86.

32. Thomas Griess interview with David G. Ershine, box 93, tape 46, p. 3, Griess Research Collection, York County Heritage Trust.

33. Griess/Devers, tape 37, p. 33.

34. Bradley, *A Soldier's Story,* 210.

35. George Marshall to Jacob Devers, 19 March 1941, Bland and Stevens, eds., *Papers of George Marshall,* 2:452.

36. Clarke and Smith, *Riviera to the Rhine,* 225.

37. In World War II, the U.S. Army was organized into three large organizations: the Army Air Forces, the Army Ground Forces, and the Army Service Forces, which provided logistical support to the other two.

38. Pogue/Devers, p.15.

39. George Marshall to Jacob Devers, 19 March 1941; George Marshall to Daniel Van Vooris, 28 January 1941, both in Bland

and Stevens, eds., *Papers of George Marshall,* 2:452, 397.

40. Blumenson, *Patton Papers, 1940–1945,* 41, 565.

41. Griess/Devers, tape 41, 12 August 1971, p. 166.

42. Griess/Devers, tape 20, p. 18.

43. Griess/Devers, 2 July 1975, p. 10; tape 27, 16 February 1971.

44. Pogue/Devers, p. 18.

45. Griess/Devers, tape 27, 16 February 1971, p. 13.

46. Thomas Griess interview with David G. Ershine, box 93, tape 46, p. 3.

47. Thomas Griess interview with Bruce Clarke, box 108, tape 16, 8 November 1969, p. 5, Griess Research Collection, York County Heritage Trust.

48. Griess/Devers, tape 107, p. 42; tape 27, 16 February 1971.

49. Griess/Devers, tapes 29–30, December 1969.

50. Thomas Griess interview with David G. Ershine, box 93, tape 46, 13 August 1971, p. 3.

51. On his success at Fort Bragg, see *Washington Post,* July 24, 1941.

52. Whiting, *America's Forgotten Army,* 46.

53. Thomas Griess interview with Williston B. Palmer, tape 53, 11 July 1972, p. 16, Griess Research Collection, York County Heritage Trust.

54. Thomas Griess interview with Reuben Jenkins, tape, pp. 38, 44, Griess Research Collection, York County Heritage Trust.

55. Thomas Griess interview with Reuben Jenkins, pp. 38, 44; Thomas Griess interview with Eugene L. Harrison, tape 70, p. 39.

56. Griess/Devers, tape 41, p.11; tape 37, p. 36; tape 55, 12 August 1971, p. 30.

57. Griess/Devers, tape 37.

58. Griess/Devers, tape 39, pp. 12–13.

59. Thomas Griess interview with Charles D. Palmer, 30 May 1974, pp. 31–33.

60. Thomas Griess interview with Williston B. Palmer, tape 53, 11 July 1972, p. 15.

61. Griess/Devers, tape 27, 16 February 1971, p. 13.

62. Devers Diary, 22 January 1945, U.S. Army Military History Institute.

4. Chief of Armored Force

1. Forrest Pogue interview with Jacob Devers, Fairchild Aircraft Corp., Alexandria, Va., pp. 12–13, Marshall Library. See also Thomas Griess interview with Jacob Devers, tape 82, p. 29, Griess Research Collection, York County Heritage Trust (hereafter Griess/Devers).

2. Jacob Devers to Daniel Van Voorhis, 30 August 1941, p. 9.

3. Daniel Van Voorhis, Notes on the Conference with the Chief of Staff, 1931.

4. Cited in H. R. Winton and D. R. Metz, eds., *The Challenge of Change: Military Institutions and the New Realities, 1928–1942* (Lincoln: University of Nebraska Press, 2000). Adna Chaffee also saw the need for separate battalions of heavy tanks to assist the infantry in overcoming machine gun nests holding together prepared defenses.

5. Hoffman and Starry, *Camp Colt to Desert Storm*, 127.

6. Adna Chaffee to Frank Murphy, Attorney General of the United States, 15 September 1939; Chaffee to Frank Andrews, 26 May 1940.

7. Hoffman and Starry, *Camp Colt to Desert Storm*, 57.

8. Gillie, *Forging the Thunderbolt*, 39.

9. Bland and Stevens, eds., *Papers of George Marshall*, 2:187.

10. Hoffman and Starry, *Camp Colt to Desert Storm*, 127–128.

11. "The Cavalry," lecture at U.S. Army War College, 19 September 1939; Hoffman and Starry, *Camp Colt to Desert Storm*, 127.

12. Ibid., 537.

13. Gillie, *Forging the Thunderbolt*, 92–93.

14. Hoffman and Starry, *Camp Colt to Desert Storm*, 128.

15. D'Este, *Decision in Normandy*, 401.

16. Jarymowycz, *Tank Tactics*, 149.

17. Ibid.

18. House of Representatives Committee on Appropriations, 77th Congress, Hearings of 14 May 1941, cited in Hoffman and Starry, *Camp Colt to Desert Storm*, 131.

19. Thomas Griess interview with Anthony McAuliffe, p. 28, Griess Research Collection, York County Heritage Trust.

20. Devers personal notebook, box 7, Devers Papers, York County Heritage Trust.

21. George Marshall to Dwight Eisenhower, 28 December 1943, Marshall Library.

22. Lesley McNair to Jacob Devers, 15 August 1941, Devers Papers, York County Heritage Trust; Greenfield et al., *Organization of Ground Combat Troops*, 69.

23. Griess/Devers, tape 41, p. 11.

24. Griess/Devers, tapes 29–30, December 1969.

25. Gillie, *Forging the Thunderbolt*, 171.

26. Pogue, *George C. Marshall*, 14.

27. Griess/Devers, tape 41, p. 11; tape 40, p. 36.

28. Thomas Griess interview with Charles D. Palmer, 30 May 1974, pp. 14–15, Griess Research Collection, York County Heritage Trust.

29. Thomas Griess interview with Bruce C. Clarke, p. 4, Griess Research Collection, York County Heritage Trust.

30. Griess/Devers, tape 4, p. 1.

31. *History of Armored Force*, 5, York County Heritage Trust.

32. Forrest Pogue interview with Jacob Devers, p. 15, Marshall Library (hereafter Pogue/Devers).

33. Patton, *War as I Knew It.*

34. *History of Armored Force,* 7.

35. Ordnance Committee Minutes, item 15842, 22 May 1940.

36. Hunnicutt, *Firepower,* 25.

37. Gillie, *Forging the Thunderbolt,* 30–31.

38. Some Ordnance Department engineers foresaw the need for a 75mm turreted gun and began preliminary design in October 1940. Numerous technical constraints led them to shelve development until the M3 could be placed into production.

39. Griess/Devers, tape 42, p. 148.

40. Handwritten notes on a typed but unpublished brief of General Charles Scott's report on the Middle East, box 7, Devers Papers, York County Heritage Trust.

41. David Sarnoff was named a reserve brigadier general of the Signal Corps in 1945. In later life, as head of NBC, he was still referred to as "the General."

42. Box 7, Devers Papers, York County Heritage Trust.

43. Jacob Devers to Richard C. Moore, 19 January 1942.

44. Griess/Devers, tape 42, 2 July 1975.

45. Griess/Devers, tape 41, 11–12 August 1971.

46. Griess/Devers, tape 42.

47. Griess/Devers, tape 42, pp. 156–159.

48. Jacob Devers to Richard Moore, 19 January 1942; Devers to R. P. Shugg, 29 March 1942.

49. Pogue/Devers, p. 34.

50. New Zealand Army Study, "Who Killed Tiger?" cited in Jarymowycz, *Tank Tactics,* 280.

51. Griess/Devers, tape 42, p. 159.

52. Thomas Griess interview with Eugene L. Harrison, tape 69, p. 20, Griess Research Collection, York County Heritage Trust.

53. Thomas Griess interview with Williston Palmer, tape 53, p. 8, Griess Research Collection, York County Heritage Trust.

54. See Hunnicutt, *Firepower,* 30–54, for details on development of the T1/M6 heavy tank series.

55. Jacob Devers to Lesley McNair, 7 December 1942.

56. Jacob Devers to Lesley McNair, 16 March 1943.

57. Chief of Staff Statement, November 1943, U.S. Army Military History Institute.

58. Griess/Devers, tape 42, p. 170.

59. Jacob Devers to Lesley McNair, March 1943.

5. The Debate over Doctrine

1. Thomas Griess interview with Jacob Devers, tape 42, p. 170, Griess Research Collection, York County Heritage Trust (hereafter Griess/Devers).

2. Griess/Devers, tape 38, p. 11.

3. Griess/Devers, tape 38, p. 19.

4. George Patton to Jacob Devers, 3 June 1942, Blumenson, *Patton Papers, 1940–1945,* 79.

5. Griess/Devers, tape 69, p. 68.

6. Griess/Devers, tape 69, p. 89.

7. Forrest Pogue interview with Jacob Devers, p. 29, Marshall Library (hereafter Pogue/Devers).

8. Pogue/Devers, p. 167.

9. Command and General Staff, "The Armored Force," *Military Review* 22, no. 37 (January 1943).

10. Jacob Devers to Lesley McNair, 18 July 1942.

11. Greenfield et al., *Organization of Ground Combat Troops,* 325.

12. The 28 May 1942 troop plan contained 59 infantry and 46 armored divisions. The troop basis approved by the War Department on 1 July 1943 was for 63 infantry and 15 armored divisions. In the summer of 1943, AGF recommended 222 tank destroyer battalions and 83 tank battalions. Of these, 101 tank destroyer battalions were ultimately raised but 23 of them had been disbanded by June 1944. Sixty-five tank battalions (roughly one per infantry division) were raised during the war. Ibid., table 1.

13. Gabel, *GHQ Maneuvers,* 120–121.

14. Blumenson, *Patton Papers, 1940–1945,* 43.

15. Gabel, *GHQ Maneuvers,* 122.

16. Lieutenant Huge A. Drum, Critique of Maneuvers.

17. "Second Battle of Carolinas," *Time,* 8 December 1941.

18. "Answer to Tanks is More Tanks," *New York Times,* 21 October 1941.

19. Greenfield et al., *Organization of Ground Combat Troops,* 70.

20. Gabel, *GHQ Maneuvers,* 176.

21. Ibid., 175.

22. Gabel, *Seek, Strike, and Destroy,* 67.

23. Greenfield et al., *Organization of Ground Combat Troops,* 325, 334, 390.

24. Jarymowycz, *Tank Tactics.*

25. Mellenthin, *Panzer Battles.*

26. Citino, *Blitzkrieg to Desert Storm,* 102.

27. George Marshall to Jacob Devers, 9 August 1943, Marshall Library.

28. Griess/Devers, tape 29, p. 144.

29. Griess/Devers, tape 21, p. 67.

30. Pogue/Devers, p. 154.

31. Pogue/Devers, p. 24.

32. Pogue/Devers, p. 46.

33. Griess/Devers, tape 27, p. 13.

34. Thomas Griess interview with Henry Cabot Lodge, 1968, tape 5, p. 17,

Griess Research Collection, York County Heritage Trust.

35. Pogue/Devers, p. 17.

36. Griess/Devers, tape 27, 16 February 1971.

37. Griess/Devers, tape 69, p. 41.

38. Griess/Devers, tape 38, p. 19.

39. Griess/Devers, tape 4, p. 4.

40. Griess/Devers, tape 37, p. 35.

41. Pogue/Devers, p. 86.

42. Pogue/Devers, p. 38.

43. Pogue/Devers, pp. 21, 22.

44. Pogue/Devers, p. 21.

45. Thomas Griess interview with Williston B. Palmer, tape 53, 11 July 1972, Griess Research Collection, York County Heritage Trust. Bruce Palmer was an early proponent of mechanized forces.

46. Gabel, *Seek, Strike, and Destroy,* 67.

47. Griess/Devers, tape 41, p. 12.

48. Devers Papers, box 4, York County Heritage Trust.

49. Jarymowycz, *Tank Tactics,* 92.

50. Jacob Devers, "Staff Data Book," box 7, Devers Papers, York County Heritage Trust.

51. Notes in Devers's handwriting appended to report of Charles L. Scott, Devers Papers, York County Heritage Trust.

52. Jacob Devers to George Marshall, 27 June 1942, Marshall Library.

53. Jarymowycz, *Tank Tactics,* 95; Jacob Devers to George Marshall, 27 June 1942, Marshall Library.

54. *History of Armored Force,* 8, York County Heritage Trust.

55. Hoffman and Starry, *Camp Colt to Desert Storm,* 131.

56. Greenfield et al., *Organization of Ground Combat Troops,* 319.

57. Gillie, *Forging the Thunderbolt,* 241–242.

58. Greiss/Devers, tape 41, 11–12 August 1971.

59. Senator Henry Lodge Address, p. 26, Additional Resources, Devers Papers, York County Heritage Society.

6. Commander, ETO

1. Watson, *Chief of Staff,* 77.
2. Forrest Pogue interview with Jacob Devers, p. 17, Marshall Library (hereafter Pogue/Devers).
3. Pogue/Devers, p. 136.
4. Pogue/Devers, p. 31.
5. Thomas Griess interview with Jacob Devers, tape 40, p. 34, Griess Research Collection, York County Heritage Trust (hereafter Griess/Devers).
6. Pogue/Devers, p. 137.
7. Palmer interview with Jacob Devers, pp. 37–38, Devers Papers, York County Heritage Trust; Pogue/Devers, pp. 29–30. Henry Stimson references the trip in his memoirs. Stimson, *On Active Service in Peace and War,* 431.
8. Pogue/Devers, pp. 29–30, 39.
9. Thomas Griess interview with Ira C. Eaker, tape 48, 1 August 1973, pp. 3–4, Griess Research Collection, York County Heritage Trust.
10. Thomas Griess interview with Reuben Jenkins, tape 33, 14 October 1970, Griess Research Collection, York County Heritage Trust.
11. Thomas Griess interview with Ira C. Eaker, tape 58, pp. 6, 16.
12. Pogue/Devers, pp. 139, 26.
13. Jacob Devers to Combined Chiefs of Staff, 29 July 1943, Chandler and Ambrose, eds., *Papers of Dwight Eisenhower.*
14. Craven and Cate, eds., *Army Fair Forces,* 2:311.
15. Tedder, *With Prejudice,* 458.
16. Ambrose, *Supreme Commander,* 249.
17. SHAEF Office, Diary, 30 July 1943, Eisenhower Library.
18. Crosswell, *Chief of Staff,* 181.

19. Crosswell, *Beetle,* 304.
20. Ruppenthal, *Logistical Support of the Armies,* 1:166.
21. Devers Diary, p. 533, U.S. Army Military History Institute.
22. George Patton Diary, 25 September 1943, Blumenson, *Patton Papers, 1940–1945,* 557.
23. Crosswell, *Beetle,* 439.
24. Devers Diary, 4 November 1943.
25. Ambrose, *Eisenhower,* 194.
26. Dwight Eisenhower to Thomas Handy, 7 December 1942.
27. Bryant, *Triumph in the West,* 430.
28. Sidney T. Matthews interview with George Marshall, 25 July 1949, Marshall Library.
29. Orr, *Supplying the Troops,* 219.
30. Ambrose, *Eisenhower,* 172, 176, 178.
31. Thomas Griess interview with Eugene L. Harrison, pp. 24–25, Griess Research Collection, York County Heritage Trust.
32. Pogue/Devers, p. 31.
33. Griess/Devers, tape 39, p. 5.
34. Griess/Devers, box 112, tape 1, p. 16.
35. Truscott, *Command Missions,* 468–469; Jeffers, *Command of Honor,* 235.
36. Keith E. Eiler, ed., *Wedemeyer on War and Peace* (Palo Alto, Cal.: Stanford University Press, 1987), 62.
37. Thomas Griess interview with Fay B. Prickett, 9 July 1972, pp. 5, 10, 12, Griess Research Collection, York County Heritage Trust.
38. Thomas Griess interview with Dan Noce, p. 8, Griess Research Collection, York County Heritage Trust.
39. Devers Diary, 4 December 1943.
40. Griess/Devers, tape 33.
41. Griess/Devers, tape 20.
42. Quoted in Oliver Warner, *Cunningham of Hyndhope, Admiral of the Fleet: A Memoir* (London: Murray, 1967), 185.

43. Bradley and Blair, *General's Life,* 210.

44. Ibid.

45. Bradley, *A Soldier's Story,* 204.

46. Thomas Griess interview with Dan Noce, 14 November 1971, p. 13.

47. Ambrose, *Supreme Commander,* 62, 178; Dwight Eisenhower to Vernon Prichard, 27 August 1942, Chandler and Ambrose, eds., *Papers of Dwight Eisenhower.*

48. Clarke and Smith, *Riviera to the Rhine,* 574.

49. Eisenhower, *Crusade in Europe,* 216.

50. D'Este, *Fatal Decision,* 483.

51. Clarke and Smith, *Riviera to the Rhine,* 29.

52. Dwight Eisenhower to George Marshall, 17 December 1943, Chandler and Ambrose, eds., *Papers of Dwight Eisenhower,* 3:1604.

53. Bradley, *A Soldier's Story,* 217.

54. Clarke and Smith, *Riviera to the Rhine,* 574.

55. Bland and Stevens, eds., *Papers of George Marshall,* 4:211.

56. Pogue, *George C. Marshall,* 375.

57. Dwight Eisenhower to George Marshall, 25 December 1943, Marshall Library.

58. Bradley, *A Soldier's Story,* 214.

59. Dwight Eisenhower to George Marshall, 25 December 1943, Marshall Library.

60. George Marshall to Dwight Eisenhower, 28 December 1943, Marshall Library.

61. Thomas Griess interview with Eugene L. Harrison, p. 69.

62. George Marshall to Jacob Devers, 28 December 1943, Marshall Library.

63. Clarke and Smith, *Riviera to the Rhine,* 29.

64. Bradley, *A Soldier's Story,* 217.

65. Ibid., 404.

66. Pogue/Devers, p. 16.

67. Blumenson, *Patton Papers, 1940–1945,* 41.

68. Taaffe, *Marshall and His Generals,* 109.

69. Griess/Devers, tape 43, p. 128.

70. Pogue/Devers.

71. Pogue/Devers, p. 43.

7. Deputy Supreme Commander, MTO

1. Devers Diary, 23 December 1943, U.S. Army Military History Institute; Thomas Griess interview with Eugene L. Harrison, p. 21, Griess Research Collection, York County Heritage Trust.

2. Thomas Griess interview with Reuben Jenkins, tape 33, 14 October 1970, Griess Research Collection, York County Heritage Trust.

3. Thomas Griess interview with Jacob Devers, p. 66, Griess Research Collection, York County Heritage Trust (hereafter Griess/Devers).

4. Forrest Pogue interview with Jacob Devers, p. 21, Marshall Library (hereafter Pogue/Devers).

5. Ambrose, *Supreme Commander,* 312.

6. Pogue/Devers, p. 59.

7. Griess/Devers, box 90, tapes 40–45, 11–12 August 1972.

8. Griess/Devers, tape 28, pp. 17–20.

9. D'Este, *Fatal Decision,* 64.

10. Ibid.

11. Thomas Griess interview with Dan Noce, p. 35, Griess Research Collection, York County Heritage Trust.

12. Pogue/Devers, p. 116.

13. Pogue/Devers, p. 109; tape 20, p. 13.

14. Pogue, *George C. Marshall,* 363.

15. Pogue/Devers, p. 144.

16. Pogue/Devers, p. 73.

17. Jacob Devers to George Marshall, 9 May 1944, Marshall Library.

18. Pogue, *George C. Marshall,* 70–71.

19. Pogue/Devers, pp. 98, 59.

20. Devers Diary, 13 September 1943.

21. Pogue/Devers, p. 71.

22. D'Este, *Fatal Decision,* 64.

23. Pogue/Devers, pp. 72–73.

24. Devers Diary, 19 October 1943, 1 November 1943; Pogue/Devers, p. 73.

25. Blumenson, *Mark Clark*, 190; Griess/Devers, tapes 40–45, pp. 11, 12, 14.

26. Performance Review of Mark W. Clark, July 1948, Devers Papers, York County Heritage Trust.

27. Jacob Devers to George Marshall, 14 February 1944, Matloff, *Strategic Planning for Coalition Warfare*, 424.

28. Troops AFSC N903/28, Devers Papers, York County Heritage Trust.

29. Sixsmith, *Eisenhower as Military Commander*, 119.

30. Thomas Griess interview with Reuben Jenkins, tape 33, 14 October 1970, p. 7.

31. Sixsmith, *Eisenhower as Military Commander*, 121

32. Weigley, *Eisenhower's Lieutenants*, 219.

33. Truscott, *Command Missions*, 288.

34. Ibid., 298.

35. Matloff, *Strategic Planning for Coalition Warfare*, 414n.

36. D'Este, *Eisenhower*, 470.

37. Quoted in Clark, *Anzio*, 63.

38. Ibid., 71.

39. D'Este, *Eisenhower*, 470.

40. Fraser, *Alanbrooke*, 230.

41. Blumenson, *Salerno to Casino*, 303.

42. Devers Diary, 7 January 1944.

43. Quoted in D'Este, *Fatal Decision*, 98.

44. John Lucas Diary, U.S. Army Military History Institute.

45. Blumenson, *Patton Papers, 1940–1945*.

46. Fred Walker Diary, 20 January 1944, FLW HIA, box 1, U.S. Army Military History Institute.

47. Mark W. Clark Diary, 6 January 1944, U.S. Army Military History Institute.

48. See Harry C. Butcher Diary, 18 January 1944, U.S. Army Military History Institute; Ambrose, *Supreme Commander*, 340–341.

49. D'Este, *Fatal Decision*, 126.

50. Kesselring, *Memoirs*, 193.

51. Pogue/Devers, p. 63.

52. John Lucas Diary, 19 January 1944.

53. Morrison, *History of United States Naval Operations*, 9:352.

54. John Lucas Diary, 25, 28 January 1944.

55. Nigel Nicolson and Patrick Forbes, *Grenadier Guards in the War of 1939–45*, vol. 2, *The Mediterranean Campaign*, 395, cited in Clark, *Anzio*, 125–126.

56. Thomas Griess interview with Reuben Jenkins, tape 33, 14 October 1970, p. 7.

57. John Lucas Diary, pp. 33–34.

58. Morison, *History of the United States Naval Operations*, 9:352.

59. Ibid., 9:353.

60. Churchill, *Closing the Ring*, 488.

61. Jacob Devers to George Marshall, Radio 9348, W-2332 Marshall 4, p. 311, Marshall Library.

62. Griess/Devers, 10 February 1970, pp. 14, 16.

63. Taaffe, *Marshall and His Generals*, 112, 114.

64. Pogue/Devers, p. 64.

65. Jacob Devers to George Marshall, Radio 882, 19 February 1944, Marshall Library.

66. Blumenson, *Salerno to Casino*, 427; Ambrose, *Supreme Commander*, 311.

67. Atkinson, *An Army at Dawn*, 356.

68. Devers Diary, 15 March 1944.

69. Pogue/Devers, p. 7.

70. Pogue/Devers, p. 59.

71. George Marshall to Dwight Eisenhower, 16 March 1944; Marshall to Jacob Devers, 18 March 1944, both Marshall Library.

72. Devers Diary, 19 February 1944.

73. Jacob Devers to George Marshall, 15 April 1944, Marshall Library; Griess/Devers, box 90, tapes 41, 11 August 1972, p. 14; Dwight Eisenhower to Bedell Smith, 8 October 1944, Chandler and Ambrose, eds., *Papers of Dwight Eisenhower,* 4:2206.

74. Pogue/Devers, p. 134.

8. The French and a Southern Front

1. Lattre, *History of the French First Army,* 119.

2. Jacob Devers to George Marshall, 9 May 1944, Marshall Library.

3. Gaulle, *War Memoirs,* 35–36.

4. Matloff, *Strategic Planning for Coalition Warfare,* 501.

5. Ibid., 502.

6. Dwight Eisenhower to George Marshall, 20 February 1944, Marshall Library.

7. Dwight Eisenhower to George Marshall, 15 January 1945, Chandler and Ambrose, eds., *Papers of Dwight Eisenhower,* 4:2431.

8. Thomas Griess interview with Jacob Devers, box 90, tapes 40–45, 11–12 August 1972, p. 23, Griess Research Collection, York County Heritage Trust (hereafter Griess/Devers); Forrest Pogue interview with Jacob Devers, p. 130, Marshall Library (hereafter Pogue/Devers).

9. Pogue/Devers, p. 87.

10. Thomas Griess interview with Reuben Jenkins, tape 33, 14 October 1970, Griess Research Collection, York County Heritage Trust.

11. Kesselring, *Memoirs,* 194.

12. Jacob Devers to George Marshall, 29 June 1944, Marshall Library.

13. Griess/Devers, tape 40, p. 23.

14. Griess/Devers, tape 40, p. 24.

15. Jacob Devers to George Marshall, 9 May 1944, Marshall Library.

16. Griess/Devers, box 90, tapes 40–45, 11–12 August 1972, p. 24.

17. Pogue/Devers, p. 115.

18. English, *Patton's Peers,* 205.

19. Lattre, *History of the French First Army.*

20. Pogue/Devers, p. 108.

21. Lattre, *History of the French First Army,* 23.

22. Pogue/Devers, p. 90.

23. Griess/Devers, tape 20, p. 18.

24. Griess/Devers, tape 20, p. 33.

25. Bland and Stevens, eds., *Papers of George Marshall,* 4:452; Pogue, *George C. Marshall,* 90.

26. Griess/Devers, tape 20, p. 89.

27. Devers Diary, 13 December 1943, U.S. Army Military History Institute.

28. Thomas Griess interview with Reuben Jenkins, p. 23.

29. Palmer interview with Jacob Devers, p. 57, Devers Papers, York County Heritage Trust.

30. Lattre, *History of the French First Army,* 75.

31. Thomas Griess interview with Henry Cabot Lodge, Griess Research Collection, York County Heritage Trust.

32. Pogue, *Supreme Command,* 231–240.

33. Griess/Devers, tape 37, p. 43.

34. George Marshall to Jacob Devers, 16 May 1944, Marshall Library.

35. Vigneras, *Rearming the French,* 167.

36. Jacob Devers to George Marshall, 10 January 1944; George Marshall to Jacob Devers, 17 March 1944, both Marshall Library.

37. Vigneras, *Rearming the French,* 168.

38. Ibid., 173.

39. Ibid., 402.

40. Bland and Stevens, eds., *Papers of George Marshall,* 4:452; Griess/Devers, box 90, tapes 40–45, 11–12 August 1972, p. 29.

41. Pogue/Devers, p. 154; Griess/Devers, box 90, tapes 40–45, 11–12 August 1972, p. 21.

42. Ruppenthal, *Logistical Support of the Armies,* 2:119.

43. Clarke and Smith, *Riviera to the Rhine,* 14.

44. Pogue, *Supreme Command,* 220.

45. Pogue/Devers, p. 80.

46. For details, see Clarke and Smith, *Riviera to the Rhine,* chapter 1.

47. Ibid., 15.

48. SHAEF to AFHQ S-55130, 6 July 1944, SGS 370.2/2, sup p. 223, SHAEF Files, Eisenhower Library.

49. Griess/Devers, tape 41, 11–12 August 1971.

50. Clarke and Smith, *Riviera to the Rhine,* 23.

51. Ibid., 49.

52. Truscott, *Command Missions,* 408.

53. Devers Diary, 21 August 1944.

54. Pogue, *Supreme Command,* 219.

55. English, *Patton's Peers,* 37.

56. Griess/Devers, tape 41, p. 23.

9. Dragooned

1. Clarke and Smith, *Riviera to the Rhine,* 574.

2. Ibid., 30ff.

3. Dwight Eisenhower to George Marshall, 12 July 1944; Eisenhower to Marshall, 15 July 1944, cable s55590, both Eisenhower Library.

4. Dwight Eisenhower to George Marshall, 12 July 1944, Chandler and Ambrose, eds., *Papers of Dwight Eisenhower,* 3:2000.

5. Clarke and Smith, *Riviera to the Rhine,* 30.

6. Ambrose, *Eisenhower,* 330; Eisenhower, *Crusade in Europe,* 281–283.

7. Thomas Griess interview with Dan Noce, p. 37, Griess Research Collection, York County Heritage Trust.

8. Ambrose, *Eisenhower,* 330.

9. George Marshall to Jacob Devers, 16 July 1944, p. 524, Marshall Library.

10. Bland and Stevens, eds., *Papers of George Marshall,* 4:523–524.

11. MacDonald, *The Mighty Endeavor,* 407.

12. Taafe, *Marshall and His Generals,* 254.

13. Forrest Pogue interview with Jacob Devers, p. 60, Marshall Library (hereafter Pogue/Devers).

14. Henry Wilson's draft report, 17 March 1945, p. 20.

15. AMERIcans in New CALedonia, technically the 23rd Infantry Division.

16. Pogue, *George C. Marshall,* 376.

17. Alexander Patch to his wife, 24 February 1945.

18. Jacob Devers to George Marshall, 20 June 1944, Devers Papers, York County Heritage Trust.

19. Devers Diary, 30 August 1944, U.S. Army Military History Institute.

20. Wyatt, *Sandy Patch,* 93.

21. Alexander Patch to Jacob Devers, 1 June 1945, Devers Papers, box 1, York County Heritage Trust.

22. Pogue/Devers, p. 108.

23. Clarke and Smith, *Riviera to the Rhine,* 33–34.

24. *History of Armored Force,* 9, York County Heritage Trust.

25. Clarke and Smith, *Riviera to the Rhine,* 22.

26. Pogue/Devers, p. 97.

27. Clarke and Smith, *Riviera to the Rhine,* 577.

28. Lattre, *History of the French First Army,* 53.

29. Alexander Patch to his wife, 22 August 1944.

30. Truscott, *Command Missions,* 408.

31. Thomas Griess interview with Jacob Devers, tape 41, 11, 12 August 1971, Griess Research Collection, York County Heritage Trust (hereafter Griess/Devers).

32. Clarke and Smith, *Riviera to the Rhine*, 47.

33. Ibid., 54.

34. Ibid., 200.

35. Ibid., 51.

36. Lattre, *History of the French First Army*, 106.

37. Griess/Devers, tape 41, pp. 108–109.

38. MacDonald, *The Mighty Endeavor*, 408.

39. Seventh Army Field Order 1, 29 July 1944.

40. Clarke and Smith, *Riviera to the Rhine*, 84.

41. Truscott, *Command Missions*, 407.

42. Griess/Devers, box 87, tape 20, p. 11.

43. Weigley, *Eisenhower's Lieutenants*, 229.

44. Pogue/Devers, p. 97.

45. Lattre, *History of the French First Army*, 56.

46. Clarke and Smith, *Riviera to the Rhine*, 27.

47. Thomas Griess interview with Reuben Jenkins, tape 33, 14 October 1970, p. 5, Griess Research Collection, York County Heritage Trust.

48. Pogue/Devers, p. 97.

49. Lattre, *History of the French First Army*, 55.

50. Devers/Breur, p. 34, Devers Papers, York County Heritage Trust.

51. Lattre, *History of the French First Army*, 135.

52. Clarke and Smith, *Riviera to the Rhine*, 62.

53. Pogue/Devers, p. 141.

54. Gavin, *On to Berlin*, 190.

55. Clarke and Smith, *Riviera to the Rhine*, 122.

56. Brehon Somervell to Jacob Devers, 18 August 1944.

57. Morison, *History of United States Naval Operations*, 11:221.

58. Winston Churchill to Dwight Eisenhower, 18 August 1944; Eisenhower to Henry Wilson for Churchill, 24 August 1944.

59. Clarke and Smith, *Riviera to the Rhine*, 154.

60. Thomas Griess interview with Eugene L. Harrison, tape 69, p. 21, Griess Research Collection, York County Heritage Trust.

61. Griess/Devers, tape 69, p. 31.

62. Lattre, *History of the French First Army*, 71.

63. Ibid., 72–73.

64. Thomas Griess interview with Eugene L. Harrison, p. 31.

65. Pogue/Devers, p. 99.

66. Pogue/Devers, p. 93; Thomas Griess interview with Eugene L. Harrison, tape 41, p. 10.

10. Up the Rhône Valley

1. Forrest Pogue interview with Jacob Devers, p. 118, Marshall Library (hereafter Pogue/Devers).

2. Thomas Griess interview with Eugene L. Harrison, tape 69, p. 31, Griess Research Collection, York County Heritage Trust.

3. Weigley, *Eisenhower's Lieutenants*, 229.

4. Truscott, *Command Missions*, 415.

5. Wyatt, *Sandy Patch*, 133.

6. *Seventh United States Army Report of Operations*, 199.

7. Wyatt, *Sandy Patch*, 132.

8. Radio 36ID to VI Corps 0130, 25 August 1944.

9. Wyatt, *Sandy Patch*, 133.

10. Pogue/Devers, p. 143.

11. Pogue/Devers, p. 143.

12. Devers Diary, 9 September 1944, U.S. Army Military History Institute.

13. Devers Diary, 30 August 1944.

14. Pogue/Devers, p. 98.

15. Dwight Eisenhower to George Marshall, 4 September 1944, Chandler and Ambrose, eds., *Papers of Dwight Eisenhower,* 4:document 1934.

16. *History of 6th Army Group,* para. 36, York County Heritage Trust.

17. Clarke and Smith, *Riviera to the Rhine,* 265–266.

18. Dwight Eisenhower to George Marshall and Henry Wilson, 31 August 1944, FWD 13445, SHAEF Files, Eisenhower Library.

19. Devers Diary, 11–12 September 1944.

20. Lattre, *History of the French First Army,* 134.

21. Clarke and Smith, *Riviera to the Rhine,* 203.

22. Thomas Griess interview with Reuben Jenkins, tape 33, 14 October 1970, Griess Research Collection, York County Heritage Trust.

23. Pogue/Devers, p. 82.

24. Clarke and Smith, *Riviera to the Rhine,* 207.

25. Pogue/Devers, p. 85.

26. Palmer interview with Jacob Devers, tape 3, p. 74, Devers Papers, York County Heritage Trust.

27. Pogue/Devers, p. 85.

28. Pogue/Devers, p. 84.

29. Devers Diary, 14 September 1944.

30. Thomas Griess interview with Eugene L. Harrison, tape 70, p. 37.

31. Devers Diary, 7 July 1944.

32. Devers Diary, 28 August 1944.

11. An End to Champagne

1. FWD 13765, Eisenhower Pre-Presidential Papers, Eisenhower Library.

2. *History of 6th Army Group,* p. 55, York County Heritage Trust.

3. Thomas Griess interview with Jacob Devers, tape 21, p. 59, Griess Research

Collection, York County Heritage Trust (hereafter Griess/Devers).

4. Ruppenthal, *Logistical Support of the Armies,* 2:349.

5. George Patton Diary, 25 September 1944, Blumenson, *Patton Papers, 1940–1945,* 557.

6. Ibid.

7. Forrest Pogue interview with George Marshall, pp. 626–627, Marshall Library.

8. Devers Diary, 4 September 1944, U.S. Army Military History Institute.

9. Devers Diary, 8 September 1944.

10. Clarke and Smith, *Riviera to the Rhine,* 225.

11. Ibid., 253.

12. Lattre, *History of the French First Army,* 195, 203.

13. *Seventh United States Army Report of Operations,* 395.

14. Clarke and Smith, *Riviera to the Rhine,* 295.

15. Truscott, *Command Missions,* 441.

16. *History of 6th Army Group.*

17. Adams, *Battle for Western Europe,* chapter 3.

18. Forrest Pogue interview with Jacob Devers, pp. 84–85, Marshall Library (hereafter Pogue/Devers).

19. Smith, *Eisenhower's Six Great Decisions,* 123.

20. MacDonald, *Last Offensive,* 15.

21. Lattre, *History of the French First Army,* 142.

22. Ibid., 158.

23. Ibid., 322.

24. Clarke and Smith, *Riviera to the Rhine,* 230.

25. Ibid., 224.

26. Pogue/Devers, p. 65.

27. For ease of recognition, French armored divisions, "division blindée," are abbreviated "AD." All other French divisions are referred to as infantry divisions

(ID) regardless of their more eloquent French titles.

28. Weigley, *Eisenhower's Lieutenants*, 402.

29. Chandler and Ambrose, eds., *Papers of Dwight Eisenhower*, 4:2146–2147.

30. Ibid., 4:2274.

31. Clarke and Smith, *Riviera to the Rhine*, 230.

32. FWD 13765, Eisenhower Pre-Presidential Papers, Eisenhower Library.

33. Pogue/Devers, p. 45.

34. Eisenhower Diary, 3 February 1944, p. 636, Eisenhower Library.

35. Crosswell, *Beetle*, 306; Griess/Devers, box 90, tapes 40–45, 11–12 August 1972.

36. Devers Diary, 23 November 1944.

37. Dwight Eisenhower to Jacob Devers, 18 September 1944, Devers Papers, vol. 4, document 1971, York County Heritage Trust.

38. Clarke and Smith, *Riviera to the Rhine*, 575.

39. Ibid., 575–576.

40. D'Este, *Eisenhower*, 483.

41. Weigley, *Eisenhower's Lieutenants*, 551.

42. Clarke and Smith, *Riviera to the Rhine*, 229–230.

43. Dwight Eisenhower to Bernard Montgomery, 24 September 1944, Chandler and Ambrose, eds., *Papers of Dwight Eisenhower*, 4:1993.

44. Devers Diary, 11–12 September 1944.

45. Devers Diary, 22, 27 September 1944.

46. Clarke and Smith, *Riviera to the Rhine*, 255.

47. Wyatt, *Sandy Patch*, 183.

48. Devers Diary, 1 October 1944.

12. Into the Cold Vosges

1. Clarke and Smith, *Riviera to the Rhine*, 231.

2. *History of 6th Army Group*, para. 55, York County Heritage Trust.

3. Ibid., para. 60.

4. Clarke and Smith, *Riviera to the Rhine*, 230.

5. Truscott, *Command Missions*, 445; *Seventh United States Army Report of Operations*, 336, 363.

6. Thomas Griess interview with Jacob Devers, box 90, tapes 40–45, 11–12 August 1972, p. 16, Griess Research Collection, York County Heritage Trust (hereafter Griess/Devers).

7. Clarke and Smith, *Riviera to the Rhine*, 292.

8. *Seventh United States Army Report of Operations*, 540.

9. Ibid., 549.

10. Clarke and Smith, *Riviera to the Rhine*, 272–273.

11. Bonn, *When the Odds Were Even*, 77.

12. *Seventh United States Army Report of Operations*, 389.

13. Ibid., 390–391.

14. Ibid., 393.

15. Wyatt, *Sandy Patch*, 153.

16. Forrest Pogue interview with Jacob Devers interview, p. 63, Marshall Library (hereafter Pogue/Devers). Recall that Edward Brooks had served under Devers in the 1920s at the Artillery School and in the early 1940s in the Armored Force.

17. Clarke and Smith, *Riviera to the Rhine*, 261.

18. Ibid., 351.

19. Griess/Devers, tape 43, p. 192.

20. Pogue/Devers, p. 89; Palmer interview with Jacob Devers interview, p. 57, Devers Papers, York County Heritage Trust.

21. Devers Diary, 21 October 1944, U.S. Army Military History Institute.

22. Lattre, *History of the French First Army*, 480.

13. Cross the Rhine?

1. *Seventh United States Army Report of Operations*, 389.
2. Clarke and Smith, *Riviera to the Rhine*, 351.
3. See Adams, *Battle for Western Europe*, especially chapter 3.
4. SCS 381, 28 October 1944, SHAEF Files, Eisenhower Library.
5. SGS 381, 28 October 1944, SHAEF Files.
6. Dwight Eisenhower to Jacob Devers, 23 October 1944, Eisenhower Library.
7. Yeilde and Stout, *First to the Rhine*, 101; Mellenthin, *Panzer Battles*, 385.
8. *History of 6th Army Group*, 158, York County Heritage Trust.
9. Devers Diary, 7 November 1944, U.S. Army Military History Institute.
10. *Seventh United States Army Report of Operations*,418–449.
11. Lattre, *History of the French First Army*, 215–217.
12. Thomas Griess interview with Reuben Jenkins, tape 33, p. 72, Griess Research Collection, York County Heritage Trust.
13. Thomas Griess interview with Reuben Jenkins, tape 33, pp. 19–20.
14. *History of 6th Army Group*, 153.
15. Thomas Griess interview with Reuben Jenkins, tape 33, p. 21.
16. Devers Diary, 11, 12 November 1944.
17. Thomas Griess interview with Reuben Jenkins, tape 33, p. 21.
18. Thomas Griess interview with Edward C. Korn, box 81, tapes 66–67, pp. 37–38, Griess Research Collection, York County Heritage Trust.
19. Lattre, *History of the French First Army*, 206.
20. Thomas Griess interview with Jacob Devers, tape 38, p. 60, Griess Research

Collection, York County Heritage Trust (hereafter Griess/Devers).
21. Devers Diary, 5 November 1944.
22. *Seventh United States Army Report of Operations*, 397–399.
23. Bonn, *When the Odds Were Even*, 113.
24. Clarke and Smith, *Riviera to the Rhine*, 388.
25. Thomas Griess interview with Reuben Jenkins, tape 33, p. 21.
26. Thomas Griess interview with Reuben Jenkins, tape 33, p. 22.
27. Clarke and Smith, *Riviera to the Rhine*, 367.
28. XV Corps Field Order, 8 November 1944.
29. Whiting, *America's Forgotten Army*, 76.
30. Thomas Griess interview with Reuben Jenkins, tape 33, p. 21.
31. Griess/Devers, tape 22.
32. Devers Diary, 9 November 1944.
33. Thomas Griess interview with Reuben Jenkins, tape 33, p. 26.
34. Lattre, *History of the French First Army*, 228.
35. Griess/Devers, tape 22, p. 19.
36. Forrest Pogue interview with Jacob Devers, p. 91, Marshall Library (hereafter Pogue/Devers).
37. Mellenthin, *Panzer Battles*, 331.
38. Pogue/Devers, p. 92.
39. Lattre, *History of the French First Army*, 281.
40. Ibid., 280.
41. Wilmot, *Struggle for Europe*, 569.
42. Clarke and Smith, *Riviera to the Rhine*, 377–378.
43. Thomas Griess interview with Reuben Jenkins, tape 33, p. 21.
44. Clarke and Smith, *Riviera to the Rhine*, 386.
45. Ibid., 432.
46. Ibid., 433.

47. Ibid., 434.

48. *History of 6th Army Group,* 189–193.

49. *Seventh United States Army Report of Operations,* 702.

50. Clarke and Smith, *Riviera to the Rhine,* 442.

51. *History of 6th Army Group,* 414.

52. Clarke and Smith, *Riviera to the Rhine,* 438.

53. *History of 6th Army Group,* 414.

54. Ibid., 413–415.

55. Thomas Griess interview with Reuben Jenkins, tape 33.

14. Throw Down at Vittel and Its Aftermath

1. Bryant, *Triumph in the West,* 254.

2. Crosswell, *Chief of Staff,* 306.

3. Thomas Griess interview with Reuben Jenkins, pp. 34–35, Griess Research Collection, York County Heritage Trust.

4. Thomas Griess interview with Reuben Jenkins, p. 35.

5. Thomas Griess interview with Eugene L. Harrison, p. 45, Griess Research Collection, York County Heritage Trust.

6. D'Este, *Eisenhower,* 659.

7. Patton, *War as I Knew It,* 169.

8. Chester B. Hansen Diary, 24 November 1944, U.S. Army Military History Institute.

9. Chester B. Hansen Diary, 24 November 1944.

10. George Patton Diary, 5 November 1944, Blumenson, *Patton Papers, 1940–1945,* 568.

11. Clarke and Smith, *Riviera to the Rhine,* 439.

12. *History of 6th Army Group,* 419, York County Heritage Trust.

13. MacDonald, *The Mighty Endeavor,* 408.

14. Thomas Griess interview with Jacob Devers, tape 41, p. 126, Griess Research Collection, York County Heritage Trust (hereafter Griess/Devers).

15. Griess/Devers, tape 41, p. 120.

16. Forrest Pogue interview with Jacob Devers interview, p. 46, Marshall Library (hereafter Pogue/Devers).

17. Devers Diary, 24 November 1944, U.S. Army Military History Institute.

18. *Seventh United States Army Report of Operations,* para. 160.

19. Clarke and Smith, *Riviera to the Rhine,* 439.

20. Thomas Griess interview with Eugene L. Harrison, pp. 36–37.

21. This and other quotations of the Vittel meeting are recounted by Devers separately to Forrest Pogue (12 August 1958) and to Thomas Griess (tape 42).

22. Recollections of conversations in Griess/Devers, tape 42, pp. 126–127.

23. Forrest Pogue interview with George Marshall, p. 317, Marshall Library.

24. Griess/Devers, tape 42, p. 127.

25. Griess/Devers, tape 42, pp. 126–127.

26. Griess/Devers, tape 55, p. 30.

27. Clarke and Smith, *Riviera to the Rhine,* 442.

28. Dwight Eisenhower to Jacob Devers, 23 October 1944, SHAEF Files, Eisenhower Library.

29. Directive to Army Group Commanders, SCAF 114, SHAEF Files, Eisenhower Library.

30. *Seventh United States Army Report of Operations,* para. 162; *History of 6th Army Group,* para. 162.

31. See Adams, *Battle for Western Europe,* chapters 4 and 5.

32. Ambrose, *Supreme Commander,* 544.

33. Clarke and Smith, *Riviera to the Rhine,* 229.

34. Blumenson, *Patton Papers, 1940–1945,* 583.

35. Chester B. Hansen Diary, 22 November 1944.

36. Clarke and Smith, *Riviera to the Rhine,* 229, 437.

37. Dwight Eisenhower to George Marshall, 27 November 1944, Marshall Library.

38. Dwight Eisenhower to Combined Chiefs of Staff, 3 December 1944.

39. Eisenhower, *Crusade in Europe,* 331, 332.

40. Ibid., 331.

41. Memorandum by planning Staff G3, Possibilities of Mutual Reinforcement, 20 November 1944.

42. Weigley, *Eisenhower's Lieutenants,* 408, 409.

43. Clarke and Smith, *Riviera to the Rhine,* 563.

44. *History of 6th Army Group,* para. 164.

45. Ibid., para. 161.

46. Thomas Griess interview with Reuben Jenkins, p. 27.

47. Pogue/Devers, p. 48.

48. Dwight Eisenhower to George Marshall, 15 January 1945.

49. Devers Diary, 5 December 1944.

50. Griess/Devers, tape 21, p. 59.

51. Griess/Devers, p. 6; tape 21, p. 60.

52. Thomas Griess interview with Eugene L. Harrison.

53. *100ID News,* February 1986, p. 2.

54. Jacob Devers to SHAEF, Main 261445 Nov, SHAEF Files, Eisenhower Library.

55. Thomas Griess interview with Reuben Jenkins, tape 33.

56. Thomas Griess interview with Charles D. Palmer, p. 23, Griess Research Collection, York County Heritage Trust.

57. Thomas Griess interview with Eugene L. Harrison, p. 32.

58. Griess/Devers, tapes 40–45, p. 22.

59. Thomas Griess interview with Reuben Jenkins, pp. 28–29.

60. Pogue/Devers, pp. 92–93.

61. Lattre, *History of the French First Army,* p. 281

62. Ibid., 200, 281, 283.

63. Thomas Griess interview with Reuben Jenkins, pp. 25–26.

64. Thomas Griess interview with Eugene L. Harrison, tape 69, p. 31.

65. Thomas Griess interview with Eugene L. Harrison, tape 69, pp. 31–32.

66. Lattre, *History of the French First Army,* 295.

67. Ibid., 295–296.

68. Jacob Devers to George Marshall, 11 December 1944, Marshall Library.

69. Lattre, *History of the French First Army,* 294.

70. Gaulle, *War Memoirs,* 162.

71. Devers Diary, 6 December 1944.

72. Griess/Devers, tapes 40–45, p. 21.

73. Thomas Griess interview with Reuben Jenkins, p. 26.

74. Thomas Griess interview with Reuben Jenkins, pp. 24–25.

75. Pogue/Devers, p. 108.

76. Lattre, *History of the French First Army,* 286, 291.

77. Clarke and Smith, *Riviera to the Rhine,* 484.

78. Lattre, *History of the French First Army,* 288.

79. Ibid., 160.

80. Devers Diary, 14 December 1944.

81. Devers Diary, 14 December 1944.

82. Lattre, *History of the French First Army,* 293.

83. Ibid., 203, 293.

84. 6AG to SHAEF, 14 December 1944, in *History of 6th Army Group,* 72.

85. Harold Bull to Beadle Smith, Enemy Bridgehead on Colmar Sector, 14 December 1944.

86. Lattre, *History of the French First Army,* 287.

87. Thomas Griess interview with Charles D. Palmer, p. 18.

88. Palmer interview with Jacob Devers, tape 2, p. 58, Devers Papers, York County Heritage Trust.

89. Pogue/Devers, p. 51.

90. SHAEF, Final Report, p. 90.

91. Pogue, *Supreme Command,* 311.

15. Nordwind Strikes Devers

1. Forrest Pogue interview with Jacob Devers, p. 49, Marshall Library (hereafter Pogue/Devers).

2. Pogue/Devers, p. 50.

3. Palmer interview with Jacob Devers, p. 75, Devers Papers, York County Heritage Trust (hereafter Palmer/Devers).

4. Thomas Griess interview with Reuben Jenkins, p. 41, Griess Research Collection, York County Heritage Trust.

5. Pogue/Devers, pp. 49–53.

6. Thomas Griess interview with Eugene L. Harrison, pp. 38, 33–34, Griess Research Collection, York County Heritage Trust.

7. Thomas Griess interview with Jacob Devers, p. 22, Griess Research Collection, York County Heritage Trust (hereafter Griess/Devers).

8. Thomas Griess interview with Charles D. Palmer, p. 22, Griess Research Collection, York County Heritage Trust.

9. "Stand in zone" allows subordinate corps and divisions to maneuver in their defensive zones in order to best stop an attack; in more modern terminology, this is known as "mobile defense."

10. Clarke and Smith, *Riviera to the Rhine,* 493.

11. Pogue/Devers, p. 47.

12. Griess/Devers, tape 44, p. 22.

13. Lattre, *History of the French First Army,* 301.

14. Dwight Eisenhower to George Marshall, 6 January 1945, Marshall Library.

15. Dwight Eisenhower to George Marshall, 6 January 1945, Marshall Library.

16. SHAEF Office Diary, 26 December 1944, Pre-Presidential Papers, Eisenhower Library; Ambrose, *Eisenhower,* 373.

17. Griess/Devers, tape 41, 11–12 August 1971.

18. Lattre, *History of the French First Army,* 309.

19. Ibid.

20. Chandler and Ambrose, eds., *Papers of Dwight Eisenhower,* 4:2224.

21. Pogue, *Supreme Command,* 398.

22. Pogue/Devers, p. 45.

23. Palmer/Devers, p. 75.

24. Clarke and Smith, *Riviera to the Rhine,* 496.

25. Devers Diary, 28 December 1944, U.S. Army Military History Institute.

26. Thomas Griess interview with Eugene L. Harrison, pp. 32–33.

27. Thomas Griess interview with Eugene L. Harrison, pp. 33–34.

28. Thomas Griess interview with Reuben Jenkins, pp. 41–44.

29. Devers Diary, 29 December 1944.

30. Jacob Devers to SHAEF for Dwight Eisenhower, 31 December 1944; Devers to SHAEF, 31 December 1944.

31. Palmer/Devers, p. 75.

32. Thomas Griess interview with Eugene L. Harrison, p. 38.

33. Palmer/Devers, tape 3, p. 79.

34. Clarke and Smith, *Riviera to the Rhine,* 494.

35. *Seventh United States Army Report of Operations,* 560, 562, 567.

36. Bass et al., *Story of the Century,* 100.

37. Thomas Griess interview with Reuben Jenkins, p. 44.

38. *Seventh United States Army Report of Operations,* 581.

39. Palmer/Devers, pp. 78–79.

40. Ambrose, *Supreme Commander,* 577.

41. Juin, *Mémoires,* 306.

42. Chandler and Ambrose, eds., *Papers of Dwight Eisenhower,* 4:2401; see also 4:2224.

43. Ibid., 4:2216.

44. Gaulle, *War Memoirs,* 166.

45. Palmer/Devers, p. 77; tape 22, p. 18.

46. Gaulle, *War Memoirs,* 171.

47. Ibid., 169–170; Chandler and Ambrose, eds., *Papers of Dwight Eisenhower,* 4:2397.

48. Gaulle, *War Memoirs,* 162, 163.

49. Ibid.

50. Ibid., 170.

51. Pogue, *Supreme Command,* 401.

52. Chandler and Ambrose, eds., *Papers of Dwight Eisenhower,* 4:2224; Butcher, *Three Years with Eisenhower,* 271–273; Eisenhower, *Crusade in Europe,* 362–63.

53. Gaulle, *War Memoirs,* 171.

54. *Seventh United States Army Report of Operations,* 581–582.

55. Dwight Eisenhower to Charles de Gaulle, 5 January 1945.

56. Chandler and Ambrose, eds., *Papers of Dwight Eisenhower,* 4:2224.

57. Pogue/Devers, p. 45.

58. Clarke and Smith, *Riviera to the Rhine,* 509.

59. Ibid., 418.

60. *Seventh United States Army Report of Operations.*

61. Clarke and Smith, *Riviera to the Rhine,* 513.

62. Devers Diary, 9 January 1945.

63. Ferguson, *Hellcats,* chapter 5.

64. *History of 6th Army Group,* 289, York County Heritage Trust.

65. *Seventh United States Army Report of Operations,* VI Corps, After Action Report.

16. The Colmar Pocket Finally Collapses

1. Dwight Eisenhower to George Marshall, S74437, S74461, both 10 January 1945; Eisenhower to senior commanders, SGS381, 11 January 1945; Eisenhower to Marshall, S74687, 11 January 1945; Eisenhower to Marshall, 12 January 1945; Eisenhower to Marshall, S74971, 14 January 1945; Eisenhower to Marshall, S75090, 15 January 1945; Eisenhower to Bernard Montgomery, 17 January 1945; Eisenhower to subordinate commanders, S75546, 18 January 1945; and Eisenhower to CCS, S75872, 75871, 20 January 1945, all Marshall Library.

2. Dwight Eisenhower to George Marshall, S74461, 10 January 1945, Marshall Library.

3. Forrest Pogue interview with Jacob Devers, p. 111, Marshall Library (hereafter Pogue/Devers).

4. Gaulle, *War Memoirs,* 174.

5. Dwight Eisenhower to George Marshall, 15 January 1945, Marshall Library.

6. Bradley, *General's Life,* 390, 403.

7. Crosswell, *Chief of Staff,* 306.

8. Clarke and Smith, *Riviera to the Rhine,* 534.

9. Thomas Griess interview with Reuben Jenkins, tape 33, p. 49, Griess Research Collection, York County Heritage Trust.

10. Thomas Griess interview with Reuben Jenkins.

11. Lattre, *History of the French First Army,* 401, 410, 413.

12. Devers Diary, 12 January 1945, U.S. Army Military History Institute.

13. Lattre, *History of the French First Army,* 335.

14. Dwight Eisenhower to George Marshall, 15 January 1945, Marshall Library.

15. Crosswell, *Beetle.*

16. Ambrose, *Eisenhower,* 380.

17. *History of 6th Army Group,* chapter 6, p. 2, York County Heritage Trust.

18. Devers's lecture at Command and General Staff College, Fort Leavenworth, given 1 July 1948, Devers Papers, York County Heritage Trust.

19. Thomas Griess interview with Henry Cabot Lodge, Griess Research Collection, York County Heritage Trust.

20. *History of 6th Army Group,* chapter 6, p. 3.

21. Thomas Griess interview with Jacob Devers, pp. 49, 50, Griess Research Collection, York County Heritage Trust (hereafter Griess/Devers).

22. Lattre, *History of the French First Army,* 341.

23. Ibid., 338.

24. Ibid., 345, 348.

25. Clarke and Smith, *Riviera to the Rhine,* 339.

26. *History of 6th Army Group,* chapter 6, p. 23.

27. Clarke and Smith, *Riviera to the Rhine,* 546.

28. Devers Diary, 23 January 1945.

29. Devers Diary, 27 January 1945.

30. Devers Diary, 26 January 1945.

31. Alphonse Juin to Dwight Eisenhower, 24 January 1945.

32. Devers Diary, 27 January 1945.

33. Clarke and Smith, *Riviera to the Rhine,* 548.

34. Pogue, *Supreme Command,* 402.

35. Thomas Griess interview with Reuben Jenkins, p. 50.

36. *History of 6th Army Group,* chapter 6, p. 43.

37. Thomas Griess interview with Reuben Jenkins, p. 49.

38. Lattre, *History of the French First Army,* 401.

39. Griess/Devers, tape 69, p. 34.

40. Devers Diary, 6 February 1945.

41. *Seventh United States Army Report of Operations,* 159, 178.

42. *History of 6th Army Group,* 306.

43. Clarke and Smith, *Riviera to the Rhine,* 535, 536.

44. *History of 6th Army Group,* chapter 6, p. 2.

45. Clarke and Smith, *Riviera to the Rhine,* 533.

46. George Patton to Jacob Devers, 21 August 1944.

47. MacDonald, *Mighty Endeavor,* 479. The obsolescence of the Sherman tank was also noted.

48. But the "book" still reflected Lesley McNair's imprint. FM17–36, Tanks with Infantry, March 1944, para. 1(g): "Anti-tank guns provide the best means of protection against enemy tanks."

17. Undertone to Austria

1. See also Dwight Eisenhower to Combined Chiefs of Staff (CCS), 7 January 1945; Eisenhower to George Marshall, 7 January 1945; Eisenhower to Marshall, S74437, S74461, 10 January 1945; Eisenhower to Army Group Commanders and Lee, 11 January 1945; Eisenhower to Marshall, 12 January 1945; Eisenhower to Marshall, 15 January 1945, all in Marshall Library.

2. Eisenhower, *Crusade in Europe,* 382.

3. Dwight Eisenhower to George Marshall, 12 January 1945, Marshall Library.

4. *Seventh United States Army Report of Operations,* 698.

5. Weekly Intelligence Summary, 10 March 1945, 6AG 401, p. 217.

6. See Adams, *Battle for Western Europe,* chapter 6, for Patton's Lorraine campaign.

7. FWD 17655, 8 March 1945, Post Overlord Planning, SHAEF Files, Eisenhower Library.

8. Dwight Eisenhower to George Marshall, 15 January 1945, S74437/SG824, Marshall Library.

9. Bradley, *A Soldier's Story,* 255.

10. FWD 17655, SHAEF Files, Eisenhower Library.

11. Note on Early Concentration for Saar Offensive, 14 February 1945, SHAEF Files, Eisenhower Library.

12. MacDonald, *Last Offensive,* 241.

13. Patton, *War as I Knew It,* 254.

14. Weigley, *Eisenhower's Lieutenants,* 636.

15. Thomas Griess interview with Reuben Jenkins interview, p. 54, Griess Research Collection, York County Heritage Trust.

16. Thomas Griess interview with Reuben Jenkins, p. 55.

17. *Seventh United States Army Report of Operations,* 737.

18. Wyatt, *Sandy Patch,* 182.

19. *Seventh United States Army Report of Operations,* 226.

20. MacDonald, *Last Offensive,* 257–258.

21. The handling of boundaries among George Patton, Omar Bradley, and Bernard Montgomery at Falaise and the Seine during the breakout from Normandy was markedly different from the manner in which Patton, Jacob Devers, and Alexander Patch handled boundaries both in the encirclement of the Germans in the Saar-Palatinate triangle in late March 1945 and during April's gallop down to Austria. At Falaise, Patton wanted to continue up from Argentan to complete the encirclement of the German Seventh Army and Panzergroup West. Bradley told him no and held him back, worrying about Patton's running headlong into the Canadian First Army. Montgomery, who had the authority to modify the boundary, did not resolve the issue. The result was an army of Germans getting away. A little later in the same campaign, Patton suggested turning the Third Army west along the Seine to create an even larger pocket, but Montgomery again did not want to move boundaries.

22. SHAEF Diary, 17 March 1945, Eisenhower Library.

23. Eisenhower, *Crusade in Europe.*

24. *Seventh United States Army Report of Operations,* 721.

25. Cited in Jarymowycz, *Tank Tactics,* 140ff, 155.

26. "I'd rather have a firm shoulder at Argentan than a broken neck at Falaise," said Omar Bradley.

27. *Seventh United States Army Report of Operations,* 738.

28. Alexander Patch to his wife, 25 March 1945.

29. MacDonald, *Last Offensive,* 268.

30. Ibid., 265, 264.

31. Seventh Army Intelligence Estimate, 17 March 1945.

32. Dwight Eisenhower to Jacob Devers, 18 March 1945.

33. Patton, *War as I Knew It,* 264–267.

34. *Seventh United States Army Report of Operations,* 743.

35. *History of 6th Army Group,* 429, York County Heritage Trust.

36. MacDonald, *Last Offensive,* 284; *Seventh United States Army Report of Operations,* 741.

37. Ibid., 766.

38. Lattre, *History of the French First Army,* 407.

39. Ibid., 488.

40. Ibid., 401, 407.

41. Forrest Pogue interview with Jacob Devers, p. 110, Marshall Library (hereafter Pogue/Devers).

42. Lattre, *History of the French First Army,* 409.

43. Ibid., 414.

44. Gaulle, *War Memoirs,* 177.

45. Lattre, *History of the French First Army,* 449.

46. MacDonald, *Last Offensive,* 335; Pogue, *Supreme Command,* 465.

47. Eisenhower, *Crusade in Europe,* 396.

48. Forrest Pogue interview with George Marshall, 13 March 1956, p. 627, Marshall Library.

49. Eisenhower, *Crusade in Europe,* 414.

50. Pogue/Devers, p. 108.

51. *Seventh United States Army Report of Operations,* 765.

52. History of the 375th Artillery, p. 85, Marshall Library.

53. *Seventh United States Army Report of Operations,* 421.

54. 6AG weekly Intel Summary #28, 31 March 1945.

55. Weigley, *Eisenhower's Lieutenants,* 704.

56. Ibid.

57. Ibid.

58. Pogue/Devers, p. 111.

59. Pogue/Devers, pp. 123–124.

60. Thomas Griess interview with Reuben Jenkins, p. 56.

61. Thomas Griess interview with Reuben Jenkins, pp. 57, 60.

62. SHAEF Weekly Intelligence Report, 15 April 1945.

63. The decision, viewed from the vantage point of many a GI's grandchild at the start of the twenty-first century, makes eminent sense despite the controversy it created in 1945.

64. Lattre, *History of the French First Army,* 192, 193.

65. Devers Diary, 6 May 1945, U.S. Army Military History Institute.

66. Pogue/Devers, p. 134.

67. *Seventh United States Army Report of Operations,* 774.

68. Ibid., 778.

69. Ibid., 779.

70. Ibid.

71. Lattre, *History of the French First Army.*

72. Pogue/Devers, p. 114.

73. Lattre, *History of the French First Army,* 490–491.

74. MacDonald, *Last Offensive,* 490–491.

75. *History of 6th Army Group.*

76. Thomas Griess interview with Reuben Jenkins, p. 57.

77. Pogue/Devers, p. 113.

78. Pogue/Devers, p. 111.

79. *Seventh United States Army Report of Operations,* 805.

80. Ibid., 832.

81. MacDonald, *Last Offensive,* 441.

82. *Seventh United States Army Report of Operations,* 855.

83. MacDonald, *Last Offensive,* 443.

84. Kesselring, *Memoirs,* 287.

85. Wyatt, *Sandy Patch.*

18. Postwar

1. Dwight Eisenhower to George Marshall, 1 February 1945, Chandler and Ambrose, eds., *Papers of Dwight Eisenhower,* 4:2271.

2. Thomas Griess interview with Jacob Devers, tape 40–45, 11–12 April 1971, p. 4, Griess Research Collection, York County Heritage Trust (hereafter Griess/Devers). Most of the material for this chapter comes from transcripts of interviews with Devers.

3. Griess/Devers, tape 41, p. 83.

4. Thomas Griess interview with Charles A. Bolte, tape 52, p. 8, Griess Research Collection, York County Heritage Trust.

5. Griess/Devers, tape 40, 11–12 April 1971, p. 45.

6. Forrest Pogue interview with Jacob Devers, Marshall Library (hereafter Pogue/Devers).

7. Griess/Devers, tape 40, p. 45.

8. Pogue/Devers.

9. Thomas Griess interview with Bruce C. Clarke, tape 16, 8 November 1969, p. 3, Griess Research Collection, York County Heritage Trust. Clarke went on to become the four-star commander of the U.S. Army in Europe during the Cold War.

10. Pogue/Devers.

11. Griess/Devers, tape 40, p. 60.

12. Griess/Devers, tape 41, p. 71.

13. Griess/Devers, tape 41, p. 72.

14. Griess/Devers, 29–30 December 1969, p. 37.

15. Thomas Griess interview with Charles A. Bolte, tape 52, pp. 11, 15.

16. Griess/Devers, box 7.

17. Griess/Devers, tape 45, pp. 53–54.

18. Griess/Devers, box 7.

19. Pogue/Devers, p. 83.

20. Griess/Devers, tape 44, p. 83.

21. Senator Henry Lodge Address, Additional Resources, Devers Papers, York County Heritage Trust.

22. Forrest Pogue, note on interview of George Marshall, 13 November 1956, Marshall Library.

23. Pogue/Devers.

24. Griess/Devers, tape 42, p. 179.

25. Griess/Devers, 11–12 August 1971, p. 175.

26. Griess/Devers, tape 40, p. 45.

27. Griess/Devers, box 7.

28. Pogue/Devers, p. 193.

29. Griess/Devers, tape 55, 3–4 April 1973.

30. Griess/Devers, tape 45, p. 261.

31. Griess/Devers, tape 44, p. 233.

Bibliography

PUBLISHED SOURCES

Adams, John A. *The Battle for Western Europe, Fall 1944: An Operational Analysis.* Bloomington: Indiana University Press, 2010.

Ambrose, Stephen E. *Eisenhower: Soldier, General of the Army, President-Elect, 1890–1952.* New York: Simon and Schuster, 1983.

———. *The Supreme Commander: The War Years of General Dwight D. Eisenhower.* Garden City, N.Y.: Doubleday, 1968.

Atkinson, Richard. *An Army at Dawn.* New York: Henry Holt, 2007.

Barnett, C. B., ed. *Hitler's Generals.* New York: Quill/William Morrow, 1989.

Bass, Michael A., et al. *Story of the Century.* New York: Century Association, 100th Infantry Division, 1946.

Beck, Alfred M., et al. *The Corps of Engineers: The War against Germany.* Washington, D.C.: U.S. Army Center of Military History, 1995.

Bland, Larry I., ed. *George C. Marshall: Interviews and Reminiscences for Forrest C. Pogue.* Lexington, Va.: George C. Marshall Foundation, 1991.

Bland, Larry I., and Sharon Ritenour Stevens, eds. *The Papers of George Catlett Marshall.* 4 vols. Baltimore: Johns Hopkins University Press, 1996.

Blumenson, Martin. *The Battle of the Generals.* New York: William Morrow, 1993.

———. *Mark Clark.* New York: Congdon and Weed, 1984.

———. *The Patton Papers, 1885–1940.* New York: Houghton Mifflin, 1972.

———. *The Patton Papers, 1940–1945.* New York: Houghton Mifflin, 1974.

———. *Salerno to Casino.* Washington, D.C.: U.S. Army Center of Military History, 1967.

Bolger, Major D. P. "Zero Defects: Command Climate in First U.S. Army, 1944–45." *Military Review* (May 1991): 61–73.

Bonn, Keith E. *When the Odds Were Even.* Novato, Cal.: Presidio Press, 1994.

Bradley, Omar. *A Soldier's Story.* New York: Henry Holt, 1951.

Bradley, Omar, and Clay Blair. *A General's Life.* New York: Simon and Schuster, 1983.

Breuer, William B. *Operation Dragoon.* Novato, Cal.: Presidio Press, 1996.

Bryant, Arthur. *Triumph in the West, 1943–46: A History of the War Years Based on the Diaries of Field-Marshal Lord Alanbrooke, Chief of the Imperial General Staff.* London: Collins, 1959.

———. *Turn of the Tide, 1939–43: A History of the War Years Based on the Diaries of Field-Marshal Lord Alanbrooke, Chief of the Imperial General Staff*. New York: Doubleday, 1957.

Butcher, Harry C. *My Three Years with Eisenhower*. New York: Simon and Schuster, 1946.

Bykofsky, Joseph, and Harold Larson. *The Transportation Corps: Operations Overseas*. Washington, D.C.: U.S. Army Center of Military History, 1957.

Chamberlain, Peter, and Chris Ellis. *British and American Tanks of World War II*. New York: Arco, 1969.

Chandler, Alfred D., Jr., and Stephen E. Ambrose, eds. *The Papers of Dwight David Eisenhower: The War Years*. 21 vols. to date. Baltimore: Johns Hopkins University Press, 1970–.

Chant, Christopher, ed. *Hitler's Generals and Their Battles* London: Salamander Books, 1977.

Churchill, Winston. *Closing the Ring*. Boston: Houghton Mifflin, 1951.

Citino, Robert M. *Blitzkrieg to Desert Storm*. Lawrence: University Press of Kansas, 2004.

Clark, Lloyd. *Anzio*. London: Headline, 2006.

Clark, Mark W. *Calculated Risk*. New York: Harper and Brothers, 1950.

Clarke, J. J., and R. R. Smith. *Riviera to the Rhine*. Washington, D.C.: U.S. Army Center of Military History, 1993.

Cline, Ray S. *Washington Command Post: The Operations Division*. Washington, D.C.: U.S. Army Center of Military History, 1951.

Cole, Hugh M. *The Lorraine Campaign*. Washington, D.C.: U.S. Army Center of Military History, 1950.

Coll, Blanche D., et al. *The Corps of Engineers: Troops and Equipment*. Washington, D.C.: U.S. Army Center of Military History, 1958.

Colley, David P. *Decision at Strasbourg*. Annapolis, Md.: Naval Institute Press, 2008.

Collins, J. Lawton. *Lighting Joe: An Autobiography*. Baton Rouge: Louisiana State University Press, 1979.

Cook, Dan. *Charles de Gaulle*. New York: Putnam, 1983.

Cox, Edward. *Grey Eminence: Fox Conner*. Stillwater, Okla.: New Forums, 2011.

Craven, Wesley Frank, and James Lee Cate, eds. *The Army Air Forces in World War II*. 7 vols. Chicago: University of Chicago Press, 1948–1958.

Cray, Edward. *General of the Army George C. Marshall*. New York: Simon and Schuster, 1990.

Crosswell, D. K. R. *Beetle: The Life of General Walter Bedell Smith*. Lexington: University Press of Kentucky, 2010.

———. *The Chief of Staff: The Military Career of General Walter Bedell Smith*. Westport, Conn.: Greenwood Press, 1991.

D'Este, Carlo. *Decision in Normandy*. New York: Dutton, 1983.

———. *Eisenhower: A Soldier's Life*. New York: Holt, 2002.

———. *Fatal Decision: Anzio and the Battle for Rome*. New York: HarperCollins, 1988.

———. *Patton: A Genius for War*. New York: HarperCollins, 1995.

Dupuy, Trevor N., Curt Johnson, and David L. Bongard, eds. *The Harper Encyclopedia of Military History*. New York: HarperCollins, 1992.

Eisenhower, Dwight David. *Crusade in Europe*. Garden City, N.Y.: Doubleday, 1948.

———. *Report by the Supreme Commander to the Combined Chiefs of Staff on the Operations in Europe, 6 June 1944 to 8 May*

1945. Washington, D.C.: U.S. Government Printing Office, 1946.

Ellis, John. *Brute Force: Allied Strategy and Tactics in the Second World War*. New York: Viking, 1990.

Ellis, L. F., et al. *Victory in the West*. 2 vols. United Kingdom Military History series. London: Her Majesty's Stationery Office, 1962–1968.

English, John A. *Patton's Peers*. Mechanicsburg, Penn.: Stackpole Books, 2009.

Esposito, Vincent J., ed. *A Concise History of World War II*. New York: Praeger, 1965.

Essame, Herbert. *Patton: A Study in Command*. New York: Scribner, 1974.

Farago, Ladislas. *Patton: Ordeal and Triumph*. New York: Ivan Obolensky, 1963.

Ferguson, John C. *Hellcats: 12th Armored Division in World War II*. Abilene, Texas: State House Press, 2004.

Ferrell, Robert H., ed. *Eisenhower Diaries*. New York: Norton, 1981.

15th Army Group History, 16 December–2 May 1945. Washington, D.C.: U.S. Army Center of Military History, 1945; reprint Nashville, Tenn.: Battery Press, 1989.

Forty, George. *M4 Sherman*. New York: Blanford Press, 1987.

Fraser, David. *Alanbrooke*. London: Collins, 1982.

Freeman, Roger A. *The Mighty Eighth War Diary*. Minneapolis: Motorbooks, 1990.

Gabel, Christopher R. *Seek, Strike, and Destroy: U.S. Army Tank Destroyer Doctrine in World War II*. Fort Leavenworth, Kans.: Fort Leavenworth Papers No. 12, 1985.

———. *The US Army GHQ Maneuvers of 1941*. Washington, D.C.: U.S. Army Center of Military History, 1991.

Gaulle, Charles de. *The War Memoirs of Charles de Gaulle*, vol. 3, *Salvation*. New York: Simon and Schuster, 1960.

Gavin, James N. *On to Berlin: Battles of an Airborne Commander, 1943–46*. New York: Viking, 1978.

Gillie, Mildred Hanson. *Forging the Thunderbolt: History of the U.S. Army's Armored Forces, 1917–45*. Harrisburg, Penn.: Military Service Publishing, 1947; reprint Mechanicsburg, Pa.: Stackpole, 2006.

Goya, Michel, and François Phillipe. "The Man Who Bent Events: King John in Indochina." *Military Review* (Sept.–Oct. 2007): 52–61.

Graham, Dominick, and Shelford Sidwell. *Tug of War: The Battle for Italy, 1943–45*. New York: St. Martin's Press, 1986.

Greenfield, Kent Roberts, et al. *Command Decisions*. Washington, D.C.: U.S. Army Center of Military History, 1960.

Greenfield, Kent Roberts, Robert R. Palmer, and Bell I. Wiley. *Organization of Ground Combat Troops*. Washington, D.C.: U.S. Army Center of Military History, 1947.

Harrison, Gordon A. *Cross-Channel Attack*. Washington, D.C.: U.S. Army Center of Military History, 1951.

Hechler, Kenneth. *History of the Armored Force*. Fort Knox, Ky.: U.S. Army, 1943.

Hirshson, Stanley. *General Patton*. New York: HarperCollins, 2002.

Hoffman, George F., and Donn A. Starry. *Camp Colt to Desert Storm: The History of U.S. Armored Forces*. Lexington: University of Kentucky Press, 1999.

Hogan, David W. *A Command Post at War: First Army HQ in Europe 1944–45*. Washington, D.C.: U.S. Army Center of Military History, 2000.

Hunnicutt, R. P. *Firepower: A History of the American Heavy Tank*. Novato, Cal.: Presidio Press, 1988.

Jarymowycz, Roman. *Tank Tactics from Normandy to Lorraine*. Boulder, Col.: Lynne Rienner, 2001.

Jeffers, Paul H. *Command of Honor.* New York: New American Library, 2008.

Juin, Alphonse. *Mémoires du général Juin.* 2 vols. Paris: Fayard, 1959–1960.

Keefer, Louis E. *Scholars in Foxholes.* Jefferson, N.C.: McFarland, 1988.

Keegan, John. *Six Armies in Normandy: From D-Day to the Liberation of Paris, June 6th–August 25th, 1944.* New York: Viking, 1982.

Kesselring, Albrecht. *The Memoirs of Field Marshall Kesselring.* New York: William Morrow, 1953.

Lattre, Jean de. *The History of the French First Army.* Translated by Malcolm Barnes. London: Allen and Unwin, 1952.

Lemay, Benoît. *Erich von Manstein: Hitler's Master Strategist.* Translated by Pierce Heyward. Havertown, Penn.: Casemate, 2010.

MacDonald, Charles B. *The Last Offensive.* Washington, D.C.: U.S. Army Center of Military History, 1973.

———. *The Mighty Endeavor: The American War in Europe.* New York: Oxford University Press, 1969.

———. *A Time for Trumpets: The Untold Story of the Battle of the Bulge.* New York: Morrow, 1985.

Marshall, Col. George, ed. *Infantry in Battle.* Fort Benning, Ga.: Infantry Journal, 1939.

Matloff, Maurice, *Strategic Planning for Coalition Warfare: 1943–44.* Washington, D.C.: U.S. Army Center of Military History, 1959.

Mellenthin, Major General F. W. von. *German Generals of World War II as I Saw Them.* Norman: University of Oklahoma Press, 1977.

———. *Panzer Battles: A Study of the Employment of Armor in the Second World War.* Norman: University of Oklahoma Press, 1956.

Millet, John D. *Organization of the Arm Service Forces.* Washington, D.C.: U.S. Army Center of Military History, 1954.

Montgomery, Bernard. *The Memoirs of Field-Marshal the Viscount Montgomery of Alamein, K.G.* London: Collins, 1958.

Morgan, Sir Frederick. *Overture to Overlord.* Garden City, N.Y.: Doubleday, 1950.

Morison, Samuel E. *History of United States Naval Operations in World War II,* vol. 9, *Sicily-Salerno-Anzio, January 1943.* New York: Little, Brown, 1954.

———. *History of United States Naval Operations in World War II,* vol. 11, *The Invasion of France and Germany, 1944–1945.* New York: Little, Brown, 1954.

Orr, John K. *Supplying the Troops: General Somervell and American Logistics in WWII.* De Kalb: Northern Illinois University Press, 1994.

Patton, George S. *War as I Knew It.* New York: Houghton Mifflin, 1947; reprint New York: Pyramid, 1966.

Perry, Mark. *Partners in Command: George Marshall and Dwight Eisenhower in War and Peace.* New York: Penguin, 2007.

Pogue, Forrest C. *George C. Marshall: Organizer of Victory 1943–45.* New York: Viking Press, 1973.

———. *The Supreme Command.* Washington, D.C.: U.S. Army Center of Military History, 1989.

Porch, Douglas. *The Path to Victory: The Mediterranean Theatre in World War II.* New York: Farrar, Straus and Giroux, 2004.

Ruppenthal, Roland G. *Logistical Support of the Armies.* 2 vols. Washington, D.C.: U.S. Army Center of Military History, 1953.

Schifferle, Peter. *America's School for War: Fort Leavenworth, Officer Education, and Victory in World War II.* Lawrence: University Press of Kansas, 2010.

The Seventh United States Army Report of Operations: France and German 1944–45. Vol. 3. Washington, D.C.: U.S. Army Center of Military History, 1946.

Sixsmith, E. K. G. *Eisenhower as Military Commander.* New York: DaCapo, 1972.

Smith, Walter Bedell. *Eisenhower's Six Great Decisions: Europe, 1944–1945.* New York: Longmans, Green, 1956.

Stacy, C. P. *Official History of the Canadian Army in the Second World War,* vol. 3, *The Victory Campaign: The Operations in North-West Europe, 1944–1945.* Ottawa: The Queen's Printer, 1960.

Stimson, Henry L. *On Active Service in Peace and War.* New York: Harper and Brothers, 1947.

Stoler, Mark A. *Allies and Adversaries: The Joint Chiefs of Staff, the Grand Alliance and U.S. Strategy in WWII.* Chapel Hill: University of North Carolina Press, 2000.

Taaffe, Stephen F. *Marshall and His Generals: U.S. Army Commanders in World War II.* Lawrence: University Press of Kansas, 2011.

Tedder, Arthur William, Lord. *With Prejudice: The World War II Memoirs of Marshal of the Royal Air Force Lord Tedder.* Boston: Little, Brown, 1966.

Truscott, Lucian K., Jr. *Command Missions: A Personal Story.* New York: E. P. Dutton, 1954; reprint Novato, Cal.: Presidio Press, 1990.

Vigneras, Marcel. *Rearming the French.* Washington, D.C.: U.S. Army Center of Military History, 1957.

Wardlow, Chester. *The Transportation Corps: Movements, Training, and Supply.* Washington, D.C.: U.S. Army Center of Military History, 1956.

Watson, Mark Skinner. *Chief of Staff: Prewar Plans and Preparations.* Washington, D.C.: U.S. Army Center of Military History, 1950.

Weigley, Russell F. *Eisenhower's Lieutenants: The Campaigns of France and Germany, 1944–45.* Bloomington: Indiana University Press, 1981.

Whiting, Charles. *America's Forgotten Army: The True Story of the U.S. Seventh Army in WWII – and an Unknown Battle That Changed History.* New York: DaCapo, 1999.

Williams, Reginald. *15th Army Group History.* Nashville, Tenn.: Battery Press, 1989.

Wilmot, Chester. *The Struggle for Europe.* New York: Harper, 1963.

Wyatt, William K. *Sandy Patch: A Biography of Lt. Gen. Alexander M. Patch.* Westport, Conn.: Praeger, 1991.

Yeilde, Harry, and Mark Stout. *First to the Rhine: The 6th Army Group in World War II.* St. Paul, Minn.: Zenith Press, 2007.

GOVERNMENT PUBLICATIONS, WAR DEPARTMENT

FM 17-33. Tank Battalion, November 1944.

FM 17-36. Tanks with Infantry, March 1944.

FM 100-5. Field Service Regulations, 1944.

MANUSCRIPT SOURCES

Eisenhower Library, Abilene, Kans.
Harold Bull Papers
Eisenhower Pre-Presidential Papers
7th Army Report of Operations
Walter Bedell Smith Papers
Strategy of the Campaign in Western Europe, 1944–1945
Supreme Headquarters Allied Expeditionary Force (SHAEF) Files
Boxes 8, 9, 19: Weekly Intelligence Summaries
Box 18: Directives to Subordinates
Boxes 22, 23: G4 (Intelligence) Reports

Box 35: Directives for Air Forces
Boxes 53, 54, 55, 77: Post-Overlord Plan-
    ning and Copies of Directives from
    Montgomery
12th Army Group Report of Operations

Marshall Library, Lexington, Va.
Cables to/from Marshall
Correspondence between Marshall and
    Devers
Correspondence between Marshall and
    Eisenhower
Forrest Pogue interviews and notes:
    General Devers
    General Marshall

**U.S. Army Military History
Institute, Carlisle Barracks, Penn.**
Harry C. Butcher Diary

Mark W. Clark Diary
Jacob Devers Diary
Chester B. Hansen Papers
John Lucas Diary
Fred Walker Diary

**York County Heritage
Trust, York, Penn.**
Devers Papers Collection
Griess Research Collection (research
    materials gathered by Brigadier General
    Thomas E. Griess for an unwritten biog-
    raphy of General Jacob L. Devers)
History of Armored Force (U.S. Army,
    unpublished)
History of 6th Army Group (6AG Staff,
    unpublished)

Index

JOHN A. ADAMS is author of *The Battle for Western Europe, Fall 1944* (IUP, 2010) and *If Mahan Ran the Great Pacific War* (IUP, 2008).

This book was designed by Jamison Cockerham and set in type by Tony Brewer at Indiana University Press, and printed by Sheridan Books, Inc.

The fonts are Arno, designed by Robert Slimbach in 2007, Calcite, designed by Akira Kobayashi in 1997, and Conga Brava, designed by Michael Harvey in 2001. All were published by Adobe Systems Incorporated.